Dear Ali...

Wish you
all the love,
in the world
and far beyond!!

GW01314794

2

LAUGHING GAS

David Field

Edited by Peter Moore

Copyright © David Field 2012
All rights reserved

The right of David Field to be identified as the author of this work has been asserted by him in accordance with the Copyright, Designs and Patents Act 1988.

All rights reserved. No part of this publication may be reproduced, stored in a retrieval system, or transmitted in any form by any means, without the prior permission of David Field

First Edition published in Great Britain on the Summer Solstice, 2012 by David Field.

Please contact the author at puppetdave@yahoo.com

Front cover photography: Dave Dobbs living outside the Guardian offices in London in his live-in, cycle powered Mayor Mobile during his 'Occupy London Mayor Campaign.' He, like nearly all the other prospective candidates outside of the main political parties, did not have the £10,000 it cost to buy into the London Mayor Campaign. After the success of his *Spoil Your Vote* campaign, Dobbs *The Man That Would Be Mayor of London*.

Back Cover: Dan Johnson.

Edited by Peter Moore

Acknowledgements

The biggest thank you must go to those characters that have directly influenced this story with their love, friendship and most of all, their character. I couldn't have done it without all that support and that love. From the very bottom of my heart, thank you.

A massive thank you to Peter Moore for his editorial and creative assistance who has hammered on through, pulling his hair out and endlessly screaming, "Say what you mean, Dave!" Thanks Pete.

May I give thanks to my brother, Ivan Massow, for his massive support through this project. I so couldn't have written a book without that help and truly had no clue of the amount of work involved. Thank you so much.

And thank you to Doogloo Ram, Derga, Tarika and my community of friends up in the mountains in India that have been such an amazing support.

Enormous thanks to Gaetan Boyer for his loving enthusiasm, especially with the front cover picture which involved getting the courage together to go and live in on the streets of London - in a live-in rickshaw. And thank you to his lovely partner, Nadine Cole, for proofreading and encouragement.

Thank you also to my father, Colin Field and my stepfather, Peter Mitchell, for their encouragement, keeping me writing.

Thank you also to Steven Ashe, author of *Qabalah of 50 Gates,* for his help getting the book laid out and available, and more than anything, through the bleakest hours, his enthusiasm. It's a big process getting a book out there. I appreciate all your technical skills and all your enthusiasm in pushing me forward. Thank you so much.

A big thank you to Susie Deadman for her support through writing this book and her beautiful understanding.

Thank you also to my long time friend, Simon Mitchell, for his enduring encouragement with endless lines like; 'don't get it right, get it written.' Thank you!

A massive thanks to Elfie and Noah. Thanks for your loving support which I truly honour. And thanks to Peter and Jenny Deadman for their enormous understanding and support through writing this book. Thanks so much Pete.

A massive thanks to *Poshratz* for his gentlemanly, encouraging support also, which, at its most enthusiastic, came in the form of a poster of *Paloma Faith,* brought thousands of miles, when I was at my most reclusive stage of this book – for the purpose of muse I can only assume. And thanks also to Tania Smith for her kind motivation. And thanks to Johnny *Melonfucker* for helping clear out the cobwebs sometimes. A big thanks to Johnny Bailhache for his enduring support also. And also to Chris Harman for sitting there and listening to me read! Thanks Chris.

Big thanks to Dennis Hickson, Dan Johnson and Jim Bob. You are superstars.

A massive thank you to Alex Kilgour for all her support and though she will not be in this world to read it, perhaps she will in the next, wherever that place is we go when we're done here. Thank you Alex!

So many people have helped me in this project that it becomes impossible to thank them all individually as assistance comes in so many different ways but for all those unsung heroes whose energy and inspiration has been instrumental in the creation of this, my first book, thank you. You know who you are!

Based on a true story.

Dedicated to Katherine.

And to my Mother, Anthea, Thank you.

Humpty Dumpty sat on a wall

Humpty Dumpty had a great fall

All the King's horses

And all the King's men

Couldn't put Humpty together again...

...welcome to The Wall.

Wednesday, 16 January 2008

It's often difficult to pinpoint the predominant aromas and sometimes almost rancid smells which greet you when you first arrive in a new country. That first breath! When you step out of the airport - or the plane if there's no sealed mobile gangway - and just tingle all over as everything rushes back to the here-and-now of a new life dawning. The olfactory senses must be the fastest memory trigger of all; literally absorbing the particles, the atoms and molecules - the very matter itself! Everything, all mixed into one rich signature that's drawn into the blood via millions of nasal capillaries and mainlined straight to the brain.

These are the thoughts passing through Dobbs's mind as he wanders down the sealed gangway at Lima International airport. He feels like he's in a decontamination unit and finds himself longing for the days of those simple mobile stairways where you actually get to the door of the aircraft and there it all is and you get that all-important first breath that lets you truly savour your destination. Whatever happened to the old fashioned treatment when you could step out of the plane and have a proper gawp at the technology that had flown you to your final destination? To really see and feel the fusion of a hundred years of aviation evolution embodied in that one vast, seamlessly gleaming flight body, all sat atop the massive knuckled crow's claws of the undercarriage. Inside this sealed tunnel he can't appreciate the full significance of his arrival - only the clinical separation from all he craves.

At last, stepping slowly out of the airport, he can soak up the freshness of the new day amongst the arriving passengers, their bustling pace contrasting sharply with his own slow, vacant gander. The air has many familiarities but the one aroma for which he unwittingly searches is missing. It's too early in the day for floral essence to have perspired from delicate buds in the heat of the baking sun and be carried off in the summer breeze. And do cactus flowers even have an aroma? Dobbs is not sure at all. Either way, the day is fresh, there's not a cloud in the sky, and the temperature is perfect.

Two guys in suits come striding towards him. They walk side by side but at a distance from one another, their arms held out slightly as if to block any competition coming up the flank. A casually dressed man stands beyond them, attempting to catch Dobbs's eye from the pavement on the far side of the main artery leading into the terminal building.

"Taxi! Taxi!" One of the men in suits demands, ushering him forward with animated hand gestures whilst subtly blocking the path to the car park where the stranger stands, and directing him to the posh taxi rank to his right instead.

He glances over at the stranger, attempting to size him up. The man doesn't smile but there's something warm in his face. He makes a slight hand gesture, raising his brow. Dobbs meets the look but badly disguises his curiosity. The two suits spin round and stare at the stranger for a moment. He says nothing, loosely holding his gaze but making no gesture. They turn their attention back to Dobbs:

"Taxi, come!"

He nods, smiling at the suits but subtly changing his direction.

"Es mi amigo," he says, pointing to the stranger and moving forward. He's ready to barge between the two men but at the last moment they both jump out of his way.

"*Quanto cuesta, Mira Flores*?" He asks the stranger quietly, giving the guy a wink when he is past the official airport taxis and has found a moment to catch his undivided attention. He's delivered the whole line as though fluent and is now looking into the man's eyes, waiting. The man rattles off something or other in heavily accented Spanish and immediately the game is up: Dobbs has no idea what has been said.

"*Si - er, claro… Err, quanto cuesta en dollars por favor?*" he stutters back.

"Fifteen dollars," the stranger says, smirking.

"*Amigo - es mucho. Mira Flores es muy cerca… Amigo, por favor.*"

The driver stops and stares at him with an amused, slightly smug expression.

"Me," he says, jerking his head towards the official taxi rank, "half!" Then he smiles and just carries on walking, knowing Dobbs *will* get in the car.

Dobbs felt a bit embarrassed by his terrible Spanish. His previous four months in South America, ten years before, have left him with a vocabulary not much greater than '*si*' and '*claro*' and a host of flailing hand movements. He should be able to do better! Still, he has a few words, so he uses one of his favourites now:

"*Vamanos!*"

10

In moments the airport is out of sight, and before he's had a chance to take in the breakneck speed at which the man is driving, his hand has found the window winder and begun winding. The car is fast but with the clearly knackered *shocks* it seems to float over the occasional potholes in the surprisingly well maintained dual carriageway. Despite the speed the ride feels relaxing and as he winds down the window the fresh, cool air begins to mix with the interior odour of a mature Japanese saloon that has spent its whole life roasting under the hot sun. Quite suddenly some kind of alchemy happens, and there it is, that scent for which he has sought so strongly: the sweet smell of adventure!

Dobbs didn't actually know that Lima lies directly on the coast. For sure, the fresh salty air has given some clues but now that the endless chromium blue of the Pacific Ocean heaves into view another little curiosity pops into his head as he stares in awe at the sight. Small dots are bobbing in the water and as he watches, first one, then another catches a white line that runs parallel and ever closer to the shore. 'Hmmm,' he thinks, as the freshness fills his nostrils and a feeling of nostalgia begins to tingle through his body, sending sparkly ripples right down to his finger tips. He brings his hands together and rubs them, as if shaking the energy free and discharging it.

"You surf?" Asks the driver, observing Dobbs's reaction through his rear view mirror.

"*Si*," he says, before pausing to think if last surfing seventeen years ago constitutes a yes. "*Claro*," he adds, half chuckling to himself.

Before long he sees sky rises, many still clearly under construction. Amongst all the development stand two glassy conical structures designed with a nautical theme, as though they might be the funnels of a modern liner. Behind them, sitting right on the waterfront, is an equally modern looking complex with sails cleverly incorporated into its architecture, and just beyond that a pier displaying the heritage of an older, more romantic period of Lima's past juts out into the ocean. It immediately reminds him of Brighton Pier, and the roller coaster ride at the end of it. When the ride finished and the brakes got slammed on, the metal wheels would screech against the tracks, making his fillings literally vibrate with the resonance. The very thought of it makes his teeth twinge uncomfortably.

Here they turn left to enter what is clearly becoming the thick of the city.

"Esta es? Mira Flores?"

"Si." Says the driver.

Dobbs reaches into the black leather shoulder holster he is wearing over a dark brown plain cotton shirt. Along with his *TK Max* designer jeans and a pair of middling-to-completely fucked trainers his travelling attire would challenge anyone to guess which side of the money he belonged, which is precisely the look he's aiming for. He grabs a piece of paper with the details of his accommodation on it as the car pulls up next to a three-storey building that looks neither modern nor old. There is not much room for a garden out front but nonetheless several large cacti and a few other, mostly potted plants, are dotted about here and there. It looks warm and cosy even for a city dwelling.

Bright, creamy-coloured concrete pavements glisten in sunlight so dazzling he has to squint his eyes to take it all in. There's a lot of trees set into the neatly shuttered concrete. It all seems very clean, and many of the well-maintained houses, apartment blocks and hotels, have a strong Mediterranean feel to them, an impression accentuated by the occasional fruit vendors selling from the back of old carts which lends a subtle sense of antiquity. And yet the scene is oddly contradicted by the many old, imported American cars - huge Cadillacs and Dodges, most now looking a bit the worse for wear - which line the street.

The front of the building is mostly windows. It would no doubt have been considered modern back in the Seventies but now looks distinctly dated. Set back slightly is a garage with aged wooden doors and to the right of this is the front door, set behind a steel security gate which, though ornamented with stylish twists and curls is clearly not just there for just decoration. Dobbs taps on the door, then sees the bell and immediately presses for attention.

He peers in through the windows and can see a large room, open plan and quite sparsely laid out with a sunny area to the rear filled with an array of even more brightly potted foliage. The front area is a spacious, open sitting room, with a TV and bookshelves. A staircase runs up to the next floor from the centre of the room with what appears to be a bar situated below, maximizing the use of space. Beyond, he can see a dining area, neatly set with gingham tablecloths and napkins. A man pops out of an open door right at the back of the dining area. He's clearly rushing, and hurriedly dusts himself off in readiness for whatever introductions may lie ahead.

Dobbs comes from the window and waits for the door to open. The man is slightly portly and appears to be of more indigenous descent than Spanish, with a round, friendly face. He is clearly still preparing breakfast arrangements and seems a little flustered. He says nothing but observes with an enthused curiosity, waiting with bated breath to find out what Dobbs wants before completely opening the door to him.

"Perdon Senor; mi amigos, Agent6 y la Brigadier, errr, *hacer habitacion aqui?* Err - *tu hacer habitacion por me tambien?"* He splutters, hoping that if the man understands nothing else, the names 'Brigadier' and 'Agent6' might trigger a response.

"Si, si!" He enthuses, gesturing for Dobbs to enter.

Moments later he's knocking on another door. There's no answer so he waits, then knocks louder.

"Hola?" Comes a muffled grunt.

"Filling in for room service, Sir. I'm afraid blow jobs are off the service list... only temporary I'm assured."

Dobbs can hear movement behind the door; slow movement. Then the stumbling of sleep-deprived feet being dragged across a wooden floor and, finally, the fumbling of the handle followed by a contradictory rapid movement as the door is abruptly swung open.

There stands Agent6, in his boxers. He's squinting whilst supporting a smile that doesn't quite manage to radiate across his whole face but more just his vocal area. Everywhere else looks a little puffy and somehow compromised but it's definitely a good effort, held a fair few moments, before a pale, cloudy glaze seeps back into his features and he retreats back into his lair.

Inside, the room is small and simply furnished. There's a pair of paintings on the walls and a couple of single beds, one of which is empty and clearly unused. The sun is at just the right height so that its bright beams reflect from the rear of the room and shine through onto the terracotta walls, mellowing the beaming radiance of the beautifully vibrant Lima morning. To Dobbs it seems like an idyllic city oasis, sprawling with tropical greenery, but it's all clearly a bit of a struggle for Agent6 right now.

Dobbs last saw him in England just a few days before but nonetheless they exchange a brief hug.

"Where's The Brigadier?" Dobbs enquires, taking a seat on the empty bed.

Agent6 climbs back onto his own bed, blinking owlishly, as if giving his eyelids an early morning workout.

He's by no means overweight but neither is he as lean as he used to be. His shoulders sit high, raising his full chest up to what seems an artificial height, but this is, in fact, his natural form. The beginnings of a cold, damp English winter has left a slight plumpness but he's still more muscle than fat. Somehow his physique reminds Dobbs of an American Indian, like a warrior or a brave straight out of a spaghetti Western.

He's often wondered where Agent6's genes descend. The only real giveaway is perhaps the fair colour of his skin. Aside from that he looks more native to these lands than to the country of his birth. His nose is large and wide, not Roman or African but set with wide cheek bones which, though perhaps not now as chiselled as when they first met, ten years prior, somehow accentuated the Indigenous impression.

"Where's The Brigadier?" Dobbs asks again, trying not to seem overly impatient for the wake-up process to conclude, as it clearly isn't going to happen any time soon.

Agent6 glances over to the unused bed then sits back and inhales. He's almost smirking whilst pouting his lips. Then he lets out a long, slow breath, simultaneously shaking his head with a gleeful look of mock disapproval in his eyes.

Dobbs flicks his fingers and gently rubs his hands together.

"You dirty bunch of *'caners'*!" He grins.

Agent6 doesn't look best pleased with himself. Not that Dobbs wants to make him feel guilty; if anything, he's quite envious that he's missed all the fun. But Agent6 is way too thick-skinned to truly take offence anyway and, shrugging it off, he drags himself out of bed and into the adjoining bathroom.

"Where's Bolivar?" Dobbs hears over the sound of the shower running.

"He'll make it in a few days, he reckons," he shouts back. He's not too interested in engaging in a conversation through a wall though, so he walks over to inspect one of the paintings instead.

There were several images from his childhood that always stood out in his mind. One was a picture in a kid's geography book of a man standing alone on a beach looking towards an approaching wave that appeared about half a mile high. The artist had obviously placed the man in the picture to give the scene a little perspective, but as a kid he never really understood that and he would just stare for ages at that unstoppable wall of water. It was clearly only seconds away from the man and yet he just stood there, his arms by his side, staring up at what, back then he would've called the 'tidal wave' - though these days of course even kids knew it was 'really' a 'tsunami'. Dobbs had always wondered what was going through the man's head as he calmly stood there, waiting to die. It sometimes seemed to him that perhaps the man just couldn't actually *see* it.

The other image he always remembered was on the wall of his grandparents' caravan. In the late Fifties and Sixties, and right through to the early Seventies, they played in their band on the caravan holiday camp where they lived most of the year. They were the star attraction by all accounts. They'd spend all summer doing gigs, mostly living in caravans, and then sail off to their house in Tenerife for the winter.

Dobbs used to stay with them in their caravan sometimes. Back in those days, big caravan parks were considered proper holiday material and the people who frequented them weren't considered 'trailer trash' or 'New Age Travellers,' like Dobbs and Agent6; they were a class act. His *Uncle* was a proper old crooner and saxophonist and would always get him up on stage with his little plastic blue guitar. Dobbs was probably not much older than three or four years of age then but still, to this day, he couldn't remember meeting a happier man. They wouldn't put him to bed until he'd fallen fast asleep by the side of the stage amidst the noise of wild festivities. Then, like magic, he'd wake up back in the caravan, and there, looking down at him, would be the picture - the very same picture that was on the wall in front of him right now.

It was a portrait of a beautiful Spanish Gypsy woman, her dark locks catching the breeze and framing her gorgeous features. Her deep brown eyes shone like majestic jewels above a blouse so loosely buttoned it could barely contain the bounty struggling to break free from such flimsy fastenings. She was sat on the back of a bow-top wagon with a whole *Constable* setting in the background and an expression on her face like the cat that got the cream. Dobbs may not have fully understood the finer points of his fascination with the female form at such a tender age, but that picture always had him captivated.

At last Agent6 emerges from the bathroom. He is now looking surprisingly fresh for someone who's probably not slept more than three hours and, noticing that Dobbs is completely lost in the painting, he wanders over to have a look for himself.

"Brings back a few memories," Dobbs says, smiling nostalgically.

Agent6 feasts his eyes on the scene as if seeing it for the first time, then scrutinizes the corner with his finger to see if it is actually a hand painted repro as he suspects. He is about to say something, but Dobbs beats him to it.

"One of yours, isn't it?" He smirks. One of their *previous incarnations* had been as somewhat shady 'art dealers' in Taiwan. Dobbs cringes inwardly at the thought now, and rapidly changes the subject,

"OK, so The Brigadier's out of the picture for a while; where's Swifty, then?"

"...Reckon we'll meet him in Iquitos," replies Agent6, shrugging those broad shoulders.

"Just a couple of days to kill in Lima then. So where *is* The Brigadier?"

A Rocky Road

The sun is even higher now but although the road is still bright the glow is toned down substantially by Dobbs's latest addition, a pair of Bono-style shades. Both Dobbs and Agent6 are returning to the hotel after coffee. As they arrive, a taxi pulls up next to them. Here comes trouble, Dobbs thinks to himself. Peering inside, he sees a pretty Latino babe wearing designer shades. She's skimpily dressed and waving to Agent6. Beside her, in the shaded recess of the battered looking car, his saxophone round his neck and beaming the naughtiest grin is The Brigadier.

Dobbs leans down and gestures greetings with a smile and a cheeky raising of his eyebrows in salute of what has obviously been a fruitful night. He can hear The Brigadier and the girl speaking animatedly in Spanish. He has no clue what is being said, but he assumes it to be a farewell conversation. The Brigadier speaks fluent Spanish and loves taking the simplest of conversations to the most complex of lingual arenas. He wouldn't think twice to correct anything said wrongly by relaying the *simple* fourteen steps in qualifying and applying a conjugation. It's quite amazing what five years in a foreign jail can do for your linguistic abilities.

In no time they're all up in the hotel room and huge rails of pestilence are lined up on the table. Time for judgment gets stuck on the back burner, prudence thrown to the wind. 'In for a penny,' Dobbs figures; there's no extra points or cash back for clean upholstery when the car finally goes to the scrapper. 'Well done for saving yourself, oh Pure One,' he thinks to himself, as the first rail disappears up the fifty Sole note and into his nostril.

"All aboard the *loco* motive!" Agent6 shrieks.

He braces himself for the toxic burn, which is normally followed by, "Oh that's really fucking smooth shit," regardless of whether it's like snorting a chainsaw or not. But, to Dobbs's surprise, it really is quite smooth. He literally feels it running round his arteries and the intense toxicity of what feels like fingers of ice contracting around his heart. No matter how deep he breathes each breath feels shallower and shallower as his heart centre shuts down and something else inflates. Suddenly Dobbs is the centre of the world - yet somehow a little disempowered all in the same instance. A few more lines though, and he's flying.

An hour later they're all walking down the road with their bags as the hotel where they've been staying doesn't have any larger rooms until tomorrow. Dobbs comes to a halt suddenly, watching The Brigadier as he, really sketchily, stashes a bottle of ammonia in a tree right by the side of the road. It's broad daylight.

Dobbs turns to Agent6 and, trying to be audible to The Brigadier, says, "What's this then, a clever trick to look really dodgy or just something to make me feel like I'm hanging out with a guy on a serious fucking rock frenzy?"

"Don't want to be caught with this shit," The Brigadier fires back.

Dobbs is not so innocent as to know that looking guilty as fuck, standing on the side of the street and stashing such paraphernalia in broad daylight probably isn't the best card to play.

"Just give it here for fucks sake," he demands, making light of The Brigadier's paranoia.

Within a few minutes they're standing outside another hotel that Agent6 had booked a little earlier. It has a distinctly Mexican vibe about it and a much smaller front than the previous place though it goes back considerably further. The building is clearly from a much older period, but beautifully maintained. Its lavish white walls are swathed in tropical greenery and a gabled porch adorned with terracotta tiles with its own little front gate leading to the main entrance which is crammed with potted plants heavy with sweet-smelling flowers. The thick, chunky oak uprights that support the porch area, aged to a deep dark solid finish lend it an air of authentic antiquity, whilst a battered old Corvette sits out the front, bathed in bright sunlight, transforming the whole scene as though some prop in a movie set.

Still feeling expansive from their earlier horse-doses of pestilence, they take what is more of a suite than a room and in no time at all The Brigadier is in the kitchen, cooking up a fuss. Agent6, who is watching him intently, removes his Che Guevara army cap and runs one hand through his damp hair. He turns and stares at Dobbs, but his mind is clearly somewhere else - wondering where all this is going perhaps?

Dobbs tries not to let it concern him too much though and accept it as just another scene in the adventure. His world has already been turned on its head. What's this going to be in the scheme of things? The Brigadier is lighting tailor-made cigarettes and, rather than smoking them, he places them carefully upright, balancing them on their filter ends like tiny factory smoke stacks.

18

"Got to be smoked on a bed of ash you see?" He says.

Dobbs hasn't quite worked it all out yet.

"That sounds more culinary than it really looks," he responds. The Brigadier just gathers up all the ash on a piece of paper. The Brigadier is now fumbling for a lighter and Dobbs remembers he's brought some clever little LED light that has a mini blow torch on the end.

"It seems it's no irony they're called crack lighters," Dobbs says as he passes it over.

The Brigadier fills a spoon with pestilence, then floods it with ammonia and carefully places it so it hangs over the side of a table before weighing down the handle with an empty cup. Then he starts heating the mixture with the intensely hot lighter. He nods at Dobbs.

"Nice," he says, obviously expecting him to beam the same enthusiasm.

Within moments the mixture starts bubbling and a waxy residue appears, floating on the top. He carefully stirs it with a wooden toothpick and the residue starts attaching itself to the end. Within a minute or two it has all attached itself and then he tips the remaining liquid down the sink and replaces it with water, gently washing away the toxic ammonia. Dobbs watches every move attentively.

"*Gotta* wash it well. Not good for you, that shit," The Brigadier grunts, observing his interest.

"Yeah, no kidding," Dobbs retorts.

The Brigadier pulls out a pipe, fills it with a small bed of ash, then scrapes some of the dry, crystalline residue off the side of the pick and sprinkles it over the top of the ash.

"Dobbs!" He commands.

Dobbs is now absolutely fascinated by the whole process. He is keen to smoke some refined pestilence and at last get some idea of what all the *fuss* is about as he's still never done it. Has he missed out? Only one way to find out.

"Draw slowly, and hold it down," The Brigadier enthuses, his piercing blue eyes scrutinising Dobbs as he fumbles with the proffered pipe.

Since it's smoked in much the same way, Dobbs is half expecting it to be like a DMT hit; to be blown almost clean out of this world, so someone has to hold on to the pipe for you as you blast off. But it's quite the opposite effect really - like pestilence, only much more intense. As the cold white flash spreads rapidly throughout his body, he begins to feel more and more distant from his emotions, and for a moment he wonders if his heart is going to stop altogether. He doesn't feel good at all, and is certain he doesn't look that good either as he can feel all the colour draining from his face.

The Brigadier, he knows, is hooked on this shit now, and once the sensation of imminent cardiac arrest has passed he catches himself almost pitying, his friend. But then, with an almost physical effort, he shakes it off; any man who feels pity for another's direct choices would be best to go and hang with the born again Christians in the Jungle telling the Indigenous to repent their sins, he chides himself. Shuddering at the thought, he projects it away from himself, attempting to disown his guilt at even having had it. Instead he turns to The Brigadier:

"All those horrid, judgmental cretins in the West, addicted to their sugar, alcohol, wheat, Prozac, sleeping pills, caffeine, nicotine and the worst addiction of all – of course – TV: The ultimate life taker. Imagine being sentenced to a life of *Dead Enders*. Years and years of wonderful life lost staring at a fucking box – poor bastards. Expressionless faces just staring into oblivion. Truly the opiate of the masses."

The Brigadier gives a scoring smile and nods with enthusiasm as he takes the pipe off Agent6 and begins loading it.

Agent6 says nothing but just looks at Dobbs, who's racking up more lines on the tabletop as he feels his energy spiraling downwards.

"Scouring their daily hate rags, thumbing through the Sins of the World, and all their shitty non-existent excuses for politics; as if such stupid left and right wing nonsense has ever really made any sense. When you live in a reality where you only have to turn 180 degrees and everything that was left becomes right. Really, when it comes to left and right, we've all only ever been in the middle; a whole crock of *shite* designed exclusively for fence sitters. You can exterminate millions of innocent people, carry out mass genetic cleansing by dumping thousands of times more waste than the Hiroshima bomb on whoever you like in the form of depleted uranium Bombshells of Redemption, and they won't even lift a fucking finger. You can bring down skyscrapers, anything you fucking like – in their name – and as long as that TV's on they'll concede to genocide and war because they can't press the off-button: Their minds just bombarded. A whole media control mechanism cleverly designed to get the masses to sit on the fence, trapped between the false choice of one total crock of *shite* or another, in a non-existent existential dimension: A digital world that extracts the masses presence from themselves, and delivers our Governments all that they ever needed; the masses unwavering, silent consent to wage war. *Wankers*!" Dobbs stops for a moment lining up more rails, then "Fucking hell," he continues, "this stuff is mad! Hitler used to do loads of this shit didn't he? Fuck, one line and I've become a totally self-righteous evangelist. It's the finger of blame isn't it? Blame feels so fantastically good on this shit!"

"Nohh man; you're not doing it, willing it, wanting that outcome, and nor are they," states Agent6, who's now being presented with the next pipe, "Where were you and I when the Iraq and Afghanistan wars kicked off?"

"Protesting!" Dobbs proclaims.

"Exactly. With millions of others. And where were you on the day the towers came down?"

"Well, at another protest actually; some demo outside a big arms fair in Docklands."

"Exactly! With loads of other people. It's this shit. You've got to be careful with this shit. It brings out the judge and jury in you. It makes you completely blind to yourself."

"It's like suddenly having the eyes of a *smirker* with the finger of a *blamer*. I feel like George Bush. I don't know if I like it at all."

He feels sticky and sweaty, as if something poisonous is pouring out of him. It's dirty, and he hates it but he kind of likes it all at the same time. He feels like he's on the other side of something; a line he's sometimes straddled, but never normally crosses.

"Shit! All I'm thinking about hot, sexy latino ladies gentleman." He, almost apologetically exclaims, snorting back one line and then immediately racking up another. "Fuck, you can't get enough of it can you?" He raves and then, pausing for a microsecond in the mad onrush, ponders; is that what I really think? Before continuing:

"The masses back home. I mean, really, that they're all just a bunch of fence sitters, aren't they? It's a bit harsh, I know, but it feels like that sometimes."

A three hour session and a whole bag later and it's well into the evening and getting dark outside. The Brigadier makes a call and next thing the pestilence is replenished and they're sitting in a

21

casino with Lobo, an old friend of The Brigadier's they've picked up along the way.

Lobo's face is soft and calming. He's wearing a plain wool hat with no distinguishing marks and is very casually dressed. He looks almost Native American, with a face like Chief Sitting Bull, and Dobbs feels totally comfortable in his presence. They're all sitting round a roulette table, paying more trips to the bathroom than even the vast quantities of free drinks could warrant. The Brigadier's on a winning streak, but he's being careless. Lobo is playing occasionally and sparingly, as if appealing to The Brigadier's calm and attempting to settle him somehow. Agent6 leans towards Dobbs.

"Lobo got lucky. The Brigadier and him served time in an Italian jail. One can only guess that certain ingredients had played a part in it," he whispers, nodding at Dobbs and simultaneously winking at Lobo. "But Lobo got on some reform program, where you go and work, farming the land. He got paid as well. Saved enough to buy a farm for him and his family when he got out, four years later. Lobo - 'The Wolf' - generally called upon as liaison between corrupt officials and gringos who just so happen to have lost all their belongings. Luckily the insurance should cover it. Speaks eight languages does our Lobo."

Dobbs just smiles at the other man, observing his winning streak. Both he and The Brigadier are building a huge pile of chips but despite Lobo's attempts to subtly pacify him, The Brigadier is beginning to look even more reckless and wild.

Dobbs is barely playing at all. He's so stoked on all the pestilence that the only thing he's really interested in is the incredibly well formed body of the Hostess With The *Mostess* who's been granted the unenviable task of waiting their table. Noticing his attention she turns and gestures with her tray to enquire if he wants a drink but the only response he can manage is to look her up and down in sleazy approval of her skimpily clad figure. She turns, totally unimpressed and just walks away.

Dragging his attention back to the table, Dobbs becomes aware that despite the pleasure of reunion and the general attitude of abandonment, there's a strange energy between the three old friends tonight. It's as if they all know that this is somehow not the same Brigadier they all know and love, but don't want to admit it to themselves. Just as the thought forms in Dobbs's head though, The Brigadier looks up sharply as if suddenly becoming aware of the unwelcome attention. Catching Dobbs observing him, his icy blue eyes narrow and he pointedly returns the stare.

"Your round Dobbs," He states. His voice is cold and flat, and Dobbs is momentarily stunned by the order.

"Give us fifty soles," he demands, ignoring Dobbs and placing his chips like a General strategically planning a great battle as the ball spins round and round, audibly slowing. But the croupier raises his hand and pushes them back off.

Dobbs looks to see how things have gone, although taking little interest overall. A pile of chips is pushed towards Lobo and The Brigadier. It seems they're both on a roll. Catching The Brigadier's eye, Agent6 gives a barely noticeable signal and they scoop up their chips. Agent6 has played like Dobbs - barely at all and mostly with the aim of just enjoying the game rather than making money; not the tactics of a gambler at all, just someone looking for a little distraction from the weight of other thoughts.

After a few goodbyes and a little wheeling and dealing on the way home they're back in the hotel room and out comes the ammonia again. Dobbs's head is already whirling from the effects of all the chemicals and alcohol running through his system. He goes straight to his bed, downs a whole bottle of water, then, lying down, pulls the sheets over him and closes his eyes. It's clear to all he's bailed out for the night but whatever noises of protest the others are making, it's nothing to the reckless chaos in his head. He wishes he had some Valium to quell the screeching hysteria and twisted torments of his mind in its withdrawal from the pestilence, but he hasn't. Time goes by agonizingly slowly, each moment dragging like fingernails down a blackboard. He knows sleep is probably hours away but he needs to step off the locomotive. Whatever they get from it, he clearly doesn't: It just feels toxic.

***

When he finally opens his eyes it's early morning and Agent6 and The Brigadier have just arrived back from another excursion. Agent6 looks sad and pale as though about to break down in tears. The Brigadier seems gaunt and almost broken Dobbs knows he cannot go near either of them.

Then, somehow, it all reaches a head. The Brigadier, who's almost haemorrhaging sadness, looks like a submarine that's gone too deep and is imploding under the pressure. Something's obviously happened, as a good night out shouldn't end like this. Agent6 hugs The Brigadier but somehow not so much with a feeling of union as almost of saying farewell, then they both retreat to their beds. Dobbs, watching the moment, feels a chill go through his body.

Contradictory to his present actions Agent6 actually disapproves of pestilence – in fact of drug abuse in general. It's not so much that he feels one shouldn't indulge at all as just exercise moderation and recognise that when the party's over, it's over: no regrets, just pick up the pieces and move on. The Brigadier, however, is lost to it all now, and Agent6 just doesn't seem to have much time for him anymore, though they've shared a lot of history and despite everything he obviously still hopes he might pull out of it. But pestilence is like a credit card; you can keep drawing all the feel-good factors from your life and never paying off the bill until suddenly you realise you've maxed out and you finally have to come down. That's the moment every junky dreads, because by then all that's left is emptiness and vast sadness.

Dobbs feels very awake. The whirling pitch of withdrawal has all but gone and he feels surprisingly normal now, and almost a little smug for having been able to bail out and pull the ripcord. He decides to take a wander down to the promenade. It's another fresh morning. He snakes along the winding path through the manicured lawns and gardens up along the Mira Flores cliff edge where all the new high rises are going up, looking out to sea. He can see the surfers are already out in the swirl. It's still early though and apart from a few joggers the only other people about are the armed guards watching over various crews of what he assumes to be convict workers. It must be a better way for prisoners to spend their days than cooped up in cells, Dobbs thinks to himself, if they are indeed prisoners.

It all seems very beautiful and tranquil compared to the previous night's activities. Mira Flores waterfront is a beautiful botanical promenade with winding paths that take Dobbs through no end of flower beds and lookout points. There's something for everyone, with kid's playgrounds, cycle pathways and skateboard ramps and hundreds of sprinklers spraying out over a feast of botanical delight. He fills his lungs with fresh sea air and can taste the aromas of the new day. Even through his pummelled olfactory receptors he feels the adventure of South America again, and draws sweet, fresh breath right down to the depths of his heart which, despite the battering it's taken, is now coming back online.

A few hours later and he's making his way back to the first hotel with the others, only this time into a bigger room, as Bolivar is due later on that night or early the next morning. He's done the most sensible thing he can think of and picked up a pack of Valium from a drugs store on the quiet. He knows they may prove handy - and not just for long bus rides.

He catches his reflection in the mirror on the way into the room. Strands of grey hair shine in the mid-afternoon light. He's getting older, he thinks, as he stops to examine his reflection; they're all getting older - even The Brigadier who, with his pale white skin, blond hair and blue eyes, Dobbs has always credited with the kind of complexion that never really seems to age. The serious pestilence abuse is taking its toll on him now, though, Dobbs thinks to himself. He's looking noticeably older and his forehead is always spotted with those tell-tale tiny beads of perspiration that don't seem a healthy sign for a man who claims he's as fit as a fiddle. Sure, there was a time when The Brigadier could always disguise it with the occasional bout of push-ups and pull-ups but these days the lines on his face and the discolouration of his skin are beginning to tell another story.

As soon as the door is shut, he turns to Dobbs:

"Give us fifty Soles," he demands.

Snake Charmer

The expression on The Brigadier's face is anything but warm and Dobbs can see he's fast approaching his flipside.

"I don't want any more. Enough now. Had a good blast though," Dobbs says, trying to make light of The Brigadier's withdrawal rattling and blatant demand.

"We treated you to a good night out, had some fun, so don't give us all that," he fires back.

Dobbs runs it through his mind and then turns to Agent6 to see where he's at with the whole thing.

"Don't look at me; I'm having a break," he says, deflecting the situation.

Dobbs reluctantly reaches in his pocket and hands over the fifty Soles and, like that, The Brigadier's gone.

"Things are going to get a little mad," Dobbs whispers, glancing over at Agent6. "I really want Bolivar to get here so we can just take off. I don't know how long I can hang out with him, you know?"

"I've had my blowout with him. What good it might have done, I can't say. You know, when we went back last night, he blew all his money in that casino: everything." There's a tone of total distain in Agent6's voice.

"Everything? You've got to be fucking joking! What's he gonna do? Fuck, he's going from the hungry ghost realm straight into the hell realm," Dobbs says, throwing a bit of Buddhist philosophy into the equation for good measure. He takes off his hat and throws it on the bed, running his hands through his sweaty hair.

"I mean, I suppose it might do him some good, but he's a serious fucking liability now," he says and then, sighing, adds, "But stuck in Lima, broke, in that state…Shit."

Agent6 sits on his bed and pulls his legs up in a very relaxed manner. "You wanted a story didn't you?"

"Yeah, but I didn't want this: a fucking pestilence frenzy!"

"Bullshit!"

"I'm on a mission to write a book, not chronicle his fucking demise."

"Same thing isn't it?"

"Shit. What to fucking do? He's like some crazy fucking Christian that's locked his sights on an all-out apocalyptic showdown. I can't help but think sticking with him is synonymous with going down with him. On his current course he's chartering a passage far away from decency to feed that thing. Shit man, he's gonna sail off the fucking edge of the world!"

"You wanted a story about why the banks are about to go down, if you're so sure they are, than what better than entering the head of a banker?" Agent6 says, glances at Dobbs then retrieves a lump of what looks like fine *Manali cream* from his pocket.

"Time to get off this crazy locomotive," he grins.

"Good call!"

In no time at all an aromatic smoke is scenting the air and they're both sitting on their beds, comfortably stoned and wondering what they're doing with their lives in the shadow of The Comedown.

"I mean, that was supposed to be a great night out and I didn't even talk to a single girl," says Dobbs. "Not that I was looking for anything but, bloody hell... I mean, great to try a bit of refined pestilence and all that but, let's face it - a girl-less bar, a barren casino, and not much else; It all just feels like a total downer."

Agent6 is silent and contemplative, perhaps reflecting on the events of the previous night. After sometime he says, "Good to have a blow out with him, though. Knew I was going to have a blowout with the old Brigadier and then maybe we could say, yeah, we've done that. Now let's move on, you know? But he's not ready to leave it; not yet, at any rate." He passes the spliff to Dobbs.

"Yeah, whatever. Call me old fashioned but, pestilence aside, where's the *chicas* from Chile? I thought having some fun might actually include a bit of getting blown away by the opposite sex rather than just sitting blowing cash in a joint like that," Dobbs conveys with a look of disappointment.

"I weren't blowing no money in that joint. The pestilence is three quid a gram and the drinks were on the house. I gambled about a *tenner* the whole night. How much did you *'blow'*?"

"Well, yeah," Dobbs chuckles, "I don't think the word 'blow' quite captures my expenditure last night."

"Exactly! We're all just feeling the comedown now and nothing more. And, well, you're just waking to the fact that he's losing it."

"Shit!"

After not much more than an hour of lolling about, the door bursts open. Dobbs is reading and Agent6 has sunk into a tired sort of lull, but The Brigadier is back, completely re-inflated, and everything is running at about 300 miles per hour again. To Dobbs

27

it's getting boring - and this is only the second day. The Brigadier begins racking up some lines on the TV but neither Dobbs nor Agent6 are interested.

"Maybe later," Dobbs says, a hint of reservation in his voice.

The Brigadier, obviously offended at this refusal of his hospitality, marches back over to the TV and, dispensing with the etiquette of a note, recklessly vacuums the lot up his nose by dragging his whole face across the top of the TV set. Then he turns around, coldly staring at Dobbs as he carelessly wipes off the vast residue of powder smudged around his face with the back of his hand. Agent6 is totally unimpressed. He jumps off his bed, grabs his sound system, and, without showing any fear of The Brigadier whatsoever, stalks out of the room, almost barging into the other man as he goes and forcing him to jump out of the way.

Dobbs, who is clearly nervous, can see that The Brigadier is absolutely seething with barely controlled anger but he just sits there, attempting to disengage from his stroppy mood. He feels distinctly uncomfortable though, and The Brigadier knows it. His ego is inflating out of control, feeding off Dobbs's fear.

"Man, you're freaking me out!" he finally manages to shout, then buries his head into his book and attempts to shut out the world beyond the edges of the pages.

The room is split into two sections and has a separate bedroom at the rear which The Brigadier has taken for himself, leaving three beds in the main section for Dobbs, Agent6 and Bolivar when he turns up. For a moment The Brigadier stares at Dobbs with eyes of fury but then, to Dobbs's profound relief, he silently stalks back to his room. Dobbs grabs his book again. It's called *The Party's Over* by Richard Heinburg and charts, in a fashion, America's third run of entering a Peak Oil scenario and the scary similarities between now and the previous two times - which led to the First and Second World Wars respectively.

He's still pretty freaked out and the irony of the book's title is by no means lost on him, but he tries to lose himself in its pages nonetheless. It seems to suggest that what is economically unfolding now is nothing more than a currency crisis propagated by war, disease, famine and terror, all funded by a credit machine out of control. There's nothing new in there for Dobbs really, but the research is thorough. It's a statistician's funfair.

It perplexes him to consider war as a viable business with today's military technology, however. The First World War started with cavalry and ended with tanks and bombers. The Second World War started with that same technology but ended with the nuclear bomb. It's not exactly hard to see where a third world war would start, though God only knows where it would end.

In today's world, a so-called 'mini-nuke' has the explosive force ten times greater than the bomb dropped on Hiroshima and they are listed by the Pentagon as 'safe for civilian use.' The present-day equivalent of a Hiroshima size bomb is called a *Daisy-Cutter*. Nobody really survives in the vicinity of one of those when they go off as it's full of sharp shards of metal. But it's not nuclear, so considered a clean bomb. It is the most awesome nail bomb ever invented. In their blast radius they cut everything to shreds – everything – thus explaining the cute little name that always makes Dobbs think of kids making daisy chains. How many Daisy Cutters have been dropped on Afghanistan and Iraq, along with all the depleted uranium bombshells, is difficult to know. The first Iraq invasion was only supposed to last a year but the bombing went on for over a decade before the next Iraq war officially started, where, in 2003 alone, 240,000 tonnes of depleted uranium were deployed. The true figures have been heavily suppressed but Dobbs had read in one blog they could be as high as forty thousand times as much radioactive waste as was generated by the bomb dropped on Hiroshima. An estimate based on the unprecedented volume of birth defects, cancers and other diseases associated with radiation exposure reported since the invasion.

It's obvious to him now: The only way to stop a third world war is simply not to start one. But how do you do that when it's never you or anybody you ever seem to know who beats the war drum? Who makes these choices, he thinks to himself. Is it really the voters? Are there normal people out there who don't directly profit from war actually voting for it? He's never met any himself. It torments him. His partner can't stand him talking about it:

"You're not a fucking economist!" She'd scream every time he raised the subject; for her it was all doom and gloom oh, and that other terrible word she hated hearing – Conspiracy!!! Anyone who looks for an answer to these questions encounters *'conspiracy theories'* within the first click of their web search. She hated them - or maybe she just hated what they did to his head; he couldn't decide. It was as though she was policing his thoughts sometimes. But then, it *was* becoming an obsession, he'd accepted that.

Coming back to the present, Dobbs realises his mind is just awash with noisy interference. He feels hostility towards The Brigadier, as though he's entangled in his anger. He drops his book down on his lap for a moment and tries to feel for the space beyond the anger, then hold himself there. Suddenly, out of nowhere, he remembers The Brigadier's a full-blown junky at the moment. Had he somehow managed to forget that little nugget? That's the long and the short of it and it has to be taken into account. He'd fully engaged with the antics of the previous night and it's affected his judgment, he realises.

He takes a breath, moving away from the bitterness, then gets up and walks over to The Brigadier's room.

"I think I'm going to get some fresh air," he says calmly.

The Brigadier is sat on the bed, just staring, emotionless, at the ceiling. Dobbs doesn't linger but instead wanders out of the room and up the iron spiral staircase leading to the roof where Agent6 is just standing looking out over the city. He seems a little lost and Dobbs guesses he is contemplating his problematic relationship with his girlfriend which, despite the fact that it is full of confrontation, still seems to persist in their absence from each other in the form of endless text messages. It's consuming so much of his time but as yet he's showing no sign of moving through the mess it's made of his head. He's clearly weighed down by it all.

They spend an hour or so just listening to music through Agent6's iPod and speaker system. Dobbs tries to make a little conversation, but his heart's not in the best state either. His own relationship back home is on the rocks as well, but right now he's just feeling total relief to have a break from it all. It's probably the pestilence comedown that's battering Agent6 more than anything else. Dobbs knows that will pass and soon, with the hot afternoon sun on their faces and the fresh air blowing in from the sea it all starts to feel exciting again.

After about an hour or so of this sunny vagueness the sound of The Brigadier's saxophone can be heard floating up the spiral staircase. Whatever tortured space he's been in has evidently lifted a little, even though his presence still feels pretty wired. But as he sways and moves with the music as though manufacturing the tones in his very core, Dobbs can sense he's making a massive effort and the old Brigadier is clearly coming through.

Dobbs knows he's not a bad man: if anything, he's normally pretty caring. He remembered a time, not so many years before, when they'd all been at *V Festival* and Dobbs had been dozing off under the sun in the early morning, recovering from the previous night's antics, neither really asleep nor awake. He'd been aware of the stragglers making their way back to their tents through his sleepy haze and just then along came a big bloke who'd peered down the gap between the trucks where they were all lying.

For some reason Dobbs had never found out the man just turned, with an expression as if he'd become an axe murderer, and paced with thundering steps towards him. The guy was so focussed on Dobbs, however, that he'd failed to see The Brigadier asleep between them and stepped clean on his head. The Brigadier had shot up and, standing directly in front of the stranger, given him a dose of his own medicine. Then, toe-to-toe, with this guy promising to perform extreme bodily harm on him, The Brigadier had said,

"Yeah, but you ain't got what it takes to have a fight with a bloke that's right up for one have you? You're a pussy. You're just a yellow pussy. You've been searching for someone to fight who you know won't fight back - because you can't fight a real fight."

The man had shaken with rage and The Brigadier had laughed in his face.

"When you're ready to fight like a man, take your first punch," The Brigadier had demanded but with every step The Brigadier took forward, the man had taken a step back until, eventually – and still spitting venom all the way – he'd been walked clean off site, backwards. The Brigadier was like a bulldog, who's nature was to protect his friends and ward off danger – normally.

Nonetheless, Agent6's face drops at the sight of him now as he obviously figures The Brigadier is going to try to dominate the airways and drown out the sounds from the stereo again. At first it seems he may be right as the melody seems to have been lost in an eclectic selection of random notes. It's not bad, but his obnoxiousness is still overshadowing the music a little. But as he strides around the roof, blowing his sax, his mood mellows and the vibe slowly becomes noticeably lighter. Agent6 looks over to Dobbs.

"Snake charmer himself," he says, just loud enough so The Brigadier can hear.

Then, as if by magic, the one thing Dobbs would most like but is least expecting happens; a beautiful young woman, her blond hair cut in a cute bob, emerges from the spiral staircase on to the rooftop, obviously drawn by the sound of The Brigadier's melodic talents. Both Agent6 and Dobbs are momentarily transfixed.

"I'll fight you for her," Dobbs whispers to Agent6.

"Not a hope in hell. She's mine..." But then, just as he's about to add something more, another girl with short dark hair, equally gorgeous, follows close behind. Agent6's jaw drops another three inches.

"Actually, you like your dirty blondes; I think I'm down with the brunette," he says.

Meanwhile, The Brigadier is walking over to the girls. Taking long, slow steps as he plays, he circles them, as though magically drawing them up. Dobbs doesn't take his eyes off the ladies.

"I wonder if they're from Chile?" He says, almost under his breath.

"I'm more worried about the numbers; we're kind of one short," Agent6 says, his tongue nearly touching the ground, and then, nodding to The Brigadier, "Hey, we're one short: keep blowing, Cowboy."

The Brigadier directs his sax to the stairs, gives a little toot, and, to Dobbs's genuine amazement, a third girl, equally attractive, rises like a genie from the stairwell. The Brigadier's eyes meet the girl's and he gives her a cheeky grin then, looking over to the others and nodding with animated glee, he circles round her, as if manifesting this vision of loveliness with the melody from his sax alone.

This girl doesn't seem as flirtatious as the first two. It's not that she's not sexy, but her face has more of an expression of friendly curiosity perhaps. Her short, mousy hair is styled in a way that suggests a youthful innocence yet at the same time there's something calmer and more mature about her. In contrast, the blonde who was first to ascend the steps clearly knows she's fresh, and Dobbs grins at her unashamedly. She's got it all going on he muses, as has the brunette, who's *got* to be Chilean. She's a skinny, super hot Latino babe wearing tight jeans which accentuate her sexy, slow stride and curvaceous hips, and Agent6 fairly laps up her moves as she wanders closer.

It's fair to say that none of these boys are shy, and if the girls want their jaws to drop, then jaws are going to drop. They both look up at the girls and then back at each other, openly exchanging nods of approval whilst sending clear messages to the ladies, who put on a bit of a blush. Dobbs glances back at Agent6 and sees the sparkle in his eyes.

"I ain't seen one line of pestilence do what that cheeky little brunette's doing for you right now. One minute you're in hell…"

But the girls are standing right in front of them now, just staring and saying nothing. Agent6 returns the stare unashamedly, looking deep into the Brunette's nut-brown eyes as though hypnotized.

"Wow!" He blatantly whispers then looks her up and down outrageously, almost undressing her as he does so and not hiding one tiny piece of his obvious lust to lose his hands up her tight T-shirt.

The Brigadier stops playing his sax and begins speaking so fast that even Agent6, who's Spanish is very good, is struggling to understand what he's saying as it seems a long convoluted sentence. The girl with the mousy hair turns to him and, with a smile, says one word, which even Dobbs can understand.

"Chile."

He and Agent6 glance at each other and piss themselves laughing. The girls look at each other with half curious expressions, smirking. Dobbs returns the blonde bombshell's friendly gaze with a look of total disbelief.

"Fantastic," he breathes.

She brushes her hair back, pouting her gorgeous full lips at The Brigadier then glancing over at Agent6 almost as if to see if he's checking her out. Of course he's checking her out; he's like a dog with two dicks and can barely contain himself, but Dobbs is clearly getting older, he thinks to himself, because whatever hold he once had over gorgeous young things like this is waning faster than he can actually believe, and all attention seems to be on his compadres.

Ten minutes pass, and Dobbs is struggling to talk with Esmeralda, the young woman with blond hair. The Brigadier is making manoeuvres on the girl with the mousy hair and Agent6 is engaged in a gazing competition with the brunette. It's quite a spectacle. She seems to draw her lips apart with a lusting, almost uncontrollable twitch that then diverts back into a periodical pout. Her lower teeth are somehow revealed slightly more than her upper teeth, with her jaw slightly extended. The overall effect is that she appears to be perpetually three seconds away from orgasm.

It's all very visual, and Dobbs has to fight back a chuckle. He watches her hold her breasts up high with her chest out and her arms just hanging loose by her side. She seems to drop her field of vision downwards periodically, as if she's trying to work out what

33

Agent6 is hiding in his pocket. Then again, perhaps she's just trying to translate the words on the t-shirt he'd picked it up on his way to the *Burning Man* Festival in America the previous year. *Las Vegas, Liquor in the front, Poker in the rear,* reads the legend, printed above a picture of a raunchy cowgirl spinning a lasso over her head, *blinged* out in gold.

Minutes later and the whole troupe are very relaxed - all apart from The Brigadier, that is, who's still looking pretty twitchy. The hotel management is one step ahead of the game however and, noticing the potential for business, is having drinks ferried up to the roof.

The Pisco Sour is one of Lima's most favoured cocktails, legendary for its citric bitterness. Dobbs, who's just taken the first sip, is experiencing a total shock-and-awe wakeup hit, followed by an immediate sweet aftermath and then something else, far stronger, that flushes through him in a delirious wave of giddiness. It somehow seems to capture the taste of this unfolding adventure; like Lima in a glass, glimmering in the golden sun.

In one moment he feels himself ascending out of the horrible head fuck of the pestilence come down and yet, as he casts his vision out to the city and the adventure that awaits beyond, he has an uncomfortable nagging thought: how can I even capture that view alone? How do I begin to write that? He shudders at the thought of the linguistic restrictions of his crap English –never mind his crap Spanish. In fact, his whole enthusiasm for writing a book seems battered by the previous night's exploits.

"Cheers," he says, proffering his glass up to Esmeralda's. *"La bar es muy poquito pero la liquor es mas fuerte. Muy peligroso. Pero, mucho gusto."* Then he shrugs his shoulders; he's almost exhausted his meagre storehouse of *Spanglish* and is now just about dead in the water.

"Si…" she says, and then rattles off another sentence he kind of understands a little but not really.

"Entiendo, err, poquito - pero despacio, por favor…"

Esmeralda giggles. *"Learning Spanish, ah?"*

"Si, claro… Oh! You speak English?"

"I used to live in America," she says, keeping her energy directed more at the whole group.

"Fuck, thank God for that. I'll make an effort here and there but it's early days," he says, holding his glass up to the gods before taking a huge celebratory gulp of his *pisco sour.*

34

"It's OK! I love an opportunity to speak English again and remind myself I can still do it."

Dobbs, still rushing from the shock of the cocktail, just nods and smiles.

"Cool!" He manages eventually.

Everything is very fluid, just like the endless flow of cocktails and the plentiful reefers that keep doing the rounds.

They run through all the normal formalities and it turns out she's a photographer. She goes into a little detail about her work. It's all sounds a bit corporate and it's clear she's looking for a springboard into something more creative.

The conversation quickly turns to art. Dobbs is no connoisseur on the subject, but the *Pisco Sour* is kicking in and he's ready to have a go.

"...can you imagine, there we were, off our tits, looking at the self-portrait of Van Gogh but, actually, what we were seeing was Van Gogh but in the flesh, just staring back at us...Like he'd somehow painted his own energetic body that projected Van Gogh in the flesh. We both saw the same thing!"

Esmeralda looks surprised by the story, but also quite unimpressed.

"Oh yeah, I love art," Dobbs adds, blundering on with his silly tale of the time he'd visited the Van Gogh Museum in Amsterdam after eating a whole box of Mexican mushrooms with his ex.

Vaguely, he realises something is wrong; Esmeralda has stopped nodding politely and is now staring at him with an expression of what can only be described as utter distaste.

"You take drugs?"

Dobbs coughs, clearing his throat, not quite expecting that. There is an uncomfortable moment of silence as Agent6 and The Brigadier both overhear and glance over at her, but Dobbs tries to sidestep the comment and not show any surprise.

"Well, I've dabbled I suppose. You...no?"

"I'm Catholic," she declares.

This time everyone turns and stares at her, shocked by the genuine sincerity of the announcement: she just didn't look the type.

"Oh...Really?" Dobbs finally says. Then he looks up and toasts the heavens with his glass again. "Fan-fucking-tastic!" He says, feeling like a stand-up comedian who's just discovered he's got an American sat in the front row.

Changing Lanes

Esmeralda brushes her hair back with that single lucky flick of her wrist and then stares into thin air, as if to bring the subject back to her rather gorgeous form. Dobbs needs no encouragement and, allowing his gaze to drop down to the delicate pale skin around her neck and just above her breasts, he lets his eyes travel slowly down the length of her body as if on a journey. She cocks her head to see where he's going and he tries hard not to pause too long at any awkward places. At last, descending down the delicious slopes of her magnificent thighs, he finally comes to a stop at his *Pisco Sour,* sitting at her feet. It appears almost in double to Dobbs now and he has to shake his head to bring his vision back into singularity.

For a moment, he's lost for words, but suddenly two just pop into his head. He pulls out his phone, casually selects 'voice recorder' then presses the green button and pops the device back in his top pocket. Without a decent microphone the device only really picks up his own voice in a muffled sort of way but that will be all he really needs to bring about some memory of events, he figures. Agent6 observes what he has just done and, winking at him, shouts across to Esmeralda.

"You know Dobbs is writing a book?"

"Oh," she says, suddenly interested. "About what?"

Dobbs stops, almost in freeze frame. Given her stance on drugs, he is wary of telling her the book is actually about a very odd blast of nitrous oxide.

"Well, funny you should mention it, but about the Catholic Church actually."

Esmeralda's shoulders drop with the anticlimax of the comment and then she pops her head up and looks at Dobbs.

"You don't like Catholics right?"

"No, not at all. I mean … yes, I love Catholics; I went all the way to Calcutta just to kiss Mother Teresa's hand once," he says with genuine sincerity.

She pulls a face that suggests disbelief but no indication of any amusement - not that Dobbs was even trying to be funny.

"No really, I did."

"And did you kiss her hand?" She says, twisting her body away from Dobbs, who senses she has her guard up even higher now.

"Yeah, but she snatched it right back. She was all about total service really. She wanted absolutely no gratitude whatsoever. She was the genuine article wasn't she? A proper saint, Catholic or not. My mum used to tell me the story of Francis of Assisi when I was really young, too. And, honestly, I'd cry every time she told me the end of it - the bit when he breaks through, past all the, well, church security I suppose, and gets to the Pope to ask for his blessing. That he could *kiss* the Pope's feet; that the Pope would ordain the tiny church he'd built in Assisi! She loved telling me how the Pope looked upon him, dressed in his rags, and how he just dropped to his knees and kissed Saint Francis's feet. So, no, I don't hate Catholics – there's good and bad in everything, right?"

For a moment Esmeralda says nothing, observing him warily. She's obviously trying to work out where he's going with this.

"I love the story of Francis of Assisi. It's my favourite story," she finally whispers.

"Kind of one of mine too, I guess," Dobbs tries to hide his relief and decides to take a different tack. "So, what – you telling me you don't break the rules like? That's not me trying to get you into bed, just curious really. You've got the look of a rule-breaker more than a rule-maker," he says, grinning wolfishly.

She squirms slightly but, to his relief, she grins too.

"Now you're making fun of me."

Dobbs is impressed. All of a sudden she's leaning back into the sun lounger and looking more relaxed, like she's feeling back in control. Plus she's got a glint of something else in those eyes, something more mischievous perhaps.

"Yeah, I break the rules sometimes," she smiles, running a finger round the rim of her glass. "So what are you writing a book about then - Catholics - really?"

More drinks get delivered by the management but Dobbs knows he needs to go easy now so, placing his half-finished cocktail on the floor, he hands out the latest delivery and then, as soon as the manager disappears, relights the spliff and passes it to Esmeralda. He doesn't point out the obvious fact that spliff it is technically a drug also.

"Well, it's about a guy who travels to South America - well, to the Amazon actually - to find the origin of Shakespeare."

"So, Shakespeare came from the Amazon did he?" Esmeralda grins, arching her eyebrows as she pulls her weight more on to the sun lounger they're both sitting on. She's definitely starting to relax now. Her English is perfect and she clearly enjoys speaking

37

it, plus she doesn't make Dobbs feel like an idiot for his lack of proficiency in her mother tongue.

"Well, maybe not Shakespeare directly," he says, beginning to get into his stride, "But I reckon he might have had a boding spirit like Ariel in *The Tempest*. You know the character I mean, the one who does Prospero's bidding? The one who creates the storm - the tempest- that brings all who have wronged Prospero to the shores of his tiny island, where he enacts his final judgment upon them?" He pauses, taking a cautious sip of his drink. "So, perhaps Shakespeare's own boding spirit was from the Amazon. I mean, I don't know for sure, but that's where the main character in my story goes to find the only thing he believes can now stop World War III."

"It's fiction then?" She says, dragging her thumb down the narrow glass until it stops with a tiny screech.

"Well, it loosely follows a true story - very loosely, of course. But yeah, total fiction really."

At this point The Brigadier, who's been getting increasingly agitated suddenly jumps up.

"I'm going to get some pizza. We need food," he declares, pacing. He looks at Perlita, the girl with the mousy hair, "Come on, let's go and grab some pizzas." He brings his attention back to Dobbs and Agent6, "Shall we all chuck in for some Pizza then?"

Dobbs looks over at The Brigadier and then Perlita.

"You going with...Perlita?" He says finally.

There's a moment of awkward silence and then Perlita shouts, "Si, vamanos!"

Agent6 and Dobbs chuck The Brigadier some cash for food and immediately he goes, taking the girl with him. The energy becomes noticeably calmer as he leaves but Dobbs and Agent6 catch each other's eye briefly as the pair disappear. For a moment everyone seems to be contemplating whether that was actually the best move and Dobbs, closing his eyes, surreptitiously places a golden ring of protection round the two of them in his mind's eye before directing his attention back to Esmeralda.

"So, you really are writing about Shakespeare?" Esmeralda says.

"No! I'm writing the story of how I became Catholic."

"No..!"

"You see that was the only bit of the whole story that was unbelievable wasn't it? Everything else is totally believable apart from me becoming Catholic! You see, you were brought up

Catholic, right? You were born into it. Tony Blair's the only person I've ever heard of that officially joined up. I mean, I'm sure people do. But it just doesn't seem very believable does it?"

Esmeralda shakes her head, wondering where he's going.

"So, what? You're going to brush up on your Spanish and present yourself as some intellectual travelling scholar and I'm going to be your token Catholic - right?"

"Oh, come on, that's not fair. You seem pretty cool to me…I don't know, it's your family religion. I'm not poking the judgment stick at those that follow in faith - Catholic or otherwise. I'm merely concerned with those that have genocide in their heads rather than love in their hearts."

Esmeralda's clearly feeling distinctly uncomfortable to have her religion placed at the forefront of the conversation again, but she did kind of bring it up, Dobbs thinks to himself.

"So why does he go to the Amazon to find Shakespeare then?"

Dobbs considers for a moment, unsure whether it's a good idea to mention the word '*Ayahuasca*' in light of her averred stance towards drugs.

"Well, Shakespeare ends up representing the origin of something that might have saved Britain hundreds of years ago when the Catholics were about to bring the Spanish Inquisition to British shores," he says, eventually deciding to play things safe.

"What…Shakespeare?"

"Well, what Shakespeare represents."

"Which is what?"

"Well…a miracle!"

Esmeralda doesn't look impressed.

"A miracle?"

"Well, back in those days, everything seemed to have gone past any point of hope. The tipping point had come and long since gone. It was one of those times in history when a miracle was the only option left on the table."

"What…and then Shakespeare came along and saved everyone?"

"Well, not quite. It's a bit of an odd thing, really. You see, I'd written this silly kind of play - a tongue-in-cheek performance for a nightclub type environment, to be performed on the night of the general election in 2005 and telling the story of a man who builds a machine that can not only turn rubbish into gold but can even recycle all the wasted votes.

"It was for a late night show so it was a bit rude - well, very rude actually…you know, lots of tunes and late night banter for an audience that are pissed out of their skulls. I guess I wanted to create the type of energy you see in those old paintings of the theatre antics of Shakespeare's time; everyone screaming out - a mob! - rather than the incredibly boring scene of people sitting in comfortable chairs looking like they're at home watching the fucking TV again. Anyway, so I wrote this play, '*One For Sorrow.*' It was an experiment, but it went well. One of my mates, Hicksy, who'd helped me write it had come up with a script that captured that same kind of crazy energy - a Shakespeare parody, complete with all the banter - like a piss-take of *The Tempest*.

It was a fantastic script, but I didn't know the original story; I'd never actually read any Shakespeare in my life. So my mate gave me a children's version of the story, as I just couldn't get my head around the original tale - it's like another fucking language! Honestly, I fell in love with the tale. It's a beautiful story; a story steeped in treachery and deceit that ends in, well, forgiveness.

"I guess because I didn't know the story I couldn't really begin to connect the dots until I read the play. And then I read my mate's play again and I loved it even more! It portrayed Tony Blair as Proslairo, the Peace Envoy, wielding his magic book of manifestoes. Well, the purpose of this book I want to write is to actually make the play happen, ironically. I've tried so many options. I think I've gone around the houses a bit." Here he pauses.

"Sounds like you like your Shakespeare," Esmeralda says, still sounding a little unsure.

"Like I say, I've still only read one of his original plays but I've always had a fascination with the story of Shakespeare. Well, for many years anyway. It was all a much bigger thing, you know? But as I dug into the research, I started uncovering a story of another tempest that happened just before Shakespeare's time: the tempest that destroyed the Spanish Armada! And I started to realize that Shakespeare's play was inspired by that great storm - the one that destroyed that Spanish Armada."

"Right?" Esmeralda sounds doubtful. She's clearly intelligent and is still showing signs she thinks that this is all likely to turn out as an attack on her religious roots.

"Imagine that time in England. The country was broken and on its knees. All our medicine women were being burnt as witches and our scholars, poets and writers executed for blasphemy. The

Catholics permitted absolutely no freedom of speech, just like they did here in South America. The country was being torn apart. So Henry VIII, King of England..."

"Ahh...Your king who liked killing his wives?"

"Yes, the very same. Although I don't think it was as simple as that. Bear in mind that those were arranged marriages Esmeralda - strategic affairs that set the course of who owned what. These were rarely unions of love I suspect."

"Perhaps being a psychopath isn't that simple."

"I'm not condoning it. It's just in the background of his legacy; the Renaissance that had really started in Germany was kicking off right across Europe. It was an uprising. So the Catholics were carrying out the Inquisition almost as a kind of act of redemption for this evil awakening that was sweeping the land. People were dying in their thousands!" He takes a sip of his cocktail.

"So Henry broke England away from the Catholic Church because it was hindering any type of development. The country was being divided and suppressed. Did you know that Henry reinstated the right of herbal medicine to be a legal practice for instance? In one single Bill a whole health care system that the Catholics had banned as evil, was reinstated. It's harsh, I know. He must have known that there would be a massive reprisal. And it wasn't just happening in England, the Renaissance was happening right across Europe; this coming back to the real Gnostic teachings of Christ - not peddled through some third-party priest class but found deep within your own heart." He shakes his head, knowing that she's listening now. "But England breaking from the Catholic stronghold came with the certainty of a massive backlash."

"So Henry executing his wives was OK? You just dismiss that?"

"No, I'm just trying to understand the motivations of a man at the helm of a country that is being torn to bits by religious extremists using what they define as 'love and light' to create divisions between every faction of society. The reality is that Henry just wanted a son to take the helm after him when retribution finally came. And when that day did come, and the Great Armada finally set sail to bring the Inquisition to English shores who did he leave?"

"A woman?"

"Yeah, a woman, Elizabeth the First, Henry's daughter. A frail woman by all accounts, too. She knew what the Spanish were intent on bringing to England. Not just taking lives - that was too easy. No, every life that was taken was used as a means to drive greater terror into the populace. Astounding torture. The only intention of that Armada; to take lives in the hundreds of thousands, destroy Henry's legacy and reverse the awakening with war." He pauses again looking at her and wondering if it's hurt he sees in her face.

"We're not talking about Catholicism really, are we Esmeralda? We're just talking about human evolution. You see, there was no way such an Armada, carrying such an army could have been stopped. It was the biggest fleet to ever set sail, even in today's terms. Nearly all the troops were already in France, just waiting to be ferried across the English Channel and right onto the battlefield to begin the killing.

Yet barely one of those ships, if any, touched English shores. Half were destroyed by a fire born of an act of faith on the part of the English captains to burn their own ships at the whim of England's Arch Wizard, Dr. John Dee. And indeed, a wind blew up from nowhere and took the burning ships straight into the docked fleet. It was the ultimate naval faux pas: **never** bring your fleet together and take them out of battle formation. Unless you really *want* to lose them." He sips his cocktail, warming to his theme, then continues.

"The other half of the fleet cut their anchors to get away from that terrible wall of burning ships that consumed everything in its path. But without those anchors they couldn't stop, and a tempest just blew them all away - and perhaps showed them the suffering they wanted to show England. The few who survived the disaster told of the most cruel conditions; disease, bitter cold, sickness and starvation. Even when they got round to Ireland the Irish wanted nothing to do with them, so they couldn't restock with food and supplies there but had to keep going, all the way back to Spain.

By the time they arrived they were broken; they'd lived out the harsh intentions they'd been intent on inflicting on so many others. The whole thing was a miracle. The largest fleet to ever set sail, just gone with the wind…"

"Nice story," Esmeralda whispers, still clearly wondering where it's all going. "Is that the official story?"

"Yes and no. The official story gives the credit to the skill of the English Navy and cunning intelligence and all sorts. Few are truly willing to really see the elephant in the room, as it were."

"Which is what?"

"A miracle."

"You seriously believe it was a miracle?"

"Yeah! But whilst one miracle was occurring there, another was slipping in under the cover of darkness - a coded message."

"Shakespeare?"

"No." He pauses. "Grammar."

"Grammar?"

"Yeah, English Grammar. The first thing Tony Blair took out of the school curriculum because of who and what he's part of. Because of what he is."

"Because he's Catholic?" Esmeralda retorts.

"You're a Catholic Esmeralda. Would you have done what he's done?"

"I don't really know what he's done..."

"He's been very foolish. He's led Britain into a trap where every country is dumping our currency and distancing themselves from us because of our stance of utter war. It's all just like what happened before the Second World War when the country was brought to its knees, and Europe distanced itself from us, and the only way to get the support of America - well, of the Federal Reserve - was to adhere to taking Palestine off the Palestinians and giving it to the Jews." He sighs.

"Tony is just repeating a very old story. He's a man who terrorizes with religion. He uses the so-called 'Word of God' to ordain murder by telling those being groomed to kill they have God's blessing. He has ordained the religious dumping of depleted uranium, in every Englishman's name, on Muslim land, all in the name of a crime we know they did not commit: it has nothing to do with being Catholic whatsoever Esmeralda. He's calling in the Inquisition again."

"I guess it's all a big part of your history."

"It's being done in my name Esmeralda. In Iraq, in Afghanistan, and probably in Iran next: who do you think they'll blame?"

"Well..."

"No, but you're right. I'm only just waking up to my own history Esmeralda. Perhaps that's why I'm so charged with it all at the moment. And, well, perhaps because we're coming into something similar to that time now maybe. An awakening. I mean, I see it through very rose coloured spectacles. I know I do. I don't know; maybe just because I'd heard of a Shakespeare conspiracy tale a long time ago but had never seen the massive impact of all that

43

was playing out - how big the picture really is. I think the dates might have a lot to do with the similarities of this time and back then. Back in the time of Shakespeare it was fast approaching 1666. Dates like that have religious extremists longing for the Apocalypse to put them out of their misery. It's just like 2012."

"You think bad things will happen?"

"Well, for instance you could consider democracy an evolutionary step, as the House of Commons opened for business just over forty years after 1666. It would have probably taken far longer if not for fear of the religious extremists threatening to tear the country apart and plunge it back into the dark ages."

"Surely it's those in your House of Commons that vote for war. Surely that does not work. It's a contradiction."

"Well, yes and no. The idea is fantastic, but the reality is flawed. You see it collects the votes but only listens to about five percent of them. The rest are wasted because there's no proportional representation. All that's needed is one tiny change in policy, one tiny Bill, like Henry's healthcare system, to correct that. Tony made thousands of rules to restrict. All that is needed is just one little Bill to more accurately represent the will of the People. You know, just to check the remaining 95 percent of my country are totally down with burying Iran under depleted uranium like we did in Iraq and Afghanistan."

"*Esta loco.*"

"*Si, pera loco lindo.*"

"Was she a good woman, that Queen…Elizabeth?"

"I don't know, really. But think of what she was up against. Think of that time, Esmeralda: Mary the First, her Catholic sister-in-law, had been crowned Queen of England and had had Elizabeth arrested on charges of conspiring with Protestant rebels and locked up in the Tower of London under sentence of death. Mary was pregnant, apparently about to give birth to an heir to the throne, but childbirth was a risky thing in those days."

"It's a risky thing these days," Esmeralda interjects with a smirk.

"Well, exactly. If anything happened to her, Elizabeth would have been next in line. But Mary had a bump in the right place and the blessing of the Pope. Remember this is a power struggle, not an attack on your faith." He tokes on the spliff that has just been passed to him.

44

"But Elizabeth's name had been smeared with every abominable crime on Earth. You know, in the same light, I wonder if Mary Magdalene was really just a prostitute? You really think she was?" Esmeralda stops to consider the comment and takes the spliff off Dobbs.

"But I thought you said Elizabeth didn't die."

Well, she was locked in the Tower of London under order of Mary, who was waiting for a mandate to chop off her head just like my country looks for a mandate to bomb Iran. Mary was the original *Bloody Mary*. She was the daughter of Catherine of Aragon, Henry's first wife, who he'd divorced. Her continuing to live or bear an heir would have kept the country in Catholic hands and the inquisition, which had more than started again, would have gone out of control. A full scale Catholic lockdown would have occurred and the enactment of *zero tolerance* served on the people: everyone is guilty, all of the time. Mary was intent on enforcing a Catholic regime upon England." He pauses, knowing she's enjoying the tale but obviously feeling slightly awkward.

"But was Elizabeth a bad woman?" He pauses, "Mary thought she was. There was Elizabeth, locked up in the Tower of London on charges of conspiring with Protestant rebels, which was what her father, Henry VIII, had initiated with his divorce from Mary's mother in the first place. You'd think, of all the people who should have most hated Henry for beheading his wives, it should have been Elizabeth - as it was her mother he beheaded. But Mary's mother lived. And yet, astonishingly, Elizabeth took on his cause. So, in Catholic eyes, she had to die." He pauses, savouring the moment and preparing for the final denouement before continuing.

"You like your history don't you?" She says with a bit of a smile.

"Well, I'm..." and then, deciding not to mention his age, "...only just discovering parts of it now. But it seems the Catholics' luck just changed like the wind once more as the screams coming from the Palace when Mary went into labour turned out not to be the cries of a woman giving birth but of a woman dying - dying of a massive tumour that had been growing in her womb."

"She died!"

"Imagine. When those guards were marching up that spiral staircase to fetch Elizabeth from the Tower of London, she would have probably been expecting to be frog-marched before a Catholic court and sentenced to die immediately. If Mary had given birth, the renaissance for England would have ended there and then. As she heard those guards coming up the stairs she would have been on her hands and knees doing only one thing."

"Praying!"

"Exactly. She would have been on her hands and knees *praying*. Probably like she'd never prayed before. I wonder what promises she made to God in that terrifying moment."

"I still don't see how it links to Shakespeare though."

"Well, the Catholics ruled by divide and conquer. And the easiest things to exploit if you want to drive a wedge between people are things like their religious beliefs, the obvious rich and poor class thing, colour and creed, and of course, last but by no means least, language.

"England was a country already divided by the natural boundaries of numerous dialects across the land. The Shakespeare conspiracy stories tell of a man who reached a level of wisdom where he found the '*whatever* it takes' to write the Works of Shakespeare. Just think of the name -'Shake-Spear'- like shaking a spear or a stick. It was what the elders held in the great circles of our ancestors. Whoever held and shook the spear was demanding the right to say what was on their mind, freely, without interruption - to be heard.

Shakespeare represented freedom of speech, something which the Catholic Church had all but banned. It was a genius - a wizard perhaps – who put together the works of Shakespeare and wrote the whole thing and invented grammar, a complex lingual system that took elements of all the dialects and pieced together a single language to unite the land against the common threat."

"Who was he then? Who was Shakespeare?"

"Well, someone very clever, writing anonymously. Probably Sir Francis Bacon, or a literary think tank headed by Sir Francis Bacon. But, really, it's not so much who, it's how? As in, how did he…"

"…or she!"

"Or *she*, indeed, obtain their vision? How did they harvest that talent? Who trained him *or her* to think like that? It's like a genius bolt of lightning. Where does that genius really come from? That's what my main character is searching for in the Amazon. He's searching for that same miracle that can stop the apocalypse."

"Nice story. How far have you got?"

"Ahh…Well, I've kind of got up to the point where the main character just got to Lima and has met this hot chica from Chile.

46

It's a really cheesy part of the book. I'm not sure how it's all panning out yet."

"I don't believe in conspiracy stories."

"Do they need to be believed? Can they not just exist with the stars, say, and be just... considered? I'm beginning to doubt it is possible to believe in anything." he says, as a mere matter of fact.

Esmeralda appears to consider the notion.

"I suppose you think 9/11 was a conspiracy tale?"

"No, not really. Conspiracy stories are cunning and clever. That was nothing more than the blundering blatancy of the real perpetrators to demand the world choose a side."

"To choose what side?"

"War or peace, one or the other. In Bush's words, 'You're either with us or against us.'"

He glances over to Agent6 and the other girl, Niki. Both are sitting on the far sun lounger, closer to the edge of the building. To no great surprise, Dobbs can see Agent6's long face making a comeback. He's obviously enjoying the company, although it seems Niki's perhaps a little more keen than he is. As Dobbs watches, he gets out his wallet to show her a photo of his partner and child back home. 'You're scaring him off,' Dobbs thinks to himself. Niki's looking a little confused too, but the truth is that neither he nor Agent6 are trying to pull, really. Dobbs tries not to laugh at the situation but can't help it and as he does so, Agent6's face also breaks into laughter.

Just then Perlita comes stomping back up the stairs looking pale and annoyed. She glances over at Agent6 and shouts,

"*Es loco, tu amigo.*"

Dobbs's understands what she's saying just from the expression on her face. The Brigadier follows behind a few moments later holding a couple of pizza boxes and in a matter of minutes, all the girls have gathered on Dobbs's sun lounger eating pizza.

There's a strange sort of energy; the two main hottest male contenders have just exited the situation by Dobbs's reckoning. The Brigadier has scared off his girl and Agent6 has been scared off on account of not wanting to make waves with his girlfriend. Dobbs is not really Esmeralda's type, plus he's in a relationship anyway. So really everyone's out of the picture. It's clear to Dobbs that all are craving a little bit of intimacy but things don't seem to be going in that direction, even though the flirt levels are cranked up so high.

47

Agent6 looks across at all the girls huddled round Dobbs and, seeing he's chatting to Perlita now, shouts across in jest,
"Watch it: Dobbs is cornering all the women!"
Dobbs is about to laugh but catches The Brigadier giving him the most ice cold stare, full of a rage, the likes of which he's not seen directed at him for really quite some time.
Leaning closer he seethes,
"Don't go changing lanes, Dobbs."

A Tempest is Brewing

"My God, look at you all!" Bolivar's deep voice is bellowing out.

It's about midday and Agent6 and Dobbs are pulling themselves out of a deep, well-deserved slumber.

"I'm here! I'm in South America!" he blares in everyone's faces as if to re-affirm the importance of the moment. Then he flings opens the curtains, allowing sunlight to flood the room, and throws his bags on the vacant bed nearest the window which is, apparently, waiting for him. Agent6 had actually already claimed the bed but somehow he's fallen asleep on the one furthest from the window instead. Now, seeing the manoeuvre, he gestures as if about to say something, but Bolivar beats him to it.

"Too late! You make your bed, you lie in it!" he roars, laughing.

Agent6 lets out a noise that could be construed as a chuckle and, surrendering the bed with a wave of his hand, he pulls himself up to take in the new day. One glance and it's clear that sleep has done its magic. He looks very mellow, in complete contradiction to Bolivar's head state.

Bolivar scrutinises the pair of them.

"Don't say I've missed all the fun, guys?"

Dobbs is smirking whilst Agent6 clasps his head with his palms, massaging his scalp with his fingers.

"Just another day in the office," he says, staring up at Bolivar and shaking his head.

"Just because you've already been living the dream, don't think you're getting away with anything less than getting completely fucked out of your brains with me tonight," Bolivar says, glaring at both Agent6 and Dobbs. Then, "they're down stairs by the way."

"Who?" Agent6 catches the comment after a few moments.

"Err…? The Chileans? Like the Chileans that are leaving - like right now."

They both chuckle and then, reaching down, Bolivar starts trying to tickle Agent6 who attempts to block the assault.

"Come on guys! I want to try some now, just to see what clean, uncut pestilence is really like. It's not too much to ask, is it?"

He's got Dobbs giggling now, knowing he's probably next in line for a tickle.

"Don't you want to take in the sights and see the wonders of Lima?" Dobbs enquires.

Bolivar stops his tickling attempts and turns to face him.

"Oh…And what sights and historical wonders have you taken in whilst being here so far then, Dobbs?" he quips, disguising his Brummy accent with something more gentrified and posh - which actually quite suits him.

"OK, pestilence it is then," Agent6 butts in.

Bolivar seems to be scouting the area.

"Where's The Brigadier anyway - or should that be obvious?" he says, looking over at Agent6, who offers a bland expression of cluelessness.

"Thought so. I can see who my partner in crime's going to be."

"I'm beginning to wonder if he even sleeps anymore," Dobbs says. But, not wanting to stir the pot, he refrains from saying more. Dobbs always chose not to cross swords with The Brigadier - or anyone bordering that state in fact - but he's often unaware of just how differently he himself acts under the effects of pestilence.

After a bit of a wake-up ceremony and an aimless meander up Mira Flores' main high street they finally settle in a little restaurant on one of the main corners, opposite a multi-storey sports store. Noisy traffic is spewing first one way and then the next to the rhythm of the traffic lights. Horns are blaring and the sidewalk is as busy as any big city. It is an exciting vibe, and a lot more upmarket than Dobbs had been expecting.

The restaurant is simple but popular, even though tiny. It has an open front, furnished with about six little tables - so small that theirs seems cramped even for just the three of them. Agent6 glances over at Bolivar, who's attempting to decipher the descriptions of the dishes on offer from a card in a laminated holder on the table.

"Go for the *menu*, man," he says helpfully. "Places like this always have a *menu*."

"Err, yeah thanks Sherlock, I now have a copy of the menu in my hands."

"Nohh," Agent6 says, his normally muted Yorkshire accent creeping through a little. "The *menu*, man! Places like this always have a *menu*. You know – like the meal they make in bulk every day? That's cheap and comes with juice and a starter? Stick to the *menus* and you can eat the best food for next to nothing in Peru."

50

Putting down the card Bolivar looks at Agent6 and then over to the waitress.

"La *menu*, por favor," he says, winking at Dobbs for recognition of this fine attempt at Spanish.

Orders out of the way, Bolivar begins inspecting the contents of a none-too-well concealed baggy he's purchased from some dodgy looking guy on the way – which by all accounts is an absolute no-no for just too many reasons. Agent6 is chuckling at him.

"You've broken the golden rule: don't take sweeties from strangers."

"No way is that pestilence, Bolivar," Dobbs says, a smug grin on his face. Bolivar says nothing. Instead, discreetly peering into the bag, he pushes a finger into its contents before licking it to taste its legitimacy.

"It's obvious just from the sheer volume he's given you. There's, like, about fifty fucking grams in there. All that for ten quid? No way, Jose!" Dobbs leans back in his chair, not even bothering to inspect the bag.

"Oh, and when did you become the connoisseur?" Bolivar shoots back. Nonetheless he gets up, walks over to a bin next to the newspaper vendor on the corner and just throws the bag away, no longer even attempting to conceal its contents.

"You should have told me before I paid," he grumbles, returning to his seat.

"That's got to be part of the fun though, hasn't it - getting ripped in Lima?" Dobbs says, smiling.

"Oh yeah, I forgot, good for the book, ah? Don't worry, I'm just warming up. By tomorrow I'll be getting robbed and raped...For the book, of course Dobbs. Are you recording now?"

Dobbs looks down and checks the recorder. "Err...Yes."

"Fucking hell! Don't know how I feel about that!"

"It's alright; I'll change all the names and call it all fiction. Maybe I'll rewrite you as the gimp. Cool with that?"

Bolivar is shaking his head with an expression of doubt and uncertainty.

"Come on Bolivar, welcome to South America; getting ripped is all part of the game," Agent6 says, dragging himself from his phone and what Dobbs assumes to be the latest round in his endless game of text-tennis with his partner.

When they eventually get back to the hotel The Brigadier has returned and is looking shaky. Bolivar doesn't even bother to go into all the big 'hello's' as he'd seen The Brigadier barely a week before. Instead he opens with:

"I just got ripped off, badly, buying some pestilence."

"I just got ripped back home for about twenty grand. You think you got it bad?" The Brigadier fires straight back. Nonetheless he is now giving Bolivar his fullest attention.

"What do you want?" he says. "Just give me the money and I'll go and get it for you now." He has a genuine look of wanting to sort the whole thing out, once and for all – or at least until the bag's empty.

And so the antics continue. More pestilence is scored and consumed as they wander from bar to bar. Afternoon moves into evening and evening into night and all the action is loosely located around the club they've decided to visit in the late hours. But as the night wears on, and the drinks get drunk, an uncomfortable edge begins to develop again.

Eventually, sometime in the lost hours between midnight and morning, they find themselves in a bar with a terrace outside. Agent6 and Bolivar are sat, deep in conversation. The Brigadier is inside, talking to two girls at a small table with four chairs. In no time, he's pumping out some tunes on his saxophone. From a distance everything seems friendly and happy, so, leaving Agent6 and Bolivar to their chat, Dobbs decides to go and join the trio.

As soon as Dobbs takes a seat one of the ladies starts chatting to him in English. She's a mature woman but she's sexy - they both are, or at least they seem so to Dobbs in his present state of intoxication. The Brigadier, however, stands and starts playing his sax obstreperously, as if warning him off, and there it is, that an uncomfortable edge again.

Although Dobbs feels he's just having a bit of fun with The Brigadier he's quite unaware of how depraved he himself can become under the effects of pestilence. Or, perhaps, he simply chooses to be ignorant to the obvious truth. Nonetheless, although the girl who's spoken to him is definitely the more attractive of the pair, he decides the quieter one is safer territory. Suddenly, however, the English-speaking woman - perhaps offended by his shift of energy - becomes luridly direct.

"I fucking hate Gringos who just turn up and think they can fuck whoever they choose!" she screams, glaring at Dobbs. "We were just here enjoying our *own* company."

Dobbs is perplexed; obviously he's misunderstood the original situation, which he thought to be passive and friendly. Now it seems anything but.

"Tu quieres me vas, no problemo. Me solo amigo, no mas. Perdon," he says, now looking only at the quieter woman, who is suddenly piggy in the middle.

He knows his Spanish is so crap that she probably understands very little of what he's trying to say but unfortunately, under the influence of the powder, he's enjoying the madness and adventure of the situation so, having finished his attempts at communicating, he turns his attention back to the angry woman, who is now going totally loopy. He waits, quietly, for her to finish her rant then, very casually, as if he's missed what she's just said, he asks,

"Que?"

"Fuck you!" she shouts, completely overheating.

"Hey, nosotros somos todos amigos. Que problem? Tu amiga es muy bonita tambien – tranquillo ah?" Dobbs says, antagonizing her further.

He's finding the situation all too hilarious now but The Brigadier, enraged, stomps down to the front of the bar, climbs up on to the stage, and starts blasting out tunes with his sax. He's just letting off steam and maybe it is pulling some calming element from somewhere as his mood changes noticeably as he plays.

It's a modern-looking joint, and not overcrowded by any means. If anything, it all looks a bit sparse.

The two DJ's, apparently playing back-to-back, see the potential of The Brigadier accompanying their tunes and lower the volume, allowing him to take centre stage, which definitely seems to calm him although it does very little for the angry woman. However, when he finishes playing Dobbs stands, turning all his attention to The Brigadier and giving him the applause he deserves - as does most everyone in the bar. By now the mood has mellowed and things seem be smoothing out a little.

Sitting back down, Dobbs turns his attention back to the quieter of the two women. In normal light, under normal conditions, it would be fair to say that she is quite rounded, greying slightly and though was once, no doubt, a fine-looking dame, in the battle between time and beauty the former is clearly making all the gains. Her face is warm and friendly nonetheless, and the reality of the situation is that she and her friend are just a couple of older women, still cool, who are being pestered by two blokes racing their tits off on a bit of pestilence.

Dobbs attempts to maintain the conversation and she now embarks on a little rhetorical feedback, giving him some idea that though his Spanish may be crap he is at least a little understood. He tries not to give any noticeable attention to the other woman now, despite the fact that she is not wearing a bra and her huge, unfastened breasts and bare cleavage are covered only by a loose, flimsy white summer dress, the seams of which are visibly hanging off her large, dark nipples as they thrust first one way and then the other with twitching pangs of impatience and anger. She knows they've got Dobbs mesmerised but he's trying hard to break free of his sex-crazed thoughts as he knows this lady might be just what The Brigadier needs.

Just then The Brigadier returns to the table to the accompaniment of applause from the audience. He looks a little more comfortable again but though he is clearly observing Dobbs's absolute detachment from the more attractive of the two women by the expression on his face, Dobbs knows he is also sensing his amusement at the situation.

The fact is, Dobbs is up to no good; he's being deliberately antagonising and, worse, he's loving it. The Brigadier pulls up a chair and sits. Dobbs knows it's all looking a bit hazardous but what can he do? Pestilence brings out his own little demon and it's all just way too much fun.

"Can you not sit there?" the woman with the white dress says, turning her whole posture away from The Brigadier and, indeed, from Dobbs. She's now staring off into thin air and obviously waiting for her friend to engage with her rather than Dobbs - or anyone else for that matter. When that fails though she stands again and, turning to The Brigadier this time, shouts:

"I want to sit with my friend!"

"I'm not sitting with you," The Brigadier snaps back with a look of intolerance.

When she sees this line of attack is getting her nowhere she holds her nose, glances over at The Brigadier and then back to her friend and shouts out, in clear English now, and waving her hand in front of her nose,

"I just can't handle it, he stinks!"

54

The Brigadier, who is fastidiously clean, looks livid and starts shouting off in Spanish, his ego utterly wounded.

This woman is clever, thinks Dobbs; she's been looking for the button and by all accounts, she's found it. The Brigadier is completely sleep-deprived and in his most ego-maniac, psychotic state. Now he goes loopy. He's not violent, but she's got him on strings. The whole banter goes off into the extremities of verbal abuse.

Dobbs doesn't understand a word of what's said, but it's the best show he's seen for quite a while. Then, at the height of the madness, The Brigadier turns to him and rages:

"This shirt was clean on and I showered right before we came out, didn't I?"

"Yeah…" Dobbs says in the highest pitch he can summon, looking at both girls and nodding seriously, "…Clean as a whistle."

A little while later and the energy has somehow started to simmer down, but Dobbs still hasn't had his fun and thinks this thing can be squeezed a little further. So, staring deep into the eyes of the quieter girl, he reaches out his hand and touches the seam of her blouse, just where it ends short of her elbow. He can see that the other woman just needs that little extra nudge and sure enough, at the sight of this slight advance, she goes pop.

Like clockwork the trouble is rekindled and suddenly she has one hand clasping her nose and the other waving to and fro, glancing at The Brigadier and then at everyone in the room as if to alert them. The Brigadier now starts swearing out every obscenity he can muster but the woman just stands up and tells her friend they have to go as she cannot handle the terrible smell. She's got The Brigadier right where she wants him - in absolute rage.

Next thing, they're all outside on the sidewalk. The abuse is absolutely over the top and The Brigadier goes one step too far and pushes the woman, who falls to the ground. Dobbs isn't clear what's been said but despite the shove, it does seem to him that she's fallen deliberately. Whatever the truth of the matter it's not a good scene though; there's a woman on the ground, screaming and shouting at a man who has, by the looks of things, attacked her. She's now the star attraction, and screaming out every obscenity under the, well, moon - if it is up - to attract attention.

"Steady Brigadier, you're going too far," Dobbs says, apparently trying to simmer the whole thing down now he's had his fun, but actually playing more like a festival security guard who's pretending to be motivated by health and safety when all he really wants is for it all to kick off.

"Fuck off!" The Brigadier screams back, staring at him with seething anger. His whole posture is set as though he is going to rip Dobbs's head clean off and he is now as close as he can get to his point of critical mass before going completely out of control. The woman is still lying on the sidewalk, screaming out like she's been mugged.

Just then Dobbs catches sight of a group of policemen. They're standing not so far away amongst a crowd of young people queuing to get into a club on the sidewalk up ahead. The woman has now got back on her feet and is screaming her head off at The Brigadier who is just standing there, hands on hips, staring at her with a look of cold intolerance. As Dobbs watches, the cops clock the situation.

"You need to get out of here," he says, turning to The Brigadier and nodding in the direction of the hordes of police twenty meters up the road, "Or you're going to end up in a cell for the night. Got anything on you that they want to know about?"

The Brigadier turns and sees all the police and security everywhere, some clearly looking their way. He freezes, registering the whole picture in a moment.

"I'm going to smooth it over, you walk away," Dobbs says to him.

The Brigadier stops and breathes. Looking around, he calms down a little. Then, without any ceremony or goodbyes, he just turns and walks away.

Eventually Dobbs manages to calm the situation and in fact is even nearly swayed to go back with the two women. In the end though he decides against it, no doubt managing to avert another looming disaster and instead nods to the ladies and starts walking away up the busy street, realising the best thing he can do now is leave them well alone.

All the same, as he makes away through the darkened streets he can't forget the crazy look The Brigadier had given him, or the eerie feeling that accompanied it.

Whatever it was he'd seen in those eyes, one thing was for sure: it wasn't

The Brigadier.

The Deal

Saturday, 19th January 2008

Dobbs allows the lowness to engulf him as he moves right down into his heart. The comedown is kicking in big time now and it feels as though the sadness might split him in two, but he keeps his course steady and straight, surrendering himself ever-closer to the core of it until he is nearly through to the bliss beyond and, finally, relaxing. The Valium is working its wonders, and he can feel himself slowly slipping away from all the mayhem of his rattling mind.

How long he'd been lying there would have been a little difficult to establish without looking at a clock. He'd been in the twilight zone: the lights left on, but nobody home. Now he is just at the point of slipping clean away when, bang! The door bursts open.

Dobbs opens his eyes and looks up to see The Brigadier, wired and wild, staring directly at him and looking psychotic. He marches over to Dobbs, who's more than a little nervous at where this is suddenly going.

"I just need to speak to someone. Can I talk to you?"

Dobbs pulls the covers over his head.

"It's really late mate. I'm so tired. I just wanna sleep now."

"Just five minutes. Please?" he demands.

Dobbs knows it is not wise dealing with The Brigadier in this state. It's crash time and they're both in bits so he tries to fend him off, pleading with him to get some sleep first, but the man is borderline psychotic. Suddenly he has an idea though and, after a short pause, pulls the covers from his face.

"Okay. I'll do a deal with you."

The Brigadier really doesn't look himself.

"What?" he says.

"I'll give you five minutes," Dobbs says, now opening his eyes and staring calmly at The Brigadier. "And then you promise me you'll sleep?"

Of course Dobbs is not using his head and considering *who* is really asking for the five minutes and whether it is wise to try to cut a deal with this monster that wants 'just five minutes' of his life so badly right now.

"Yeah. Absolutely," The Brigadier says.

"Then take three Valiums before we talk. And then I'll know you're going to sleep."

The Brigadier shakes his head in a sort of snotty fashion,

"I don't do Valium," he snorts.

"What? So you'll take pestilence, smoke spliffs, pop pills, eat shit and everything else but downers are above you, right?"

"I hate downers."

"Well, no deal then Bro. Because right now you're scaring the shit out of me, and everyone else. You can't go up unless you're willing to come down. So, no Valium, no deal. Sorry."

At this The Brigadier becomes even more wildly obnoxious, waving his arms around and looking about the room in a frantic search for something to smash to a trillion bits. Dobbs just holds his breath, hoping those psychotic eyes don't suddenly stop on him.

Agent6 has taken a few Valium himself and he is out like a lamp but Dobbs is concerned The Brigadier's antics will wake him because, in this state, Agent6 is liable to absolutely annihilate him.

Suddenly, though, The Brigadier spots what he's really looking for; Bolivar's pestilence, slightly concealed, is on the dresser next to his bed, and now The Brigadier makes a bee-line for the bag. Immediately, the dozing Bolivar pulls his head up.

"Hold on," he says, almost as if guarding the stash in his sleep.

But to both men's astonishment The Brigadier just grabs the pestilence then pulls back the bed sheets and, in a rage, pours the entire contents in a careless pile over Bolivar's bare belly before recklessly snorting the lot, like a monster tearing into his intestines. For a moment Bolivar just lies there, stunned, in shock and disbelief, but then, as The Brigadier lifts his head to stare coldly into his eyes, pestilence smudged all over his face, he grabs the covers and pulls them back, staring at The Brigadier with a half-enraged half-perplexed look of utter shock at how his space has just been so seriously violated. For a while he just stares in total silence, then his face relaxes a little and, in his deepest, sternest voice he says,

"Fuck you, man. That was just...nasty." Then he just closes his eyes and lies there.

Dobbs is totally unimpressed but The Brigadier is just pacing about like a trapped animal now and all of a sudden he comes running towards him like a mad man.

"Five minutes, Dobbs. That's all I'm asking of you. You fucking cunt! You fucking selfish bastard!"

Dobbs has seen The Brigadier in a rage many times before but there had always been some element of control, however tenuous, over his anger. Now he's near to the point of becoming totally crazy however and suddenly Dobbs remembers what he least wants to remember; he's directly contributed to the initiation of this crisis by deliberately antagonising The Brigadier whilst he's in this state. It's tantamount to creeping up behind the biggest, hungriest lion you could possibly find and kicking it in the nuts before screaming "Fuck you!" at the distressed animal with a megaphone. Despite the seriousness of the situation, he finds himself fighting off a smirk at the thought.

He knows that this is all about overcoming fear and taking responsibility. With hindsight perhaps not taking any pestilence at all might have been the most *responsible* thing to do, but abstinence is not what he believes to be the definition of responsibility. As a wise man once said:

'The road of excess leads to the palace of wisdom and prudence is a rich, ugly old maid, courted by incapacity.'

No. Recognizing exactly what crazed addictions you have become involved with, what you have colluded with, he knows, is the only way to move through this dynamic. And this wasn't a new situation. It was something that had been brewing up for a long time - two years in fact, steadily moving to this final climax.

At least until about a month before, there had always been containment but The Brigadier's girlfriend had been taking the brunt of his withdrawal until then, and with her he could sail a relatively straight course most of the time. But when he'd popped, she'd been in the front line.

Star was a gorgeous, bubbly West Country girl, with absolutely no communication problems. She and The Brigadier had once been so happy but as the pestilence had taken hold, their relationship had gone clean under the wheels of it. Her love for him was a love of utter conviction - something truly commendable to Dobbs and, indeed, most people who knew them, and knew what she endured, .but eventually that love had became his ego's containment, allowing him to buffer himself from the realisation of the treacherous path his life had taken until he was truly lost. In containing that rage, and condoning it, her sweet, innocent humanity had taken a beating and finally the seams of her love for him gave way. Ultimately, all containment is temporary.

His jealous tendencies combined with his massive comedowns had obviously exacerbated the speed these things work; every time she talked to another guy when he was on a comedown was dangerous to say the least. Worse still he would always think, when he was most rattling, that one or another of his friends was fucking her. This made things difficult - for Dobbs especially - as he often gave her work at Christmas, selling puppets.

She was one of his best sellers actually. If you really want to sell puppets, you have to love them. And she loved puppetry like she loved The Brigadier. She didn't see his flaws. She'd fallen in love with something else, with the dream of living the highlife with him perhaps. She'd fallen in love with the story of The Brigadier and the wild adventure of his pirate lifestyle. But he'd finally ripped her storybook to pieces. At the end, in the final throes of their relationship, the violence started to spill out until, six months before, in Agent6's home actually, he'd completely lost it.

Agent6 had given him his house for the winter whilst he was away the previous year. It was one of his big 'rock' comedowns and by all accounts it was bad. He insulted everything about Agent6 in front of Star, who was apparently screaming her head off at him to chill out. But he'd finally pushed Agent6 to the limit and a massive fight had ensued in the front room which ended with The Brigadier in a headlock, having his head smashed against the wood burner until he was subdued. Dobbs, on the other hand, isn't a fighter at all – a complete pacifist in fact - and his only line of defence right now is Valium.

Maybe Star could've calmed The Brigadier down and brought him back, but she loved him. He was an odd specimen but he called a spade a spade. He always had a hidden agenda but it was never too difficult to work out his games and they were usually not dangerous or done with too dire an intention. Jealousy was his demon's spell book but you generally knew which way the wind was blowing with him and, as the saying goes 'better the devil you know!'

What's happening now is clearly not going to be a breeze though: this thing is a tornado – a raging tempest. Dobbs knows it, and in the realisation of the potentially violent finality of what is unfolding he suddenly remembers another line of defence: the little protection technique he sometimes uses. It is possibly his only other option now, as the situation has reached critical.

60

Closing his eyes, he tries to visualise golden rings of light surrounding him, then begins a whole sequence of other techniques taught to him by his mother, holding the absolute silence and totally relaxing his whole body from any tension, even as The Brigadier stands towering over him, face smudged with the residue of pestilence, tensed as if ready to utterly smash him.

Though he feels the other man's energy trying to terrorize him Dobbs knows he must become totally unthreatening now, yet absolutely impervious to fear: whatever happens now, he cannot pander to the fear, so he just sits there, eyes closed, waiting. Time seems to slow to a standstill as he waits for the first blow to fall but at last, to Dobbs' profound relief, The Brigadier finally speaks.

"Where are they then? Where the fuck are they then?"

Letting out a long, slow breath, Dobbs takes the packet from under his pillow and holds it up to The Brigadier.

"I want to see you take them before we go and talk," he says. "That's the deal. You know you need to come down. And you know that, when you wake up, you're going to feel rested and ready for us to move on to the next phase of this trip. Even if you've got fuck all you're still a skilled man with all your languages and your means of persuasion – with your music! But you've got to come down first, Bro. We're you're friends, man!

We've all had a blast together; now it's time to come down, recuperate and recover."

The Brigadier is shaking, running his hands through his fine, short-cropped hair. It normally has a light curl to it which makes him look almost boyish, complimenting his bright blue eyes and the cheeky gap in his front teeth. He has such animated features, like a little kid, addicted to naughtiness. It's one of the things that Dobbs most loves about him: naughtiness is The Brigadier's only real hidden agenda. Now his hair is longer, damp with humidity and perspiration from his hands where he's swept it all back almost flat behind his ears as he stands, battling some agonizing internal process. He looks as if he's going into complete meltdown and finally screams out, in rage and frustration,

"I just want to go back to fucking jail!"

Dobbs holds the packet closer to him.

"Don't need no jail to get through this shit, man. You just need some determination, and a bit of conviction, and a genuine desire to get past this little hurdle in your life. But, first, you need to down three of these babies, and then I'll listen to all you've got to say. I just can't go there with you if not though Bro: what goes up must come down. It's not rocket science, is it?

And if you struggle doing it for you, then do it for me. Do it for your old mum. For Agent6 and Bolivar. Come back down and just slip into sleep. It's everything you need right now."

He holds the pills out closer to The Brigadier, who's looking at them, hesitating. Finally, he grabs the whole packet, and charges out the room.

Dobbs lies back on the bed, contemplating what to do. He wants to witness The Brigadier take at least three pills. 'Just knock the fucker clean out,' he thinks to himself. Every warning system is going off in his body. 'What to do? What the fuck shall I do?' he asks himself. 'I need answers.'

When he opens his eyes, the first thing he sees is the water bottle on the TV.

'Make him drink water,' he thinks. 'Get as much water into him as possible. And Valium. Get as much Valium into his system as possible, and just finish the fucking job.'

With this the way ahead is clear and, jumping off the bed, he grabs the water bottle and goes to make his way to the roof. As he approaches the door he looks round to see Bolivar staring at him though; he's shaking his head with an expression so utterly grave Dobbs can hear his very thoughts screaming out to him: 'Don't go! Whatever you do now, do not go up there!"

He pauses for a moment but he knows that, like it or not, he has already participated too much in this process to back out now. Instead he closes his eyes as if somewhere else momentarily, then turns and disappears through the door.

The Tempest

The sun has not yet risen but it's already bright and fresh outside. It's a spectacular morning, although still quite cold. The clarity of bird song, with little audible interference from the still-sleeping city, is pristine. Dobbs marvels momentarily at how the sound saturates his senses; it's so clear, so incredibly beautiful. Most of Lima is still dozing but alarm bells are, no doubt, starting to ring out in bedrooms across the city, thinks Dobbs to himself. As his eyes fall on The Brigadier, looking lost and angry, alone on a sunlounger, they begin to ring in his own head.

He's dangerous now, and Dobbs can sense it so, closing his eyes and drawing a breath, he pictures a golden ring running around The Brigadier from left to right then another circling from above his head, forward, and, finally, one exactly the same as the first only horizontal, like a gyroscope, completely encapsulating him. Then he does the same round himself.

Next he constructs a pyramid, its base formed by himself on one side and The Brigadier on the other, it's apex rising above them both. He asks for unity of their souls in the higher plane and all who work with them to come together and help bring this situation to a state of peace. He knows he has to give permission for Spirit to enter this equation as he cannot handle it on his own. His mother once said to him that choice is the mechanism of manifestation on Earth and if you want help from the higher planes you have to ask for it: *wanting* help and *asking* for it are not the same thing.

Finally, looking at the pavement four stories below, and acknowledging that right here, and right now, falling off – or being thrown off - represents the greatest physical danger to him, he places another golden ring around the whole edifice on which he and The Brigadier are both standing. Then he just takes a moment to absorb the whole scene, the rooftop, the sunrise, and The Brigadier silhouetted, alone, against the spectacular backdrop of early morning Lima sprawling beyond.

He realises he needs to tell Spirit what outcome he is trying to achieve.

'What is the exact outcome I want?' he asks himself. And then he wonders what his mum would do. She'd say a prayer, he thinks; she'd be praying by now.

'Dear God, please help me solve this problem. I want a win-win situation. All my guides, his guides on the higher plane that truly have his well-being at heart, as well as anyone out there who can genuinely help bring love, light and peace into this situation. Please: all hands on deck! Please! Thank you.'

Then he just maintains his space, observing The Brigadier in his sphere of utter protection and trying to feel where he's at.

As he focuses, he slowly begins to sense pain. Perhaps it's The Brigadier's pain, or perhaps his own. In this state it's hard to differentiate, but there's an enormous sadness there, the polarized opposite of the splendour of this new day that's dawning, and The Brigadier is the only cloud on the horizon, hunched forward, in absolute hell. Dobbs knows he needs to help him carry this burden for a while.

He wants to break down in tears but he knows that to do so now would only be a distraction. Instead he tries to just feel the pain with his whole being, to breathe through it. But the sadness is so intense he can feel that oh-so-important first tear that somehow doesn't drop. It's as though it's balanced more on his breath than the ledge of his eye, clinging like a scared child by its tiny hands of surface tension alone, scared to take that leap into the deep blue pool below that will wash away the sadness and bring back all the joy and laughter again.

Dobbs senses that the dividing line between the tear that hangs and the sweet pool just waiting to wash away the pain is nothing but fear now - pure fear. He can feel it; see it, like a wall. Taking a deep breath, he steps forward, and through the wall,

"Go on then, pop some of those and we'll talk," he says, attempting to keep his tone jovial.

"I have," The Brigadier coldly states.

Dobbs wanders over to him and takes the sun lounger adjacent.

"Sorry man, no offence, but I don't believe you."

The Brigadier opens his mouth for display, extending his tongue out, and sure enough there are the Valiums just sat there on his dry tongue. Dobbs attempts to pass him the water, keeping himself as calm as he can whilst he does so.

"What you gonna do, suck 'em? You want to get some of this down you as well, then you won't wake with a kicking headache. You'll just feel fantastic. Down that whole bottle if you can. Get some fresh water in ya," he says, offering the water a little closer.

The Brigadier takes the water, hesitates, then swigs it back.

"I want to see inside your mouth, man. Sorry."

Sure enough, they're gone, swallowed. Job done - nearly - thinks Dobbs, taking a deep breath.

"I'm tired man, really tired," he sighs.

"You promised me five minutes."

"I did promise that, and a little more maybe - right up to the point you feel like you wanna sleep. And then we'll go down together, get some quality rest and sleep this fucker off our backs."

The Brigadier's not looking much concerned with what Dobbs is saying though. He spins round, staring at him.

"I done my side of the deal, now it's your turn. You got to listen and not say a fucking word. Not a fucking word. You're agreed to that?"

Dobbs sits down next to him and makes himself comfortable. He's been in this position with The Brigadier before but never sensed his rage directed so utterly towards him. It's like he's two completely different beings, as though his ego is in its final phase of dying and, terrified, is desperately reaching out one last time to get a hold of something. And if that something isn't found in the next five minutes all will be lost.

It's a state of panic, of absolute hell, as if the sadness is now a monster coming over the hill faster than the sun; an agony that no amount of pestilence can offset any longer. His ego has become a mothership of hugely inflated nonsense, beached on the shores of his sadness. It's checkmate, and all-out crash time.

Dobbs senses this thing is unlikely to collapse into its own footprint - not without some serious assistance at any rate - but there's no real room for any defensive tactics either: he has no martial arts moves hidden up his sleeve. So, saying nothing, he just nods in affirmation.

"Me and Star are finished. We're finished, right?"

The Brigadier, Dobbs realises, is testing him; trying to make him break his word and give him an excuse for more rage. Instead he just runs his thumb and index finger across his lips as though zipping them up. Cocking his head to one side, he opens his hands out in a gesture of understanding, whilst simultaneously shrugging his shoulders. He truly does not know the answer to that most painful of questions burning within The Brigadier's mind but he is truly trying to share the pain of it nevertheless.

"We're finished. I told her we're through. I can't do it anymore."

Dobbs can see he just wants to cry his eyes out but the whole emotional mammoth he's got hemmed up inside of him is too massive to let go of in one big chunk. It would be like letting go of Niagara Falls and he just doesn't know how to release that torrent. But just as it seems he's approaching the perimeter of his pain, and almost shaking with the effort, something else takes over and he jumps up, staring at Dobbs and starts pacing round him, rage in his eyes.

Dobbs relaxes his body and reaffirms the golden ring of light around himself. He can feel this strange dark energy that has taken over The Brigadier and the panic that it is trying to generate inside him. The Brigadier looks like he wants to smash him to pieces but Dobbs looks him full in the face, all the time allowing his whole body to relax away from fear and tension.

Finally The Brigadier screams out in rage. Running towards the wall at the front of the building, he jumps over it to sit on the ledge on the far side, his legs dangling over the long drop below. Then, looking at Dobbs, he points to a space directly beside him.

"Sit here," he orders. His voice is so chilling that for a moment Dobbs feels the core of his bones momentarily turn to ice and involuntarily visualises them breaking like glass at the thought of falling off the drop beyond.

Dobbs looks at him and shakes his head, pointing down and then drawing a finger horizontally across his throat with a half smirk, trying to make light of The Brigadier's terrifying tone.

"Sit here. Fucking sit here now!" The Brigadier screams at the top of his voice.

There is no way Dobbs is going to sit right next to a terminal drop with The Brigadier in this state. He shakes his head then makes a gesture with his hand in front of his mouth and points to The Brigadier, telling him to keep expressing his thoughts and feelings. But The Brigadier's face becomes expressionless. He turns his head slowly towards Dobbs, seething white cold anger projecting from his piercing blue eyes, their pupils sharp as pins points.

Then, abruptly, he stands and, placing his feet half over the ledge, leans forward ever so slightly. Dobbs knows he has to say something; they're four stories up and falling off would almost certainly mean death, or at the very least serious injury. It's as if The Brigadier's literally leaning against the golden ring he has placed round the building.

"I want you to come away from the ledge, man. Please Bro."

The Brigadier turns his head slowly and as he does so that cold sensation occurs again. Dobbs feels like he's in a horror movie.

"You promised me you wouldn't speak. You're a liar. You fucking wanker; you just broke your word!"

He hisses.

Dobbs is struggling to find his breath. The situation is about as much as he can emotionally take. His knees are trembling and his fingertips are beginning to tingle.

"If you jump, there's nothing I can do to stop you man. But I *can* tell you, now, whilst you're still alive, that you have so much to live for. You can get past all this," he says, appealing to The Brigadier to take back control from this thing that has taken him - or that he has, unwittingly, given himself to.

Below, a man walks on the pavement with his dog. Unaware of The Brigadier standing on the ledge four stories above him, he is the only other soul in sight as they embark on this new day.

"No fucker cares if I'm going to fucking die!" The Brigadier shouts out, trying to attract his attention.

The man looks about discreetly but, failing to find the source of the noise, he just carries on walking - albeit with a slightly increased pace. The Brigadier leans forward even more and stares down into the abyss.

If he fucks this up he's dead, and Dobbs knows it.

"Please Bro. This is so cruel on all those who love you. I don't want to live with this, man. I don't want to watch my good friend take his life. It doesn't have to end here, you know. All this will pass and you'll still be a young bloke with so much valuable life experience under your belt and all your life ahead of you. This is a blip man, just a little rock on the highway. The masses out there - they're addicted to all the same shit but they just don't know it. You know the chains that bind you - you can see them now – and you can pull those shackles clean off if you've got half the courage I know you have. You're the bravest man I know, Brigadier… if you want to, man, you can just cruise past this."

The Brigadier stands, motionless, for what seems an eternity but at last he steps away from the ledge.

"I haven't got the balls to jump anyway. I'm a fucking coward," he says quietly, as much to himself as to Dobbs.

"You ain't no coward, man. Not by a long shot. Come away from the ledge and we'll talk, together. You're going to start feeling sleepy soon, and everything will calm down."

Then the strangest thing happens. He turns his head, cocking it to one side, and Dobbs can see it – it's back - that *thing*.

In a much more energetic fashion now, The Brigadier jumps back over the wall and stands, staring at Dobbs with pure murder in his eyes. Dobbs knows he's not armed, and the only danger is the drop, so he places the golden ring around the building again.

His mum had taught him all these techniques and though he knew many people would just consider them silly tricks they, he believed, were infected with a doubt that rules their being. His mother had told him that prayer, through honourable intention, is what enacts a human's power to choose whether they wish to invite in help from the higher planes. She always said "You don't have to believe in miracles, but you'd be a fool not to - especially if a miracle is your last hope."

Even to Dobbs it sometimes seemed like just a load of hippy nonsense and yet there had been times in his life when he'd really depended on these 'tricks' - and it looked like this was certainly going to end up on that list.

"You gave me your word you wouldn't talk. You gave me your fucking word, you *cunt!* You *fucking cunt!*" The Brigadier spits the words, almost as if they are an angry mantra he's using to convince himself that Dobbs deserves to be punished.

Suddenly he's striding forward again, staring at Dobbs with eyes of the coldest hate. Whatever it is that has taken The Brigadier is now completely present. His head is dropped low like a predator ready to pounce and he has come within a few feet of Dobbs and is pacing in a semi-circle round his golden ring, which is blazing so bright it seems almost tangible. It's as though this thing that has taken The Brigadier can see it too. It stops, staring directly at him.

"Your girlfriend…is fucking your best mate." The tone is seething and dry, like it's trying to drag Dobbs down into this hell it inhabits.

Even though he knew that his girlfriend was in love with another man - a man he loved and admired immensely also - this thought has never truly crossed his mind.

"I don't blame her. She's a beautiful woman. And I've been a right cunt of late."

His ring of protection remains strangely solid without so much as a flicker. He holds his state, wondering whether this gold ring is really doing what it looks like it is and yet continuing to hold it even as he questions it. It feels as if it's perhaps suspended on his breath, of which he's suddenly become very aware now. His diaphragm feels as if it is moving in almost circular, shallow cycles, juggling these rings of golden light as though juggling balls between his breaths, and somehow merging them, like the merging of two worlds enacting something almost alien within him. Meanwhile he's just staring at The Brigadier, holding the space in his most utter inner stillness.

Suddenly, a missile of thought takes him from nowhere and before his mind has a chance to give him the *incoming* alert, the thought breaks through; it could be *any* of your mates. Before he can deflect the attack a single syllable breaks out of his mouth.

"Who?"

As soon as the word is uttered The Brigadier comes charging straight through his ring of protection to stand, staring him in the face, with an expression like Dobbs must be a fucking retard for asking such a stupid question. Closing his eyes just for a moment, he pictures his protection moving back to give him the space he craves, until it extends right round the building again. He can't see it now but he trusts it is still obeying his intentions. When he opens his eyes The Brigadier is still totally in his face but, despite the terror that threatens to overwhelm him, he holds still, trying to maintain his strength of intention whilst keeping his face expressionless.

The Brigadier makes a noise like a vampire, like he's going to bite him or something. It's almost silly. In fact it is silly, he starts to think, and suddenly almost wants to laugh. The Brigadier, sensing his defiance to the fear, immediately just turns and runs, straight to the sidewall this time, almost as if standing on the very edge of Dobbs's golden ring again. The whole thing seems so stupid, like some kind of cartoon. He's standing with a lunatic on top of a high building, encircled in golden rings of light. 'Which of us is crazier?' he finds himself thinking. But even though he can no longer see the rings he can sense them, almost by The Brigadier's apparent fear of them.

The Brigadier is now standing on a wall with no parapet beyond, just a two-metre gap to the next building with a vertical drop to the pavement far below. If he stumbles there's a chance he could jump and get his arms over the next wall though he'd have to leap as he fell. But right now, it isn't The Brigadier's health he's most concerned about - it's his own.

69

"You embarrass your girlfriend," he says, his voice taunting. Running along the wall on tiptoes like a ninja he turns to stare at Dobbs again. Dobbs feels terrified. He wants to get away but he knows that whatever's going on, this thing is feeding off his fear. He knows he could run but The Brigadier is ready to pounce and what he'd do in this state is anybody's guess. He should have taken Bolivar's advice and kept well away.

'Please God, help me now and help my friend. Please help me rise above my fear,' he says in his mind. As he prays, he becomes aware of his breathing once again and it gets easier and deeper.

The Brigadiers eyes narrow with wild rage but Dobbs is careful not to show any facial expression. He knows he has to remain emotionally neutral.

"I know I embarrass her. I probably embarrass you, too. I haven't got a cool bone in my body. I believe in a whole load of spiritual crap that makes her cringe, the same stuff that made my old mum cringe all those years back when she was young, before she became a channel." And then he pulls a somewhat dismissive face, "but you know what, Bro? If she don't want me, she don't have to have me, does she? I'll get through it. We'll all get through it. And anyway, you know me, man - *Dobbs* - your mate; I've always been a bit of an odd ball, ain't I? Unlike you trend setters, ah? If I make her cringe, let her fucking cringe."

The Brigadier jumps off the wall and runs at Dobbs as though he's going to launch a full-scale violent attack, but Dobbs doesn't move a muscle.

"I'm not scared of you, Brigadier; not scared at all," he lies. "I'm your friend. And you're being a total fucking twat."

He knows he has to get away but now The Brigadier leans forward, bringing his face right up close. Looking into his eyes, Dobbs, tries to remember the protection he has up, but whatever has taken control of his friend is trying to penetrate it; push through it, and violate his space with fear. Using all his will power Dobbs slows and regulates his breathing again, drawing the air slowly through his nostrils until he has regained control.

The Brigadier's face is as cold as ice and as hard as a hatchet. He's become something he has no clue he becomes. He barely remembers anything when he's in this state and, judging by the expression on his face, he seriously wants to harm Dobbs right now. It's like he's been possessed by something demonic which is scanning Dobbs's mind for snippets of fear.

He wants to push the notion away but The Brigadier's girlfriend had talked of it and he'd heard this monster down the phone once when she'd come over to his place, hiding from The Brigadier when he'd been totally sleep deprived and completely gone with pestilence abuse. The rage he'd screamed down the line then was truly terrifying. It was just before Star had started to work with Dobbs selling puppets.

Suddenly, he thinks of the time she'd stayed with him in his van. As his mind stops there, on that night, The Brigadier's eyes, staring coldly into his, almost catch something and suddenly his whole face fills with rage.

"Star worked for you at Christmas didn't she?"

Dobbs doesn't delay for a moment, though he knows exactly where this is going.

"She did –yeah."

Star had desperately needed the work. She'd had to leave The Brigadier altogether, changing her mobile number and breaking all contact to escape his torrent of desperate calls and raging anger. One night, when she'd worked late and they'd been out for a drink in the pub after, she'd spent the night in his truck with him. Nothing had happened - she'd slept in the bed next to the wood burner - but The Brigadier would never believe that. Even though she and The Brigadier weren't actually together any more Dobbs knew it would have been totally wrong for him to get involved, on just way too many levels.

Star was emotionally unstable with all the abuse she was taking at the time and he just couldn't have gone there with her. She needed her friends, and Dobbs was a genuine friend. But not only that, he was a genuine businessman, and she was just too good a seller to lose over a drunken tumble. Besides, Dobbs was in a long-term relationship at the time. He tries to push it all out of his mind but it's like The Brigadier is peering in on his thoughts.

"And she stayed in your truck one night, right?" His whole posture is seething with hate and blame.

Dobbs knows denial would be the most dangerous thing he could do now; he has to maintain the truth and hold himself together without fear.

"One night she did, but not in my bed. She stayed in the kids' bed next to the wood burner. When we're on the road everyone ends up staying in my truck or Agent6's at some point. It's my home, man. You know me, man - everyone's welcome in my home."

"In your fucking bed!" It's not a question, it's a statement, and as he watches The Brigadier's eyes start literally rolling with rage.

"You really think I'd fuck your girlfriend? Is that really what you think of me? I guess you'd prefer I hadn't helped her when she was on her arse, just trying to make ends meet - just so you wouldn't feel any jealousy? Is that fair on her?" Dobbs says, not raising his voice but speaking as assertively as he can without being antagonistic. His pose is relaxed - loose and unconfrontational - but he can see the rage moving through The Brigadier in tense shudders, literally like something growing all over him, eating him up with anger.

"You had sex with my girlfriend, in your bed," he screams.

Dobbs's eyes are locked on his.

"I've never had sex - or slept with - your girlfriend, Brigadier. She slept in the bed next to the wood burner. It's as simple as that. I wouldn't do that to you and I wouldn't have done it to her. She was in a total mess back then. The man she loved, the man she wanted to live out her dreams with, whose children she wanted to bear, had gone off the fucking rails. She needed a friend, not some letching *wanker* trying to get in her fucking knickers."

The Brigadier turns and runs back to the wall on the far side of the building and jumps up onto it. Beyond is an unobstructed drop down to the ground.

"You *fucking* bastard!" He screams.

"Why are you doing this to me - and yourself?" Dobbs tries to soothe him. "What have I done to deserve this? I have never done anything with Star, or anything to deserve this. What is this really about, anyway? You know she loves you: she always loved you. But all the pestilence is pushing her further and further away from you. She needs a friend right now, not some wanker taking advantage of her situation. Do you think I'd risk my own relationship for that? I'm happy with Ruby. I'd have lost her over that. Maybe I've lost her already. But that would have been too low man.

"I mean, you've emotionally pulverized her, haven't you? She knows it's not really you, it's just the drugs. But she believes you can make it through this. That's why she's stood by you for so long. You *can* make it through this."

Dobbs senses that bringing his own girlfriend's name into things has had a slight soothing effect, so he tries to drive home the point:

"I love Ruby mate. I'm not looking to jump into bed with another woman. That's why Star comes round – it's as much to see Ruby as me. I mean, think about it: we're quite solid, aren't we, most of the time?"

The Brigadier seems almost dazed for a moment. It's as though he doesn't know where he is and he nearly falls backwards but catches himself at the last moment. It seems the Valium is at last starting to kick in, but the monster inside fights back.

'This thing is a stubborn little fucker,' Dobbs thinks to himself as The Brigadier runs along the wall opposite to the building beyond, which has a wall at the same height as their hotel. But the property has an exposed stairwell that ascends to the roof where the outer wall is lower.

The Brigadier stops, staring at the stairwell, clearly calculating the manoeuvre. It could be jumped, but it's risky.

Turning to Dobbs and giving him his most psychotic look, he turns and leaps with his arms high and flailing, like a crazed cat. Nevertheless, he lands successfully on the steps of the far building then runs up to the roof to stand, staring again, at Dobbs, his chest out and his arms tensed like a boxer about to enter the ring.

Dobbs stares back at him. He's beginning to tire of the whole saga now, and can feel the Valium he's taken himself properly kicking in. He finds himself wondering how the poor fucker is going to get back? Maybe it would kick in for The Brigadier over there. At least there's some sun loungers he can pull into the shade, he thinks to himself. Suddenly it all seems comical again, and Dobbs can feel himself about to giggle. But then The Brigadier turns and walks away from him on the far roof.

Dobbs knows exactly what's about to happen so he places his golden rings around himself and the building again, wondering when the hell this thing was going to let up. Sure enough, as The Brigadier comes to a halt at the far end of the opposite roof, he turns on his heel.

"You fucked my girlfriend!" he screams out for the whole of Lima to hear. Then he starts running.

Approaching the far property's dividing wall, he jumps with one stride onto it, and is suddenly leaping across the divide. He lands like Spiderman, with his arms latching over the wall but somehow he manages to use his legs to stop him rather than impacting with his torso. Almost seamlessly, he springs his whole lower half over

73

the wall and, in one fluid motion, breaks into as print towards Dobbs.

Dobbs braces himself for a heavy impact but finds The Brigadier more sort of throwing himself round him than smashing into him. To his surprise, he is not really hurt at all, but The Brigadier begins squeezing him tighter and tighter like a boa constrictor – all the while staring into his eyes with a look of wild hate.

"Feel that?" he demands, the seething rage contorting his face into an ugly grimace. "That's love... Did it feel like that when you fucked my girlfriend?"

Dobbs tries to remain as calm as he possibly can under the circumstances but the hug keeps getting tighter and he can feel The Brigadier's arm coming over his shoulder to force him into a headlock. Still he does not resist. But The Brigadier keeps contracting his hold until it becomes a strangle hold. Then he starts edging towards the rear wall.

Dobbs slowly walks with him, trying to show no resistance, and within a few steps they are both looking over the edge. He is still doing his rings of protection but, strangely, he doesn't feel panicked at all. In fact he has to fight back a giggle.

"Brigadier, all joking aside, do you really and honestly believe I would have done that to you, to Star, or to Ruby for that matter? I mean, really. And for fuck's sake, if I've got to die, at least let it be in the fucking jungle, deep in the Amazon somewhere. Far easier to get rid of bodies there as well! I mean, come on man, do you really and honestly think I fucked her? What I mean is, do you really believe that or are you just in need of an excuse to murder a mate?"

At this The Brigadier's grip softens slightly. As it does, Dobbs begins to pulls his head free. He does not need force now, as it feels like The Brigadier has just given up.

"You don't, really, do you?" he says gently.

The Brigadier sways a little, loosening his grip."No," he almost whispers.

His grasp is almost limp now, and Dobbs pulls his head free a little more.

"So shall we go and get some sleep, man? You look really tired."

As The Brigadier releases Dobbs he almost falls backwards. "Yeah."

"Cool man I'm off to bed," Dobbs turns and makes his way down the spiral stairs.

74

"Five minutes is up, ah…?"

Hot Pants

He doesn't know if The Brigadier will follow him and the turmoil will continue but his feeling is that it is over. Nonetheless as he descends the stairs his hands are trembling, his whole body in shock from the ordeal.

Dobbs's mother had once told him that if you open yourself to the lower astral plane you invite negative energy into your life and to Dobbs, now wearily making his way down the steps, it seems clear that with the vast quantities of pestilence they've consumed both he and The Brigadier have not so much opened the door to uninvited guests as blown it near off its hinges.

He knows that The Brigadier has been well out of order but equally he feels some responsibility for some of the anger that's been brought up; he'd known from the beginning that The Brigadier was unstable and he realises he has taken things way too lightly.

Down in the room, Bolivar is awake, just lying on the bed. Agent6 is still asleep.

"That was a bit intense," Dobbs says, shaking his head. "In fact that was really very scary."

Bolivar rubs his eyes. "Where is he now?"

Dobbs shakes his head in disbelief at what he's just been through. He's exhausted, but very awake.

"On the roof, I think. To be honest, I don't care anymore. I got him to take some Valiums but it was a tough deal though."

"It's gonna take elephant tranquilizer to bring him down," Bolivar says.

"He's dangerous in this state. More to himself than anyone else, I think. I've never seen him this bad. But I have kind of toyed with him, so I feel like I'm in it - actually in the storm with him, I mean. I'm actually tempted to pack my bags and just get out now, but I'm so tired...," He climbs into bed and is just getting comfortable under the sheets when The Brigadier wanders in, looking psychotic again.

It seems it's not Dobbs's case he's on now though as, approaching Agent6 whilst he's fast asleep, he pushes his thumb into his forehead before flicking his knuckles across his head hard enough to wake him up and seriously piss him off.

Like a rocket blasting the body deep into sleep so that whatever we are in our astral state can roam free to go wherever it goes every night, the Valium Agent6 has taken has clearly been having the desired effect. But suddenly, just at that magic point, he is unceremoniously wrenched back to reality.

"You fucking wife beater!" The Brigadier is shouting in his face.

Like a corpse arising from its coffin, Agent6 rolls upwards into a sitting position. Despite the rude awakening he sits, apparently contemplating The Brigadier's words but looking strangely peaceful under the circumstances. The verbal onslaught begins, as The Brigadier starts laying into Agent6.

Dobbs knows The Brigadier is trying to ignite Agent6's rage – in fact anybody's rage really - so he visualises a golden ring around Agent6 and prays he won't rise to the bait.

Agent6 just sits there, doing nothing. Then, without so much as acknowledging The Brigadier's presence, he says,

"I was in such a beautiful deep sleep." Then he stares at Dobbs again, holding the moment.

"Wife beater?" he says, shaking his head, and then lies back down. He knows he can't get back to sleep, but he's relaxed. Nonetheless, it's clearly the end of the road for him and The Brigadier. There will be no more helping hands and no more friendship after this; it's all too dangerous and risky now. The Brigadier has some very simple and yet hugely difficult choices to make. Stories of his recklessness are becoming all too common. He's been burning bridges faster than he could ever begin building them. He's on complete self-destruct.

Agent6's complete lack of engagement in the face of such provocation is just too much for The Brigadier. However despite his tolerance so far Dobbs can sense that if The Brigadier keeps carrying on like this, Agent6 is just going to annihilate him. Even in his shameful state it seems The Brigadier knows it too, and without saying another word he steps out of the room and ascends the stairs again. This time Dobbs does not follow but relates the tale of what just happened on the rooftop to Agent6 and Bolivar.

Not much more than fifteen minutes later however The Brigadier is back. Staggering down the stairs, he stumbles into the room, his face very flushed and seemingly totally out of it, although he's still completely wild. He stops and stares at Dobbs, then Agent6 and then Bolivar, propping himself on a wall whilst knocking things off surfaces, flailing and stumbling, raucous and frenzied.

"You alright, Brigadier?'' Dobbs says, sitting up. "Why don't you lie down?"

"Fuck off," he screams in seething anger.

This is not the effect that a mere two or three Valiums should be having, so Dobbs decides to go upstairs and see if the Valium packet is still about. Sure enough there it is, lying on the ground next to the sun lounger. It is now empty. After a brief mental calculation he works out that The Brigadier has probably taken about seven pills but they're double the normal strength. He's going to be out for some time, Dobbs thinks to himself.

Going back downstairs to relay the jovial news he arrives in time to witness the amusing spectacle of Bolivar attempting to help The Brigadier into bed. At present he is kneeling, passed out, with just his upper torso actually on the mattress. As Dobbs watches, a spreading pool of wetness begins to appear round The Brigadier's crotch.

"Holy fuck, he's pissing himself."

Undeterred, scoops him up, and tosses him on the bed. Even on auto-pilot The Brigadier is still at war with the world however. He throws punches like some terminator robot with a near flat battery but they are nothing more than flailing arms really now, and deflect weakly off Bolivar's chest. The Brigadier makes one more attempt at a punch and finally passes out.

"Fuck me, he's just downed a hundred and forty milligrams," Dobbs says.

Agent6 peers in the room and nods in satisfaction at the sight of The Brigadier, out cold.

"Fan-fucking-tastic," he says.

***

Dobbs is feeling shaky and tired. The Valium he'd taken has long-since kicked in, but the intensity of the experience he's just been through has completely overshadowed its effects. Now the whole, in-depth account of the affair on the roof to the others and the constant rechecking of The Brigadier's health state has all petered out and there is nothing left. He feels empty and exhausted, but at the same time strangely elated. Rays of sunshine are bursting into the room but he knows he must sleep now and crawling into bed, is out cold in moments.

No more than three hours later and the blinding radiance of the new day wakes him to find Agent6 and Bolivar lolling about with a lost vagueness. He just lies there for a while, in a strange state of bliss almost, staring out the window and listening to the drone of Lima mingling with the bright sun rays. It is as though the light carries the resonance of the adventure he's seeking. It seems to be drawing him out of bed. He clambers out from under the bed sheets, throws on some clothes, and makes his way up to the roof to take in the fresh air.

His mind is, strangely, crystal clear. There is a brave new adventure dawning within him. He can feel it birthing, like a portal opening inside his core and spreading through his body, right out to the tingling tips of his fingers. Life is screaming out to him again, and a wild story awaits. He knows it. He's waited his whole life for this somehow and whatever is about to unfold is going to be about as big as it gets. But somehow, on some crazy level, he's ready for it.

Heading back down to the room, Bolivar can see his head is whirling.

"What we gonna do about this bleeding Inca Trail, Dobbs?" he asks in a fashion that implies he doesn't give two hoots but feels he needs at least to show interest.

Dobbs doesn't answer. It doesn't even register. He just stops in the centre of the room, looking around as if there might be something he needs and then, seeing nothing, he nods at Bolivar and turns to walk towards the door.

"Fuck knows."

"Where you going?" Bolivar calls just as he's disappearing through the door.

"Not sure. I'll tell you when I get back, in a while." He closes the door behind him.

People are wandering here and there in the hotel and a few eyes catch Dobbs's as he goes to leave the premises but he dons his shades, puts on a happy but assertive face, the sort that is on a mission and can't stop for anything, and is clear of the building in seconds. Now he's walking on the bright concrete sidewalk flooded with radiant sunshine everywhere. It's another spectacular day.

He's feeling fantastic; crystal clear. Walking down to where the end of the road joins the main artery running up from the pier, everything seems so new again. A modern metropolis bolted onto the ancient City of Lima. Glass towers and brushed stainless steel shop fronts, big names and classy boutiques. He has no clue as to what exactly he's searching for but he's sure he's going to find it.

When he finally arrives back at the hotel, Agent6 and Bolivar are still lolling about, playing backgammon. They seem almost a little shocked when Dobbs comes bursting in through the door. Their energy still feels a little low and despondent as if they're in a limbo state, not really knowing what to do and not really caring either. The Brigadier, sprawled across the bed, is still out cold.

Dobbs's new-found enthusiasm and sense of direction is what makes their heads pop up initially, but that is immediately overshadowed by what he's wearing. Jumping up to check out the scene, Bolivar flicks his fingers like one of the *boys from the hood*. "Hot pants. You funky devil! I want a pair of those."

Dobbs is stood there in these blue, tight-fitting girls' tracksuit bottoms that are wrong with a capital 'R'. So wrong, in fact, that Dobbs knows they are right. He'd tried them on in the shop just for a laugh but, to his amazement, their flamboyance was completely offset by the reservation of his brown shirt, trilby and modest green trainers. Dobbs had always had a natural talent for combining things which, individually, would be of unforgivably bad taste but somehow, together, could be pulled off. Not that these could be so easily pulled off though; peeled would perhaps be more appropriate. If you'd pricked his arse with a pin, it looked like they'd probably burst. He'd had to have them.

"I've changed my mind about everything. Sorry guys. And it looks like the Inca trail's going to have to wait 'til my fifties."

Agent6 is just staring down at the backgammon board, saying nothing. Bolivar is trying to look surprised, but he's so stoned it's clearly a struggle.

"Oh. And I ain't going anywhere with The Brigadier right now. No way, José."

"Where you thinking of going then? What's the plan, Dobbs?" Bolivar finally pipes up.

"I just went down to the bookshop to have a read-up about the Inca trail and it's rainy season now. It's all closing up as we speak. Plus, I ended up in the woman's section of that department store and bought these: they're so wrong they're utterly right.

And then I discovered that surf season is starting up north somewhere - got the town written down in my book. We need a surfing holiday before we think about hitting the Amazon, guys. We need some fruity fitness."

Agent6's response is non-vocal but he does, however, select 'Peaches' by *The Stranglers* on his sound system. By the looks of things everyone is kind of warming to the idea.

"Just think of it: long, beautiful sandy beaches and gorgeous Latino…" he pauses for a moment "…*ladies* everywhere.Surfing, getting fit every day. Fruit salads in the morning and fish barbies at night under the stars. And proper waves man – the real deal. Tomorrow, I'm gone."

Bolivar starts singing along to the music.

"Walking down the beaches, looking at the peaches."

"Da-na-na," Dobbs sings out. "I'm going guys, with or without you - though preferably with, obviously. I've got to do it - for me, for England. And if you guys aren't down with it then I'll meet you in Iquitos. I think I need this; brush up on my unbelievably bad surfing and my Spanish and go rent myself a long board.

Come on guys, you know you want this. You need this! Then we'll fly on into Iquitos. No, fuck it, we'll be right up North - we could jump on a boat! It's a fucking epic journey that, man: we'll sail down to Iquitos! Let's just get out of Lima, guys."

Bolivar is actually on his feet now, looking a little excited.

"Man, I didn't really have the money for Cusco anyway."

"What - like we would have paid anyway?" Agent6 muses with a chuckle.

"But this is north as well and that's at least the direction for the Jungle; Cusco's in completely the opposite direction.

"Where is it up north? What's the name of the town?" Bolivar asks.

All of a sudden a renewed feeling of adventure is replacing the despondency caused by the morning- after-the-week-before. Dobbs starts hunting through his bag, looking for the book with the details written in the front. He pulls it out and is struggling to pronounce the word, "Man…" when Agent6 completes the sentence with a wide grin.

"Mancora?"

"Yeah, Mancora. You know it? You been there?" Dobbs is almost shocked he's got anything out of Agent6; for the last three days he's been about as present as world peace.

"Yeah. Passed through there nearly fifteen years ago, just before I ended up in jail. You know where the Chileans were off to, don't you?"

"No way!" Dobbs says with a cheeky grin.

"Yeah, that's where they're headed." Agent6 is actually sitting up now and his eyes look sharp and awake. Even more amazing, there's a naughty smirk just brewing up in the corner of his cheeks.

A button has been pressed and suddenly he's back on-line. Jumping up, he claps his hands together and before Dobbs can do anything, he's run over and slapped him on the arse.

"And Dobbs has got his hot-pants ready!"

Soul Anomaly

Agent6 is twisting up a half-rolled spliff. It's a precision operation. He's carefully tucked the gummed edge of the rolling paper under without first licking it and now he runs the tip of his tongue right along the length of the spliff where the gummed edge lies just one level of paper below. He allows just enough saliva to soak through to the glued layer below, cementing the two together, then he sets fire to the overlap, holding it up at a forty-five. The flame moves along its length in a moment, leaving a perfectly rolled spliff using the bare minimum of paper. He holds it out to Dobbs:

"One last spliff for the road."

"Oh, nice one!" Dobbs says, sitting on his bed after packing his things. All that's left to go in now is his book, *The Party's Over*. Other than that they're all packed, bar The Brigadier, who is still asleep but now close to coming round. Bolivar gets up and checks him out.

"What about The Brigadier?"

"What *about* The Brigadier?" Dobbs says. He's clearly having none of it anymore.

"I ain't travelling with him; it's too dangerous at the moment. He's a liability. I mean, look at us all. We're all over the fucking place. We *gotta* raise the frequency guys. What do you say Agent6?"

"No. I'm done with him. He won't walk away from it: he doesn't want to, yet. When he does, well that's another story," Agent6 says in a tone of total detachment.

"Let's cross that bridge when he wakes," Dobbs says, more whispering. Then, catching sight of his book, "You know what?"

"What?" Bolivar retorts.

"I think I've finally worked out the riddle of the statistics I've had going through my head ever since I picked up this bloody book."

"What?" Bolivar is perplexed.

Dobbs's holds up *The Party's Over*.

"Look, there's a graph in this book that's been twisting my head up and the mention of a word which has caused an odd train of thought. Somehow the penny's just dropped; it's like the clearing after a storm."

"Go on Dobbs, spill the beans" says Agent6.

"Well, I think I've discovered a *Soul Anomaly*."

"A 'sole anomaly'?" Agent6 enquires; a note of genuine curiosity in his voice.

"I like it, it sounds good. A little bit sci-fi maybe, even." Bolivar takes the book, looking at the graph where Dobbs has his finger.

"So go on, pray tell us - what exactly is a Soul Anomaly?" He says it almost with bated breath, as if taking the piss slightly.

"Do you believe in life after death Bolivar?" Dobbs asks.

"Not sure."

"Well, take someone like myself, having parents that channel. Do you know who most frequently visits my parents?"

"No," Bolivar says.

"People who are terminally ill or people who are losing - or have just lost - someone they love. Most of them are old and just need a helping hand to change their minds about what they believe. What I mean is, when times are good you don't need to believe in life after death - or karma for that matter, do you? It all just seems like unnecessary nonsense really, like, it doesn't seem to matter one way or the other, right?

"But being brought up in that world, coupled with some of the odd things that have happened in my life, well, personally I have no doubt about reincarnation; absolutely none whatsoever. But that's just me and my life experience. It makes no odds whether you believe or not, really, does it? It doesn't change the quality of the experience you or me are having now, does it?"

"No."

"So it's not something that can threaten your comfort zone particularly, right? It's something that can't be proved either way as, whatever our souls are; they seem to be made of a different substance than that of elemental matter, right? As in to say, just because you can't see it, it doesn't mean it's not there."

"Yeah, I guess. So?"

"So, we can only talk of these things in terms of ideas, concepts and out-there ball park figures - 'X's in our formulations, right?"

"Yeah. Go on, I get the picture." And then Bolivar starts laughing in his deep, bellowing voice. "He really does love his foreplay first, doesn't he?"

Agent6 laughs with Bolivar. "Yeah. Why don't you just rape me, Dobbs!"

"OK, so here we go: The Soul Anomaly: If you're a person who considers that life after death is part of the human cycle on Earth, that our souls come and go and that we have all had hundreds, if not thousands, of lives on this Earth, right, then this graph here

84

poses a problem. It demonstrates the existence of this Soul Anomaly I talk about."

"So what's the graph?" Agent6 enquires.

Bolivar picks up the book but before he can start reading, Dobbs says,

"Well, it shows the impact of a wave that started from the Peruvian coastline, just like the ones we're about to go and surf. Except this particular wave is known as '*Guano*,' a word which is probably familiar to every organic dope grower under the sun. It's a wave which has picked up a bit too much momentum and grown into an economic tsunami – a tsunami which is about to crash down upon the shores of humanity."

Bolivar stares at the graph which demonstrates Humanities population explosion.

"The graph shows the effects of the discovery of *Guano*. Well, it's a bit like the discovery of the Americas, full stop, actually. It shows what's happened since the White Man's discovery of nitrous- based fertiliser. The indigenous had used it for centuries."

"What?" Bolivar says, attempting to make some sense of the graph. "So what's this? 'World oil production from 1600 to 2200, history and projection, in millions of barrels per year', and… err, 'World population from 1600 to 2200, history and projection, assuming impacts from oil depletion, in millions.'"

Dobbs nods. "Yeah."

"What's that mean - no oil, no food?"

"It means tsunami. No matter which way you slice it. It even looks like a huge wave about ready to crash in the graph, doesn't it?"

"I don't get it," Bolivar says, flicking through the book. He's clearly not liking the look of so many words all at one glance and throws it down on the bed. "How the hell did you pull 'Soul Anomaly' out of that?"

"Well, *Guano* was the world's first nitrous-based fertilizer. It was discovered here, off the coast of Peru, back in about 1850 when the world population was not much more than a billion people.

"That's to say that, up to that point, you'd have to gather cow and horse shit and all the compost you could get together to make fertilizer." He pauses, "And then suddenly they discover this enormous pile of the finest-grade fossilized bird shit, created over millennia by billions of anchovy-munching birds: twenty million tonnes of it to be exact - or, more specifically, twenty million tonnes of fossilized fertilizer that anyone could get their hands on, as long as they had the money.

"Britain had the shipping monopoly on it all. That meant no more leaving whole fields fallow anymore, so the natural bacteria could grow in the soil and shit out nitrates. That natural process of soil regeneration, which could take a couple of years, could suddenly be replaced by one little sprinkle of *Guano* - which is no longer sloppy bird shit but has become a fossilized mineral, full of ammonia - instead.."

"So that shit's slow release," Agent6 quips.

"Exactly! And '*Hey Presto!*' bumper crops every time. Every time, that is, until it virtually ran out at the end of the Nineteenth Century. That was right about the time scientists worked out how to synthesize it in the lab – '*it*', basically, being ammonia, which it turns out is the precursor both for fertilizers and for high explosives, ironically. For the British government it was a win-win situation. Although it takes vast amounts of energy or, more specifically, fossil fuel to make ammonia."

Bolivar's nodding now.

"This is a good bit of history then; we're going to be doing historic research on the waves. I like it. So what you're saying is: a nitrogen explosion kind of equals population explosion."

Dobbs nods. "Exactly. And we've increased our nitrogen manufacture by using vast quantities of oil, nearly all bought through a system of credit powered only by the movement of US dollars. It's like a machine, completely out of control, and the only thing that gives the dollar its value is the worldwide faith in it which, in turn, derives from the movement of that oil. It's crazy, but the value of that oil drives the credit cogs that enable it to be purchased in the first place. It's like a massive scam, enforced only by war - a machine set on self-destruct.

"The only thing that holds it together is the seemingly smiling faces of the politicians shaking hands with one another when everybody knows that, really, the gun's always under the table. That's what gives the dollar its value, right?"

Agent6 and Bolivar seem to be agreeing with him, but only in their facial expressions.

"Fuck man, if the dollar becomes overloaded with hyper-inflation because America gets too greedy and borrows too much and the world finally gets tired of being a slave to their blind greed then there's only one choice left: dump the currency and use another."

86

He makes an odd face as if considering his own words. "The world will carry on - learn from its mistakes - but carry on."

"But if the credit system collapses it means no oil and no oil means no food," Bolivar says.

"That's the tsunami, yeah. That's what I saw on a blast of nitrous oxide, I think. Well, part of what I saw, as mad as it sounds which is maybe why I'm so fascinated by nitrogen."

Agent6 has grabbed the book and is leafing through it, looking at more graphs.

"Yeah, I like it but it's not new is it? And where's the 'Soul Anomaly' in that, anyway?"

"Well, years ago, when I was on a ferry in Hong Kong heading back to my home on Lantau Island, and I read an article in one of these glossy magazines. It contained one of those astonishing figures that stays in your head. It was talking about the population explosion Earth has experienced and it claimed it was so big that, of all the people that have lived and died and all the people that are still alive, those that are alive represent forty-five percent of the total combined."

"What?" Bolivar says.

"Population explosion," Agent6 says. "That getting on for half of everyone that has ever lived on Earth is still alive today?"

"Exactly," Dobbs says.

"You believe that's correct? It can't be right." Bolivar asks.

"Well, it's not about believing or not. It's merely a window; a looking glass on the situation. No one truly knows and all our history notions so far are, well, I don't rate them too much anyway. They're all just a shot in the dark, ballpark figures aren't they?"

"So go on Dobbs, where's the Soul Anomaly, then?" Agent6 says.

"Well, obviously, in truth, there's a line there somewhere, right? No one knows the real truth - well, no one that we know of anyway - although I wouldn't doubt that Great Spirit keeps quite an accurate ledger of all that have come and gone, and all that still remain. But, for instance, using the figures in this graph here, let's think about it. For someone like me, who's of a mind to consider that maybe each soul incarnates maybe ten times, probably more like a hundred times, maybe a thousand times. Who knows, right?" He says pulling out his phone and fumbling for an application.

"But, using that figure, without using a calculator, and suggesting world population is roughly about six and a half billion people living now; if that figure represents forty five percent of everyone

87

that has ever lived then the total amount of all that have ever lived would be coming on close to, well, fifteen billion people. That's like everyone who's alive now plus all that *have* lived and are now – well, dead. Can you see the Soul Anomaly now?"

"Not quite Dobbs," Bolivar gestures with a vaguely interested shake of his head.

"Well, it would be about 8 billion that have lived and died using those figures. And of all those humans - ballpark figures remember – through the eyes of reincarnation, how many souls does that give you? I mean it's almost impossible to conceive because we can't see the bigger picture from this perspective but, as a random looking-glass, how many souls does that give you?"

"So you're trying to work out how many souls have incarnated on Earth?"

"*Yeah.*" Dobbs says slowly.

"Well, if you thought each soul had an average of a hundred lives, then you'd simply divide that eight billion by one hundred I guess," Bolivar says, "If you believe in reincarnation."

"Yeah and we're not looking for the correct figure, we're just playing with the numbers. I ain't looking for commitment to believe here, Bolivar. It's all Unknowns. But if we divided that figure by one hundred…"

Agent6 raises his hands with the seemingly obvious notion,

"Well, just take two zeros off. One zero off would bring it down to eight hundred million."

Dobbs nods. "Yeah, that alone would be like each soul having an average of ten lives and would be the equivalent to just under the present population of India."

"For a hundred lives, you'd drop another zero," Agent6 calculates. "And that would make eighty million. Fuck, that's such a small figure."

"Exactly, through the eyes of reincarnation, if all the souls were present that had ever lived on Earth, given an average of say a hundred lives each, you couldn't go much above the size of Britain in terms of world population. Sure, you can slide that marker up and down between the living and the dead but the figures just don't add up with the size of the population explosion Earth has experienced somehow. And if you were to suggest that each soul had had maybe a thousand lives, impossible figures to play with really, I suppose, but that would bring it down to…"

Agent6 nods at the notion. "Well, a thousand lives would make it eight million."

"Probably about the size of London perhaps," Bolivar says.

"So where are you going with this then, Dobbs?" Agent6 says, clearly kind of liking the concept.

"Well, for someone like me who does not doubt reincarnation in the slightest, it can mean only one thing. Well, actually maybe two."

"What?" Bolivar is now clearly finding the whole thing quite funny judging by the expression on his face.

"Either reincarnation is total bullshit - or Earth's got visitors!" Dobbs finally says.

"Visitors?" Bolivar says laughing off the connotations.

"I think what he's saying, Bolivar, is you might be an alien," Agent6 exclaims with a smirk.

"Shit, yeah man. That would explain loads."

"Fuck, you think I might be an alien Dobbs? I mean, I didn't want to say anything, man!"

"Well, there you go though: The soul anomaly; the 'X' in the equations. Who are they and where do they come from?"

"Generation 'X' man!" Agent6 exclaims. And then suddenly looks puzzled by the notion of the suggestion, "What, like new souls?"

"Well, it seems there's more souls about than can be accounted for. Where do they all come from and what the fuck are they doing here? Just visitors perhaps. Maybe they're just here for the crack, to watch it go down. Or maybe they're here for something else - to *do* something, specific," Dobbs finishes, putting the book into his bag ready to leave. Then, zipping it up, "Who knows, maybe they're just here to help."

"Do animals have souls?" Bolivar asks after a contemplative break.

"Yeah, of course!" Dobbs says. "In fact, the last incarnation in the animal kingdom before a soul can become human is cow!"

"What?" Bolivar asks laughing at the notion.

"Well, so the Hindu's kind of believe anyway. I'm not so sure at all myself. But the notion is that the cow's life is total service to humanity. Well, that's one take on it. But again, down here, humanity is the last to know what's going on, right? As in, all our knowledge and history, mistakes and everything are screened off from us, so we have the chance to create ourselves anew. Well, that's what my old mum would tell me."

"Well, OK: If animals have souls and humanity expands to take all the land - where all the animals lived before," Bolivar says, still clearly contemplating the notion, "What do they come back as if there's no place to come back as an animal?"

Now Dobbs has stop to consider this notion.

"Shit. I like it. What an interesting idea!" Dobbs says approvingly.

Even Agent6 likes the idea:

"Yeah, that would explain loads!"

Just then The Brigadier, perhaps sensing that a shift is about to occur, emerges from his room rubbing his eyes. He looks like a lost little boy.

"Did I sleep a bit?" he says.

Both Dobbs and Bolivar can see that though he is trying to play it like everything is cool he's sort of feeling like he might have missed something.

"Did you sleep?" Dobbs chuckles, "Yeah, you could say that - just a little kip."

Bolivar is smiling at The Brigadier who is completely straight-faced, waiting for him to elaborate.

"Just a little thirty-hour kip, to be precise."

"Get out of here. No way," he responds, genuinely not believing he's slept for so long.

"What's the last thing you remember?" Bolivar is not fussed one bit that the hairs on The Brigadier's back are up a little at the sight of a completely packed-up room but his tone is not one of blame, more humour if anything.

It's easy for all to see The Brigadier's slight nervousness at his own confusion as to his last conscious activities. It's also clear to see he's in a slightly scary place. He's twitchy, with the pestilence withdrawal, no doubt, now fast kicking in. But the comment has stopped him in his tracks momentarily.

"Do you remember anything of just how out of order you were? What you said and what you did?" Dobbs says, walking over to him. He turns, obviously feeling cornered and in a strop.

"No," he says, and walks back into his room, slamming the door.

After a brief pause Bolivar pipes up,

"You might want to change your clothes, man; you wet yourself."

A painful silence ensues as the boys sit on their beds wondering how to break the news to The Brigadier that they've booked a flight out and they'll be leaving in about an hour or so. It was never going to be easy but after not much more than a minute or so Dobbs gets up and walks into The Brigadier's room, closing the door behind him. 'Shit, back in the den,' he thinks. But what he says is:

"We're going up north to do some surfing and get some exercise. Thought we'd meet you in Iquitos." Dobbs is not feeling comfortable about dealing with The Brigadier. He doesn't know what to say, but one thing's for sure – something has got to be said. Taking a deep breath, he begins.

"You went too far, man: you lost it. You placed yourself in incredible danger. You forced me to watch you try and top yourself. You were viler than I think you'll ever know.

"I know it's not you, it's the pestilence; it's taking all your best, man. But we can't do it anymore. We came here for something better than to experience that. We're better than that - and so are you.

"When it comes to studying and learning, you've got all the gifts. You've got the looks and you've got the talent, but if you don't get over this hurdle we're going to lose you, man. You know that, don't you?"

The Brigadier is a man who can assimilate language in ways Dobbs could only ever dream of. He could learn a language in two months and has developed complex rules for understanding grammar and structure to enable a rapid learning process. He's like a walking dictionary. If he's in the mood he'll correct everything you say all day long. To Dobbs, he's truly the Hundredth Monkey.

"Look, I'll tell you what I'm going to do. I'm going to cut you a deal, man. I'm going to buy you a ticket and you're going to get on a plane, fly to Iquitos, go to the land and wait there 'til we get there. And you're going to go clean for two weeks – a month if you can handle it." He pauses, "Yeah, it might half kill you but you need it, man; a tough spell in the jungle, just you and that other self to battle it out. Dose yourself up on Valium for a couple of weeks, man. You'll be a bit dazed by it all but then you can start fresh again. In South America: new life, new start." Dobbs pulls off his hat, wiping his sweaty hand through his already damp hair. The Brigadier just stares at the ceiling.

"You were that close to killing either me or yourself last night. Someone nearly died. You've *got* to get past this, man. You know that. Or we're all going to lose a dear and valued friend.

"So that's the deal, man. I ain't giving you a penny of cash. If you don't want this hand of support than you can work out another plan yourself. Just don't get stuck in Lima," he says, sensing that it is not even registering. "Come on, let's go down and book a ticket for Iquitos now. Grab your passport and we'll do it now as, well, our flight leaves in a few hours and we won't have time to do it later."

The Brigadier still hasn't apologised or made any attempt to take any responsibility for his actions. Instead he's just lying there, cold-faced, staring at the ceiling.

"I think I'll just take the cash for the flight and sort out getting some cash sent over," he finally says.

"You didn't hear me properly. That ain't what I'm offering. What I've offered is all I'm offering, and nothing more. From me, you don't deserve fuck all. And I sure as hell am not travelling with you anymore. It's too much for me right now. You've got some serious work to do. Anything else, as far as I can see, is just a distraction."

The Brigadier looks directly at Dobbs, seething.

"Well, I decline your offer."

"OK, that fine. We're out of here man, but the offer remains open; if I get an email or a text from you saying 'Dobbs, I need that fucking ticket now, man' I'll buy it for you. It ain't no gift man. You'll owe me that money. It will be a loan. Are we crystal clear?"

The Brigadier says nothing.

"Either way, we're out of here and if you've got any sense you'll get out of here, too. Two weeks on that land, man, and you'd be clean. You know it." Dobbs begins to step back towards the door, "Then you'll be out busking with your sax and probably making good money, teaching a bit of English. For fuck's sake man, you'll be teaching Spanish, plus you can probably earn a bit of cash taking people to the land. You've got to get past this, and you've got good friends that are willing to help."

The Brigadier stares at him. He is clearly almost wild with rage but also totally bewildered as to his antics of the previous night. In the end he just stares back at the ceiling.

"I can't do this with you man. None of us can. Sorry dude."

The Brigadier looks wounded; thoroughly insulted that his friends are dumping him.

"I just want to go back to fucking jail."

"You don't need jail man. What - to be locked away and have to live with the regret that you didn't just take a chance and head off into the jungle? You need fresh air, wild adventure and to be free of that shit. How often do you see me or Agent6 go near it – honestly? Yeah, sure, at a wild party maybe. But even then it's not energetically where we're at. It never used to be where you were at," Dobbs says turning to the door.

"I fucking hate that shit. Really. Sure it's a blast for a few days when we come to a place like this where it's clean or at some crazy party, once in a blue moon, but it's not cool though, is it? Ditch it now man. Just let it go. We've all had a laugh, but it's time to say enough is enough and call it a fucking day now.

"The jungle's waiting for you, man; take loads of biscuits, some sweets and some tools to whittle wood maybe - and your sax. Do whatever you need to do to distract you from the big rattle that's going to kick in as soon as you let this shit go. You're strong enough to get through it if you want to. It'll be a breeze for you."

"Well I *fucking* don't want to, do I? So fuck the lot of you."

Dobbs goes to exit the room but turning to The Brigadier one last time he says,

"Well, fuck you too, man. But like I said, the offer stays open."

Outside the room Dobbs turns and looks at the others. He knew there was no way Agent6 could have done that; he's tried too many times already. There's nothing more he can do now without The Brigadier wanting to give it up but all the same he feels relieved; lighter, clearer and above all finally ready to leave Lima.

"Time for a spell on the beach," he whispers to the others.

They start hauling their bags out the room but just before they leave The Brigadier surfaces again, this time holding two books.

"Dobbs...thank you, man. I'll think about the offer, but can you do me one favour and look after these in case I lose them?"

Dobbs recognises the books immediately. One is his poetry book and the other a breakdown of his Spanish lingual articulations and learning techniques. He doesn't really want to take them as he knows they will tie him to The Brigadier and though he really doesn't want that responsibility right now, he realises that maybe that's a comfort he needs on some level.

"Sure, I'll do my best," he says.

They all say their farewells and as they do so Dobbs closes his eyes for a moment, placing a golden ring of light around The Brigadier in his mind's eye, just like his mum would have probably done. He gets the feeling Agent6 is doing so too.

93

"I'll check my email tomorrow, so you can sleep on my offer. Get out of Lima man - for your own good. You need a bit of tough jungle life to sweat that shit out of you so you can make a fresh start. Good luck man."

They all give a nod and a smile of final resolve that they can exit the situation leaving The Brigadier with options and not just a feeling of total abandonment.

And then they're gone.

Sorry

It's a very modern plane - like, Brand New. Everything's immaculate.

Dobbs pulls a bit of an inquisitive face at Bolivar.

"Loads of people on here, ah?"

"Yeah, I suppose so," Bolivar replies noncommittally.

Having never flown into the Amazon before, he has nothing to compare it with. Dobbs has never flown in either, but all the same he is surprised to find the plane crammed with loads of men in suits that don't look at all like tourists.

"They look like politicians!" he whispers.

"I thought you were a politician!" Bolivar jests.

"It takes one to know one maybe."

Dobbs feels the frontal elevation of the aircraft drop slightly and experiences a momentary feeling of weightlessness. Peering out through the cabin porthole all he can see is dense rainforest extending to the ends of the earth, a blanket of emerald green glowing and shimmering in an ocean of golden sunshine. A feeling of unimaginable vastness fills his soul, his spirit seeming to bask in the almost unlimited possibilities for adventure it represents.

"Looks like this heavy chunk of metal's about to make its final descent," he says finally, sitting back with a satisfied sigh.

"I'm not keen on descents at the best of times, especially final ones," replies Bolivar a little nervously.

"Don't panic mate, anything goes wrong, the ground will always break our fall," Dobbs smirks back.

"Cheers, that's comforting."

Agent6 has moved to another window seat to enjoy the view and as the aircraft finally does that bit of levelling out just before the wheels touch the ground he looks over with an expression of anticipation. Then comes the judder and they're down; they've finally arrived in the Amazon for real. What's more, this time it's just the way Dobbs has been craving: no mobile gangway, no flashy fix-linked bridge, just a flight of steps straight down to the tarmac and a proper gawp at all that impressive technology.

To his surprise the airport complex seems quite modern and built-up, though small as one might expect. Behind the main building however a decommissioned DC10, slumped on one wing with half its undercarriage removed, fuselage covered in dirt, provides an atmospheric backdrop against the rampant green wilderness beyond.

They're very quickly through the airport security but as they approach the exit they meet with a spectacle none of them could ever have expected. Just outside the exit door of the airport a whole bevy of beautiful, half-naked local lovelies are performing what appears to be a ritual dance involving an anaconda.

The huge, glistening reptile is curled across the torso of one of the women while the others gyrate wildly around her. It seems somehow a more African style of dance than anything Dobbs has seen in South America before, with painted tribesmen chanting and beating drums whilst dancing a hypnotically repetitive stomp. Apparently these ladies - from what, Agent6 thinks, is the Borah tribe - are serenading them as they arrive in Iquitos.

Dobbs is laughing, whilst Bolivar grabs his camera from his bag. All are properly perplexed at the sight, but Agent6 catches Bolivar's eye.

"I made all the necessary arrangements for your arrival!" he winks.

Dobbs looks at the other two with total astonishment.

"I don't know, but this seems like the VIP treatment to me; I think there must have been some important people on that plane," he shouts across the commotion. "I feel like Elvis, arriving in Hawaii!"

Bolivar chuckles at Dobbs,

"You kind of look like Elvis with that bloody ukulele," he says dourly.

Agent6 moves closer to get a look at the girl with the anaconda wrapped round her. The massive snake is spiralling up between her full naked breasts and as he gets closer she brings it closer to her face, gesturing with her lips and undulating its head in her hand. He spins round to look back at the other two and tries to say something but he's speechless; it's some show.

They jump in a *collectivo*, one of the little share-taxis which are the ubiquitous form of local transport. In this case it's a motor-rickshaw, an odd contraption like a motorbike only with two rear wheels instead of the normal one, a tiny body shell sitting over the rear axle, and a canopy that runs forward to cover the driver.

Long gone are their days of travelling light and it seems difficult to believe such a flyweight vehicle could possibly carry the three of them and all their luggage but soon they're racing along with the wind blasting in their faces and in no time that old feeling of

96

imminent adventure is completely back. Dobbs clings on for dear life as the machine hacks along, the driver kicking through his gear box as he winds the engine up to its maximum revs before each shift, weaving through the dense traffic past heavy trucks belching thick black smoke.

There's a moment of distinct nervousness as they overtake what looks like a proper, old fashioned coach-built bus, its body made mostly of wood. It seems appearances can be deceptive though as, when they finally get past and can start to breathe again Dobbs realises it's actually a relatively modern Japanese flatbed truck and the coach-built box section is just bolted on to the back. It looks very handmade and, glancing around, it seems there are loads of similar vehicles about but he just hasn't noticed them because they blend in so well with the surrounding architecture.

Everything seems so alive and frantic in the back of this mad contraption. With the driver feigning pole position Dobbs feels like he is in an episode of the *Wacky Racers* cartoon, an impression amplified by the countless rickshaws being repaired by the side of the road as if having a pitstop. Dobbs catches sight of a dead dog lying in the road and even its carcass seems to have become part of the rally; an obstacle to weave around without losing penalty points or speed.

The city is dated, but it still looks like a happening place and in what seems like no time at all they're speeding into a thriving central district humming with noise and pollution from the frantic traffic. The road is bumpy and he feels the need to cling on as it is quite broken here and there, but it seems in far better condition than he remembers from ten years before.

Most of the houses are old and they seem a little cluttered, set as they are between the even older, more majestic remnants of the city's imperial heyday which, though long-since passed, is still surprisingly well-preserved. To Dobbs it seems that this architecture, constructed during the great boom of the rubber trade a century before, has become a spectacular epitaph of an exuberant bygone era which renders the whole scene totally captivating, as though it's been dressed for a period film set. There was a massive British influence back in those days but the architecture seems more Portuguese in style, an impression perhaps attributable to the vibrant tropical greenery crammed into every nook and cranny, which lends a distinctly Mediterranean air to the place.

It feels almost like he's experiencing time travel; a whole city, never really knocked down to make way for something more modern. Every street is just drooling in character. Everywhere he looks Dobbs spots old colonial architecture; rows and rows of terraced houses with elegantly tiled bay windows and ornate balconies. But the city looks tired, like the paint is the main thing holding it all together.

There's no feeling of financial difficulty though; the whole place is absolutely humming with people running about on their daily errands and, by the looks of things, business is booming. On his last visit - considerably younger and perhaps a little more cautious - he was here, alone, for much of his stay. Now he can't decide whether his recollections of the town back then are just a reflection of himself all those years ago or things really have just gone crazy since he was last here.

Finally they arrive at their hotel. It is not old but neither is it modern: just a large, whitewashed block sat on the river front. They're right next to the fish market down at the far end of the promenade where the splendid, Regency style homes seem to peter out into smaller, more humble dwellings, little ramshackle shop fronts and shack-like market stalls. There are many more shack-like structures in front of the hotel but they're lower down the slope and built on stilts. Effectively, they're built in the river – well, at certain times of year anyway. This is how the indigenous people live all along the river in Iquitos.

Bolivar jumps excitedly out of the rickshaw.

"Fuck bro, we're in the Amazon!"

They begin dragging their bags into the hotel foyer. The place is very basic and most of the family that runs it are just sat in front of the TV, the kids playing in the street out front. Agent6 greets the old man who runs the place and they're clearly pleased to see each other. He glances back at the others as the old man goes slowly ahead of them up the stairs and, as soon as he's out of sight, whispers,

"I know it doesn't look like much but it actually has the best views in Iquitos, especially on the top floor - which is exactly where we're going."

Eventually they reach the top floor and a large room overlooking the expanse beyond. It's big, but it only has two double beds. The floor looks like old parquet and is wet - with kerosene, judging by the heavy, petrochemical aroma saturating the air. Dobbs assumes it is used as a cheap means to preserve the timber and kill bacteria. Agent6 is deep in bargaining mode with the old landlord, but Bolivar and Dobbs are more interested in the spectacular view. It's an unobstructed panorama; the shantytown running along the banks of the river and beyond, the endless jungle, consuming the horizon in every direction. They both just stand and stare in disbelief at the epic scene. The Amazon: right there, in front of them. Neither of them can quite believe it.

The room itself seems a bit rundown at first sight but Dobbs knows from his last experience that this place will seem like five star digs after just a couple of nights in the jungle. The old guy is desperately trying to hold his ground and insist they need to take another room but he has obviously forgotten that Agent6, who glances over now as if to get a little support, is virtually impossible to negotiate with.

"Got to have three beds in here or one of us gets mediaeval on Bolivar's arse, right?" he says.

Dobbs nods at the old man.

"Ah – amigo, si, claro, - por favor?" he says, grinning and shrugging his shoulders.

The old guy is shaking his head to all demands, but the way Agent6 howls his intolerance at the old man's terms makes him laugh and he's clearly enjoying the banter. Eventually he gives in and Agent6 just sends him on his way to get another bed, chuckling and shaking his head to himself as he goes.

"So where's Swifty then?" Bolivar says, looking around.

Dobbs looks at him sheepishly and immediately Bolivar starts laughing; apparently The Brigadier has also come up to Iquitos with Swifty, who arrived in Lima the day after Dobbs and the others left to go surfing.

"Where's The Brigadier, more to the point?" Dobbs says anxiously. "I've just got to get this shit off my chest."

Agent6 turns to Dobbs.

"He gave them to you, Dobbs."

Bolivar is pissing himself with laughter every time it gets mentioned.

"Just a series of unfortunate events Dobbs," Bolivar splutters. He's clearly enjoying every second of Dobbs's discomfort.

"The crazy thing is I've still got my notebook, and on that first morning I arrived and we were all up in the hotel I was telling The Brigadier about how I was going to write a book and that I wanted to find a story here, and he wrote a poem in my notebook. So I've still got *that* poem I guess. You know the one, 'When our eyes see our hands doing the work of our hearts…'"
Agent6 is nodding along; he knows the poem well, and now he finishes it:
"'…a circle of completion is created inside us. The door to the unknown opens up and loves comes forth, healing every living soul.'"
Dobbs is staring at Agent6 as he recites the end of the poem.
"Yeah, that's the one. Shit man, I'm just going to tell him as soon as he walks in through the door. No way do I want something like that hanging over me."
"You *wanted* to lose it Dobbs," Agent6 says in a patronising, almost cutting way.
"That's not fair; I didn't make that flood happen, and I tried to dry it all out afterwards, which is why I ended up forgetting it. But then, maybe I did. There *was* a part, inside of me, that was truly angry with him, that's for sure. But I was more curious as to what or - more to the point - *who* that being is that he channels when he goes into that state."
Agent6 knows what his priorities are and the first thing he unpacks is the sound system and his huge iPod speakers. He has it all set up in moments and soon the room is rocking to some sweet sounds.
"I'm only joking with you. I know you wouldn't want his books to be lost. It *was* an odd sequence of events though; they were the only things that actually got damaged in the flood."
Bolivar is still laughing as he unpacks.
"Oh, any second now he's gonna walk through that door. I can't wait to see your face."
"No, don't say that. Let's just forget about it," Dobbs says.
"Look, he asked you to take responsibility for his stuff because he was worried he'd lunch it out," Agent6 says, obviously attempting to retract from the abrasiveness of his previous statement. But Dobbs can see he is losing patience with the way the energy is getting sucked into the whole Brigadier drama again so he says nothing, just gesturing with his hands as if to say 'what to do?'

100

"So we leave on Monday, which means we pick up all the supplies tomorrow. I reckon I'll go over and see Juan tomorrow too, and pick up the motor for the boat," Agent6 says, changing the subject. Bolivar and Dobbs just nod.

Dobbs wants to phone the hotel where he left The Brigadier's book. He knows his Spanish is not going to be good enough to be properly understood and he'll need help, but it's clear the others have had enough of the subject and indeed of The Brigadier in general. Instead he just searches for their business card, which he's made a point of keeping.

Just then, as if the next scene of a play is unfolding, the door bursts open and in walks The Brigadier, dressed in a camo vest and shades, his saxophone round his neck. He seems noticeably calmer since the last big blow out and something has shifted slightly. He's clearly happy to see them, although still kind of hiding behind his shades.

Swifty follows behind shortly after. His energy is much softer, which is by no means the norm, but he's calm beaming a warm smile. Dobbs's doesn't know how long he's been hanging with The Brigadier but he seems pretty unfazed. He is wearing a camo safari hat, rolled up at both sides and fastened with heavy-duty poppers. Dobbs can't decide if he's gone for the rugged, outdoor look or is just giving his ears the space they deserve to display all his piercings; it's all a bit *Jack Sparrow*. He's unshaved and looking particularly gung-ho in an army green T-shirt and a pair of NATO tank pants.

"Alright," he grunts calmly as he plods in. His almost sheepish mildness seems oddly contradictory to his appearance, which Dobbs immediately puts down to The Brigadier Factor.

The room is suddenly full of chit-chatting and crossed-line conversations. Everyone's trying to catch up on everything all at the same time, but all Dobbs can think about is when to drop his bombshell. He knows this is probably not the best time, but then again, is there ever a good time to break bad news?

Meanwhile, Swifty has pulled out a shiny, chromed flute. He shows it to Agent6, who inspects it with enthusiastic curiosity.

"You playing?" he inquires.

"A little. I'm learning. I'm gonna learn," Swifty nods.

The Brigadier cautiously edges over to Agent6; he knows he's not in his good books at all at the moment.

"So you meet up with…"

101

"…Niki?" Agent6 finishes his sentence, but seems to retract his energy immediately after.

Bolivar's raucous laughter breaks the momentary tension.

"So go on then! Spill the beans. Tell him how you boned her over the bonnet of that old American sedan we drove up to Mancora in!"

Agent6 smiles modestly, but he's obviously not ready to bury the hatchet yet and just continues his conversation with Swifty instead. Bolivar shakes his head and sighs as he looks at The Brigadier, who he can see is feeling a bit excluded.

"Boys on the beach. You know how it is."

"Did he bone her?"

"Nahh. But we had some fun. I think that's all everyone wanted really. A bit of *Peach* Life. Nothing new to a man like you," Bolivar says.

The Brigadier puts on his filthiest face, nodding with his cheeky grin.

By now Dobbs is beginning to feel like he really needs to say something because all this is obviously going to move to a bar very soon, and he wants to see Iquitos before the light fails. He catches The Brigadier's eye.

"How you doing man? Did that Valium help in the end – d'ya manage to get a spell with just you and none of the other shit?"

The Brigadier flashes Dobbs a look of total purity, which triggers doubt in him from the outset.

"No, we ain't done nothing!"

Dobbs feigns authentic enthusiasm for The Brigadiers efforts and trying not to be judgmental, keeps a neutral face. He's had to wash his hands of things a bit - they all have - but who is he to point the finger? He knows how easy it can be to get dragged in. Not necessarily to the point of addiction but that feeling that somehow you're missing out because you're not snorting - as if you can't enjoy yourself without it. That's where the slippery slope starts. Most don't get it bad, but some seem to surrender their all to it and can become dry, sinister and generally a little lost, especially at social events when it's not about.

The Brigadier starts laughing at the sight of Dobbs's attempt at a sincere nod of total belief, as if to say 'who the fuck am I kidding?'

"Well, we did have one blow out - okay - a couple," and then starts chuckling.

Dobbs is impressed with his honesty. That's the key to controlling the whole thing, he thinks; not lying to yourself or your friends so everything is out in the open and there's no guilt. It's the denial that becomes the backbone of the guilt when it does get you, and in the end it's the guilt that sustains the addiction. He smiles at The Brigadier who, he can see, feels lighter.

"Well done. Really - Well done. Small steps, man." And then Dobbs starts laughing. "Actually, I really want to get a smoke."

The Brigadier laughs too.

"We'll go down later and get some. Whatever you want!"

Bolivar's face lights up and Dobbs bursts into laughter as The Brigadier lets out a guilty little, dry chuckle.

Swifty, who's been deep in conversation with Agent6, starts to put his flute away but Dobbs and Bolivar can both sense he needs a bit of support in his intended endeavour so they join in for a while to give him some encouragement.

The Brigadier breaks into a story about their week in Lima, going twenty-to-the-dozen.

"We had this night: we come out with Lobo, like. Swifty brought his flute along and we were out, the three of us, and we meet this Canadian bird. She plays trumpet. We all end up on stage in this bar and Swifty's just making stuff up, being a bit instrumental. But it worked, it really worked. He was like a proper snake charmer!"

At this Swifty gives a little head waggle as if to say 'yeah, whatever' and Dobbs realises The Brigadier's energy is off down the road of excitement again. He knows where that road is likely to lead to, so he figures it's now or never. Taking a deep breath he tries to eliminate any signs of laughter and give The Brigadier his straightest face, as he often ends up giggling when the shit is really about to hit the fan. It's been the bane of his life - like Tourettes, only he laughs instead of swears.

"I've got to get something off my chest," he blurts out.

The Brigadier is standing in front of him but he can see Bolivar in the background, pulling a face, and already he can feel a snigger threatening to crack the carefully composed mask of his sincerity, even though he knows how much the books mean to The Brigadier, who is now saying, in his deepest, most forbidding Yorkshire accent,

"Go on then. No time like present."

"Yeah, I know," Dobbs says, suddenly horribly aware of the rictus grin that has fixed itself to his face.

"Go on. I don't care how shocking it is, I still want to hear."

Suddenly Star pops into Dobbs's head and he realises The Brigadier is most probably expecting he's about to confess to sleeping with his girlfriend. For a moment he's relieved but then, he suddenly thinks, The Brigadier would, secretly, probably welcome the thought that someone else was responsible for his girlfriend leaving him. So now, not only will he have to deal with the bombshell Dobbs was about to drop on him, he would also have to shoulder the blame for that one again.

"No. I think you might man."

The Brigadier is starting to get jittery now, and Dobbs knows he has to spill the beans. Bolivar makes himself comfortable, waiting for the show.

"Go on. Get it off your chest like."

By some Herculean effort Dobbs manages to keep his face completely straight and now Agent6 and Swifty have also gone quiet and are waiting to see how he will deliver the bad news.

"Well, you see, there was a terrible flood…" he leaves the sentence hanging, and for a moment there is a silence as everybody watches the wheels in The Brigadier's head whirl. Eventually the cogs start to grind and jam up and a white flush spreads across his face. He stares at Dobbs, in total disbelief.

"My books? They're wet?"

Dobbs looks at The Brigadier as sincerely as he possibly can, but the rictus grin is back.

"They got wet, yeah. But then I lost them. Well, the poetry's lost."

In truth Dobbs doesn't know for sure it's lost, but he always feels it's better to start with the worst-case scenario and backtrack rather than open up a black hole that just keeps getting bigger and bigger. The Brigadier's face has dropped to an all-time low; those books were everything to him, absolutely everything.

"No. No, you can't have done."

"Well, I did dry them first," Dobbs tries to soften the blow a little. Perhaps, he thinks, the thought that they're out there, admittedly lost, yet still legible and able to benefit some other poor soul on their path rather than rotting in a state of squidgy pulp fiction might bring a little hope in this moment of sadness.

"What?"

"Well, that's how I ended up losing them. Well, the poetry book anyway - that was the wettest.

I put them in the bottom of my bag where I thought they couldn't get damaged in any way and then there was this massive storm and the roof leaked like a sieve. We'd kind of downed a couple of Valium that night – purely medicinal you understand - and when we woke up everything was absolutely saturated. I found my bag lying in about four inches of water and of course the first thing I thought of was, well, your books."

The Brigadier is now about to pop and Dobbs knows this is going to be the hardest part. The tension is becoming unbearable and the closer The Brigadier gets to the edge, the more Dobbs finds himself on the verge of absolutely pissing himself with laughter, just out of sheer nervousness. He's learnt all sorts of techniques to cope with moments like this - running off to the bathroom or screwing up his face to hide the offending expression of amusement – but in this case he has to just settle for partially covering his mouth with his hand until the giggle has subsided.

Bolivar's still badly hiding his own smirk and his face is taut with the effort, which only adds to the hysterical hilarity of it all. Dobbs looks away from him and back at The Brigadier, who's now almost beside himself.

"I don't know if we've lost it permanently. I mean, I, err, we … left it on top of the wardrobe. We didn't want to dry it in direct sunlight in case it turned into a brick you see – I mean that would've been the end of it, wouldn't it?" he says helpfully. "But we do have the number for the hotel, don't we –you got their card?"

He turns to Bolivar, whose face immediately becomes as straight as a die.

"Yeah, right here," he says.

Dobbs has been trying to get the card off him for the last few hours. Now he takes it and passes it, at arm's length, to The Brigadier.

"Please, can you ring them? Your Spanish is perfect," he says meekly.

The Brigadier is on the defensive now and, sensing that this is an attack on him via his prized possessions, he scowls at Dobbs.

"No! You fucking ring them!" he screams.

Dobbs does his best to look The Brigadier straight in the eye whilst holding his phone out to him.

"Listen," he says, "what happened was a result of overly-looking after your stuff. What I mean is, sometimes the fear of dealing

105

with the consequences of our actions plays a big part in the way things pan out, doesn't it? And I was always a little worried about taking responsibility for your books. Now, I haven't got the Spanish to explain that I ... we, left the poetry book on top of the wardrobe, drying, to the hotel manager. But you have! Just ring them, and offer them a reward to post it on to us here or else we just fuck it off: I'll pay the reward and the cost of posting it. Those are some of your most beautiful creations, man! It was a genuine accident; there was never any question of deliberately losing them. Think about it - it's an easy little earner for them to send it back ain't it?"

Dobbs is almost pleading now, holding out the phone and the card.

"It's fucking gone, isn't it!" The Brigadier angrily declares.

"You don't know that's the case. I know how much they mean to you. All of our personal possessions got drenched. It was a proper flood. Shit happens. Let's at least find out if they are properly lost first, or just ... delayed."

Dobbs has put his all into the speech and in the end The Brigadier gives in and rings the hotel. Initially it's all looking positive: some Argentinean guests have apparently found it, but then it turns out they've gone off with it and though the word is that they might return, in the end the prospect of an emotional reunion all seems about as vague as a politician's promise.

Nevertheless, the notion that the precious poetry book has indeed been picked up and is, even now, in someone's care seems to have planted a little seed of comfort in The Brigadier's mind; it may be missing in action but it's at least still out there somewhere, working its magic.

Eventually the drama seems to be drawing to a conclusion and the tension is dissipating. But just then The Brigadier turns to Dobbs.

"What about the Spanish book?" he says.

"Ahh...?" Dobbs suddenly remembers the Spanish book, with all the words washed away.

"Oh, I've got that *safe*."

It's Just Shit

Rummaging through his bag, Dobbs passes The Brigadier his Spanish book. Externally, it looks exactly the same as when it was given to him. Inside, a disaster awaits discovery. To Dobbs's infinite relief, The Brigadier just takes the book, folds it over and sticks it in his back pocket before walking out of the room. Bolivar chuckles at the expression on Dobbs's face as he watches The Brigadier leave.

"What?" Dobbs says, rounding on him.

"That one can wait..." Bolivar replies, making no attempt to hide his smirk.

"Yeah, right."

`He begins pulling things from his bag, his head tilted forward and his brow furrowed, scowling like an old school master.

"...until he opens it!"

"Perish the thought," Dobbs shudders.

In truth, much of the text is still just about legible under close examination and, thinks Dobbs; if The Brigadier was so inclined he could always write it out again, perhaps even elaborating it into a book so a wider audience could appreciate his amazing learning techniques. Also, he's sent much of his poetry to various friends who probably still have some of it in emails and old correspondence and Dobbs has promised to put the word out for everyone to have a look and see if any of it turns up.

Nonetheless, it's a tragic loss. The poems are living proof that, behind his rugged façade, beyond the addiction - and even, mostly, during it - The Brigadier could still be a being of incredible beauty, even at a time when he'd been locked up in a dark and terrifying dungeon, far away from home. Then again, maybe that was not as terrifying as the freedom to indulge his vices, Dobbs muses. Because strange as it may be it seems now, in his most desperate hour, that that is what he most longs for: to have the 'monster' locked away, like a bird in a cage.

The heat and humidity is almost, though not quite, unbearable and Dobbs is still in a sweaty mess from carrying his bags up the stairs. Most of the others seem to be in a slower gear, although The Brigadier knows he wants to go out before the light fades completely. He has a craving to just stand down by the river and take it right into his core. Being here, in the centre of the Amazon Rainforest, feeling the intensity of its energy; it's overwhelming.

He jumps in the shower and immediately feels fresher. He's happy that he's got that load off his chest and though it's still not clear whether the other hotel will be able to return the book he has tried his best to sort the situation out and The Brigadier seems satisfied at least some effort has been made to get it back. Now all Dobbs wants to do is get out into the fresh air.

"What say I meet you guys down there?" he says. "I'll be in the most havin' it bar closest to the waterfront. Just look for the hottest Latino babes you've ever laid your eyes on and I'll be there before you, sipping cocktails."

The Brigadier nods in approval.

"Yeah, come on. I'll walk with you," he says. "Let's go."

"Wicked!"

Agent6, still engrossed in sorting out odds and sods, is about to say something but he knows the expression on Dobbs's face; he's out of there.

"See you at the bar on the front then. We'll be there in half an hour," he says, winking at Dobbs.

"I'll be there - sippin' cocktails man," Dobbs gests with approval.

"And Dobbs," Agent6 adds as he walks through the door, "Be careful Bro; the ladies do all the chasing round here."

They set off along the promenade. The Brigadier is fully equipped, shades down, saxophone at the ready. Dobbs has donned his hot pants, a green camo sleeveless vest, and his feathered trilby, all set off by the silver chain round his neck. For the most part, he has kept this covered up but now it seems to be taking a more central role in his attire and hangs almost like a medallion in the centre of his chest.

From a distance it's a rough, teardrop-shaped stone fastened with a coarsely finished, almost annealed band of silver folded around its top like a ribbon. Under closer examination, however, the texture of the metal seems to mimic the texture of the stone, a small, once-molten shard of Moldavite.

It has a deep, mysterious green opacity almost like a crystal and yet you only have to glimpse it to see by its shape what it so obviously is: a shooting star bound on a silversmith's anvil. Many know exactly what it is at first glance but similarly, somehow struggle to believe it is what it so appears to be. Dobbs half believes it can make wishes come true but then he's also of a mind to be careful what he wishes for. Crystal buffs generally show a degree of caution to it as they say it's a double-edged sword but perhaps that's just the story of the world.

He'd seen it on a display whilst loitering about with his hand up a monkey's backside, selling puppets outside the Roman Baths in, well, Bath. Some old feller and his wife had it on their jewellery display. Dobbs kept going back to see it, always looking at other things and trying not to give it too much attention but he couldn't quite believe how beautiful it was: a tear-shaped molten droplet from a massive asteroid that smashed into the Earth's crust millions of years ago in the region now known as Moldavia. A fallen star, shattering into millions of rugged molten gems rapidly cooling in their flight path as they exploded outwards from that initial, cataclysmic impact.

It must have been a few Christmases ago when he bought the stone, come to think of it, about six months before he lost the plot following a heroic dose of nitrous oxide (although it will be another couple of years, and a different story, before he finally begins connecting those dots). Suffice to say - for now - Moldavite doesn't fuck about. Some say it's the stone that inspired the Superman comics, others that it's from a planet long since destroyed and brings with it the wisdom of the erstwhile inhabitants' errors.

Whatever it is though, right now it's looking better than it's looked in a while. Dobbs feels fantastic; a little bit of a tan, a week on the beach and a splash in the sea have all conspired to give him back that something he's been craving. He hadn't surfed that much, but he'd had a lot of fun on those sandy beaches.

They're still some distance from their destination, a hive of activity that can be heard all the way from the far end of the old promenade. It's a good fifteen minutes of slow gander away though, and as they wander along The Brigadier seems very quiet. Dobbs can guess what's coming next; it's pretty inevitable, but glancing away down the promenade he sees somewhere he thinks might be of interest to The Brigadier and a good place to sow a seed in his mind. He's just waiting for the perfect time to deploy the notion. In The Brigadier's mind, Dobbs knows, he probably kind of owes him one, especially after he's lost the poetry book. Maybe he does, but as The Brigadier tries to move in for the kill,

109

Dobbs plays for time by pretending to be dumbstruck by the view, though in truth he doesn't have to play too much,

"What's this river here, then?" he says, feigning ignorance.

The question stops The Brigadier in his tracks.

"It's the Amazon, that is."

"Silly question I suppose."

"Not really. Loads of different rivers round here," he retorts.

"I'd forgotten how wide it is," Dobbs says, taking in the freshness of the breeze coming in over the jungle that's been slightly chilled by the cool expanse of the vast river. For Dobbs, breathing this air is like drinking fresh water straight from a mountain spring. It is the sweetest of summer wines. This is what he came here for. This is where he can find his adventure – where he can find the book he's somehow been looking for all his life.

The Brigadier just stares out at the river with Dobbs and then half chuckles; he knows Dobbs too well.

"Man, that's nothing. In some places you can barely see the other side. We'll show you a fucking river or two mate - don't you worry about that. We got the old *Christina* don't forget."

Below them, light spilling from within the wooden huts and shacks dimly illuminates the shanty town. A few houses are floating right out in the river on rafts, selling gasoline and generally catching passing trade. The rest of the river dwellers live mostly in houses stood on stilts set into the mud. The houses are very tightly packed and connected by a network of thin planks creating walkways that leave no space inaccessible. They are all crammed together down the long, gradual incline of the riverbank and well into the water itself. He pulls his shades off to get a better view, balancing them on the brim of his hat.

The houses have a distinctly higgledy-piggledy thing going on due to the subsidence of their supporting stilts and the chaotic angles of what were once probably horizontals and uprights. The whole thing looks like some sci-fi animated water world, an impression accentuated by the warm glow of tungsten lighting which seems to capture an element of simplicity. But to Dobbs this is not a vision of poverty. Rather it is something tribal; a scene of true community.

"I was blind to all this somehow, last time I came here," he says at last. "I think I was a little too nervous; I couldn't relax into the ride. Perhaps because I'd come from a land where someone would beat you up not to rob you, but just for the sake of it. You might get stuff robbed here but it's unlikely they'd want to hurt you, right?"

The Brigadier doesn't answer but continues to stare out at the expanse with Dobbs.

"You know what I mean though? I see it now, man. How beautiful they are in their tiny wooden huts. I used to think their lives were so simple but I was wrong; their lives are so complex. It's *our* lives that are simple. I mean, how complex is going down to the supermarket and chucking some bog roll and a pre-cooked meal in a trolley before heading home to just vegetate in front of the TV?"

The Brigadier nods.

"Yeah, I know what you're saying."

"It seems so civilised to me now," he muses, taking in the whole panorama. "It's like two polarised extremes, divided by the promenade. Yet they're all living in perfect harmony: the poorest of the poor, the *Indigenous*, literally on the water's edge, and the richest and most powerful in their big houses up above. Yet neither wants to be where the other is and they're all, seemingly, happy with their lot."

The elegance of the waterfront feels like it's transported him back in time by a hundred years. It all seems so regal, so steeped in the imperial wonder of a bygone age.

"I can picture lords and ladies wandering up here. Iquitos has changed, man. It looks more like Brighton seafront now, don't it?"

"You know Iquitos is an Island? It's a whole city built on a mud island and surrounded by rivers."

"I'd heard something along those lines," Dobbs muses. "So this is the Island we all get washed up on after the Tempest."

The Brigadier just nods.

"It seemed almost like a bit of a ghost town before. But now it's, like...booming." Dobbs says, attempting to take it all in.

The Brigadier stops to talk to one of the local lads. It appears they both go back a way, like they're old pals. The youth seems nice enough to chat to but he's got trouble written all over him, and Dobbs knows if they pick him up it's certain to add a twist to the tale. They're both talking fast, in colloquial Spanish, but Dobbs can just about make out that the stranger's telling The Brigadier he's joined the army now and is on leave. He doesn't get involved though, being content just to take in the view and allow the conversation to come to its own conclusion.

111

"What was that all about?" Dobbs asks genially as the guy walks away.

"Just saying hi. Kind of looks like he's on the *pasta* though."

"Thought he looked a bit out there on something. What's *pasta* anyway? Somehow sounds a lot worse than a bad wheat diet."

"After they wash *it*, there's loads of shit left, which is almost worthless, toxic crap. They refine that a little and you get this second-grade shit that fucks you up worse than anything. It's the shit of the shit."

"Shit!"

"This place is saturated with it, man; from the cheapest and dirtiest to the absolute very best," The Brigadier continues casually. "It's where most of the money is coming from."

"It seems I've only got eyes for the ladies." Dobbs says absent-mindedly. He is a bit taken aback by all the gorgeous girls that are now saturating the walkway as they near the busier end of town and somehow feels he is failing by not being a bit more culturally captivated by the old Regency style houses fronting the promenade. With an effort, he pulls his sight back to the architectural wonder at hand.

"Man, look at all the cracks; you can really see the whole place is just floating on mud can't you?"

Indeed there are many cracks in the pavement, some quite huge. Most have been, or are in the process of being, repaired. But there are also large sections where the promenade appears to have broken free completely and is being drawn down into the river. It's the later part of dusk, and the sky has darkened to a deep velvet blue. He can still see the jungle far across the watery expanse but it's lost its emerald glow now and is just a silhouette.

The promenade is busy to say the least but the crowd is mostly teenagers hanging in groups and seems quite unthreatening. There's random stragglers wandering about and a fair few couples snogging here and there. Every which way Dobbs looks he sees gorgeous ladies and as they wander past one group of girls The Brigadier shouts out some crack and they all start giggling. He's got that cheeky grin across his face like he just scored for England and he gives them a parting blast on his sax for good measure. Dobbs knows things are likely to get a bit rocky before too long but all the same he decides to try to avert the inevitable - for a little longer, at least.

"So all these buildings stem back from the days of the rubber trade, don't they?" he observes, gesturing to the grand houses and apartments, many with an almost ambassadorial style of architecture, that are now coming into view along the far side of the promenade.

The Brigadier nods, grinning.

"*Caucheros*," he fires off with a Latin twist and all the emphasis on the 'cheros' which, as Agent6 had explained to Dobbs earlier, is how they speak in this neck of the woods, apparently.

Dobbs smiles, adopting a similarly arch expression.

"Ah, The rubber barons. Us British coming to do business with mafia-style tycoons that had no qualms about enslaving the *Indigenous* in work camps."

The Brigadier shrugs his shoulders.

"They weren't no different to the drug cartels that run this place now," he says, his tone heavy with fatalism.

Dobbs remembers reading on his last trip about how English ships crossed the Atlantic loaded with boxes of sterling pound notes piled up on the gangways to purchase the precious rubber. They were cunning however, and when the competition intensified and prices became too high the British Government commissioned a man by the name of Henry Wickham to bring 70,000 seeds from the rubber trees here in the jungle and take them back to England. Apparently after propagation fewer than 3,000 trees survived but nonetheless they proved sufficient to seed a plantation in the British colony of Maya - now part of Malaysia - which eventually flourished, and broke the *Caucheros'* monopoly on the rubber trade.

Here Dobbs stops to properly take in the old buildings. The neighbourhood they are now passing through seems to be composed almost entirely of palatial-style mansions as evenly spaced as the palm trees and other plants standing in neat rows beneath their large, Georgian-style balconies. Despite the British influence prevalent at the time of their construction they seem to have more of a Portuguese or Spanish feel to them, with brightly coloured vintage tiling tastefully incorporated into their stately facades. Their sheer size gives them a regal air yet something - perhaps the myriad of plastered-over cracks in the white-washed frontage - lends them a lived-in feeling, as if that imperial antiquity has never really died.

The promenade is equally romantic, with huge overhanging palms and other jungle foliage crammed in every nook and cranny. Walking along with The Brigadier in his Indiana Jones style get-up, it all conspires to transport Dobbs back to a time of wild-eyed explorers and doomed expeditions into the heart of darkness.

"So you reckon the rubber barons built these do you?" Dobbs repeats, now trying to sound a little more culturally informed, but The Brigadier is obviously not too interested in participating in some middle class property developer rant and brushes off the comment.

"Yeah. Guess so."

The silence resumes, but now there is a bit of an edge to it; they are getting closer to the point Dobbs has pre-selected for his speech, and it looks like The Brigadier is going to make his move right on cue. He stops, looking down at the river bank just below the promenade and trying to work out exactly where he'd sat last time he was here, all the while saying nothing and waiting for The Brigadier to ask what he is sure to ask. There is a short pause then, like clockwork, he starts.

"Listen Dobbs, I kind of got up here under my own steam and all that so I was thinking, like; that money you were going to give us for the flight …well if you give us that then we're square."

Dobbs knew this little tete-a-tete was coming and he has planned his moment to perfection. Now he points down to the bare riverbank without looking at The Brigadier,

"See that spot just down there?"

"Yeah?" says The Brigadier, nonplussed.

"When I was last here, I went there to smoke a spliff and have a ponder on whether to risk taking a load of pestilence back to England. You and Trouza were both doing it, and stood to make a small fortune. I was really paranoid at the time as I'd already had a run-in with the cops back down the river a few days before." He pauses, still not looking at The Brigadier.

"Man, I remember it like it was yesterday. The place was totally silent, no one about, and then, literally two *tokes* after sparking up a spliff in my room, this cop appears. It was as if he'd been just hiding in the dark outside, nose at the ready for the first scent of smoke. Crazy thing was he was like straight out of an *Ayahuasca* vision. Immaculately dressed; you could see your face in the reflection of his polished shoes. Another story but I got away with it. But it was a warning telling me not to get too stoned in this part

114

of the world. So I decided right then and there that the next spliff I smoked in the Amazon would be down by the river where - so I thought - no one would give a shit. How wrong I was," he chuckles, shaking his head at the memory. "So, anyway, I bail out of there and get to Iquitos. I'm gagging for a spliff but I'm still really paranoid so I decide to take my own advice, keep it discreet, and head down to the river - just down there, to be exact." He nods to the muddy bank below.

"So, there I am, having a quiet smoke and wondering whether to risk the big one and you know what it's like man, you ignore all that shit in your head and you just stand at the threshold of the rest of your life and you make your choice. You don't know how you know which way you're going to go and which decision you're going to make. But you just ...*know.* You know, right? I mean, last time, you weren't choosing nothing but jail, right? You even said it to Agent6."

The Brigadier says nothing but just nods very slightly.

"So I'm smoking this spliff and contemplating: couple of hundred grams. Got to be worth a few grand, and that's a fucking decent truck. I wouldn't have taken much more than that – or maybe I would...I mean, I don't even know whether I could have really done it...just to consider it was exciting enough! But as I sat there, contemplating, I felt this wave of paranoia go through me, like a shudder. And you know that shudder man. Like your worst fear."

The Brigadier just nods again.

"And I looked round and right where we're standing now, there's two cops just looking down at me smoking a fat reefer with all my dope on me. I'm fucked, I think to myself, and I turn away and just freeze: I don't know what to do!

"So I'm looking around in a state of panic, knowing I've got this grass on me, and trying to think of a way to lose it somehow, and the first thing I notice is this big pile of shit, right there, in front of me. And then I see another. And then another. And just like that I realise that, basically, I'm sitting in the local shitter. And I suddenly laughed to myself as I realised those cops would have thought that I was just having a shit. And, let's face it; in a sense I was having a shit, wasn't I? I was having a shit thought! And sure enough, I turn round and they're gone. They'd left me in peace, to have my shit thought."

Dobbs turns to The Brigadier.

115

"You know the mad thing is, I went back and checked my mail after that and I'd had a message from Trouza, telling of the bad news that you'd been busted. I was going to do a ceremony and drink that same evening, and you were in my mind the whole time so as I was coming up, I decided to ask the brew why that had to happen to you.

"Immediately, in my vision, I saw two armed guards in the distance silhouetted against the black background of the dark forest. Crystal clear they were. At first they seemed very far off but they were marching towards me with a Gestapo type of marching step, just like you see in that video, Pink Floyd's *The Wall* - you know the bit. When their boots came up as they marched towards me they got massively and rapidly bigger, like they were covering fifty metres with every stride and suddenly there they were, right in front of me, standing to attention. Short, dark hair, massive, chiselled chins, big barrel chests in grey uniforms with rifles over their shoulders. I knew I had to go with them.

"I was scared but I knew I had to overcome my fear, so I focused on my breathing and tried to remember my intention - which was to find out why *you* had to go through this, what you were going to have to endure. So I agreed to go with them but as I got right between them, I saw who they really were.

"It was so strange; they had long, flowing hair running down their backs and the back of their uniforms were the hessian robes of *Arawaku* Columbian *Indigenous*. Their huge, shiny bovver boots suddenly looked like clogs as I could see their naked heels and the thin strap of their sandals. I realized that I was simply passing through fear, through one of the many doorways into the Dream-world. And, as I moved through and in, the feeling went from fear to incredible love and understanding, and the voice I heard in my heart just said to me: 'The Universe has many doors and many door handles.' It was so beautiful."

The Brigadier signals a knowing expression but Dobbs wonders if he really understands or it's simply a knowing, perhaps, that cash is not going to happen.

"And you *know* what happened next: Trouza read my mail the next morning just before his door was kicked down by the cops -kicked down with his Mum and Dad *in* the house. I mean, can you *imagine* what that was like for his folks? They literally bust the fucking door down with a battering ram, man. Him, upstairs, a good couple of days down the line and happily thinking he's home and dry but, just like you, they'd had his number from the very start. You know how that horrible game works.

"But I realised then that message was for both of you. And in that moment he really got it and the whole experience turned his life around. And when he came out, well, you know the story; he went to university and got his life together, basically."

The Brigadier lets out a long sigh. He is now, Dobbs can see, totally sure which way this is going to go.

"So, to cut a long story short, I'll be straight with you," says Dobbs, now turning to look him square in the eye.

"I'll make sure you don't starve but I ain't giving cash handouts. My intention here is to help you and to get you out to the middle of the jungle and onto that land you've worked so hard for, and to keep you there until you've had the type of break that gets you off that shit. Plus – and let's be frank here mate - you don't fucking deserve it. I know that sounds awful, but no way am I going to fund something that is proving to be near fatal for me as well as you. I know we're going to have a blow out for a few days before we go - it's inevitable - but I still ain't doing it. No way.

"We'll all buy you drinks and what-have-you but you've got a chance to get off the merry-go-round here, mate. I want to get the old Brigadier back. But there's a hardcore little fairy lurking in that powder that won't let you go until she's stripped you of everything you are and everything you've got. You are opening yourself to massive psychic attack; it's like a complete possession when that thing takes you man. Either you're going to leave her at the gates of heaven, or she's going to leave you at the gates of hell; which one it's gonna be is up to you, man. But I'll tell you this: you're going to have to fight with everything you've got to reach the escape velocity necessary to get that bitch off your back, and I mean Everything man."

"I hear what you're saying Dobbs, and I appreciate the sentiment, but you said you'd sort me out!" The Brigadier angrily states.

"No. That weren't never the deal, man. I was never going to give you cash. I was only ever going to buy you a flight to Iquitos - nothing more - and even that was only going to be a loan. We both know where the cash is going to go if I give it to you now, right?

"You don't realize just how much that shit has you. But you will if you do a stretch in the jungle and go clean. People like you and me don't get expensive rehabs unless we're part of some criminal

117

reform package. This is going to be your best port of call or your absolute fucking worst man."

And indeed, it really was. Some of the finest grade pestilence comes via Iquitos and it's as cheap as chips and as clean as it comes – well, some of it anyway.

"You just have to understand," Dobbs says, looking at The Brigadier. "Pestilence isn't good or bad, or right or wrong. You must know and realize that now. It's just Shit. It's fun in big doses on the bluest of moons, if at all. Beyond that - and even within that - it's just Shit."

Dobbs has said his piece now, and without waiting for a response from The Brigadier he just turns and walks towards the bright lights and the high-pitched squeals of excited *senoritas* beckoning him from the crowded waterfront.

"Come on man, let's go and get pissed instead," he says. "The drinks are on me: if you can't snort your troubles away, at least you can fucking drown 'em."

The Circus is in Town

It's Friday night. The promenade is rammed and it's going off like a firecracker. There's a tiny auditorium, like a little speaker's corner positioned in front of all the bars in the busiest region of the walkway. About a hundred or more travelling street-performer types are gathered around, intermingling with the young and havin' it scene. Crusty-looking Travellers are beating djembes and an assortment of other drums whilst cheering on a guy with no arms or legs who's somehow break dancing using just his torso - and doing it well. People are throwing down money and the guy's absolutely going for it. Dobbs just stares in disbelief.

"Fuck me, man! That's amazingly cool."

There's lots of what look like Brazilians fly pitching their jewellery and also a couple of puppeteers displaying hand puppets made of sponge. Dobbs is fascinated by the puppets and wanders over to have a play with one of them, a beautifully executed effigy of the Inca Sun God. It has a selection of finger-holes cut in the back and simple hand movements make it possible to achieve the most surreal facial expressions.

"Your puppets are beautiful," he says to the girl of the pair. Then, with a bit of effort, he manages to repeat the phrase in Spanish, and also to ask her the name of the indigenous tribe living along the river banks.

"*La Shipibo!*" Comes the answer.

Dobbs looks around at the volume of people, trying to take in the full spectacle of all these wild festivities taking place against the awesome backdrop of the Amazon. He nods at The Brigadier and then looks back just in time to see a guy dancing by on his hands and feet in a full-body puppet suit that gives the illusion of a man and a woman dancing together. It all seems very well rehearsed.

The Brigadier pulls out his sax and blows a few notes and then turns to Dobbs with a grin,

"Fucking circus is in town," he grunts.

"Let's go and get a drink," Dobbs says. Then, catching sight of the guy they'd spoken to earlier hanging about nearby he adds, "And tell your man there to go and get us a smoke. Just a spliff or two - and nothing else man."

The Brigadier does a little hand gesture to the guy, who approaches. They talk for a short while then he turns to Dobbs.

"He wants the money first."

"Yeah, I fucking bet he does," Dobbs says, grinning at the man.

A busy bar right beside all the commotion on the promenade is cordoned off with red rope to give patrons some feeling of exclusivity as they knock back expensive cocktails. They take a seat and, like magic, attract a handful of rather attractive ladies. The Brigadier pulls the raunchiest grin, which somehow amplifies the money gap between his two front teeth. He nods at Dobbs then sets about making the girls feel welcome. It's all starting to seem stupidly surreal again.

"How much is a cocktail here then?"

"Less than a quid!"

"Fuck man, spending the last pennies of ancient sunshine!" Dobbs says, not even attempting to hide the grin on his face.

"Hey, amigo!" he shouts out to the waiter, who's already well on the way. "*Caipirina's*, ah? Gracias amigo," he says, swinging his finger round and letting him do the maths.

There's a man with shoulder-length blond hair. He is tall and, though not exactly well-built is by no means skinny. He has a friendly face and though his origins appear at first glance to be quite Nordic, looking closer Dobbs somehow recognises him as another wild-eyed Englishman. He reaches across to shake the man's hand.

"Dobbs"

"Julio," the man says. "You guys look new in town."

His accent confirms Dobbs's suspicions; it sounds somehow of Celtic origin. Dobbs sits back in his chair, getting comfortable.

"Nice to meet you man. Yeah, we're kind of straight off the boat - well, plane."

He turns and shakes all the ladies' hands, performing all the relevant introductions befitting such lovelies, to the now-customary accompaniment of tittering at his crap Spanish. The mood is vibrant and it's easy to see an interesting night lies ahead.

"I thought we should at least pop down to the local bar before unpacking. Well, my first thought anyway. The Brigadier here spends quite a bit of time here anyway. I've been once before, but that was ten years back. But, yeah, we literally just arrived. What you doing here then? You've got that wild-eyed Mr Livingston thing going on, like you're busy doing stuff."

Julio nods with excitement.

"Funny you should say that, I am a busy man."

"Oh yeah?"

Julio points down towards the water's edge in the opposite direction from where they've just walked, and a floating structure that seems quite huge relative to everything else in its proximity.

"I've been building that thing."

Dobbs peers over to get a better look at the floating mass of timber. It resembles a raft of sorts, only on a very large scale. Its base is perfectly square and its structure rises far more in the centre than anywhere else. Even to the casual observer it seems obvious that its design is bordering on the mystical.

"What the hell is that thing trying to be?" Dobbs frowns.

Julio stops to consider the question almost like it's the first time anyone has asked such a thing.

"Well, I wanted to bring a lot of different things together and I sort of felt that a floating pyramid might do the trick."

Dobbs stares back at the huge structure. He is surprised it didn't catch his eye on the walk down, although it does look more like a large pontoon than any kind of vessel he's ever seen. He tries to picture just how big it will finally be from the size of the base, which from this distance looks to be over a couple of hundred metres square.

"You crazy mother fucker!"

"I sold my house back home and just thought, it's now or never. Plus, I've got a little funding now as well."

"Shit man. You're building a fucking pyramid! Far out!"

The drinks arrive right on cue. In fact everything seems to be happening right on cue tonight, as though they've entered into some kind of harmonic relationship with the jungle, which now seems to be resonating through Dobbs's moment-to-moment existence. He distributes the drinks round the table and holds his glass up to Julio,

"To you man: what a vision!"

Reaching over, he clinks glasses first with Julio and then the girls.

Just then Bolivar rolls up and it's big smiles all around. Swifty and Agent6 follow close behind, looking very calm and relaxed. It's such a heavenly scene; the only thing missing is a fat reefer. But then, as if Nature herself is answering his every half-formed whim, The Brigadier's mate arrives, bearing gifts.

A few drinks later and, even though he'd been sure that he'd had his fill and wasn't going to do any more pestilence, Dobbs finds himself in the loo with his finger in a wrap. He's a bit over it by now but it's very clean. 'What the hell,' he thinks and surrendering to the chaos of the night sticks the crystal-coated digit into his mouth and waits for his gums to go numb.

He knows the jungle juice is a severe *cleaner-outer*, so to speak, especially when it comes to the toxic residues of pestilence. He knows She'll be harsh with him; he knows how She works. She'll be real nice with him the first time, and maybe even the second too. But then She'll be brutal. And if She's really brutal, like She sometimes can be ...well, he'll probably survive. Ultimately, everything always turns out better than you plan it, he reassures himself. He knows there's a price to pay for everything, it's just that the more he drinks and the more pestilence he consumes the less he cares; payday is always tomorrow. Right now, he's hammered and he can't take his eyes off all the sexy women vying for his attention.

Agent6 was right; these jungle ladies really come on strong and don't seem at all put off by the fact that he's so obviously ridiculously aroused by the combined effects of the stimulant and their own overwhelmingly erotic aroma. He tries vainly to bring himself back to the here-and-now and the enjoyment of just hanging with his pals, rather than his present fixation of hanging with *her* - and hanging with her now - but just when he feels he's broken the spell of the siren sitting to his right, whose hand keeps somehow landing on his lap and brushing past his painfully sensitive crotch, he looks into her eyes and sees she has the tiniest, naughtiest grin in the corners of her mouth. Game over: she has him captivated.

'Wow,' he thinks to himself, catching Bolivar's eye over all the noise and commotion. He's sitting next to Agent6 who's being chatted up by the hottest little *chiquita* Dobbs has ever seen and has the *baddest* grin across his face. This girl's so hot it hurts, and Dobbs has to keep looking away, but he watches Agent6 peering periodically at her as they talk. She's making it very clear she's very available.

Occasionally Agent6's eyes meet with his and where there's normally playful glee there's now a look of total bewilderment. He's almost powerless in the face of Pure Temptation and it feels as though they're both only just holding on to the tattered scraps of their consciences by their fingertips. Agent6 starts fumbling with his phone, which is normally his get-out-of-jail-free card; a place into which he can dive and disappear from the rest of the world.

122

But now he's scrutinizing the screen with his face screwed up almost in shock.

"Good news or bad news?" Dobbs says, leaning forward.

Agent6 doesn't answer. He manages to keep with the flow of events, but something has just come in and Dobbs can see the cogs whirling.

"I think she's with someone else," he says eventually, looking over at Dobbs.

"What?"

Dobbs places the *Caipirina* down on the table and pushes it away from himself, nervous of what the monster inside of him might unleash if he keeps sipping and tooting the way he has been. Agent6 just shakes his head and passes over the phone for Dobbs to read the text. It doesn't look good but, ever the diplomat, he tries to soften the blow.

"Man. I don't know what to say to that. Just because she wants to try other partners doesn't necessarily mean she's with someone else. Maybe it don't mean that…" He knows he sounds lame though, and his voice trails off before he can finish.

"I know what it means. It's pretty *fucking* obvious," Agent6 coldly declares.

Realistically, thinks Dobbs, the way Agent6's relationship has been going it might not be such a bad thing if he and his Missus had some time apart to discover if the difficulties they've been experiencing are because of their relationship, or just stuff they would've gone through anyway. It's easy to blame someone else for your own pain, as Dobbs knows only too well, but the question is always: whose shit is really whose?

Being an old friend of Agent6 and his partner, and knowing how much they mean to each other and how much they've been struggling lately, Dobbs can't help wondering if the text was deliberately worded to sound so ambiguous. It does kind of read like the intro to a New Age 'Dear John' letter, but he knows he has to let Agent6 translate it the way he chooses as, whatever the actual facts of the matter, it's subtext is clear. What's not really clear is whether his girlfriend is asking for the green light for herself, or somehow giving him permission to go off with someone else.

Dobbs knows how Agent6 has been handling his relationship and he also knows that he needs to be careful not to say something now which might sway the outcome of the battle between heart and hard-on that is currently playing out between his friend and the siren sat next to him. It's a proper quagmire, and no mistake.

Bolivar and Swifty are looking calm and relaxed, just chuckling at Dobbs and Agent6. Agent6 pops his phone back into his pocket and then glances at the girl. 'My God,' Dobbs thinks to himself as he watches Agent6 surrender himself to the whirlpool of her eyes. Dobbs knows Agent6 hasn't got a fucking chance, almost as though she'd been dispatched by the gods to be there to help shoulder the blow or perhaps just blind coincidence but Dobbs struggles to believe in such notions these days. Either way, one thing is for sure; that text could not have come at a more peculiar time. It defies all the odds and made the course of this thing basically unstoppable now: like *Titanic* meets iceberg only in this case the water's distinctly warm and sinking into it will be oh-so agreeable – at least until the morning, anyway.

Agent6 is clearly trying to focus on the pain to distract himself from the seductive powers of the luscious Latina love machine luring him in with the sweet promise of some easy pleasure. No matter how hard he tries to stay with his grief, though, it's obvious the strategy stands no chance of success and every time he looks up there she is; absolutely beautiful, young, fresh, her gravity-defying breasts floating weightlessly on the ever loaded moment, just offering herself to him. Finally he snaps and, standing abruptly, just grabs her hand and drags her away with him.

Dobbs and Bolivar's eyes meet as he disappears and all the sound and fury signifying nothing which has reigned around the table throughout the evening so far is suddenly put into perspective by the immense communication that takes place in that one, silent moment - a communication now devilishly amplified by the knowing, lascivious looks on the remaining ladies' faces - especially the one whose hand has just landed, smack bang, on Dobbs's all so sensitive crotch again.

Back at the Bar

Dobbs is surprised how fresh he feels considering the previous night's antics. He's almost forgotten that he's smack, bang in the centre of the Amazon, but it's well and truly light and the day has more than happily begun without his knowing.

From somewhere nearby he can hear the noise of metal grinding away and pick up the smell of oil mixed with that strange aroma emitted by electric motors which always takes him back to the *Scalextric* set he'd played with as a kid; he's of a mind to think it's ozone. The grinding noise is mingled with the sound of children playing in the road below. Their voices seem to dance in the glistening beams of light flooding the room giving the stained, whitewashed walls an impression almost like some kind of crystal palace.

He sits up, stretching, and peers out at the open expanse of the Amazon River below, resting his arms on the grime-filled runners of the aluminium window frame. The unobstructed view of the river and, beyond, the jungle splaying out like an emerald carpet is simply epic.

The river is full of activity; from a few large, battered cargo ships and the occasional small, ferry-like speedboat darting here and there, all the way down to tiny dugout canoes. Mostly though it's small vessels with thatched roofs like the *Christina,* one of the many contributions brought in by The Brigadier to the project in which Agent6 has negotiated with the *Indigenous* to loan him land for his endeavours. So far Dobbs has only seen film footage of the vessel: it reminded him of Hawaiian girls, dancing in grass skirts

Immediately to the left of the building a flat roof extends back from what appears to be the rear of one of the large old terraced houses a couple of doors up the street where a domed steel pavilion sits on top of the roof. It looks like an old fashioned birdcage straight out of a Tom and Jerry cartoon with a lady inside hanging up washing and generally pottering, though her activity seems not to bother the two birds that are sitting on top of the cage. It seems such a perplexing scene set against the epic backdrop of enormous expansive freedom and somehow it contrasts sharply with the looming sense of adventure in his core.

Seeing Dobbs lost in the scene Bolivar gets up and drags himself over to the window at his end of the room. Noticing the lady in the birdcage, he immediately dashes back to grab his camera, even though he's clearly not yet quite awake. Once the picture's taken though he just lolls forward, flopping down on the window ledge and staring at the woman with the birds still happily perched on the cage. To the watching Dobbs it appears as if he's taken a deep breath and surfaced after a long swim under water.

"Do you think we should free her?" Bolivar asks.

"She looks quite happy," Dobbs replies, a perplexed grin contorted across his face.

Agent6 is just lying there, awake but looking a little lost following the previous night's encounter. The lady he'd brought back had disappeared before any of them awoke. In contrast, Swifty is rushing to and fro, looking very switched on. It's clear that he's in no mood to motivate anyone else though; he's just on a mission to generally flap and fetch supplies so they can all get off to the jungle and get the show on the road – or, rather, on the water!

Eventually Agent6 rouses himself and he and Swifty head off to see Juan, the *curandero* they're hoping will accompany them to the jungle, and make a precise list of everything they need. If everything goes to plan, they're hoping to set off the following morning into the jungle.

For Bolivar and Dobbs time seems to go very fast and, after a few coffees and a spot of very late breakfast, they find themselves in the same bar again, sipping cocktails. Dobbs feels twitchy. There's a paranoia growing in the back of his mind that his whole book idea is just going up his nose. Already he wants to go off to the bathroom for another quick toot.

'Ah,' he thinks as he rests his hand on the pocket containing the pestilence, fingering the tiny lump, 'just one last time.' But then he lets his fingers move on past, pushing his palms into his lap and away down towards his knees.

'No...No more, you stupid fool.'

He knows that's exactly what he doesn't need. Whatever the craving is now, it's separate, like a crying child that just won't give up. It wants to be nurtured, but though it is crying out for attention he cannot give himself up to it; it's just not him! Instead, he focuses on the withdrawal and looks around him, attempting to regain his control and comfort himself against the rising rattle.

'It's OK,' he affirms to himself. 'It's all OK'.

He finds himself wondering why he went and did another line in the first place - especially just before going to drink. So stupid! For him, pestilence is the polar opposite of *Ayahuasca*. Now he can feel that deviant little gremlin that rises up in him and turns on him in those rattling moments, that gremlin he only knows how to quell with Valium. That same little screaming monster that's always lurking deep within him somewhere, that turns from fun and cheeky into downright rude and depraved. He can feel it, right now, soaking up the lustfully sensual body language of the ladies sitting round him, and he knows they feel his lust too.

He's sitting with Bolivar, drinking copiously. The Brigadier has finally risen and is wandering around the table, blowing tunes on his sax. He seems a little lighter to Dobbs at the moment, which means he's had plenty of sleep. It seems to be a good sign when he gets up late, as anyone who does lots of pestilence needs loads of sleep. That's a big part of the process of getting off it, or at least maintaining a life whilst on it; not just rest, but sleep - quality sleep - which translates to quality dream time. Then the body has more of a chance to repair the toxic damage caused by the drug. That and trying to do the cleanest pestilence you can find. For Dobbs though there's no getting round it now; no matter how well it's washed, it all just feels the same: dirty shit, taking him to the same dirty place.

Right now all his plans for finding a story seem so unachievable. It's like this thing's consuming his ambition and drive, as though it's living off his dreams, draining them of their energy. It feels like he's pulled out the cosmic crowbar and wrenched open a space in his life to follow and fulfil a dream but now he's squandered it. He stares out at the river being consumed by the darkness of the fading dusk and ponders his actions. How frustrating to find himself here and then blowing it all out for a binge on this shit.

'What the fuck am I doing?' he thinks to himself: 'living the dream, or just draining the dream's magic away?' He shudders at the thought.

He's always felt he's a man of action, and though he's never had a lot of cash he never really felt he needed it. He's long considered that the real fingerprint of the wealthy is not their big houses and flashy cars but rather the time to enjoy those things. The time to simply enjoy is what the wealthy most envy of the poor. Their wealth often robs them of their most valuable asset: in the rush of it all they forget that the only means to follow your dream is with time. Money sometimes helps, but as often as not it consumes time as much as buys it. Just like pestilence, money kills dreams if you have too much of it.

Now the pestilence has become a crowbar in itself, wrenching his dreams from deep within and allowing him the ability to completely experience their wonder without actually fulfilling any of them. It's just like that credit card: he can sort of experience and get the high factor from what he dreams of doing and then pay it all back later, only with regret.

Pestilence is a deal with the devil himself: have all your dreams come true now with one quick toot and a big showdown and then it's time to pay the piper. But his dreams don't glisten and lure him anymore. They've become just vacuous illusions, empty caskets. Suddenly it seems too harsh a treatment to get to the end of a night's binge and feel every ounce of his dreams pillaged and raped. The only hope is to get some quality sleep and start the process of getting them back. He knows he can't live without them and if *he* doesn't fulfil them, who the fuck will?

Why has he gone and done more? How will he now find his way back to that euphoric natural high he'd realised within himself? Why has he let the whole thing fall victim to that nasal dream killer? It feels like a squadron of biplanes is circling his heart as though he were King Kong on top of the Empire State building, clinging to the tower of his plight and fighting off doubt and negativity as though trying to duck and fend off terminal firepower.

He feels the withdrawal rattle move through him and experiences daggers of worthlessness coming right at him. It's like a monster that wants to tear apart his pathetic dreams and useless ambitions. Now he has no shields left and so, as painful as it is, he just stays with the pain and allows himself to fully feel it: he will not go and do anymore, no matter the rattle. And with that resolve, he's suddenly through it. But just when he thinks he's clear, in comes an attack of doubt again:

'I haven't even got the slightest story yet.'

He suddenly remembers his golden rings of light and fires one up around him. He can barely visualize anything but he's made the effort.

'You've got your voice recorder and you've got your intention to find a story,' he thinks. 'That's a good start. And you're here: You're up for it.'

128

In moments he's deflecting the attacking rain of fire and the exploding shards of doubt are just background noise, as though he's deflecting it all with a breastplate wrought of iron. He triumphantly surfaces with a feeling of defiant bliss.

'No...You can't have me you little fucker,' he says silently to the rattle in his head. 'You'll have to try harder than that. Scream as loud as you like but I'm not going to play this game with you.'

'What *are* you anyway? I'm going to find out who you really are 'cause you're sure as hell not me: I don't have tantrums. How dare you scream in my head like that you pathetic little fucker. It's *you* that's really doing all this shit isn't it? It's you that's tearing my world to bits. Maybe that's why I'm doing this; just to find you. But I'm not scared of you; I know you're there, you sly little powerless motherfucker.'

And like that, the noise just disappears.

Dobbs is lost in his own world, almost like a madman. In many ways, he now is a madman. He's obsessed with what is happening in the world and how that relates to what is occurring inside of him. It's as though he's going through a transformation and has become a victim to an obsession that his partner cannot handle one tiny bit. And probably for good reason. The Amazon is the only place he knows he can find a cure for this crazed notion of imminent turmoil that plagues his peace.

He wants to know if this thing that he saw on a blast of laughing gas could really be what it appears to be: A wall; a karmic wall. Because if it is, he figures, then perhaps this is not the end of the world but simply the end of an era or, more specifically, the end of a *soul contract*. Could it be that what we are witnessing is simply the settling of an old ledger and the rise of a new soul contract so much higher in operating vibration to the present one that, from humanity's current perspective, it behaves like a wall – a karmic wall? It seems to Dobbs that there is no place in the future to offset negative karma now, and humanity could be simply experiencing a karma train pileup on the Earth Super Soul Highway. Or, more simply put, a barrier to low-vibrational activity.

The town has lost its lure for him now and he craves only the secrets hidden within the emerald lair of the vast Amazonian plains beyond the winding river. The expanse is so full and vast it almost feels like it is drawing his soul from his very being but just as it seems his mind will drift away completely it is snapped back as

Agent6 suddenly appears from behind him. He's looking calm and collected although a little distant.

Swifty follows close behind, looking very sweaty and tired out and, by the grin and knowing nod he gives Dobbs, it looks like he's got a gripe brewing. Possibly Dobbs and Bolivar are being, at the very least, a bit lazy on the running around front. Swifty can't really hold gripes. When they come they just come and he just shouts it all out. It can seem quite threatening, especially with his nose splayed halfway across his face (the result of some distant punch-up) and his feisty, impatient South London accent. It's sometimes difficult to realise he's the pussycat most know him to be, although from the sounds of it he'd bitten off slightly more than he could chew that week with The Brigadier in Lima. Possibly they all should have warned him that The Brigadier had come clean off the rails. But if Swifty's got issues no doubt he'll voice them. Dobbs isn't too bothered; it's only the first day - well, the first full day - since their arrival in the jungle.

Agent6 takes a seat next to the lady he'd taken home the previous night, giving her a warm, comforting smile which she's clearly pleased about. Swifty pulls up a chair too. He has a look of proud satisfaction about him now he's sitting down with a stiff drink in his hand. It all implies it's been a successful mission at Juan's. Dobbs is used to seeing him when he's on a money-making mission, running round in a manic rush, which is such a different space from where he is now. The idea of a relaxing holiday with his feet up just seems a little alien to his character. In Dobbs's experience relaxing, to Swifty, normally means applying maximum effort and screaming at lots of people who should be working but are in fact scratching their heads and watching him do all the work. The truth is that Swifty absolutely loves throwing a good tantrum and huffing and puffing about like an old troll. It's all, as Dobbs has come to learn, really quite harmless - and often hysterically funny. In just one blast of his temper, he could probably throw up five marquees all on his own.

He's quite the opposite of Agent6 which, Dobbs muses to himself, makes him the perfect foreman for their land project. Agent6 is far happier to let other people run about doing all the work. Then he can properly relax: feet up, gently rocking in a hammock, obviously phone in one hand, a constant stream of texts coming and going, selecting tunes on his iPod with the other, all whilst

130

juggling a spliff between the manoeuvres. Agent6 is a good project manager, far more so than Dobbs.

Now there's a quietness about him however; he's not with the others at all. He's not even with the girl he took home the night before. He's not even lost in the pain and anxiety of his troubled relationship. He's already out there, in the jungle, waiting for everyone. Just one trip to the *curandero* and the jungle has become a going concern again to him. Sure, he's sitting there sipping cocktails but in reality he's not there at all. His soul seems to have scooted off ahead.

Swifty takes a closer look at Dobbs, who's just sitting and staring off at the waterfront. He's also somewhere else, and has been for some time.

"Alright then Dobbs?"

"Yeah!"

"Snortin?"

Dobbs cocks his head to one side; no one likes to say yes to that, do they? Swifty just gives a half nod and a friendly grin,

"We setting off early tomorrow then?" he says.

Dobbs is not sure if it's a question or a statement.

"Yeah, I guess so?" Dobbs answers with a non-committal grin.

Swifty tries to catch both Agent6 and Bolivar's attention.

"No. We *are* setting off early tomorrow," he says, almost shouting. To Agent6, it's like water off a duck's back. Bolivar and Dobbs look at each other, raising their eyebrows, and try to nod enthusiastically without pissing themselves laughing. They've both discussed the prospect of leaving on a Sunday and pretty much concluded that it just won't happen, but there's no crime in wishful thinking so they just nod and try to summon the enthusiasm they feel Swifty truly deserves for his efforts.

The Brigadier's still playing his sax and this indeed seems to be his medicine. It calms him and he calms the people around him when he plays. It's odd melodic bursts more than whole tunes but they're timed perfectly and somehow seem to be helping Dobbs escape into the magic of the moment. At least, that is, until his reverie is broken by the sound of an unbelievably annoying pitch from a man who seems to be trying to sell something. Dobbs isn't sure, but whatever it is, it seems the man has no clue he's talking *at* someone rather than to someone. Perhaps it's that pestilence talk that has the desperate need to be heard over everything else like it's a competition, or perhaps the man's hard of hearing and is simply unaware of the volume of his own voice. Dobbs knows he sometimes does the same thing when he's on the phone, like he assumes he has to shout because whoever's on the other end of the blower is are miles away and he somehow doubts the science of telecommunications. Whatever it is, it's an annoying drone, as though the man's trying to speak louder than the noise in his head. But it could also be the American accent that accompanies the drone that is so annoying.

Bolivar is half engaged in conversation with the girl he's sitting with and half with the American sitting on the table to his left. He's not as torn between the two as much as perhaps the American might believe though; the lady's energy is much softer and clearly luring Bolivar with blatancy he's kind of liking. He's almost being slightly camp and silly with his deflections to the American's sales pitch and Dobbs can feel the battle. The American is sitting directly behind him and making him feel nervous and now that little demon in his head pops up again. The naughty rascal; the silly little piss-taker.

Dobbs turns around to take a look at the man. He's older - a good ten or fifteen years on Dobbs anyway - and his eyes are piercing. He's not sure at a glance the guy is just a wild-eyed crazy explorer or a crazy pestilence junky but either way he's a character and his jaw is going off twenty or thirty to the dozen. His strategy seems to be to lure in the listener with compliments when they throw disagreement into the equation, as if constantly trying to patch his grating monologue with a stream of compliments. He won't give up the whining pitch for love nor money though, and Bolivar is clearly getting frustrated, but the more Dobbs listens the less he is agitated and the more it begins to amuse him.

"I'll tell you man, this is the best piece of jungle you'll find - and the lodge? Oh man, you wait 'til you see this place. It's one of the best, most isolated lodges ever built," the man pleads.

He is an advert for America without doubt, though not the average American exported to the world through the movies and media; this guy's the real deal. He's wild and eccentric, just out on a limb. But he's not quite reading the situation that is occurring between the man he's addressing and the woman that man would probably like to undress. It's a nervous thing that's leading into a self-fulfilling prophecy as Bolivar is struggling to deal with him and the man's putting up his defences a little which is clearly a cycle, a routine, or perhaps what could be better described as an old

132

program he runs that just goes round and round but only results in pushing that which he wants ever further away from himself. All that's really needed is some sellotape.

The man can clearly see Bolivar is cutting the chit-chat and about to bail out on him but as he begins his energetic severance the man pipes up,

"Let me tell you something, man."

Bolivar sighs.

"That intuition you have about people is very correct... You should trust in those intuitions. I mean you don't even know me."

Bolivar sighs again and looks at the American, and then over to Dobbs, who's sitting in front of him.

"No, I'll tell you man, I'll show you this place; I'll take you there. And I'm not selling anything my friend."

Dobbs comes in here, adding,

"No. This guy's for real man. Chill, man."

Bolivar is relieved that someone else has come into the equation as the man is simply talking at him.

"No, I'm just like a woman. You got to warm me up. I need foreplay. You can't just move in on me like that. Foreplay, man," he says.

Dobbs laughs at the way Bolivar states his case so bluntly.

"He's just being colourful and expressive."

The American is clearly feeling a little under attack now and it's as if his thick skin has become soft and sensitive. But Dobbs can see it would take a lot more to truly deter him, and sure enough the man now begins to plead his non-profit intentions.

"Hey man, come on, you didn't come here for just this right? You're not just here just for the nose candy and pretty ladies, right?"

Dobbs looks over at Bolivar.

"The man's on fire. He could sell the *Titanic* to the deep blue sea."

"He's got me reaching for my wallet," Agent6 shouts across at Dobbs.

Dobbs looks him straight in the face.

"So, realistically, what you're trying to say is, you just need a donkey to carry a couple of K's, right?"

The man looks shocked at Dobbs's suggestion.

"No fucking way man. No fucking way!"

Dobbs looks at the man with a softer smile.

133

"I'm joking. Really. I'm just taking the piss. We're not used to the heavy sale, that's all. But go man, sell it to us. You're close man, you can close this baby."

The man starts laughing now and sees the funny side to it.

"Look you're not paying nothing."

"So if we're not paying nothing, how much are we paying?" Bolivar enquires.

"You're just paying for your fucking selves on the way up there. What am I getting? I'm getting absolutely nothing!" The man exclaims.

Now Bolivar is laughing. Not that he's that bothered by him, but it's good to have some backing in a situation like this.

"Dobbs, did you see that, he had his eyes on your hot pants."

"Hey man, that's not my game. Stop it," the man pleads, trying to be serious.

"He's joking man," Dobbs jests. But the man doesn't respond to that sort of humour at all.

"So no dodgy business with the old nose candy then?"

"That's not my line of work round here. It's cut throat man. I knew a guy, they almost killed him. Fuck man, they tried to kill me once."

Bolivar is looking doubtful now and starts chuckling.

"We've already got a good place to go though, up the river. But thanks man."

The man raises his hand, trying to save the sale.

"Hold it there man. What I'm offering you is a no-charge trip. I'm taking you to a place that is so fucking unique; that's been there for millions of years. Trees that are thousands of years old; a fucking lake you can drink the water it's so fucking pure."

Bolivar looks at the man inquisitively.

"And what's your intention when you get us there?"

The man goes into a wild, wailing defence that leaves Bolivar and Dobbs pissing themselves laughing and then the man starts laughing himself, finally seeming to exit the old program. Dobbs looks across at the two of them.

"Give him a cuddle Bolivar. That's all he needs. He's feeling a little nervous, that's all. The jungle's been tough on him. You can hear it in his voice."

But just when it looks like the Yank is chilling out, he suddenly pipes up again.

"Gee, you can die out there like *that*."

"No!" Dobbs retorts.

"Like fucking *that* man. Fucking *dead* man," The man shrieks whilst simultaneously clicking his fingers.

"Shit man, I've seen them come and go - like *that* man. You got to get with the right people, man."

"Is it dangerous in the jungle then?" Dobbs asks as innocently as he can muster.

Bolivar immediately breaks out laughing.

"Are you fucking kidding? Are you fucking joking with me?"

"What, you could properly hurt yourself?"

"Fuck man. Are you kidding with me?"

Dobbs tries to hide his amusement.

"Lots of mosquitoes biting you, I suppose?"

"Lots of fucking mosquitoes?" he exclaims with astonishment. "Fucking fairies compared to what's out there, man. Fucking fairies. You got snakes. Big fucking snakes man, and they'll fuck you man. And if you don't know which one bit you and you can't identify it, and its bite's deadly, then you're fucking dead man. I mean chances of getting you to a hospital in time are virtually zero anyway man."

Dobbs and Bolivar look at each other and Dobbs starts laughing.

"He's going for the fear sale. I was wondering how he was going to close the deal, where the final leverage would come from. Clever, man," Dobbs says.

The American is shaking his head.

"No man, I wouldn't worry too much about the snakes. It's the insects. Some of the things that bite you out here or just leave a tiny little rash that doesn't look much but just gets seriously worse. Huge spiders hatching out from under your skin or literally crawling out your fucking eyes man. Creatures that live under your skin; parasites of every kind out there man, attacking you on every front. Some that literally swim up your piss and then crawl up your fucking cock. Think I'm full of shit, right?"

"No man, it's all part of the show, right?"

"Let me show you something," the man says. Taking his cigarette, he nods to the man sitting to his left who, so far, has seemed quite unconnected to him.

The man holds up his arm and the American holds the burning cigarette above the skin. As he does so, movement appears below his skin as something underneath crawls away to escape the heat. It's a disturbing sight. Dobbs has seen some pretty disturbing

135

things in his time but this is pretty rough. Bolivar, too goes considerably paler at the sight. The Yank just smiles.

"Insects, my friends," he says, now with a somewhat sinister laugh. Dobbs looks at Bolivar with an odd, slightly freaked out expression then diverts back to the American.

"So you got a monopoly on the medicine, or the luck?"

"Just been here a long time. Just know some of the things that people do in emergency situations and some of the things that aren't too clever and some of the places that are very beautiful. Sometimes you've got to go a long way but sometimes not. Just depends what you want to see, man."

Dobbs can't help be the piss-taking Englishman and nods with an understanding.

"Yeah, I think I'm getting that picture now. Thanks for that," he says knowing their agenda is already full. But the sentiment has nonetheless been noted as such considerations haven't been largely accounted for on his part, other than a bottle of *deet* to ward of mosquitoes.

The man, however, seems a little calmer now he's made his point. Bolivar returns to chatting with the lady sitting next to him. It seems they can all relax now, but as Dobbs turns round to rest his neck from craning round so much he is met by the sight of a lady in an absolute league of her own. In fact at first he has to look away as she is so shockingly beautiful he can barely look at her; it's as though he is not worthy to even lay eyes on her. Sure, she's sexy and fit, but she has something else going on too - a type of sweet serenity.

She's facing towards Dobbs but she's not looking at him; rather she's looking beyond him toward the river and the vast sprawl of the jungle, now cloaked in the deep turquoise darkness of the night. Dobbs follows her gaze for a moment, taking in the wonder of the Amazon set beyond the shantytown below, and as his eyes adjust from the city's light pollution he notices the scene has turned from emerald green into the deepest, darkest sapphire. It lifts him into another space of euphoria, and he almost trembles with excitement at the sheer wonder.

He turns back to observe the woman but as he does so he is momentarily shocked to find she is no longer staring out to the river; now she's staring straight back at him.

Emotional Mass

Dobbs can only stare at the woman's face in something bordering shock. She's so utterly beautiful, he feels overwhelmed at the feeling of just being in her presence. It's as though she's shrouded by some sort of protection, as if she can exist in the city and yet hide in the jungle all at the same time. It felt to him as if she'd cast her presence out and beyond, to the jungle, and it was not until he'd felt that dark expanse lurking beyond the glistening shimmers of the fast moving water that he'd been able to find her.

Now, turning back to her and staring into those eyes, Dobbs realises why his soul is suddenly so present: it's here to meet her. He has an odd feeling - a feeling he's had many times already in this life - that he never quite catches up with himself and his soul is always one step ahead of the game, as if the Universe knows exactly what it wants to happen and has carefully organised everything; he simply has to make the right decisions. And if he makes it through some of the odd things that life keeps throwing at him, then he gets chucked a biscuit - if he stays focused that is. To Dobbs it seems focus is his dharma. On one hand it seems to be about moment-to-moment existence but on the other he always feels like he's only on the tail end of life most of the time. Like his soul always has somewhere important to be.

But right now, time seems to stand still. It is as if the carriage of his soul has finally arrived at its destination and everything has just stopped in the absolute here-and-now and all his guides and angels in the great orchestra in the sky simultaneously breathe sighs of relief, and are silently high fiving as he enters the emerald gate of the moment, wondering exactly what has just happened in that gargantuan introduction.

Still almost disbelieving the vision before him he's suddenly perhaps a bit too explorative with his eyes as he looks her up and down because when his eyes return to hers, she drops her head to one side ever so slightly. But all the same, he sure he can detect a little twinkle of curiosity there, almost as if she's curious to know the findings of his little exploration.

He really can't believe it; she's a proper Amazon Queen: she's on fire! Yet she wears not even the tiniest bit of makeup and hides behind the simplest of city-like façades. She needs absolutely no added accessories. She's utterly gorgeous to Dobbs.

She seems to be of indigenous descent but though he can so easily see her deep jungle roots her face also carries some perhaps European ancestry, Spanish or perhaps Mexican in appearance. Even sitting down Dobbs can tell she's tall; an impression somehow accentuated by straight back and perfect posture. She's observing him, almost as if energetically sizing him up with a soft, curious smile and Dobbs doesn't know where to let his eyes rest, locked onto her deep brown eyes or luxuriating in her delicious Spanish Gypsy lips. But whichever way he looks, it's clear she's properly done him; he doesn't even need to look at Bolivar and Agent6 to know they have more than clocked the situation, and besides he dare not make eye contact with anyone else; right now his eyes are all hers.

"Wow. You just popped out of nowhere. How did you just do that I wonder? *Err...Perdon; un momento, nada, y ahora tu es aqui. Muy loco! Muy mal Espanol. Perdon.*"

She cocks her head to the other side, still just observing him. It's doing his head in a bit, as she's just way too much to take in all in one go. She seems so relaxed it makes Dobbs feel a little nervous. To him, she seems like a sunflower, just like his mother. She has that something special about her that's wide awake and shining; a simplicity that nevertheless cannot mask something else so very sophisticated it bears all the traits of the true super science of spirituality and drives him to a sense of wonder.

She's dressed in a plain, custard yellow top that appears like a boob tube, the thin straps supporting her perfect breasts being mostly concealed by her long hair. Her shoulders are bare, revealing a strong, supple frame. Her hipster pants, made from a thin, off-white linen, are cut like jeans that sit very low accentuating her slim waist and womanly hips. Everything about her is a picture but most especially her face, which is perfectly framed by long, black hair, cut to a fringe at the front. It somehow gives her a cute, almost innocent appearance but for those eyes, which seem to swirl like deep, fearless whirlpools, drawing him in. Her hair is cascading over her shoulders and down her front to stop just short of her gorgeous, pert breasts. Her ears, just poking out of her hair, lend her a slightly animalistic vibe, like a cat perhaps, or a panther who could tear his head clean off with single, serene flick of her paw. It's as if she's a hunter, and he's the prey, cornered and yet captivated by the spell of her fearlessly intense beauty, as hot as high noon, and yet as cool and collected as the vast river, with all its concealed undercurrents.

Dobbs is not so innocent though. She can't have just popped out of nowhere, she's just too drop dead gorgeous for that. In his experience all such people come with some complicated story, some caravan of emotional *baggage*. He has a theory that the more present one becomes, the more flowing 'emotional mass' one conducts and thus the more 'story' one attracts, as life is nothing but a story being told. One look at this sultry jungle jaguar and Dobbs can tell she comes with a story. And he feels the fear, that hidden knowing, that to play with fire is one sure way to get your fingers burnt.

Nonetheless he nods at her, running his thumbs across his fiery fingertips and smiles his most winning smile. Baggage or not, it's now or never.

"*Caipirina?*"

She is sitting, it seems to him, in an odd position, totally open, with her posture somehow exposing everything about her in a most unnervingly relaxed way. Her chair is literally pointing directly at Dobbs, almost like his father sits when he's channelling. She's facing him head on with such a perfectly straight posture, like she's either properly meeting him or properly seducing him. With her sexy little, perfectly white, slightly funky trainers it all seems to add up to a single picture telling him one rather fantastic story. But despite the sex appeal it's those mystical eyes, set like glistening stones bound in a pendant that hold him so captivated, they seem nothing less than portals. As if staring into them could transport him to another world completely, and they're trained on him right now.

He feels naked beneath that gaze and, somehow almost filthy, as though she can see the effects of the pestilence leaving nothing but the residue of rattles and withdrawal to shame his inner being. But there's nowhere to hide except in silence, so he holds his tongue and just takes a deep breath.

She seems to be observing the same silence herself, as if considering not only whether she wants a drink but a whole lot of other things besides but finally it seems she's finished her screening of him, and makes a slight sound.

"*Si...Gracias.*"

"Thank God for that," he sighs. Then, remembering his Spanish and looking up to the skies, "*Gracias*!!"

Agent6 is sitting quietly, watching Dobbs with the *Woman Who Fell to Earth* without saying anything. The girl sitting next to him isn't very talkative either. She's young - early twenties at the oldest - and it must be a little overwhelming for her surrounded by all of these men, Dobbs considers. But then perhaps it is the newcomer who is making her a little shy, slightly shutting her down with the power of her presence. The stranger seems to sense her tension though and, turning, whispers something in her ear. Immediately the girl giggles in response and now it's Dobbs's turn to feel like the odd one out.

Suddenly all the girls are giggling at him and it's almost overload in Dobbs's head. The feeling he's sensing is very rare; it's like love, only terrifying as there seems to be an impossible divide that cannot be crossed between them - she's out of his league in just too many ways. And yet he knows he's snared by her and, even if he wanted to, where could he run to escape the lure of those eyes?

Taking another breath, he attempts to overcome his rising rattle.

"So where did you just come from, I wonder?"

She just stares, slightly smiling, as if she understands what he just said and now he has no choice but to reveal his crap Spanish. He tries to splutter along stupidly,

"*Donde tu…*"

To his relief, she steps in to save him from total embarrassment.

"Out of nowhere, maybe."

Now she's properly done him.

"Wow, you speak English."

"I had an English boyfriend for many years."

"Really?" Dobbs says, nodding attentively.

Agent6 rolls his head back, almost as if wanting to say something but not wanting to intervene as they seem to be doing okay on their own. It's strange; the woman doesn't seem particularly interested in anyone else, she just has some fascination with Dobbs, and it isn't necessarily attraction; it feels more like he's an odd specimen, being observed.

"You here with…?" She motions with her head towards Agent6.

Dobbs nods and Agent6, picking up on the gesture, catches his eye. "Dobbs," he says, regarding the woman with a warm, knowing smile, "Meet Gatita. Gatita, meet Dobbs." Then he somehow exits the whole process as smoothly as he'd entered. Dobbs feels a little uncomfortable. He is wondering just how much, if at all, he can enter into a story with this woman. He can't speak the lingo and

140

though it's clear she's a cool bunny she's likely to prove a serious distraction to everything he's doing in Iquitos. Plus, he's already in a relationship. Or is he?

He'd dismissed what The Brigadier had said about his girlfriend sleeping with another man - or so he thought - but suddenly the notion that *she* was sleeping with *him* suddenly pops into his head and he realises that he hasn't forgotten it at all; he just hadn't wanted to deal with it. And more to the point, for multiple reasons, he didn't give a shit anymore. It had become so much bigger than that now as, for the first time in his life; it was only their sanity that mattered now. She was drinking like a fish and 'caning it, and he'd somehow inherited this odd tortured state that he was constantly having to fight off with the only weapon he knew how to use - an attempt to understand why all this shit was really happening in the world and find out if there was any way to prevent the terrible vision that he'd seen on that fateful blast of laughing gas.

To her, he'd hit a brick wall. To him, it was as if they'd both hit a brick wall at the same time and weren't able to give each other the same level of support they had when things were good. They'd known such happy times together, like when he'd lived with her and her two children in his truck. Their whole relationship had all been summer wine, right up to the point he'd started saying that all the banks were about to go pop and this crazy thing was all about to go down, beginning with the big boys up top beating the drum for an all-out war he knew could never be won and in which, he believed, in our hour of need, Britain would be deserted by her allies because they knew what we were doing was morally indefensible. That Britain was being used as a *Trojan Horse* by the Federal Government to cripple Europe, or what really threatened the US dollar: The Euro. Why he had to sit and witness the whole thing play out in a few moments, at *Reading Rock* on a blast of nitrous seems equally insane and yet he is completely entangled in the vectors of its 'emotional mass' that has his mind - or perhaps his heart - trapped in this obscure web or notion. She didn't want to hear it, whilst he couldn't stop thinking about it. They'd run into an invisible wall that was somehow forcing them through a life changing process.

Their failure of their relationship could so easily be rooted back to their individual problems in their individual lives. Neither of them was in denial, and neither was in such a bad way; it wasn't like she was some totally lost *caner*; she was just pushing boundaries - as was Dobbs. She was pushing the boundaries of intoxication a little too hard and too regularly which in itself was not a problem other than the terrible midweek comedowns. He, on the other hand, was pushing the boundaries of what he was willing to conceive as feasibly possible in terms of what she considered doom and gloom. One minute things were going smoothly and the next minute they were going very badly. To her, the notion that the global situation was about to severely fuck up was exactly what she didn't want to hear.

It was the last thing he wanted too: he had always been the eternal optimist but now he was plagued with this horrible fear, and she didn't like that one bit. It pushed her away from him and destabilised her, which had resulted in him staying up until the early hours trawling the web each night trying to get a take on the bigger picture. And whereas once he'd always been Mr Positive about everything, suddenly it seemed to him that the way things were panning out, it was moving inexorably towards a showdown with very little possibility for a positive counter movement. In Dobbs's head the whole thing was reaching a tipping point.

Dobbs feels he has the mind of an unconventional scientist, operating in the little known laboratory of spiritual experience. It is to this laboratory which he drags back his nuggets of research to brush off, observe and dissect. He believes that he, like many others on the planet right now, is engaged in constructing a new set of psychic instrumentation through which to view the universe and he considers that spirituality is a science that exists on the edge our current understanding, a science that has only recently begun to be opened up by pioneers of the super-conscious potential of humanity such as the *Nassim Haramein's* of the world that open a new take on science, thus opening themselves to a far bigger picture.

A mindset that opens the fifth, or quintessential element, the realm of spirit itself right up to the Earth dimension. A mindset directed towards mapping a single, unified field in which consciousness and matter are subject to the same principles through the medium of the absolute nothingness that encompasses all the fields. In attempting to understand atomic science, all that *is* can take place only within the context of the 'void', that no-thing-ness of space which is the far bigger picture and yet remains so poorly understood.

At the human level this quintessential matter, or 'emotional mass' as Dobbs terms it, equates to the really big feeling that fills him whenever he touches the stillness at his centre, a feeling that's filling him now and saturating his being as he sits in the presence of this beautiful woman. As he observes her he knows he has to honour the principles of this understanding: it is the undercurrent of his intention which has to be clear from the beginning, the resultant direction of the various vectors at play in the dynamic of his own emotional mass. The trouble is that, looking into this woman's eyes, he doesn't know his intentions anymore – or at least he's just too scared to admit them.

Sitting there however, basking in the brilliance of Gatita's beauty, he can feel some part of his mind ransacking his memories, looking for the evidence it craves. It's almost as if he has given his permission for that deviant part of himself to access the sacred files of all his most precious memories, and it's tearing them down, quantifying the information and coming up with potentials and possibilities he's previously locked away from conscious thought, screened off from viewing under the premise: 'if she goes, she goes and if she stays, she stays. The only thing bringing her back to my bed is the strength of her desire to share herself with me rather than someone else.' And in that, he'd always found peace, even in his most *munted* state at some festival or party, when they were both out there independently, holding on with only their finger nails. He always trusted her and she always trusted him. And now suddenly he wants to believe the complete opposite or merely the truth.

Suddenly he's staring at Gatita, wondering - and half hoping– that his partner is having an affair. It'd probably be the best thing for her.

'Fuck...' he finds himself thinking as he stares into the deep water of Gatita's eyes '... it'd probably be the best thing for me too.'

Witch Hunt

Dobbs catches the waiter's eye as he's emerging from the bar ferrying a tray of drinks.

"*Caipirinas!*" he shouts out, signalling 'six' with his hands. The waiter nods.

It's now a heaving Saturday night, though the crowds are mostly gathered round the tiny amphitheatre and in and around the bar sitting just behind. Beyond, everywhere seems sparse and quiet but in the localised eclectic commotion strangers have the cover of the drunken crowd with which to disappear into each other's gaze without too many dangerous connotations.

"You're not trying to get me drunk are you?"

"No!" Dobbs defends his good nature. Then he recants his statement with the cheekiest grin he can muster. "Well, maybe a little tipsy."

"You have the face of a Spanish gypsy girl somehow. It's like I've seen you before. Like I know you. Gatita," and he savours the word. "Nice name."

She looks away from Dobbs for a moment and then back.

"I'm a cat," she purrs seductively.

"Yeah, I can kind of see that." He pauses for a moment. "You have the look of a *curandero* slightly, something else going on."

Suddenly he's thinking, 'what a silly thing to say.'

"Well, you've got the eyes of the jungle. And you've got other stuff happening. You must drink the juice? Of course you drink it. Silly question."

"I used to drink, and I tried to learn the medicine ways, years ago. I used to do a lot of ceremonies but I haven't for a long time now."

"Did your ex-partner used to drink?"

"No. Not everyone comes here to drink. Some are nervous. Not all stories you hear are good stories."

"I've heard loads of stories also. But nearly always from people who've never been near it. They tell the darkest stories about it but few who've truly drunk tell bad stories and those that have told me about bad experiences they've had personally...well, at least they were still around to tell the tale. So it can't be that bad – surely?" Dobbs says with a cheeky grin.

"Mind you, I kind of stopped for quite a few years myself until very recently. So much had been happening in ceremonies and then it all just seemed to stop. I'd drink and just sit in silence other than the noise of people throwing up; I'd get absolutely nothing whatsoever. So I kind of felt like it was telling me to go and get on with it; to bring the wonder of what I'd seen in those previous experiences actually into my life. But I did take some recently with Agent6 back in England. Two ceremonies. And they were just as strong and as fruitful as I can ever remember. So shockingly so in fact that, well, here I am back in the jungle to find out what the fuck's going on."

He cocks his head to one side slightly.

"Are ceremonies as powerful beyond the jungle. Does the medicine travel well?"

Those last two ceremonies were. It's all becoming illegal now though. Getting the medicine into the UK through legal routes is getting harder by the day. It can't go via the States basically and soon it will be completely illegal. But the last couple of ceremonies...very beautiful ceremonies – yeah."

Gatita is quiet just observing Dobbs. It makes him feel self-conscious.

"Did you do some protection thing earlier by the way?" He finally says. "It sounds crazy, but I didn't sense you arrive and even when I saw you it was like you weren't there. You slipped in past my radar. And the next second you were *so* there that I nearly fell off my chair!"

And then he chuckles, offering his hand to shake.

"Nice to meet you Gatita; you certainly know how to make an introduction!"

"Mucho gusto" she says, shaking his hand. Then, pulling it back, "You don't use protection in places like this? Iquitos is a crazy city, *muy* loco."

Dobbs chuckles and looks away, embarrassed at how their conversation must sound to anyone listening. He can barely take his eyes off her and finds himself staring with a curious satisfaction to see someone else using this 'protection' that would be deemed quite daft by the masses back home in Britain, even as they get *dicked* over in their millions and become the weapons of those whom they so despise, all the while refusing to accept the reality of the lower astral attack being directed at them.

"Yeah. I use protection all the time. It's just rare to see someone else using it so effectively, especially when they kind of hide from *me*."

145

He closes his eyes, taking a deep breath and visualises a golden ring round him. Although most times he can't see it in his mind's eye at all, this time it's beaming quite clearly. Not that seeing it or not bothers him; he knows that because he has attempted to do it - not just thought about it but actually taken the time to do it - even if he can't see it, it's still there because it is powered by his intention alone.

In Dobbs's mind, whatever's going on, certainly on the plane of his human experience and awareness, he always seems the last to know what is happening down here; his soul evolution seems to be a very different thing to his human evolution. Down here, it's as though his soul is flying blind. It's like his soul is playing a big game with him and all he has to do is stay with his feeling and not let the noise in his head interfere too much. It is enough just to enjoy the gift of sitting and looking into this beautiful woman's eyes.

"There, I just did a golden ring of light round myself," he says to Gatita. "I can see you better now, although I can't hide - my cover's blown."

Now, he can somehow sit in this silent comfort with her and just enjoy the serene space she is occupying. It's rare he can truly share that space or understanding with someone. Especially with the ongoing witch hunt in Britain and the endless incarceration of its shamans, to do, or indeed even talk about such things would no doubt be looked upon with scorn. Even to him it all sounds silly sometimes; the notion that one would wish to track their own intentions back to a peaceful, wholesome resolve and attempt to root out the blocks in the flow of that mystical power, the 'emotional mass', the energy of which remains, as yet, scientifically unproven, and can only at best be marked 'X' in any equation, for it is the unknown factor. What we commonly perceive as 'space' is actually the largest component in our atomic structure and perhaps the very fabric of Soul itself. From this perspective, for Dobbs, even pestilence is just another tool for the *curandero*-minded human, an opportunity to sharpen their awareness whilst immersed in the darker side of duality, which destabilizes the user's mind with doubt and cynicism when attempting to reemerge. A wager with the devil himself that can turn good men and good women into *smirkers* and *sneerers*; that judgemental mindset which can only be defended with the moment-to-moment awareness that can stop such low level mental activity pervading a peaceful mind or that state of vector equilibrium, and be pulled off course by something that would be most commonly termed; demon.

He feels comfortable, sat there with Gatita, as spirituality is not alien to her at all.

"So this is your first time to Iquitos then?"

The sentence is slightly loaded.

"No. I've been before and I think it's been calling me back. Mind you, I don't remember so much of it really. Well, the ceremonies I will never forget. In fact, I'd come here after working on this massive airport project in Hong Kong, where I'd met Agent6 and The Brigadier in fact. And previously to that, I'd been editing a architectural magazine. Seems like a distant life now."

"You're an architect?"

"Err...no...not at all. Sort of puppeteer come blagger. To be honest, I don't actually know what box I fit into anymore. But last time I came, the only thing I seem most to remember, outside of the visions, is the close encounters with the cops and *Caso de Fierro*. It was a members only club last time I came here but I was quite struck by those massive imperial chunks of iron. I had coffee in there earlier today but there's a whole new city that has popped out in front of me that I somehow missed last time. Mind you, *Caso de Fierro* kind of looks a bit better from a distance doesn't it?"

"I never really notice it now."

"Well, it doesn't really capture the iconographic imagery of the meaty structures Eifel built does it? Just captures the essence of the industrial revolution I guess. Maybe just a symbol of exuberant wealth: A flat pack palace no less."

Gatita looks utterly uninterested but the *Caso de Fierro* stands regardless, admittedly at of eyeshot, literally just round the corner to where they now sit.

But it impresses Dobbs, if nothing else, for its longevity and it's defiance to obsolescence and the fundamentals of designing things that fit sustainably into the rules of entropy. Certainly it was not all that uncommon to find an instruction plaque in or on one of Brunel's structures that states, 'grease every hundred years.' Certainly the *Caso de Fierro* is an impressive iron imperial palace built by Gustave Eifel nonetheless, who was the equivalent of Britain's Isimbard Kingdom Brunel at the time. Dobbs has always been fascinated by structural design, not that Eifel's Tower ever did *that* much for him. But huge ships, like the *Titanic*, the *SS*

147

Great Britain, suspension bridges and things like aircraft wings, that are so thin and yet can support hundreds of tons. He was fascinated in techniques that use the absolute minimal of material to make a structure lighter in weight and yet contain super strength in its design.

Not that the *Casa de Fierro* quite fell into the category of light weight however. Very far from it, in fact. It was a large, heavy gauge iron building. Indeed there was no real structural genius in the building whatsoever in fact. It was more the captivation of an era with all those huge separate sections of what appear to be individual cast iron panels, with their intricate imperialistic embellishments set into their designs like a Knight's standard set into his shield. And yet, within it all, it was the large round rivets which somehow captured the history of it all or perhaps the volume of paint under which they are all buried. Really, it was just an expensive fashion accessory for the stupidly rich. It captures the riveted veneer of the industrial age and was built as nothing more and nothing less, than an exquisite piece of art.

Dobbs remembers from his last trip, when he wasn't out in the jungle, sipping coffee in a cafe on the far corner, rain pouring down outside and observing the thick pressed steel panelling all riveted together which makes the exterior walls, which for some reason reminded him of very old fashioned radiators. The whole building seems to be set into a structure of thick gauge cast iron pillars and arches rising up several floors with open balconies of wrought iron. Apparently, it the equivalent of *IKEA* flat pack house back in the day, designed for wealthy *officials* working overseas in French and British colonies in Africa. A pop-up palace. Slightly bigger and heavier than the lightweight flat-pack houses of today's world, which caused all sorts of problems getting the thing to its present location, as the ships kept running aground with the enormous load as he brought it up the Amazon River.

It's clearly not Eifel's finest structure like the internal structure of the Statue of Liberty and some of the bridges he built, after he designed Paris's biggest pylon. None of course were admittedly as grand in design as anything Brunel designed, Dobbs had always considered, but then Dobbs was English, and was perhaps unfairly biased. Plus, he used to live in Bristol, right next to the Clifton Suspension Bridge. The first suspension bridge of its kind ever built in fact. It always seemed a shame that it was one of England's a top suicide spots and Dobbs had wondered how many people had been distracted from their suicidal pangs by the epic structural design.

"It's what I most remember of the city last time I was here, for sure. But then, I didn't see Iquitos through the eyes I see it today. I was quite nervous I think. Plus, it was a total vision quest. In fact, the protection techniques I began to learn here are what I most remember. They seem such crazy ideas sometimes and other times, they're like everything; like all you've got. I came up river last time, and just before I got into the jungle I was attacked in my dreams by a crazy old lady."

The waiter arrives laden with cocktails. As Dobbs distributes them he senses Gatita observing him, and finds it strangely empowering. Sitting down again, he offers up his glass up for a toast:

"*Que mas*!"

He sits back, holding the glass in one hand and the cocktail stick in the other, peering over the rim at Gatita. The talk of attack via dreams seems to have either unnerved her or interested her as she moves her position very slightly to her left. Immediately the intensity of her presence subsides and he can breathe again.

"How do you know it wasn't all your...?"

"Shit! All my own shit?"

Gatita just makes a head gesture as if not needing to reply.

"It was a warning. Two warnings, in fact. One, getting caught by the cops, which was perhaps telling me to stay present and beware of losing my focus in this town. The other was being attacked in my dream. All just before arriving in Iquitos. And it was definitely her that attacked me."

"But how did you know?"

"She made it very clear. It happened in this small town just about where the roads end and the jungle starts. There's this Inca fort there that's supposedly just like Machu Picchu - not that I've ever been to Machu Picchu so I couldn't say - but this fort, or what I thought was a fort, was built just above cloud level so it just looks like there's snow everywhere. Like a palace where God once lived, up in the clouds; orchestrating the world. Weird it was. There's a part where the cloud sits exactly level with the ground, as if you could step off the world and stand on it. I mean, you can stand right on the edge with your toes overhanging and lean forward without fear, but it's a vertical drop: certain death, if you lean too far.

149

"It's like a gateway through fear into another world. I mean, modern historians would say it's a place of sacrifice or execution probably, as the natives were viewed as savages back then."

"They still are."

Dobbs considers the comment,

"But, standing on that ledge, you don't feel any fear. The feeling was like it was where the elders left this world. They could step clean into another world and leave their old tattered bodies as an offering of thanks to the vultures. Who knows, maybe the vultures lend them their eyes for a few hours in exchange."

He pauses for a moment, chuckling,

"Crazy place; a one horse town, no tourists and this odd little shop that rented the rooms above...well, hotel doesn't really cut it: *muy tranquillo*! So, anyway, I was sitting in this kind of shanty-shop with two other mates and this old woman just waltzes in and starts wandering about; into the kitchen at the back, behind the shop counter, like all over the fucking place. Perhaps it wouldn't stand out under normal conditions except for the fact that this woman was filthy. Her clothes were torn, she was absolutely covered in dirt and grime, her hair was all greasy and matted; she was a mess. But she just wandered around in that shop like no one could even see her. I was, like, 'what the fucking hell is that?'"

"Was she real?"

Dobbs chuckles at the notion.

"Yeah, I think so. I watched her do a complete circuit of the whole ground floor, her hands up in front of her as though searching for something in front of her. I mean, she did look like a ghost straight out of a kids cartoon or something."

Gatita starts laughing.

"She sounds like a ghost."

"Maybe she was, but I don't think so. I think the people that ran the place were scared of her. Or, more specifically, scared of her intentions, and they just ignored her completely. Probably a good move!

"But just as she was headed back to the door to leave, she stopped, then span round and stared at me with these eyes that sent the coldest shivers down through my bones. It was like she'd suddenly found what she'd been looking for."

Dobbs pulls off his hat and runs his hands through his hair.

"Fucking hell...That night I had a dream, a proper nightmare. All these *hips* that were..."

"Hips?" Gatita asks with a tone of humoured curiosity.

"Yeah," and he places his hands on his hips. "Weird, I know, but there you are. Loads of hips cornering me, with no upper bodies or legs or anything, just *jiggy-jiggying* towards me like they were going to...you know?"

Gatita laughs. Her deep, husky tone is thoroughly seductive.

"So funny to think about it now, but so *not* funny at the time. They were all just coming at me and I was thinking 'Shit, this is a bit wrong.' But then I realised: 'Fuck! This is just a dream; someone's trying to fuck me in my dream!' I tried to open my eyes but I couldn't make my body wake. It was like someone was trying to take it but it was so consumed by fear I couldn't get back to it. So I'm screaming at myself, shouting, 'Wake up! Wake up!'"

Gatita seems more amused than anything else.

"But I can't wake myself. So I have to rationalize what's happening, and explain to my sleeping self that I'm being attacked so I can come back to myself. Like reaching into my own hands and try to make them move and then, eventually, I started feeling my eyelids, but they were weighted as though with lead. Anyway, I finally push them open and wake up, a little shocked by the whole experience. So there I am, sat in this dark room with my mates, asleep, and I can see moonlight or some luminescence coming through the window shutters.

"So I get out of bed, go to the window and open the shutters right up and peer out. And there she is, the old woman, standing barefoot in her dirty rags, staring up at the window as if in a trance, chanting some dark mantra in the dead of night...It was her all right. And suddenly I realize that she's still doing it! So I look at my mate and he's tossing in his sleep, like she's locked on to him and he's having a nightmare. So I woke my mates up and the one that had been stirring had been having a nightmare too." He pauses, "I needed to see that, Gatita. Agent6 had a similar thing happen when he first came here. It seems to be the nature of the universe to warn; how can someone believe if they've never seen it with their own eyes?"

Gatita just stares, over the top of her cocktail.

"So she was an angel really, as she gave us a warning. I didn't believe that someone could actually attack you with their intentions. But now I realise that people can attack with their intentions because they have been conditioned to believe someone else is in the wrong, and perpetuate a negativity that ultimately

151

disempowers them through their own conditioned hatred. She was warning me."

Gatita smiles at Dobbs's enthusiasm for it all, his excitement at being here in the jungle. She can see he's a man living a dream right now.

"Were you scared?"

"No, I was excited. But I constantly put up my golden rings of protection after that because many people do what this woman did, although rarely do they make their intentions so clear and many do not even understand their own intentions, mostly because what they believe are their intentions are merely social conditioning. That's why she was such a gift."

Gatita just sips her cocktail, perhaps considering what Dobbs has said.

"I certainly didn't engage with her on any level; I disengaged her if anything. But the following day I built a dream catcher. By the time it was finished night was falling again and, you wouldn't believe it, but as I held it up to the paraffin lamp to inspect it, out of nowhere she suddenly appeared again."

"She was actually there?"

"Yeah, there in the flesh. Very weird. I just respectfully nodded at her, but peering through the dream catcher. And I mean, really, it was literally like that; I just held it up and there she was and she couldn't touch me."

"There's lots of black magic here. You have to be careful."

"There's lots of black magic everywhere, I think. Most people don't even stop to consider that their anxieties could actually be the result of psychic attack. I think that's why no one is allowed to have such views in Britain; it's as if people are being sacrificed to the fear. I mean, ultimately, it's just people learning about their energy and how to hold it," Dobbs says, trying not to let on that he is close to a comedown and his own energy feels dangerously low now, though he feels somehow protected just sitting in his little bubble of bliss with Gatita.

"There's more black magic at work in England than anywhere I've ever seen. The disempowerment of the masses is beyond belief right now. It's like being in a science fiction movie. And the mad thing is that people look at a character like me and think I'm weird. I suppose to them I am, but I think the masses, well, the world at large is about to hit some sort of karmic wall, and it will be

152

interesting to see what they do then. Whether they'll finally throw down their guns or think they can smash right through."

"So what are you doing here then? You're here for the *Ayahuasca?*" Gatita asks with an amused expression.

"Well...it's a big 'just', Gatita!"

Gatita just holds her gaze and says nothing, almost as if waiting for him to come out with something.

"Well, I'm kind of here to write a book. Well, not to write one but to find one, I guess."

"You're a writer?"

"Yeah, well...I suppose I am a seeker of stories. I guess we're all seeking a story. You know how they catch a monkey in Africa? I saw it on TV."

Gatita shakes her head.

"The tribesmen drill a hole in a tree and then bores it out larger inside and chucks some nuts in. It's all done in plain sight of the curious monkey that they want to catch, of course. Then they just walk away. But you know how inquisitive monkeys are: they absolutely *have* to go and investigate to see whether there are nuts really are just up for grabs. But as soon as the monkey closes its fist around the nuts, it can't fit its hand back through the hole because the grip of the free goodies makes its hand too big. So it's a choice between letting go of something it wants or letting go of someone that wants it. If the monkey makes the wrong choice, or takes too long deciding what to do, the tribesman has time to go over and stick a noose over its head and do whatever they do with monkeys."

"So you're writing about catching monkeys," she says with a giggle.

"Well, I'm trying to understand what's happening in the world at the moment and I thought I'd kind of put the question to the *Ayahuasca* and see what *it* says. I mean, I'm another frustrated writer I guess. I feel like I'm in a story at the moment really though, rather than looking for one. It seems to place so much more pressure on every moment. It's almost like it's all been worked out already but I've got to have the balls to see live it out."

"I know that feeling."

There's almost a noticeable duality in Gatita's face; it seems to flash from one character to another. One minute she seems more indigenous, the next a far more Latin identity comes through. When she speaks her tone is low, like a cat purring. Her words are

153

minimal but she listens intently. Quite the opposite is true for Dobbs, who speaks more when he's nervously disposed.

"Yeah I bet you do. You look like you've got a big story."

A boy, no more than five years old comes by and stands, staring at Gatita. His clothes are dirty and he has the look of a street kid. A moment later and another child; a small girl of a similar age, joins him. They both focus their attention on Gatita.

"I wonder why they both come to you to ask for money?"

"They're not as alone as they look. They're mother is nearby. She's using them to earn money because she doesn't know how to herself."

"Well, she does, but you just don't like her technique very much I guess. It's a pretty tough way of making a living, even if they're the ones who do the work for her."

"I don't like to see this. She should get a job."

Somehow that grates with Dobbs. Reaching into his pocket, he pulls out a few soles. Showing it to the children, they immediately turn their attention on him.

"*Bailar para mi,*" he says, then looks back at Gatita. "Will they dance for me?"

The children just stand, waiting, expecting the money for nothing.

"No?" Dobbs says, pretending to wash his hands of the whole thing. "*No bailar, no soles.*"

Finally the children make an attempt to do a little performance. It's not the best effort he's ever seen but Dobbs hands them some loose change and suddenly he's the centre of attention. The cogs are clearly whirling in the kids' heads as they suddenly realise that the newcomers, whoever they are, appear to be more pliable than the locals. Dobbs can't help smiling as they peer over at Bolivar and Agent6, who drop them a few soles also.

Dobbs points to the travelling street performers that are selling their wares and performing carnival theatrics near the tiny amphitheatre and tries to get the kids to see the link, that they could perform for cash rather than just beg for it.

"Thing is, this is their lives and their situation, and the downfall of the situation is the mother. Maybe she's more desperate than we can understand but all the same the losers are the children because they end up becoming beggars. But what happens if they become street performers? Would that be so bad?"

"No."

"It's the mother you're angry with. Not these kids."

"But she'll take that money off them."

"I know. But learning street performance would be a career move for these kids and something she can't take so easily. Street performance is the last bastion of a disenfranchised society."

"They should be in bed. They should go to school."

"Sure but if your mother asked you, when you were five, do you want to go to an academic school or a circus school, where would you have chose to go? Honestly!"

"I would have gone to the circus."

"We would all have gone to the circus."

"Years ago, I was desperate in Hong Kong. I was young, didn't know the place and had arrived, like so many of the Brits who got washed up there, with no money. So I went down to the ferry terminal - there's loads of them in Hong Kong - and stood there in the morning rush hour, asking commuters if they could help me with my ferry money as I'd lost my wallet.

"So the first guy just gives me the equivalent of about a hundred US dollars, just like that. It was nothing to him. I nearly fell off my pony I was so shocked that someone could give that much!

"That day I took loads of money. So the following day I went to do the same thing, but just as I started to approach the crowd the very same guy approaches me, only this time he doesn't stop. Instead he just walks by, and as he's passing he said, 'What happened? Did you lose your wallet again?'

"I died of embarrassment. But that guy was an angel in my life, he must have been. I couldn't do that shit. I mean, I can do a lot of shit but that was an education to me. No school can teach you that. These kids aren't here learning *nothing*."

"What, so this is OK, what they're doing?"

"No. But maybe this is the best she can do in her circumstances. Maybe she's fucked up on that pasta shit, whatever that is."

"They should be in bed."

"I know."

Really, Dobbs is just hiding behind his own comedown by being antagonistic. After all, she was right; the kids should have been tucked in bed, ready for school in the morning. But maybe, also, in the mother's mind she didn't have a choice. Who was he to be passing judgment? Maybe they haven't even got a mother, he suddenly thinks.

Agent6, who's been looking more and more tired, and in no fit state to make small talk with anyone, quite randomly just gets up and, without making any fuss bids farewell to the girl he's been sitting next to.

"Right, I'm off to bed," he says, and exits the scene.

Swifty jumps up to follow.

"What you doing Dobbs?" Bolivar asks.

"Badly chatting up Gatita I think," he says, not feeling much like concealing his intentions.

Bolivar winks at Gatita, who smiles warmly but minimally over her cocktail and there's a moment of discomfort that Dobbs can only sit through.

"I'll see you back at the hotel. Nice to meet you Gatita," Bolivar seems to almost whisper. Then, after saying a round of farewells to the ladies he's been sitting with, he takes his leave.

More people have gathered round the bar now and the band of merry street performers are displaying their wares. The Brazilian girl, Ilena, a proper crusty-looking Traveller is there with her puppets. In no time they're all chatting and, almost as a final flourish to what has been a fairy-tale evening, the two children return and start playing with her, like some seed has been sown. By now it's getting very late however and as the waiters signal it's time to go and begin dragging off chairs the remainder of the throng starts meandering its way back down the promenade.

Dobbs walks with Gatita for a while, but he's exhausted now, and is feeling a little uneasy and his restricted linguistic abilities have begun to become a little tiring. He tries to make more conversation when all he really wants is to just walk away, but somehow he feels oddly tied in his emotional connection to this woman. So he stays and walks until they come to a bottleneck where the whole crowd has gathered at the bottom of some concrete stairs leading down from the promenade to the shantytown on the river bank below.

By now, Dobbs is feeling like his whole evening has been compromised by the pestilence and he is being consumed by pangs of paranoia that maybe he's been coming on too strong, plus feelings of betrayal toward his partner are flying round in his head, making him track his intentions. Does he want to take her back to his bed? If not, why the fuck is he still here with her?

The whole, twisted mess in his head seems almost like some animated scene, with The Brigadier taking centre stage on his Sax amidst the old muddy stilts supporting the shantytown. He suddenly feels so awkward being here with her, trapped in this intense attraction that seems to have him ensnared. He feels like that monkey holding on to the nuts.

Finally he can bear it no longer.

"I'm tired," he says, turning to face her, "But can we hook up another time maybe? After our trip to the jungle perhaps?"

Gatita just nods.

He takes her number then kisses her on the cheek. It feels strangely awkward to just walk away, as though he's trying to break out of a spell. He turns to The Brigadier, who's not really engaging in conversation with anyone in particular and is just generally climbing about the place as though it were a kid's playground.

"I'll see you tomorrow, man. We're going to do our stint in the jungle, right?"

The Brigadier catches his eye and then turns away from him.

"I ain't going," he says.

"I don't reckon we'll even leave tomorrow anyway to be honest," Dobbs says.

"I ain't going anyway."

Agent6, Dobbs realises, hasn't spoken a word to The Brigadier the whole evening, so perhaps that's what's causing this sudden objection he thinks. Or, perhaps, this thing that happens to him after heavy pestilence abuse is kicking in again. The thought of having to watch The Brigadier crash and burn again was indeed a sobering one.

"Well, you'll be sorely missed," he says after a moment's thought. It sounds lame, but he just doesn't know what else to say.

"I'm off to bed man."

"You always leave me," The Brigadier shouts across at him as he turns to go and though it's said as if in jest, there's another tone there; a cry for help - a fear of abandonment.

An impossible dynamic is twisting Dobbs's head however, and all he can think of right now is escaping to be alone and ride out the intensity of the storm, so he turns and, with not much more than a wave, is gone.

Juan's Home

As the rickshaw engine races and the driver pushes the machine to its max, Dobbs is rapidly coming to the conclusion he's not quite as awake as he'd perhaps thought. The engine sounds like it's going to throw a rod as they hammer round a sharp bend trying to overtake another rickshaw with a *Che Guevara* stencil on the back. Somehow it seems to perfectly capture the spirit of South America. It's been a slow rising and several cups of coffee has barely touched the sides. Dobbs is only now really coming to, speeding along at breakneck speed in a motor taxi with Bolivar behind Agent6 and Swifty's rickshaw, which is a little way ahead. None of it is quite as stimulating as the overtaking manoeuvre the driver is now attempting however, which places them about ten feet away from a head-on collision with a truck coming the opposite way.

Slightly unbelievably, the screeching motor manages to power the rickety contraption through the rapidly closing gap between the two behemoths before and behind, and as they make it through, Dobbs and Bolivar look at one another, nodding in acknowledgement of the sudden awareness of the here and now again, grateful for the wonder of life as they both take a breath and check their hearts are still pumping.

It's not early by any stretch of the mark, but Swifty's still adamant they're leaving today and it seems apparent that the rickshaw driver has picked up on that sense of urgency. Dobbs, however, will be happy to arrive in one piece whatever day of the week it is. Now he leans forward to pat the driver on the back.

"Amigo, tranquillo, ah!" he says, and immediately the man kicks the machine down into fourth and the anxious tone of the engine subsides.

Dobbs recognises the road partly because it's next to the airport but also as it's the same route he'd taken ten years earlier to find *Sachamama*, the location of the lodge where he'd drunk with Fernando and Fransisco on his last trip. Iquitos is more of a big town than a sprawling city and this, one of the few main highways is a built-up road that peters out more and more until it eventually comes to an abrupt end a few kilometres outside of town.

Close to the airport they turn off into what appears to be a rural village where a series of dirt tracks connects a cluster of shack-like houses. There's something very sweet and rural about the whole

159

area and the kids playing on the mud tracks lends the place a comforting sense of community.

The rickshaw pulls up behind Agent6 and Swifty's *collectivo* and drops them off at the bottom of a track, which Dobbs assumes to be the entrance to Juan's garden. It's nestled amongst an eclectic collection of similarly fenced-off plots, each with its own no-nonsense wooden dwelling in what seems quite a sparse but sprawling indigenous estate. Some houses are so basic they look like nothing more than crude garden sheds. Others are bigger and set on larger pieces of mostly undeveloped land amongst the arterial network of tracks. The whole estate sits just a stone's throw away from the city and literally a couple of minutes from the airport, although apparently this only experiences air traffic in daylight hours so the noise probably doesn't interfere with Juan's ceremonies.

Juan's house is larger than most but still very basic. It is constructed of aged, rough-sawn timber, most of which is painted a sky-blue colour. It's all, seemingly, set on two floors - although it's a bit difficult to tell exactly what's going on from the outside by the chaotic selection of beams and planks - and has a series of extensions and annexes coming off, as though it's grown out of the ground as organically as the many trees surrounding it. The gentle subsidence occurring here and there lends an added quirkiness to it, and somehow reminds Dobbs of an old battered boathouse. It seems a warm and humble dwelling.

The front garden - if you could call it a garden - is neither excessively manicured nor particularly overgrown. Basic functionality seems to be the order of things, with signs of habitation everywhere. There are sparse patches of grass and trodden-down muddy areas amongst an equally spare dotting of trees, shrubs and bushes. In occasional spaces there seems to be a carpet of the tiniest, bright pink seed-like things which are so dazzling they look as if they are dyeing the very mud magenta.

Each patch of pink seems to be circling something that looks like a rubber plant and Dobbs squints in perplexity at the intensity of the spectacle. The strange, rubbery texture of these plants apparently springing out of the bright pink soil all looks so alien that it almost feels as if this is the place Dorothy's house actually landed. Somehow it has such an eerie feeling that it sends shudders through his body and he has to do a double-take, looking back at Bolivar and scratching his head. He can tell that many ceremonies

160

have been done here; the place feels like it has an odd aura about it, as if it's become a portal.

Portal or not, it's certainly a hive of activity though; quite a few Westerners are knocking about here and there and another chap who looks perhaps Arabic or Israeli, even though he's naturally fair-skinned. Though Juan's an old *curandero* who works mostly with the local *Indigenous,* some of his income is no doubt generated through teaching his craft to these newcomers. There is a massive spectrum of medicinal herb knowledge and many healing songs or *icaros* to placate the spirits, but this is all just the tip of the iceberg of his practice; a total dedication that is ultimately all just a means to humbly knock on the doors of the Other worlds, beyond the Earthly plane.

Dobbs wanders up and just hangs with Bolivar out the front. Despite the apparent activity and all the *gringos* knocking about there's also an odd quietness and other than the occasional nod of acknowledgement there's no real exchange of pleasantries with anyone. Instead Dobbs now turns his attention to the old Jeep some indigenous-looking guy in overalls is tinkering with out the front.

After a short while Agent6 emerges from the house with a man who Dobbs recognises as Juan through photos he's seen. Swifty is following behind them, pacing about like a frenzied mad man and looking uncomfortably busy. It's part of his character but it doesn't necessarily help him get things done; he just sort of runs around in a flap and everybody gets busy around him. No doubt he will make a good foreman, Dobbs thinks to himself, although he's relieved he won't really be on the building side of things.

Juan looks relaxed. He is of average height for an *Indigeno*, which is not tall by western standards. It is impossible to determine his age, other than to say he's not a young man but he's clearly still strong, especially in his upper body. His eyes look old and wise and his face is worn with life, but he has the frame of someone who is fit and active. He is wearing tatty jeans, a tired old T-shirt and wellingtons that are folded short at the top.

Agent6 and Swifty have the energy of men getting down to business and there's a moderate degree of commotion, but Juan clearly isn't buying into it. He's a mixture of soft nods and moments of contemplation and although there's lots of people running about in preparation for the expedition, it's clear to Dobbs that there is no chance of leaving today. Agent6 obviously approves of Swifty's motivation and it seems clear that though the

161

idea of postponing departure till tomorrow has been discussed though perhaps not yet fully been accepted, but the reality is that they still need a lot more supplies.

Dobbs just wants someone to tell him what to do really, but though everyone's intentions are mutual he's not being too forward in offering assistance as it seems most of the hard work is already being done right in front of him. It's a complex thing to pull together; as well as chainsaw operators and chainsaws they also need a whole host of other workers - carpenters, labourers and thatchers to name but a few - plus someone needs to repair the boat, which has apparently sprung quite a serious leak.

Then there's the cook to run the kitchen and all the food, drinking water and pots and pans and, he has no doubt, a whole load of other stuff that they probably won't realise until it's too late. It's all going to be a bit of a mission getting the whole thing off the ground and it will probably take a few trips to and from the land before everything really gets cranked up. All that without even considering the intention of doing a ceremony whilst they're out there. Plus it's a Sunday today and almost everywhere is closed. All in all though, Juan looks very relaxed and in control of things, as if he is running at absolutely the appropriate speed for a late Sunday morning.

A strange-looking dog appears, and greets Dobbs. It looks like he's straight out of some old black and white horror movie, like *The Hound of the Baskervilles*. He's big, and suffering from chronic alopecia which makes him a little less attractive to give affection to as he's in need of some serious scab care but he's got a gentle temperament and when Dobbs runs the tips of his fingers down his crown to stroke his grizzled nose, the old dog laps up the affection like the warmth from a wood burner on a cold winter's night.

Dobbs wants be introduced to Juan but there's a lot of commotion going on, and he feels a better time will come. Juan, he can see, has the eyes of a *curandero* - warm and wise. Perhaps it is the wisdom of the jungle, he thinks; he'd seen the same thing in Fernando's eyes the last time he'd drunk in the Amazon. Then again maybe it's just that he's seen a thing or two: apparently Juan had fought in Vietnam for the Americans and seen some terrible things in that senseless war; a war conducted solely for profit that allowed the enemy weekly slots to rearm themselves for the following week's assault. A war solely designed to consume a steady flow of weapons and soldiers; huge egos flying in, dead and broken soldiers shipped out, many with the sad realisation they were only ever there as cannon fodder. Wherever it's come from though, the wisdom is there, and it's easy to spot.

Dobbs turns his attention to inspecting the sea of pink seeds from the unusual plant. So intense is the colour it almost appears fluorescent in the bright sunlight. Something about the particular tone or the odd texture reminds him of the Dream-world he sees when he drinks sometimes, in which everything is set in darkness yet seems illuminated from within by its own energy. Dobbs has only ever seen such colours on the wings of butterflies in this world.

Juan has been watching him in his reverie. Now, approaching, he nods at the odd plant.

"*Arboli*," he states, as if telling everyone.

"Muy loco, so bright." Dobbs replies. Then, turning his attention to Juan's old fashioned, but well- maintained four wheel drive Jeep, he pats the front wing.

"*Bueno*. Original?"

"*Si*, wartime classic."

"Wow. You know what 'Jeep' stands for?"

Juan looks with curiosity and shakes his head.

"'Just Enough Essential Parts.'"

Juan stares at the old Jeep, slowly nodding. Then he smiles.

"Just enough essential parts, ah?"

Dobbs just nods and then, with a sweep of his glance that takes in Juan's humble home, his basic garden, and eventually the man himself, he chuckles and offers his hand.

"Si," he says, shaking Juan's hand, "Dobbs!"

It's a humid day, and Juan removes the baseball cap that he is wearing back-to-front, running his fingers through his dark sweaty hair as if attempting to keep his head clear amidst the commotion happening around him. It is thick and black, without the slightest sign of greying. He looks back at Dobbs, seemingly considering something for a moment but then he just smiles, nods a brief acknowledgement, and turns back to the task of gathering together bits and pieces for the mission ahead, and organising things with Agent6.

Dobbs spots Bolivar walking into the house and decides to follow, entering through the front door that leads directly into the main sitting room. It is very basic, with a moderate-sized, low wooden table and a few plastic chairs up against the wall, which somehow gives the vibe of a waiting room. The inner walls are of the same unlined timber as the external; rough cut by chainsaw, and darkened to the darkest brown with age.

Dobbs is a little perplexed at first to notice there are no windows but then, as he steps across the threshold, he realises it's clearly where they drink, as the energy of the place sends shivers through his body almost as if he's feeling the shudder of that first taste of *Ayahuasca*. Not that the intention is to drink here at the moment, but rather to take Juan and his young *curanderos*-in-waiting off to the jungle with them.

There's probably about five or six men and women of varying nationalities, but communication is not so forthcoming between any of them so far. It's not really in a rude way, but there's always anxiety before drinking. For a moment he becomes a bit paranoid, thinking that perhaps he should've toned down what he's wearing a little. But then, 'Naah,' he suddenly thinks.

There is often an odd vibe in the build-up to a ceremony: whether it is fear or apprehension of the ceremony or perhaps just the anticipation of the properly rough taste of the brew itself is difficult to say. Possibly it's the effort of trying to hold a balanced energetic state in order to bring all the focus right back to the rawest intention, discarding all the noise and nonsense of the mundane mind.

Then again, he thinks, they're probably days away from drinking, so perhaps it's just the knowledge of what going off into the jungle for more than a few days can really mean, and the visions that conjures in the mind's eye, especially for those who know it a little already – which seems to be most of them this time. It's unclear where the vibe comes from, but whatever it is, the energy feels slightly eerie.

Dobbs offers his hand to the Israeli-looking guy, who glances down at his hot pants and then back at his face, almost as if not properly registering him. It's as if there's a barrier up or a vibe in the air which Dobbs initially puts down to his crap Spanish.

"Yahu," the man says, accepting the proffered hand, but he disappears as soon as Dobbs attempts to speak English with him. He's clearly not impressed, but though Dobbs feels perhaps he should be doing better, nevertheless he feels there's something sickly cool about the guy, and he shakes his head in almost disbelief at the abruptness of his disengagement.

Bolivar immediately laughs out loud.

164

"Dobbs, you're just not cool enough mate. Sorry."

Dobbs chuckles and watches the man for a while, wondering what it will be like drinking with him. He's tall, quite thin, and very naturally pale, yet something about his hair or his eyes looks Israeli. His energy is delving into the *cool,* but it's a type of cool that Dobbs has never been comfortable with; the type that makes people around feel as if they have to shut up or something. It's like his head is screaming out silent obscenities.

But then, thinks Dobbs, the guy's only young and if he is Israeli, which is pretty guaranteed, he's probably done military service, something which is obligatory in Israel, and perhaps that gives him the cold edge. Certainly Agent6 won't be able to suffer him if his energy is too abrasive – at least not without being equally abrasive himself. Then again, maybe Dobbs's energy threatens him in some way?

Then, Dobbs takes sight of Carlos, who has only seen in photos, who has just caught sight of the newcomers loitering lamely in the kitchen at the back of the house. He wanders over. When Carlos got involved with the land project, it was much to The Brigadier's bitter disappointment, who seemingly saw his involvement as a bit of a threat. Apparently he'd had to endure enormous verbal insult from The Brigadier, and Dobbs can't help wondering if his presence is the real reason why The Brigadier is not accompanying them on this first trip.

Dobbs knows the answer is to get The Brigadier out on the land, away from the pestilence, but he was blind to it all at the moment, unable to see that those around him simply wanted to help and they understood that much of the shit that comes up in that process is not personal, even though it's so nasty sometimes. It is one of the truly ugly sides of pestilence addiction, however, and The Brigadier's not alone in it: so many are going through the same terrible addiction in the West, and Britain is absolutely saturated with it. What's more, it drives the banking world, and most people behave like total *bankers* when they're on it.

Regardless of The Brigadier's opinion however, Carlos has worked on the land with Agent6 for some years now whilst studying the ways of the *curandero* with Juan, and in his mind at least, he's more than shown willing in the project. His energy is certainly a lot lighter than the Israeli's but, Dobbs suddenly thinks, if Yahu had heard about some of the intensity he might be expecting from Agent6's mates, it might account for his attitude. Then again, he

165

grins to himself, it could just be the hot pants which are freaking him out.

It seems in one way or another they're all strong characters, which is always a good ingredient for a bit of adventure, but whatever the dynamic they've just walked into, Carlos seems relaxed.

"Oh hi, Dobbs right? Agent6 has talked about you. You're thinking about writing a book or something?"

"Yeah, well maybe just record one first. So, yeah, say 'hi' to the dictaphone, man!"

"Shit. Is that thing recording?"

He has a strong, intellectual American accent but it's soft, and he's clearly overcome any need to speak *at* you, in that All American way.

Dobbs presses the screen on his phone.

"It is now!" he says, holding the phone up to Carlos. "Care to add anything?"

Carlos takes a breath and looks at the device.

"Err, yeah. Hi."

"Nice, thanks. Every little helps!"

They all have a chuckle.

"This is Bolivar by the way."

"Nice to meet you man."

Somehow everything slows down again to a loiter; they all know they'll be stuck in the boat for hours the following day, and now is really just checklist time. Kids are running about screaming their heads off whilst they're kind of just hanging in the front room and kitchen. Bolivar holds up his tobacco, which to Dobbs represents a spliff break. They make their way out the back and Carlos joins them. With Dobbs's crap Spanish and everyone talking too fast for him keep up, it's much more relaxing just to stay out of the way.

Emerging out the backdoor and into the garden, which is more of a Fifties backyard, they are immediately greeted by the sight of two butterflies having sex on a leaf. They're properly going for it, and Bolivar grabs his camera.

"I want to get the cum shot," he grins.

"Oh nice," Carlos muses.

Even with all the bushes and trees about it all seems a little oddly barren at first sight but then Dobbs sees the chickens and ducks, or at least what look like ducks, although admittedly smaller, and he realises the reason for all the bare earth and mud. He's kept chickens himself, and knows how they can tear a garden apart, but

166

apparently that's nothing to what ducks can do. There are still quite a few trees and bushes here and there, but beyond that, everything has been thoroughly ravaged by the poultry. It all has the feeling of a proper old back yard rather than any sort of manicured garden, and a perfect place to come and comfortably throw up when the *medicine* is getting to work, and it's time to purge.

Juan has a big family by the looks of things and the house is the central hub of that. However the whole family, coupled with the *gringos* staying in a room off the main front room does give the place a bit of a manic vibe, which feels ungrounded and slightly unsettling. There is a tingle of something in the air, a feeling of transience which somehow makes it hard to relax, although perhaps that's just because everyone is about to take off to the jungle.

"You been in the jungle before?" Carlos asks Bolivar.

"Yeah. In Africa I have."

"What were you doing there?"

"Oh, you know, teaching adventure sports, like white water rafting and taking people on safaris and stuff."

"Wow. What's the worst experience you've had in the jungle?" he asks with a grin.

"Waking with a condom hanging out my arse," Bolivar fires back, looking Carlos in the face without so much a hint of a smirk.

"Nice," Dobbs says, looking at Bolivar grinning and not quite believing what he's just said.

"No, your worst experience?" Carlos quips.

Bolivar laughs more than Dobbs at Carlos's rapid response.

"Well at least they *used* a condom," Carlos says, not falling to one side or the other of Bolivar's humour.

"I got malaria a few times. The best trip I've ever had. A whole week of tripping that lasts what seems not much more than an hour. Oh, and I've had to dig maggots out my arm on one occasion."

"Well, hopefully we won't have anything as exotic as that on our trip over the next few days. But in truth, you never know," Carlos says.

Dobbs and Bolivar smoke a joint and then return to the front of the house to find Juan preparing the motor, or *peci-peci* as he calls it, for the boat. He's attaching the long propeller shaft by bolting it onto the block of motor, which is all looking very clean and tidy. Finishing the attachment, he primes the motor and, with one pull of the cord, fires her up. Looking up at Agent6 and Swifty, he nods with a satisfied expression. All look delighted by the sound, which seems somehow to be the cherry on the cake for the day's proceedings.

It's an exciting moment, as now they know for sure the journey can move forward. All that's left to do is make final arrangements for meeting the following morning at Belen Market to do the food shopping. Dobbs has only the vaguest memory of the place – a big fruit and veg market with lots of little shanty shops – but it's right next to the port from which they'll set sail and whatever they need, they'll find it there he reckons.

The boys are still pottering about, phoning people and discussing this and that, whilst Swifty is carefully writing down what they still need and everything they've spent so far. It looks almost like he's keeping the minutes of a meeting to Dobbs which, it's fair to say, he finds thoroughly impressive. Dobbs himself is not really present, however. It's not that he's being lazy really; preoccupied would better define his head state. If someone was to give him a job, he knows he would deploy immediately but he knows he could easily complicate matters also.

It's clearly all going to be a massive runabout in the last five minutes, which will no doubt stretch their scheduled ten o'clock departure to mid afternoon tomorrow before they actually set sail, and the reality that they probably won't arrive until night fall. Dobbs doesn't need to be a fortune teller to work that out. Agent6 sure as hell knows it, but having Swifty in a flap is a winner either way. There's a massive volume of boxes that will have to be ticked, but right now, he's here, with everyone, and that's probably the important thing. His role in this process will no doubt become apparent. Perhaps it is indeed a book. But he's not sure what the story is yet and seems to be getting further from any story he's been toying with in his head.

Suddenly it becomes a bit of a looming prospect to Dobbs to think he has to live the story he wants to write. And he certainly hadn't thought about writing a romance.

"You're not with us at all are you Dobbs? I know who you're thinking about. And it's not Ruby is it?"

"It's all just so complicated isn't it?"

Bolivar doesn't answer, but the way he cocks his head to one side looking at Dobbs seems to imply he thinks that perhaps it isn't actually that complicated at all.

Lovingly Fearless

It's now late in the day, and dusk is fast approaching. The Brigadier is deep in conversation with Swifty, who is sweaty and clad ready for the jungle - even though they haven't actually left Iquitos yet. Agent6 is similarly attired in rough, torn green army surplus pants and a thick, baggy cotton lumberjack shirt. The bagginess will allow his skin to breathe in the sweltering humidity, and also afford a distance between the fabric and his skin below which, apparently, most creepy crawlies can't traverse with their fangs and spikes.

They're all back at the hotel, having stopped for a bite to eat, but Dobbs feels a bit distant from affairs. He's like the fly on the wall, just watching. Agent6 is so excited that it's all coming together. He's expecting the estate to be a little overgrown when he gets there, but he's also hoping it's been maintained as it's supposedly being looked after by an indigenous family, and he has a reputation from a previous project in Iquitos for being a little harsh with slackers.

He'd abandoned that venture after the local guy he'd negotiated the land agreement with started lying and ripping him off. It seems that whilst he was away he kept getting phone calls asking for more cash to buy materials and such like, but when he turned up it was to find the place completely overgrown and untouched since his last visit. It was then he realised his business partner was a liar and a cheat, but by all accounts even though he was, to say the least, livid, apparently he didn't shout. Instead he just walked off without saying a word, leaving the man thinking that he'd got away with stealing all the land and the *maloka*, or roundhouse, they'd built for him and his family to live in whilst they were in the jungle.

The following day, however, he turned up with a work crew and disassembled every part of the maloka, leaving absolutely nothing behind. He took everything, including the dignity of his erstwhile business partner who was forced to watch, in front of his wife and children, as the fruits of his deception came home to roost. After that he stopped working with the man completely. As Dobbs's stepfather had always told him: 'you can trust a thief, but you can never trust a liar.'

Watching Agent6 going back to his project – this dream which has been going on now for nearly fifteen years - is a fascinating sight for Dobbs, who's known him throughout that period. What's really interesting to him though is not so much Agent6's achievements in developing the land, but rather the recognition that in this process his friend has become quite a shaman, or *Curandero* himself.

Now, however, with this latest assembly of troops to take out and recommence the project, he seems more like a little boy, just hours before going off on a summer holiday. He's excited because he's living out his dreams! In truth, it's the only way he kind of rolls, Dobbs thinks to himself, and tomorrow will be like going from one world to another. Even as he feels the sense of adventure pulsing through his veins though, he could never guess just how true that notion will turn out to be.

Nonetheless, he just sits on his bed, listening to one of Agent6's old childhood stories again that seems to come to the surface of our memory pool when we're embarking on adventures and indulge in that excited state we feel we should refrain from in mature day-to-day life. Now Agent6 is looking as happy as Larry with a fat spliff in his hand and his music playing.

Dobbs feels like everything is finally coming together, that heading off into the jungle to ask his big question to the gods is exactly what he's here to do. He knows that the magic happens in the journey and not necessarily just the destination though, and the kind of answers he's seeking for only come through pilgrimage. He feels like he's a tiny cog in a far bigger engine, and yet at the same time unified in that picture. Even the fan, squeaking in the corner, seems to morph with the tune playing in the background with its ironically titled, 'This was supposed to be the future', by the Nextmen. The tune seems to empower and capture the richness of the moment with a seductive Cafe Del Mar sounding chill-out riff.

Everything around him seems to be harmonising with this looming sense of adventure, as if he's believing something into being, and some part of him can sense that, whatever it is, it's going to be earth-shaking. The thing is; it's no longer so much thoughts about the jungle that are whirling round in his head as fantasies about Gatita. Bringing his attention back to the room however, he keeps his feelings to himself as Agent6 tells the story of how he nicked a pallet of food when he was a kid which turned out to be tins of spam and how he and his friends had to set up a covert spam distribution ring. It's a funny story of teenage naughtiness that he got away with.

Dobbs wants to bring his thoughts away from Gatita and begins,

"I ended up with all this cash on one occasion. When I was a kid we used to bust into *Butlins*, to hang out with the girls and use the swimming pools and what have you. Avoiding the Red Coats was hilarious. Sometimes we'd grab a collection box off the front counter if the place was full of pensioners and do the pretty 'boy scout' thing, then pocket the lot. Terrible I was.

"They'd get to know your faces after a while though, and I remember this one occasion they'd seen me and I made a run for it into the amusement arcade. I ran down and hid behind a bank of one-armed bandits and lost them. So there I am behind this line of machines, and I can see all these small metal doors on the back of them, which I immediately thought must be the end of the rainbow like.

"Then, lo and behold, about five or six machines up, I see a machine that looks like the door's ajar. So I crawl up, and sure enough it is. And as I pull it open, there's literally a bucket full of 50p's: more than my body weight, probably.

First I filled my socks, like, all round my ankles, then my jean pockets and then I used the front of my T-shirt. Then I had to get out of there. The whole thing was quite an ordeal; my old man would have lynched me if he'd known I'd nicked it, which I didn't really - the door was left open, and the Red Coats practically chased me in there. I mean, what's a kid to do in a situation like that?"

"It was entrapment, Your Honour: the Redcoats chased me to the money!" Agent6 shouts out.

"But that was the only real time I stole and got away with it. Normally I got caught for almost everything I nicked, or at least people sort of knew it was me, as I've always looked more dodgy than I was."

"Sounds like you looked as dodgy as you were!" Bolivar muses over a chuckle.

"Funny, I used to nick from my mum's purse and never got caught and then it got to the point that every day, as soon as they went out for a walk along the seafront, I'd be straight in my mum's purse and nick a pound or 50p."

"Ohh, nicking from your ma; not good," Swifty tones, who was adopted by a high court judge, though seemingly he has little or no contact with his parents now. The comment causes Dobbs to pause in his story, as he considers how that must sound to someone who doesn't even know their biological mother.

"Yeah, properly wrong. After a while I started to feel guilty, but I just couldn't stop myself; it was like it could almost take me over, and that really started to bother me. I started to feel like I was addicted to it – addicted to stealing!

"Then, one day, they'd gone for a walk and I'd nicked a pound and I just couldn't handle the weight of it anymore. It was all so covert and calculated. I used to run into their bedroom where I could see if the coast was clear before I nicked anything. But the weight of nicking this pound was just overbearing. I had to put it back. So I ran back into their bedroom and saw them just come round the corner. They were, like, seconds from walking through the door, but I decided to make a run for it and put the pound back, and just when I'd got the money back in her purse, the door opened. My old man saw me and knew something had gone down. He sensed my guilt. Well, I reckon he did anyway. But that was the last time I ever nicked money from my mum's purse. Then, a few months later, she tells me how pleased she is that I'd stopped stealing from her!"

"She knew!" Swifty exclaims.

"Yeah, she was clever like that. I felt so embarrassed that she'd known all along, but she took a weight off my shoulders also," Dobbs chuckles.

"Oh shit, actually I did do one thing that was really quite bad: I broke into the church at the bottom of our road in Lewes when I was about five or six and snapped the cross off the collection box to use as a crowbar to bust the thing open, and once I'd got the money out I went and ransacked the old ladies' tea room: smashed everything to bits in there. I hated those old ladies with their snobby attitudes. I could hear everything they used to say, the way they bickered and moaned. It was like I could hear their thoughts."

"That is properly wrong," Bolivar bellows.

"Never got caught though. That would have been a proper blight on the landscape. Even worse, I was standing on top of the garage my old man was building, helping him a bit I suppose, and the bickering old ladies came round, whining like witches, and I was just standing there like the good policeman's son, like butter wouldn't melt in my mouth, listening to them bicker about the terrible state of the world and knowing inside that they *were* the terrible state of the world. How dark is that? The horrible noise that came from their heads. The dark judgment."

"You could hear their thoughts?" Bolivar asks.

"Well, I was really young. But I'd look at some of their faces when they were gossiping and they'd suddenly go quiet and that's when I'd hear. It was like in their heads they were seething about wastefulness and spoilt brats."

"Maybe the noise was just in your head," Bolivar suggests.

"Yeah maybe. But I don't reckon. Who truly knows whose thought train we're following?"

"'I', is nothing more than an assumption my friend. You might not be who you think you are Bolivar."

"That's just weird Dobbs. You guys were *so* bad! I was a little angel who just used to get beaten up a lot. I was bullied all the time," he says, half-joking and half-sincere. He's quite a big chap, and from the way he scooped The Brigadier off the ground when he was losing it in Lima, and just brushed off his punches, it seems he's clearly learned something in the process.

"*Oh*, Bolivar," Agent6 tones in mock sympathy.

"I think a lot of the stuff I did as a kid was quite dark though," Dobbs continues. "Not violent, and never - or at least rarely - cruel really, but I was very calculating and devious. I don't reckon I was a good brother."

"Ahh," Agent6 tones in amusement, "Kids can be nasty. But how else do you really learn?"

"And you carry that stuff you did wrong when you're a kid, just like when you're older don't you? Well, I did – for years anyway," Dobbs says.

"Did you text her by the way, Dobbs?" Bolivar throws in out of nowhere.

"Who?"

Bolivar throws the book down he's just picked up and laughs so loudly that Agent6, who obviously knows what he's talking about, bursts out laughing too.

"Who?!" Bolivar almost shouts, doubling over.

Dobbs tries not to rise to it.

"Ye-ah," he replies as casually as he can.

"So when's she coming then? I want to ask her if she can help me sort out the paperwork on this land to make it a bit more official," says Agent6.

"I don't know if she will come," he says, on the defensive now.

"Maybe she's shy, maybe you need to encourage her. Go on Dobbs, ring her up. I want to watch you in action," Bolivar grins.

"If you don't ring her, I will - and then she'll be totally confused as to who's on her tail," Agent6 adds mischievously.

Dobbs's competitive gene is twanged by that one, and so, pulling out his phone, he selects her name from the address book.

"Too much pressure!" he wails, half-laughing.

But no one says anything as he holds the phone in his hand, deliberating.

"Shall I?"

Bolivar has a huge smile from one side of his face to the other and then straightens his face completely as if he's suddenly having nothing to do with Dobbs's little game.

"You know you want to, Dobbs," he says, before immediately retreating back to his book.

The others watch gleefully as Dobbs takes a deep breath then presses the green button on his phone. There's a brief pause, he speaks, and then he immediately terminates the call, all in a motion that lasts no more than two seconds. There's a moment of quiet while the others just sit, pretending not to be interested, but Bolivar can't bear the anticipation.

"So? What's she doing?" he pipes up.

Dobbs doesn't answer but just sits there, staring at the door.

"She's here, isn't she?" Bolivar intuits. Then he jumps up and starts dancing round the room.

"Dobbs is getting his rocks off, Dobbs is getting his rocks off," he mocks in a schoolyard sing-song.

Dobbs suddenly feels as transparent as sheet glass.

"Shut up for fucks sake! I *gotta* keep it together."

And then, like that, Gatita's standing at the door. She looks completely relaxed and comfortable with herself and Dobbs jumps up and greets her with a kiss on the cheek, which is about as much as he can handle, considering the pressure of expectation he feels under from the others. He doesn't like the feeling of being so exposed one tiny bit but he allows her to take the only chair in the place, next to the window, where she immediately starts to build a spliff. Even now, without any stimulants she seems so utterly beautiful he finds himself struggling to so much as lay eyes on her.

For the next few hours they all sit, talking amongst themselves. Agent6 is chatting away about his land but the conversation is mostly in Spanish, and though Dobbs can understand better than he can speak, he still feels a little left out. To be fair, he's so overwhelmed by Gatita's presence that even in English he would struggle.

He feels completely out of his depth with the way people seem to go about things in South America; there's a hands on, no bullshit attitude here that's the complete opposite of the English way - well, English like Dobbs at any rate. In comparison, his mind seems so convoluted and constipated with calculations that sometimes it seems almost impossible to just get on with it, and do what he really wants to do. He feels so tightly wound he can barely look at her, but she would probably not bat an eyelid if he told her he wanted to pull her knickers off with his teeth alone.

'In fact, she'd probably prefer me to just do it without saying anything!' he thinks, castigating himself for his accursed politeness.

It's not that his feelings are purely sexual - far from it - but certainly his attraction toward her is adding to his confusion, as every time his mind goes there he finds himself thinking about his partner and the mess of that whole situation. For now all he can do is just sit, occasionally glancing at Gatita, who stops every now and then to stare at him, as if wondering why he's so quiet. He's so overwhelmed he just can't bring himself to talk to her though, and feels like anything he says will just come out wrong. What's worse, he's painfully aware that everyone else is watching him to see how he's going to make his move; even she seems a little perplexed by the looks of things.

As the hours pass the tension mounts. It feels like there's a battle is raging in his head: she's so close to him, sat right there on the chair at the end of his bed, and he's desperately thinking of a way to move closer. He's imagined a thousand scenarios and run through a million lines, but everything just feels so contrived. Finally he just thinks 'sod it' and, deciding to just take the plunge, blurts out:

"Can I kiss you?"

He can't quite believe what he's just said, but now the die is cast. The room has been plunged into silence by the comment, and as everyone waits with bated breath to see what will happen next, Gatita just turns in her seat and, giving him a look of pure seduction that totally wipes him out, calmly says,

"No."

Lying on his side, his head supported by his arm, staring at her, he knows he should be collapsing to the depths of despair now, and yet completely the opposite is actually happening: rather than

175

dying of embarrassment, he seems to be rising to heavenly peaks. It's such a relief just to know that she knows his intention and how he feels about her and that now there can be honesty and openness. He can see she feels more comfortable too, knowing he's riding on an even keel.

Bolivar is looking at Dobbs with absolute bemusement.

"Did you just ask Gatita if you could kiss her? Did I get that right?" he says, then claps his hands together.

"Nice line, Dobbs."

But then Gatita drops a line which quashes even Bolivar's jesting as, ignoring the others, she stares him right in the eyes as if he's the only person in the Universe and says in a deep, aphrodisiac intonation,

"Not yet."

Agent6 and Bolivar immediately break out in a cheer, while Swifty's chuckling at the whole situation and The Brigadier gives a grin so cheeky it's almost a scowl, but to Dobbs the others seem to have just receded into the background as, peering deep into Gatita's dark eyes, he sees the fearlessness in their depths.

Time seems to stand still. It is the last few minutes of dusk and the sun has long since dropped below the horizon, but the last, stray rays are bending round the globe to bathe the room in crimson bliss. He rolls onto his back to bask in the notion of it - kissing her! As he does so, she twists her head round to look at him, holding the spliff she's just finished rolling and signalling him to take it. Reaching across, he still can't quite get his head round just how drop dead gorgeous she is; it's like the painting in his Granddad's trailer has stepped out of the frame and is sat there in front of him, and she's absolutely fearless. Lovingly fearless.

Ice-cream

Dobbs realises, lying there, that without having any wine in the gaff he's at a disadvantage. He wants to go out and get some, but for some reason he feels a bit nervous being on his own at night with his crap Spanish and his lack of knowledge of the area. Suddenly, he realises the fear is creeping in again. He shudders and tries to shake it off, but he recognises that thinking he can engage with Gatita like this is setting himself up for a major fall. It's too much, too soon; he's giving her all the 'sell signals' but he's not even for sale. His head is becoming a cluttered mess worrying about all these projections of what may or may not happen, so he decides instead to focus on the one silly little fear he can move through right now.

Getting up and going out into the night on his own in this crazy little town might be the best thing to do, he thinks to himself: move through a fear, eradicate it, and see what's on the other side. With that he jumps up and, glancing at Gatita, says in his most proper accent,

"*Tu quieras vino?*" He's even dared to ask her in Spanish!

She cocks her head to one side and pouts those gorgeous lips of hers. It feels as if only she and Dobbs are in the room; he's not asking the others if they want wine! Of course they want wine. Somehow, every moment with her seems stupidly precious, but alarm bells are ringing in his head: Gatita is clearly an easy lady to fall in love with.

"You will go?" she says.

"*Si, claro*," he retorts assertively, trying to conceal his absurd anxiety.

Agent6 bursts out laughing at his classic reply.

"Where you *gonna* go, Dobbs?"

Dobbs is feeling paranoid that either Agent6 or Gatita will pick up on his fear, which only serves to amplify his need to do it. The truth is, it's all too intense for him to sit with her in this environment; he needs a drink.

"You want some money?" Gatita asks.

"No, no!" Dobbs immediately answers, then, "I feel like I've forgotten something. What have I forgotten Swifty?"

"I don't know. A woman maybe?"

177

Dobbs chuckles at the pointedness of the comment, then peers at Gatita. The corners of her mouth rise ever so slightly, but Dobbs is not sure if it's a smile or she's simply observing his intentions. He hopes it's the former, as right now he's not sure of the latter himself. He feels transparent, like his whole process is laid bare. Does she realise how nervous he feels around her?

Leaving the building, he flags down a motor-taxi and takes off to a nearby corner store. Grabbing a couple of bottles of wine, he's back within ten minutes, feeling oddly surprised how easy it was, and a little foolish about his previous misgivings.

On his return however, he finds that there's no corkscrew and so he goes back downstairs to find one, but the only person around is an odd-looking European man, sitting out the front. He's a strange looking older gentleman, German at a guess. He looks either very well weathered or a little jaded by life. He is skinny, with a gaunt, almost calloused-looking face and very chiselled cheekbones. Catching his eye, Dobbs can see he has a cynical look about him, like he's seen it all before.

"You don't have a bottle opener on you I suppose?" he says.

"No. But they will have one over there in that house. Here, give me your wine. I will open it for you."

Dobbs doesn't know how he feels about this; it could take longer than he's anticipating and he's keen to avoid complications, but the man's holding his hand out, waiting, so after pausing for a second, he passes over the bottle.

"Sure," he says. "Thanks."

With that the man promptly takes off with the wine, leaving Dobbs standing by the road, scratching his head, thinking, 'why the fucking hell did I just do that?'

He takes a seat on one of the plastic chairs where the man was previously sitting, and settles down to wait. Half an hour passes, during which time every thought passes through Dobbs's head as to why he's just let his wine disappear. He is almost ready to jump into a motor-taxi and go and get another bottle when the man finally comes back with the wine and two plastic cups. Dobbs wasn't expecting that.

"Oh, nice one," he says, trying to hide his disappointment, and wishing he'd just stuck his thumb down into the bottle to open it instead of complicating the situation.

"Well, I suppose we should have a quick drink then," he sighs in resignation, filling the plastic cups.

He doesn't immediately tell the man he has a lady waiting upstairs, as experience tells him that if you find yourself in a situation like this, there's normally a reason. They sit quietly, and as he drinks he tries to let go of his feelings of impatience and adjust to the idea that there's no rush. It's not easy though, and he's no more than half way through his first glass before his impatience gets the better of him.

"I'll have to go in a second," he says to the man. "I have a gorgeous lady waiting upstairs."

"Don't get involved with the ladies here," the man replies, eyeing him balefully. "Most come here for the ladies and the pestilence. They just…" he pauses, staring at Dobbs with an expression of distaste that sends an involuntary shiver through him "…fuck and go. How easy it is, or should I say, how easy it all seems. But there's a price: you can't just fuck and go man."

"No-no, of course," Dobbs exclaims, reaching for his bottle wanting to get clean away from the man suddenly and then looking at the man, Dobbs lets out a slow sigh. He's another wild-eyed traveller who looks like he might have done too much of something along the way, but then again maybe not. Whatever it is, though, he appears to have become a little jaded by the passing years.

"This whole town is built on pestilence and sex," the man offers, shaking his head mournfully.

"Oh really," he says, but leaves it at that. He's thinking about Gatita, and all the other girls he's met since arriving in Iquitos. He remembers, uncomfortably, himself on the pestilence, being drawn into the sexual vortex of all the girls the night before he'd met her, and how close he was to going off with one of them.

"So what are you doing here?" he asks in a more upbeat tone, deciding to change the subject and find out why this man has crossed his path and whether he can offer any real reason why he shouldn't go with the gorgeous lady upstairs. Not that he's even planning on that, as even though his relationship seems such a mess now, the very notion tweaks his sense of loyalty to his partner.

"I'm working with a herb that cures asthma," the man immediately answers. There is something about the way he says it, as though it were rehearsed and practiced over and over, which implies this is not to be questioned but rather just a simple matter of fact.

"Oh, wow, you're a herbalist," Dobbs responds. He is just about to say he's studied Chinese herbal medicine but then he suddenly bites his tongue, thinking that opening up that avenue might prolong the conversation unnecessarily.

"Have you had some successful results treating anyone?" he asks instead.

"Yes, of course. But I'm a long way off yet."

"That's fantastic. Really fantastic. Well, you're not here for the pestilence and women then, so that's something," Dobbs offers supportively.

"Everyone's here for the pestilence and women. You have not taken any since you've been here?"

He chuckles, then says with an uncomfortable tone of dry inevitability,

"Everyone fucks and goes - or fucks and stays."

Dobbs looks down at the ground and realises that as blunt as this obnoxious German is, he does seem to have a point. Now he wonders if he really should go up and entertain Gatita or stay with the jungle program. She could be a massive distraction from what he's here for. He runs the whole thing through his head and then stops to feel the man's emotions. What he picks up is a massive sense of loneliness and he looks in his face, curious as to what the man's intentions are right now.

"Here, let me top you up man," he finally says.

Nodding at him ever so slightly, he adds more wine to the man's cup, then jumps up.

"Well, I guess I'm going to take my chances with the beautiful lady...cheers for opening the wine," He says, then takes off, leaving the man sitting there.

"Where the hell have you been? I opened the other bottle with my thumb and we've drunk the whole thing," Bolivar shouts out, an empty bottle in his hands as he re-enters.

"Not to worry, there's more," Dobbs says, putting on a mock Irish accent to hide his feelings of awkwardness to find Gatita sitting on Agent6's bed, and trying to cover his confusion over what he should do about it. There's no choice really, though; it would make Agent6 uncomfortable if he sat on the far side of the room and they were all huddled together smoking. Immediately he sits down on the bed, Gatita gives him the warmest smile and moves round to get closer to him. He immediately feels better, and somehow he knows Agent6 does too.

180

He's not quite sure what to do next, but after a moment's thought he decides that there's nothing to do really, except enjoy the night and keep breathing. Still, it's hard: his head seems like spaghetti junction with too many thoughts piling in all at the same time, leaving no space for him to just sit, and be there with his friends and this beautiful woman.

They chat for a while, then Gatita suddenly gets up and, without a word, walks out of the room; not to the toilet, but actually out of the room. There's an odd silence and a void, apart from music in the background, and Dobbs becomes aware how central she's become to the energy pattern of the gathering.

"What's this then - an interlude?" Dobbs says, looking round at everyone lost in the sudden silence.

"It's like the ice-cream break in the cinemas, isn't it? Shame they don't do that anymore: I used to love that bit. You know, the mid-film anticipation - that wondering where the story's going. And then they'd start it up again, just before where it left off so you properly felt like you hadn't missed anything. Made it feel like a proper show like," Dobbs muses.

Swifty looks over at him.

"What you doing then? You going for it?" He says in his deep, calm voice. Then he shakes his head with amusement, "Can I *kiss* you? Is that your best chat-up line?"

Dobbs drops his head in utter shame at the comment even though, secretly, he's over the moon that he'd said it.

"I didn't know what else to say. I'm not cool, calm and collected like you. You'd just take her by the hand and lead her to the bedroom, wouldn't you Swifty?"

Swifty waggles his head from side to side, like some Indian *baba* answering a query about whether a particular train is due in the next few minutes or days.

"Well, we're kind of in the bedroom already mate; you're not doing so bad!"

Dobbs shakes his hands with an embarrassed excitement.

"I feel like a little kid or something. You think I should? You think I can? I feel like a naughty little boy. I'd fall in love with her. Shit, I'm falling in love with her. She's a fucking...bombshell."

Agent6 looks as if he's going to say something but then pauses as if trying to choose his words carefully, and Dobbs immediately becomes aware of how compromised he probably feels about being piggy in the middle between the man he's pondering might be

181

having an affair with Dobbs's partner and Dobbs himself. In the end he says nothing, but his silence says more than his attempts to speak, and falls heavy as a lead weight upon Dobbs's heart.

Dobbs shakes his head in total confusion, rubbing his forehead as if to clear away the fog that feels like it's blinding him as to which path to take.

"Come on," he says, "You guys know what's going on with Ruby, don't you? I feel so out of the picture of my own fucking life."

Bolivar shakes his head.

"No. We don't. No one's spoken to her, and he hasn't laid it plain on the table either."

But Swifty and Agent6 are keeping quiet, and that bothers Dobbs.

"So why are you guys so quiet then?"

There's no immediate response but they're clearly uncomfortable.

"It's okay, you don't have to answer that. Right now I'm more scared you'll say she isn't or that you don't truly know. Truth is, right now I'm seriously fucking hoping she is. How fucked up is that? She is, isn't she?"

He pauses.

"Actually, don't tell me. No, fuck it, tell me. Oh I don't fucking know anymore. Gatita's a lady. Fucking hell!"

"Dobbs!" Swifty says like a wet flannel.

"What?"

"Your woman back home's a lady ain't she?"

Dobbs sits back and considers the comment then moves forward slightly, straightens his back and raises his shoulders, immediately becoming a gentleman.

"Yeah," he sighs, though he's wondering how that comment really helps him. "You think she could understand, given the circumstances?"

"Fuck knows," Swifty shrugs as if suddenly washing his hands of any responsibility or where that was perhaps going.

But then Agent6 suddenly bounces the ball straight back into his court,

"Go on Swifty, tell him what you told me."

Swifty suddenly goes from man to mouse as silence again consumes the moment.

"I don't know Dobbs. I don't know what I saw. Some festival, and they were closer than I kind of thought."

Dobbs wants to know more but somehow he doesn't at the same time. It somehow feels like an intrusion into their private life, plus

182

he didn't want to pressure Swifty, and in truth he didn't want that image in his mind's eye. At the end of the day, he just wanted some honesty more than anything else, but it seems Ruby wanted more of a whole lot of things Dobbs had lately been falling short of. It all felt like such a sticky mess.

"Look," sighs Dobbs eventually, "I was at a *Bob* party and he was off his tits and clutching her arm and she was a bit *twatted*, but I saw it. Just the way he held on to her and the way she was there for him. I saw it in her eyes: she's in love with him."

Bolivar, who up until now has been mostly engaged in conversation with The Brigadier suddenly weighs in.

"Look Dobbs," he calmly asserts, "What goes down in Peru stays in Peru."

Dobbs has more than a sneaking suspicion that that might not be the case though.

"I'm just looking for justification, aren't I? That's the real truth: I need justification because I haven't got the balls just to go and give and receive love without fear."

Bolivar laughs like a banshee,

"Err…no Dobbs, that's just hippy shit. You're looking for some *action* and don't tell me you're not. I've only known you for a little while now but I've never seen you like you are with her. Yeah, you're a bit of a flirt but you're not actually going there are you? None of you are. But there's something's different with this one."

The Brigadier lets out a rhythmic blast on his sax, nodding along and staring at Dobbs with his blue eyes and a look of wicked delight across his face,

"He's right Dobbsy," he says, pulling the sax away.

Agent6 is nodding whilst selecting yet another tune. Though seemingly engrossed in his iPod, he looks up and says in a slow deep tone,

"But just remember Dobbs. If you get someone like Gatita warmed up, you ain't gettin' off 'til the ride's over and she's good and done."

Now Swifty's nodding too.

"Dobbs, if you're going to pull the rip-cord, now's your last chance."

And then, just like it's all some cheesy soap opera, Gatita walks back into the room. As she walks back to the bed and sits down Bolivar looks back at Dobbs and then around the room, as if talking to no one and everyone.

183

"What goes down in Peru, stays in Peru."

Gatita glances at Bolivar then down at her lap. She seems to pause for a moment, then looks up at Dobbs, who's acutely embarrassed to think what she's made of the comment; after all, she's certainly not daft. He observes her face anxiously. On the surface she seems totally unaffected by it, but as he looks more deeply in her eyes he can see those two faces again. The super sensitive Indigena from the deepest core of the jungle, and the wild and carefree Spanish gypsy girl. One seems terrifyingly free with love and passion and the other is acutely vulnerable. Suddenly, in that moment, he knows, it's not her that's dangerous: It's him who is the dangerous one, for he is the one with all the complications. She should be the one with the cogs grinding in the baggage allowance system, not him.

He's aware that she knows everything that's going on on some level and very probably on every level. Gatita is enabling him to look at what has been happening in his own relationship that he's chosen to be blind to. He doesn't truly know if his partner is having an affair but he knows there's a lot of love between her and his friend. He knows his relationship has hit hard times and he's been blind to that too. But he also knows that if he sleeps with Gatita, which at this stage feels almost inevitable, it will bring the whole scenario to a head. Perhaps it will balance the equation – or perhaps it will break the scales. Do most people give so much thought to the prospect of having an affair, he ponders, or do they just jump in and wade through the aftermath at a later stage?

All those hours spent on *Limewire* are really paying off, as Agent6 is rocking out the tunes now. Meanwhile, Dobbs and Gatita are just lying on the bed, seemingly completely detached from the others, who are all either chatting or somehow busy. The Brigadier is playing along here and there on his Sax and seems to be holding a steady even keel.

Dobbs just doesn't know what to say. He knows that now would be a fine time to make his move but it feels like the chains of his attachment are holding him back. He feels somehow restricted yet totally transparent; embarrassed by his lurid desires as he steals a glance at her immaculately formed breasts. She's so relaxed and free that somehow he feels a little uneasy. He catches her eye and starts to say something, but is not entirely sure what will come out.

"It's funny. Staying here a month seems such a massive amount of time. But it's not, is it?" As soon as he's said it, he thinks 'what a stupid thing to say.' Then immediately after, manages to knock over the wine that he's already spent what seemed like hours first obtaining and then opening. It all just amplifies how jittery he's feeling as he cleans the mess up with an old newspaper.

She looks down at the spliff she's rolling, fumbling with grass and tobacco,

"Most people are just passing through this place. That's the way it goes I suppose."

She has tiny dimples each side of her mouth that he thought only showed when she smiles. But they mean something quite different now, though he's not sure what yet. Maybe reluctance - or was it regret, and sadness? He knows he's being almost comically careful: after all, it seems that if you like someone in this neck of the woods, and you think they like you, it seems fine to just make a move. Gatita's not a young girl; she's late twenties, perhaps even early thirties.

"I'm surprised a lady like you isn't married off."

She glances up from the spliff she's rolling and then back down.

"After my last relationship, which lasted for years, well, now, if I like someone...that's OK and I don't care..." she pauses, looking directly at him, "Even if they do have a girlfriend back home."

"No!" he says, shocked and immediately regretting the speed with which he'd reacted to her comment but grinning inwardly at his own naivety all the same.

She looks up at him calmly though.

"I mean if I was with them, properly, I might. Well I would." It was the Spanish gypsy speaking at first but that last comment, he knew, was the warm, sensitive Indigenous jungle girl: one didn't care, but the other so does. He realises that sweet, Indigenous Amazonian desperately wants something so much more substantial than what Dobbs feels he can give her, but the effects of the alcohol whirling inside of him allow him to take the comment without feeling too overwhelmed.

"Yeah, I can understand that," Dobbs nods, but the truth is, he's not quite sure what to make of it all. He would like to think he can empathise with her logic, but he's just not sure he's evolved enough to deal with it in practice. He doesn't want to take the subject further though so he decides to take a different tack.

"Do you take the pestilence?" he asks, then, kicking himself, 'why did I ask that? I really am a total twat. She wouldn't go near it in a month of Sundays.'

185

She looks up at him sharply, obviously inspecting his eyes to see if he's on the powder himself.

"I hate it. I've never done it. People are not real when they take that. You?"

'What a twat, I walked right into that,' he thinks to himself again.

"It's all cut to fuck in England, so I don't do it there but we wanted to try out the pure stuff so we had a few nights on it here. It was a blast, but I'm a *toker* more than anything really. But, you know, once in a blue moon. What I mean to say is 'never say never', I guess, but I want to be clear for the jungle juice now."

As he says it, he suddenly prays that he'll take no more on this trip, if ever in fact, as if he's honest with himself he doesn't actually enjoy it. It just makes him feel like he's having palpitations.

"It doesn't work for me really. Actually, it never really did work for me. I don't need it."

"No, I feel the same, but I don't mind if others do it. So what, I smoke," she says calmly.

Dobbs just feels like he's making excuses though, like he's in an interview for a job. Shaking his head as to where this is all going, he suddenly feels like it's all turning into a mess again. It's like his mind is just not cooperating.

'What is all this restriction that's making me be such a stupid analytical twat?' he chides himself.

He tries to shut his mouth and quiet his mind, and allow himself to just take in the vision of this gorgeous woman and enjoy it without letting his ego pore all over the experience, like some insensitive city kid trampling a patch of wild flowers in a beautiful meadow, but still the voice in his head nags him: 'Where is all this shit you're spouting coming from? What are you so scared of?'

Clenching his teeth, he just looks at her and breathes. It feels as though there's an invisible chain holding him back, so he tries to visualise that chain tying his hand back from touching her. With a little effort he manages to see it clearly in his mind's eye and then, raising his other hand, he imagines the fingers as a pair of scissors and just snips the chain. She's watching him curiously, obviously fascinated as to what he's doing and as the ties that bind him suddenly fall away. He looks into her eyes, and quite deliberately places his hand on her ankle. At his touch she pouts her lips very slightly and there are those dimples again, as the flicker of a smile appears at the corners of her eyes. But then, just as mysteriously as before, she suddenly gets up and disappears again.

186

Agent6, who has, until now, seemed otherwise preoccupied looks up at Dobbs.

"Ice-cream, Sir?" he tones, inclining his head.

Dobbs shakes his head in bewilderment.

"Do you think she does this just to give me talk-time to help me work out what the fuck I want to do? Did you hear what she just said?"

Agent6 shakes his head.

"No. What did she say?"

"Man. I just don't know why this is all so intense. You didn't hear that? When she said she doesn't care about other partners?"

"That's good isn't it?" Agent6 half frowns.

"When I was a kid, my mum took me to a pantomime and at some point in the performance, one of the cast offered out lollipops and literally looked right at me, beckoning me to come and take one. I was close to the stage and I so wanted to just run down and grab a lolly but it was like I was chained to that seat. My mum was, like, 'Go on. Get a lolly!'But I was terrified.

"All the other kids were the same, apart from one kid, who got up and took first one lolly and then, seeing that no one else was taking one, he went back over and over again. Every time he took another lolly, I felt so much anger towards that kid - for taking *my* lolly. But it was all my own fault: I just didn't have the balls to get up and take the lolly myself."

Bolivar shakes his head.

"Your mind, Dobbs! How does it work?"

Just then Gatita waltzes back in and sparks up the spliff she'd rolled earlier. She stares at Dobbs a little quizically and this time he doesn't wait around, but just lifts his hand, puts it on her ankle and runs it up to her knee.

As if on cue, everyone just gets up and walks out the room, but just before the door closes Agent6 pokes his head back through.

"Dobbs!" he says, speaking like the true Yorkshire man he is, "Looks like we're sleeping next door...*pull* bed away from the wall, mate." Then he shoots Gatita a naughty little wink and pulls the door closed. Now it's just him, and Gatita.

Suddenly, he feels a little overwhelmed.

Honesty

Unlike Dobbs, Gatita doesn't so much as flinch with embarrassment to be so utterly alone with him and all the thoughts of all that could suddenly occur in this all so powerful moment. He's the little boy staring at the lady with the lollipops, so excited to be alone with her at last. Certainly it's sexual - her presence makes his body tremble - but there's also something more. She's like a whirlpool, completely relaxed, but at the same time drawing him in.

He feels transparent in front of her, and weirdly compromised. Actually, he doesn't want sex right now, or at least he wants it, but he's afraid it will just complicate things. What he really wants is to make love with her - which is arguably the same thing, and arguably a world apart. Whatever it is, he's nervous, and a little uncomfortable, and somehow her tranquillity just amplifies his own anxiety a thousand-fold.

"You remind me a bit of my mum, you know."

She looks away from him as soon as he's spoken the words, and suddenly he has to have a quiet word with himself again.

'Why did I just say that?' he thinks to himself: 'women hate being compared to mums: especially ones being hit on!'

But then he has to stop for a moment and ponder; actually, who was hitting on whom? It all just felt so complicated.

'I'm getting myself in trouble,' he thinks. But, when he breathes, all he can feel is the beautiful undercurrent of just being here with her. He takes another breath and tries to relax his body by lying out over the bed, though not in her space. She's just sitting in lotus position, with her back very straight, and now he's not quite sure if her unnatural calmness is helping him keep it together or making him fall apart.

"She used to have her hair just like you when she was much younger," he persists, somehow following a hunch despite his mental misgivings about the subject matter. Still she says nothing as Dobbs deliberates: a slap round the face would probably have gone down better than all this stuff about his mum. It's not that he's really trying to work it anyway at present, but cogs are turning and, he hopes, possibly something will click into place.

"Not that it's that which stands out," he adds. "She's a medium - a channel. You know of this?"

188

"Your mother's a channel?" Click! Her response is one of almost shock, like she wasn't expecting that.

"My father too. Well, my stepfather. But my real father is too, actually. He taps into something profoundly wise, but he can't differentiate between himself and his guide - a bit like me. Our heads are like spaghetti junction, and we tag them all as Self, which is really just a central hub. I'm never quite sure what the hell's going on up there - or down there for that matter, if there is a down there. I used to have a take on it, but recently it's been upping the ante, and now it's very close to blowing my mind. It's like this big other thing that I have always known about is now reaching into my life. Well, like it has me by the fucking balls actually." He stops to consider the thought.

"So you know about channelling then?"

"Of course I know about channelling. This is Iquitos: it should probably be me asking you!"

Dobbs looks at her with a new curiosity now.

"Yeah, I suppose so. I hadn't thought of Iquitos like that. That's quite exciting. It is the kind of shamanic central hub of the world I suppose."

He suddenly realises he's been distracted from his mental process, and finds himself right back in the here-and-now. Looking in her eyes, he knows he could touch her if he wanted to, but still he's aware of his baggage and the fact that his feelings are not clear. 'Why do I complicate things so?' he wonders.

"You know, I'm very attracted to you Gatita - ridiculously actually - but there's something else going on - something quite overwhelming about who you are, or what you represent. I don't quite understand what's happening between us, but it's very strong and I'm a little afraid of it - which is probably why I've been acting like such a twat.

"You know, when I first saw you in that bar the energy was quite base, but you were completely outside of it. You just sat there, staring out over the water, on another frequency altogether. You don't even pay lip service to that vibe, do you?"

"You say that: my mother thinks I'm a drug addict because I smoke grass."

"Really?"

"She just doesn't understand…how things are here."

"How are they – things here?"

189

"Things are slow - and fast; some things never change..." She looks at him, "...and others are here today and gone tomorrow."

She's smiling now, and those dimples are clearer. Maybe they're the dimples of a deeper knowing, Dobbs thinks. There's an inevitable silence as the implications of what she's just said sink in, but somehow it's a feeling of comfort that she could speak her truth, as well as the fact that she had described the likely trajectory of their meeting.

"I think maybe I channelled once," she says, moving on. "I took a *collectivo* and at the end of the journey the driver begged for more money, saying his wife was sick and he needed to pay the hospital. I gave him a hard time because I felt he was lying to me, trying to manipulate me with this 'poor-me' story, so in the end I told him to take me to the hospital and show me his wife if he really needed the money." She pauses for a moment, "But sure enough, we go, and I can feel he's very uncomfortable, because he knew I didn't believe his story. So anyway, we drive to this hospital and he tells me to wait while he goes inside, but then he just disappeared up the stairs and I never saw him again.

"So after a while I decide to go and look for him. I walk up the same stairs he went up and there's a doctor standing there. He walks over to me, and goes to ask me who I'm looking for or whatever, and just like that, suddenly I'm floating, or maybe sitting, in these beautiful clouds up in blue sky and I'm just up there, hidden from the world below by this cloud I'm sitting on and then, just as suddenly, I'm back, staring at this doctor, feeling like something very strange just happened to me."

Dobbs is not shocked by the story; he's been surrounded by channels most of his life, and that sort of thing isn't particularly unusual to him.

"That's where my mum goes when she channels sometimes; up into the clouds," he says. "In fact, she met her ex-partner up there as well, right after the funeral."

He looks deeper into her dark brown eyes, losing himself in the bliss he feels with her,

"So what did the doctor say when you came back? Did you channel for him?"

"Well, I said sorry because something strange had happened to me and he just looked at me and didn't say anything. He was just staring at me."

"What did you say to him, did he tell you?"

"No. He just said: 'You just became my guide.' And that was all."

"Wow! And you don't drink *Ayahuasca* anymore?"

"Well, not for a long time, but 'never say never', right?"

"You going to come out with us and drink?"

"If I'm invited, maybe."

He nods at her.

"Oh, you're more than invited Gatita. I'm almost intent on dragging you off there against your will. You've got something else going on and I'm not sure what it is but it's very special."

The sharing of these intimate stories has brought them closer, but part of him still feels he's deceiving her by hiding the fact that he's in a relationship back home. He feels cruel, opening his heart to her like this, and allowing her to open her heart to him, and suddenly the silence is overbearing. Dobbs knows he has to come clean.

"Look Gatita, there's something I've got to tell you … I've got a girlfriend."

Immediately, he feels like a total idiot, ruining the moment and destroying everything. 'What a twat,' he thinks, 'she didn't want to hear that.'

"Why did you tell me that?" she says, hurt in her voice. "Does it make you feel better to tell me you have a girlfriend somewhere else? Does that relieve your guilt?"

"Would you really rather have not known? Is that fair on you?"

"Would you want to know if I had a boyfriend?"

"I haven't asked you. Should I?"

"Would you care if I had?"

"I just feel I have to be honest with you, that's all. I have something going on elsewhere and I don't want to fuck you about or play games with you. Even if that means you walk out now, I'd still have no regrets."

"So you do feel better?" she says with distaste.

He ponders on that question, looks at her then looks away.

"Yeah. I guess I do. I feel honest."

"Do you love her?"

"Yeah."

"Does she love you?"

"She thinks I'm cuckoo. And she's having an affair with one of my mates; I guess I should have laid off the laughing gas."

"Look, sorry Gatita. I'm honest, that's all. No illusion, and no lies. That doesn't necessarily mean I'm not going to fall in love with

191

you, throw in the towel and elope to the jungles of Northern Peru with you or something mad…It just means you know what's going on… and it doesn't mean this hand will have any difficulty getting under that sexy little top of yours either…It just means you know where I'm at."

There's a moment's silence, and he places his hand on her knee and moves it up towards her thighs, still looking at her face.

"Look, all I'm saying is this: given the choice, would you prefer to live the truth or live a lie? The truth for me is that my girlfriend is having an affair with someone else, and meeting you has suddenly made me celebrate that rather than grieve the loss of her. But I can't do anything with you unless you're aware that, technically, I'm still in a relationship. Maybe that's all in the past now; I just don't know. But I don't want to lure you in on any false pretences. I want to do everything I can with you, but I also want to be absolutely honest. Is that possible?"

Gatita just sits there, looking like she's in a state of shock, but despite the fact that Dobbs feels he's probably blown his chances, strangely he still feels better about things - lighter. She's looking at him like he's a total alien.

"Does it really change that much to have a bit of honesty?" he says, spreading his hands and giving her his most winning smile.

She leans back, resting on her arms, and puts her legs out straight. Somehow she seems more relaxed now too, and to Dobbs's complete surprise she just smiles,

"No."

"I could live a lie with you and tell you that there's no one else but it would be a lie, a deception. And I certainly wasn't expecting to find you!"

They both seem lighter now, though Dobbs still feels he's blown it on some level. Gatita just looks at him, and smiles.

"Laughing gas? You took too much laughing gas?"

"Yeah! You know; Nitrous? 'Hippy crack' they call it at the festivals. It's the stuff they give to women in labour."

"You *lost it* on that?"

"Well, I had a vision and saw some things that I kind of didn't want to see – about eighteen months ago. It took me nearly six months to get over the trauma of it all."

"Like what?"

She seems relieved that the subject has finally moved away from his mother and girlfriend, so Dobbs presses on with his story.

192

"It was all very short, and it seemed like it wasn't so much in my head, but more in my heart. It's kind of still there now."

He's a little afraid to elaborate however; if everything he's said so far hasn't blown it, drug induced insanity probably would.

"Is that why you came here to drink?" she says, a soft smile playing around her lips.

"I want to understand what I saw on that day - what I felt. It was a feeling, and a whole lot of shit, all focussing around the most painful sadness you can ever imagine. A life-shattering sadness. I didn't understand it at the beginning because it was so crushingly intense, like I'd been destroyed. I just sat there, crying my eyes out, with all my mates thinking I was just being a total twat, and literally the first thing I said when I'd stopped crying and managed to breathe, with the pain weighing right here in my solar plexus, was: 'All the banks are about to go down.'

"Well, that was the first part of what I saw, but it was absolutely nothing to the second, which was the *effect* of the banks going down, and what they're really orchestrating, and the feeling of loss experienced by the people. But that was utterly inconsequential to what happened last. The first was a sense of confused, almost exciting loss and bewilderment to the prospect of change, which compared to the next was the reality of that kicking in I think; like an economic tsunami because of the way it sweeps to rapidly. It's a feeling of utter loss and desperation and then BOOOM!!! It was like a dagger being plunged into the Earth itself. It was only a flash of pain but it felt like the Titanic had just fallen on me. Whatever that was, it made everything else look like barely incidental. It was almost like one was a catalyst for another. And yet the feeling I was left with, the feeling that, in that moment, there wasn't a being on this Earth that did not know what had just happened. And it wasn't surprise, or even disappointment, It was…"

Gatita doesn't speak, but she's waiting to hear.

"…shame. And the irrevocable feeling of utter loss. Total and complete destruction and only loss remained. I mean, it kind of looked like a war starting after the bank crisis but I can't imagine what, in war, could cause what I saw. It was…geological, I think. It was all happening in my heart. Like, when we saw those kids last night begging. We don't have to carry the emotional weight of that. We can see and we know it's wrong and feel it's wrong but it's not like seeing your own kids in that state. Imagine turning you head and seeing your own child right there. You couldn't emotionally disengage from that. This is like that... like I was witnessing my own child suffer. It had bypassed all my filters. It wasn't a *head-fuck* it was a *heart-fuck*, like a knife going right through me. It was like I died there and then. For my girlfriend back home, I'd gone mad. And I suppose I had; because after that big blast of Nitrous, everything changed.

"Funny, I never thought I'd touch psychedelics again and then, about six weeks ago, Agent6 asked me if I wanted to do a ceremony at his place. It was being organised by a woman - a Peruvian woman actually - who lives in England mostly now, another *curandero*. It was a birthday present, so I felt a bit nervous to say 'no' but I had to: it had taken me a year to get over that blast of Nitrous. I couldn't risk going back into that pain. But then, two days before the ceremony, I had a dream.

"I was cuddling a cat, a huge cat, like a leopard. It had its back to me, spooning into me as I lay there. I had one arm under the animal and the other kind of going over the top and in my hands I clutched a dagger and I was, like, 'No, I don't want to do this!'But I had to, and I plunged the dagger into the animal's heart, but the blade went straight into my own heart and I woke, right back in that terrible pain I'd felt when I had the blast of nitrous. Whatever it was, it had me by the fucking bollocks. The next day, I phoned Agent6 and told him what had happened and that I'd changed my mind and I wanted to drink.

"So there I was in this ceremony. I was so scared, and the *curandero* this Peruvian woman works with asked everyone to offer some insight into their intentions. Many of them waffled on a bit, which is okay, as it helps to hear different peoples intentions, especially if there's genuine conviction, but I just said: 'OK, if the shit has to hit the fan and, we have to go through this change, what will it look like afterwards, and will it all be worth it in the end?' That's all I wanted to know."

"And what happened? What did you see?"

"Oh Gatita, it was so beautiful! It was kind of like I was looking down from above, and all these kids were playing in these fields. They were dressed in old fashioned English sort of clothes, like Victorian or perhaps even like the Indigenous wear in Guatemala - rich fabric and so many colours. And ribbons trailing off from some of the girls, just blowing in the wind as they played. I could see for miles and miles; beautiful rolling hills, with all the hedgerows intact, natures own wildlife corridors stretching off as far as the eye could see. They'd all been put back and it was green and lush like you can't imagine and then I heard a voice say: 'And you'll have visitors.'

"And I looked, and I saw this huge, walking tree. It was like in the form of a man, only huge, and his face was so wise and beautiful and he trod so carefully, so as not to step on any of the kids running along with him, trying to keep up as he stepped clean over the hedgerows. He was easily thirty meters high, and magnificent. The kids couldn't follow and had to run up the hedgerow, out of my field of vision, as even with his slow steps he was moving at massive speed."

"And then, of all things, a bike just bombs past me and I realise that I'm no longer just floating in the sky but looking from a nearby hill. I only get a glimpse of the rider and his bike as he speeds past, but I can see the gears on the back wheel and it's a really complex little assembly, and just then I hear the word: 'Technology.' And I realised then that we're not going backwards with the transition we're going to go through."

He moves closer to Gatita,

"So then Agent6 says, 'why don't you drink again?' So I did; a couple of days later I drank again, and it was just as mad. I saw this rhinoceros-like thing. A massive creature that stands like a man: not on all fours, but literally like a man. I can't see its head, just its massive body, and it has these two huge fat spiked horns coming from its elbows."

"I'm scared, so I put a golden ring around me and it just makes it brighter and I feel its beautiful presence. It's kind of to my left, and it turns right round so it has its back to me and then sits on me. I'm like, 'fucking hell, what the fuck?' But it doesn't sit *on* me. It sits *in* me, and suddenly I've got rhinoceros skin and theses two spiked horns coming from my elbows. See 'em?" And he shows his elbows to Gatita, who chuckles.

"I see something," she says with a smile.

"Yeah, a fucking mad man. But just when the vision was ending and I was just falling into bliss, I saw myself walking down this country track in a tunnel of trees and there's my cat, my huge leopard, just walking slightly ahead of me, looking mighty fine. So, you see, I didn't kill her after all; the cat's cool. It was in that moment that I knew I had to come back here to Iquitos, the only place I know that really lays it all bare. So here I am with the notion that Shakespeare has something to do with the whole thing for some obscure reason, and that kissing you has something to do with my mission here as well."

Gatita doesn't respond to that. She just stares, expressionless.

"And now you're writing a book."

"Well, I haven't found a story yet, and I haven't written a word either. Maybe you're my story Gatita. Would you like to be in a story? I don't know if you have much choice one way or the other."

"What sort of story?"

"Well, I don't know. But whatever it is, I've decided I have to live every part of it. Where do you reckon this chapter should go? I know where I'd like it to have gone, when I'm finally sitting at my computer, reminiscing about what happened from now until I leave you tomorrow morning. What d'you reckon Gatita, can I have that kiss you promised me, or what?"

She looks at him with a passion bordering on anger, almost like she wants to rip his head clean off, but in contradiction her lips are fending off a smile.

"Yes," she purrs, "You can have your kiss now."

Dobbs gestures her to come to him, but she doesn't budge. Her form is perfect, her eyes dark as night and mysterious as the deepest depths of the jungle - all except a twinkle, like diamonds glistening, or a distant world, sparkling far off in the inky blackness of space. Slowly, she shakes her head.

"No. You come here if you want your kiss. You want your story... come and get it."

She pouts her lips seductively and arches her spine, leaning even further back so that her breasts seem even more pert and her nipples more prominent beneath the thin fabric of her tight-fitting top. Everything about her is drawing him closer and he takes the greatest pleasure in undressing her with his eyes, piece by piece, touching her with his gaze alone.

Tearing off his top, he pulls her closer. He's still holding off from kissing those gorgeous lips as he's already in a state of bliss, but the tension is becoming unbearable. Pulling up her top to bare her breasts, he draws her close until her nipples are touching his chest, then runs his hands through her hair and down her spine, caressing her satin-smooth skin as he senses her energy rising in wave after wave, until their souls feel like they're merging and all the doubt and worry just dissipate like mist on a sunny morning. Now, at last, there is only him and her and the noise in his head has just dissipated. It's more than merely sexual. Still he holds back from the brink, savouring her sweetness as he runs the tip of his tongue across her lips, which she has slightly drawn apart until finally he can bear it no longer. Their lips meet, and the pledge is sealed, gently at first, then ravenously.

***

'Bang-bang-bang' goes the door, rousing Dobbs rudely from his reverie. His night with Gatita is over and it's time to get the show on the road.

"Come on Dobbs, we're going," Agent6 is calling through the keyhole.

He's barely slept a wink; they'd made love all night long, and it seems no more than half an hour ago since they fell asleep in each other's arms, but he's awake immediately.

"I'll meet you down at Belen Market," he shouts out.

"Ok, but we ain't waiting about Dobbs."

"I'll be there!" he shouts back and then slumps back down to snuggle Gatita, who's lying next to him, half awake.

"Shame, I feel so rough; I just want to lie here with you and curl up in a ball until the end of time, kissing those gorgeous lips of yours…" and he kisses her, "…over and over and over again."

His head is a curious cocktail of starry-eyed honeydew wonder, hangover and sleep deprivation but it doesn't stop him making love to her one more time before he crawls out of bed and drags himself into the shower.

He still needs to pack, but it looks like this trip to the jungle is going to be a rather under-equipped mission, as he's not really prepared anything apart from a solar charger for his phone. The only really important item he's missing, he thinks, is a good mosquito net. Other than that, he's narrowing it down to the three primary essentials, namely food, water and spliff.

Last time he went into the jungle all he had was a torch, mozzie net and some spices to add a little flavour to the otherwise very basic fish dishes. The memory that stuck most from that trip was of searching for his torch one evening when, preoccupied with getting all the nets and hammocks up, time seemed to have lapsed and, quite suddenly, it was pitch black beneath the shadow of the forest. Having found it and switched it on, by chance he'd shone it on the ground next to the leg of the girl who was travelling with him and there in the spotlight, just inches away and slowly moving closer, was a massive tarantula. The most perplexing thing about it wasn't the spider though, but the girl's reaction: she'd just sat there, motionless, until Dobbs told her that now might be a good time to think about getting up or something.

'Torch; shit, I'm going to need one of those,' Dobbs makes a mental note with a shudder.

Emerging from the shower, he finds Gatita standing there in just her knickers and top. He pulls her close and lifts her top, but she pushes away from him, exposing her gorgeous breasts in the process. She makes no attempt to cover herself however, and he slides his hands up from her waist, cupping the soft flesh and thumbing her nipples to hardness.

She inspects his face, as if scrutinizing every part of his intentions, then smiles.

"You'll wear them out," she says eventually.

"Now that's something I'd like to try," he replies, grinning wolfishly and pulling her closer. At first she offers a little playful resistance but then she succumbs, allowing him to lose himself once more in her hot, sweet, salty taste.

"So Belen's where I've got to go and meet them is it?" he says trying to pull his head back down from the cloud of soft sensual affection it's in danger of floating away on.

Gatita just nods.

"So I guess I can just get everything there and not worry about a thing ... Keep it nice and simple, ah?"

He pulls her close again, running his fingers through her damp, dark hair, "You know they'll take ages getting ready. I'm in no rush."

"Depends what you need for the jungle," she says, breaking away. "I'm going to take a shower. You should leave with them. If I stay here now I'll be late for work and you'll be no good to anybody - and they probably need your help."

"'Help' is what? *Olvidar*, right."

"No."

"No, that's 'forget'."

"Help is '*ayudar*'. It's funny that you remember 'forget', and forget 'help'," she quips.

Dobbs ponders that one for a moment.

"That's the story of my life!" he says eventually.

"Something inside tells me that meeting you is a bit of a blessing."

He pulls her close again, keen to lose himself in the intoxicating scent of her moist hair mingled with the soft morning breeze

198

blowing in from the Amazon, which, with the first, shimmering light of dawn is slowly emerging from the darkness. She pushes him away again, but leaves her hand resting on his heart as she fixes him with a look which is at once both infinitely compassionate, yet deadly serious.

"Go," she says. "Go to the jungle...and find your book."

Belen Market

Separating from Gatita is harder than Dobbs could have believed, even though she's virtually kicking him out of his own room; he knows they won't set sail for ages yet, and given the choice he would've preferred to just lose himself in her sweet embrace for the next few hours, drink a litre of water and then perhaps take a valium when they finally set sail and just shut down for a while. All this passion has kind of blown him open and all his systems are approaching overload. Sleep is all he craves now, to be spooned up next to her, stroking her silky soft skin and basking in the warmth of her wild Latin love.

That reality soon disappears however, and suddenly he's bombing along in another motor-taxi back to Juan's. Sat next to Bolivar, he's not feeling on form at all, like he might be fighting something or maybe just didn't drink enough water and properly flush his system. He's dehydrated, and he can feel his liver's inflamed.

Within no time they've arrived at Juan's to find him looking under the bonnet of a big American pickup, and Dobbs catches his eye as he walks up the dirt track. Glancing under the bonnet, he is surprised to see a Nissan six-pot instead of the big-block Chevi lump he would have expected. He nods at the engine approvingly.

"Nissan? *Que bueno!*"

Juan just nods whilst calmly raising his brows and then looks at the mechanic, who has the distributor in his hands and HT cables all over the place.

"*Uno, cinco, tres, seis, dos, quatro. Corretamente?*"

"*Si!*"

They both chuckle, not so much because he knows the firing order of a six-pot – he is a trained motor mechanic after all - it's just that counting to six represents a marked improvement in his Spanish.

In fact he can now count to eight and above, but he still wouldn't have had a clue of the firing order of the original eight-pot General Motors engine he was expecting to see. Dobbs had always considered that to be a very nasty piece of junk - a bit like General Motors' share value, although since that's one of the main leverages on the US petrodollar hegemony it will probably muddle through and come out wearing diamonds and pearls.

As far as he can see, GM are solely intent on designing engines with twice as many moving parts as the average four-pot in most every other car around the globe so that they need double the amount of maintenance. Twice the parts, double the odds of failure, vastly inefficient fuel consumption and then all stuck onto an automatic gearbox just to squeeze out a little more inefficiency.

Chevi-fans will no doubt disagree and wax lyrical about the fat sound of their beloved gas-guzzlers, but the real truth is, General Motors are just making toxic sound boxes.

Returning from his musings, to look around, Dobbs can see the whole front yard is a commotion of people running about, dragging bags, chainsaws and all sorts into the back of the pickup and Carlos's smaller van, which is packed to the brim also.

Dobbs looks over at Bolivar.

"How big *is* this boat?"

Bolivar brushes the comment off, and he is none too interested in the pickup's motor either. They're both a bit hanging.

"You're looking a bit like I feel Bolivar," Dobbs observes.

"You're the cat that got the cream," Bolivar says, hiding behind his sunglasses. He is about to add something else, but nose dives into a yawn instead.

They both know they should be looking lively and hobnobbing with the others to help keep the motivation up, but they're not at all with the program today and just stand there with arms dangling, like reluctant school kids.

"Ahhh, I feel wiped out: I might be the cat that got the cream but I didn't get any sleep. I'm just going to curl up in a ball and crash as soon as we got on that boat."

"Yeah - if you can find any bloody room to curl up," Bolivar states over another yawn.

Juan's wife has put some boiled eggs, bread and coffee out for everyone, which definitely helps a bit, but Dobbs is still struggling to make a connection with the group.

The 'Westerners' - a bit of a misnomer really, as they're all either Northerners or Easterners - all seem university types. Academics are always fascinated by *Ayahuasca* as it's not considered a 'recreational drug', like acid or MDMA. It only really works in ceremony and is considered a medicine as it facilitates lucid dreaming. It contains a similar chemical to that excreted by the pineal gland, or 'third eye', which stimulates the *rapid eye movement* state of dreaming sleep. Personally, Dobbs considers

201

dreaming to be the Creator's - Whoever or Whatever that really is - own means of genetic update: Universal Mind's calibration facility.

All the students look a little closed to Dobbs although, half-cut as they are from the previous nights antics, he and Bolivar do probably look like the average recreational user, to be given a wide birth. No matter; academics always rub him up the wrong way anyway. Not that he wants to generalise, but he feels they tend to get uncomfortably sensible at the first sign of adventure and should perhaps spend less time intellectualising about life and more just getting down to the wild business of living it.

Bolivar looks a bit more on the case after coffee and walks out to the back yard to find Dobbs sitting slumped on the concrete perimeter track at the back of the house.

"Did you have coffee?" he asks.

"Yeah, but it hasn't done anything," Dobbs says, resting his head on his knees.

"Thought you had to spend a good few years with a woman before this happens, Dobbs."

"I've got what my old man would call a liver head. I think I must have a liver the size of a pea. Some alcohol it can handle just fine, but what we drank last night? Fucking hell, maybe I'm just dehydrated. It's like my eyes are being pushed out from their sockets. Don't get me wrong man; I'm on cloud nine, and Gatita's lovely, but I've got a bastard headache pounding behind my eyes."

Bolivar's got a smile on his face.

"Don't start bragging Dobbs."

Dobbs lifts his head, squinting at Bolivar to restrict the unfeasibly bright rays of sunlight breaking through the trees overhanging the back yard.

"It's the only thing that's making me feel better, although I think that a judicious bowel movement might be wise before I get on that boat."

"Nice, good luck with that."

It looks like Dobbs's dump will have to wait however, as all of a sudden there's an exodus and everyone squeezes into Carlos's van or the back of the pickup to weave their way back through all the chaos and traffic of the city to Belen.

The port is exactly how Dobbs remembers it, though just the scent as they approach is enough to bring back visions of the place: river air, diesel smoke, dried fish and the tang of burning charcoal. An almost audible hum of activity seems to arise from the chaotic tangle of wooden shacks made of higgledy-piggledy odd sections of dark timber and corrugated iron food halls.

Some dwellings are very large, with rough-looking tables and benches outside, and others just little shacks. Most of the occupants seem to be traders, although there are many others just selling their wares from simple carts. The constructions closest to the river are standing on stilts and everything is curved and twisted due to the endless subsidence of the supporting posts sinking into the river bed. In between a network of gangways and planks leads from one to another, like a rickety wooden spider's web. The whole market, though not especially overcrowded at any particular point, is still absolutely full of people coming and going, and lots of long, narrow hulled wooden fishing boats, many with thatched or corrugated roofs are all crammed together in what looks like one big floating mat of vessels.

Most of the fisherman have long-since unloaded their catch and are busy mending their nets or getting on with other tasks. There's something timeless about the scene, and at first glance, only the *pecki-peckies* on the back of the boats and the jeans and old worn-out T-shirts the locals wear offers any indication as to the current era. There's a happy, self-sufficient feeling of lots of individuals making their living about the place: a proper community.

Big business would happily come here and wipe this out in a few short moments given the opportunity, Dobbs has no doubt, although the Indigenous would be hard to undercut, so perhaps it would survive. Undercutting is the fundamental principle of big business - before it ups the prices and forces legislation upon its competitors that they can never afford to uphold. Monopolise the business, strangle the competition, and finally finish the job by blaming the effects of the downturn on the community itself, thus manufacturing more reasons to enforce further legislation and tighten the stranglehold in an ever-tightening vicious circle.

The corporate disease of big profit is the very nemesis of the Indigenous life style, and the Amazon at large, but the corporations are eyeing up the candy and licking their lips, and it seems the only way to fend off such an attack by piratical capitalism is for the Indigenous to have virtually nothing. But even with nothing else to take there is always the land and its resources. Oh, and their lives.

All around the market, stallholders are barbequing and frying all sorts of different fish, crocodile and other even odder forms of life on small charcoal fires. Dobbs doesn't know if he should be fascinated or repulsed: one of the vendors is cooking what appear to be huge, brown maggoty things that look like the most unappetising meal imaginable. His reaction to the sight makes the family running the stall giggle.

At first he is surprised at how little rubbish is about, but then he notices that the food is all served on plates made of leaves. It all seems so independent and self-sufficient. In Britain this kind of life has been all-but banned, as it would damage corporate profit. Health and Safety would have this place closed down in a week, but to Dobbs it's such an incredibly beautiful scene of real community that, even though he is still feeling a bit green about the gills, he's totally enthralled by it.

It's not just food stalls though. There's everything one might need for an expedition into the jungle: lots of hardware, pots and pans, knives, and fishing tackle. Dobbs stops to inspect one of the fishing hooks as he can't see any hole through which to thread the line. He points a finger at the top of the hook with a questioning frown and the old lady running the stall, who boasts just one front tooth, squawks with laughter. She takes the hook and wraps the end of a piece of fishing cord round it like a hangman's noose, which binds tighter the more it's weighted. It's simple but very clever, and he takes a little selection of hooks and line for a spot of fishing when he's out on the river.

Some of the slightly bigger shops running down each side of the street leading into Belen offer bigger selections of hardware supplies and there's many tiny dining areas, as well as some very open and spacious ones like those on stilts close to the river. Everything's cheap, too, as it caters for the simple lives of the Indigenous; to them this *is* the big city.

At last, having traversed the market, they walk right down to the waterfront and there she is, the gorgeous and most illustrious *Christina*. She's beautiful; a simple and traditional fishing boat, her hull all handcrafted timber with a full thatched roof on top. She looks like she's sailed straight out of *The African Queen*, and Dobbs half expects to see Humphrey Bogart sitting in the back, smoking a fat, sweaty cigar.

The blue paint that once covered her has long since weathered away from its last overcoat and all the bare internal timber and rough cut hardwood uprights supporting the roof have darkened almost to black. The dirt and grime from what, no doubt, must be

204

thousand of pairs of hands and feet clambering over her throughout the years has left a deep, polished sheen, nowhere more so than on the gunwale running around the edge of the hull, which is really just rough-sawn planking, and serves as bench seating.

Though old and very traditional, she is surprisingly slender, almost like a stretched version of an old Fifties speed boat. From the bow, which sits high out of the water and has a tiny forecastle on it, the line of the hull sweeps down to a stern so low it is almost level with the water, giving the somewhat unnerving impression that one tiny wave could sink her. In reality, however her hull ends almost three feet short of the tiny square stern deck where the pecki-pecki is mounted, perfectly aligned to the top of the rear gunwale and extending out over the stern.

She looks like a floating fairytale, and as they clamber across a weave of similar bobbing fishing boats to board her, Dobbs is hit by an intoxicating aroma is of old rope, fish and diesel mixed with the scent of damp canvas. Though pungent, it is a savoury delight for the senses, and he fills his lungs. To him it seems one of the most romantic smells in the Universe.

Stepping into the boat, Dobbs can't help contemplating The Brigadier's refusal to come. No one's paying his room rent at the moment and he's got no cash himself though, so as far as Dobbs can see it's just a matter of time before he realises this is his only option. The energy between The Brigadier and Agent6 is not very productive at the moment though, and after that scene on the rooftop in Lima, Dobbs is not going to budge on his stance either. The Brigadier knows he went too far, even though he barely remembers any of it. Perhaps that's not surprising, as he really wasn't himself that night, but as far as Dobbs is concerned he's still responsible for the choice of whether to open the door to whatever that entity is or not; if we give our car keys away to a complete stranger, then we only have ourselves to blame if the car gets totalled. He's just not willing to make the change yet, and though Agent6 blanking him clearly hurts him deeply, Dobbs thinks he needs that tough love to move him forward.

His head is pounding as he drags his load onto the boat, and everything seems such hard work, but he sits down on one of the benches running down her breadth and tries to consciously relax his senses and soak up the vibe. his olfactory sense seem the easiest route to the optimum feel good potential, cramming in the most information for the absolute least exertion of energy and so

205

now, propping himself up on one of the supporting beams of the roof, he closes his eyes, and savours the intoxicating cocktails of aromas. There's the freshness of the air coming in over the Amazon and the smell of the market, the dampness in the hull, the fuel, the charcoal, the dung from the cattle and - hangover or not - that old smell of imminent adventure is back. He sits in the feeling of it all, bathing in it, feeling the cooling breeze and the bright sunshine beaming down on him.

Quite naturally, he begins to differentiate sounds; the comforting clatter of all the work that's going on about him, and, the complex symphony of little squeaks and groans of the boat gently rising and falling as the work crew load up all their kit. Now, opening his eyes, he checks them out. They're all Indigenous, and none of them look like big men really, especially with their baggy T-shits and loose fitting jeans and wellies, nearly all of which are folded over at the top to stop them chafing. Their hands look strong and calloused, telling a story of hard work, like their strong shoulders.

Somehow being half cut seems like an advantage, because he's normally Mr Social and for once it's good to have an excuse not to have to talk to anyone. He knows first impressions count though, and as he sits there silently massaging his furrowed brow he's aware the first impression he's projecting is of a lazy, hung-over, possibly obnoxious Englishman.

Bolivar offers some motivation.

"Come on Dobbs, let's go and get some supplies and then you can roll up into a ball and sleep."

There's still no sign of Swifty or Agent6, who've gone off to get tools and various other odds and ends. Dobbs can't help thinking it was obvious before they started that all that was going to take ages, and could have been balanced with far more important cuddles, kisses and sleep.

Just then the kitchen crew turn up, and as everyone and everything gets loaded into the old boat, questions start being raised as to if there is enough room. She's a big boat really - a good five metres or so long – but she's not much more than a metre wide, and all the activity and moving about is too much for Dobbs in his fragile head state. Squeezing himself into a little space near where Carlos is sitting patiently awaiting departure, he squints at the American through half-closed eyes,

"You're not looking quite set for an expedition into the jungle," Carlos says.

"To be fair, I'm not feeling like an expedition into the jungle either. It'll pass, though," Dobbs says in the most upbeat tone he can muster. Then, changing the subject, "Would you still have wanted to come if The Brigadier had come along?"

Carlos thinks to himself for a moment.

"Yeah, I think so," he says eventually. "My motivations shouldn't be his problem. And if they are…well, the Amazon's a big place."

"If he feels he's losing control of a project he panics and I think that's what he was nervous about when he met you out here last time. He seems to be losing control of himself more than anything else at the moment, though."

They sit quietly for some time, and Dobbs nearly falls asleep. Well, not sleep but disengagement from the world. It's a stupidly bright day and he's got no shades. His eyes feel like they're being burned out of their sockets.

"Can I get a fag off you Bolivar?"

"For fuck's sake. We haven't even got to the jungle and you're nicking my fags."

Dobbs ignores the comment and decides to make an introduction to the lady who will be running the kitchen.

"Hey, mucho gusto Majorie."

The woman doesn't speak but just beams a radiant smile, and puts her arm round her daughter, who's huddled up next to her, observing the foreigners.

Over two hours goes by and still there's no word from the boys. Dobbs knows it's pointless ringing them though, as they're the only ones in a hurry.

Eventually they arrive, huffing and puffing at the head of a small army of porters. Agent6 is wearing thin, green hessian army pants which are so worn and ripped they look as though they've endured some proper work. Dobbs can't help but wonder if they actually belong to him, as he finds it hard to believe Agent6 has actually done the work that it looks like those things have seen. He's more of a delegator than a labourer, although when there's proper work to do he'll definitely pull his weight.

Swifty's looking particularly rough too, and dressed like a proper scallywag. His rugged, unshaven features, rough-looking camo attire and mullet, which is slightly hidden by his hat all paint a picture of wild outdoor adventure. It's all a far cry from Dobbs's hot pants.

207

Immediately Agent6 sees Bolivar and Dobbs looking vacant in the boat, he shouts out:

"We didn't get any water, Does someone want to go and get some butts?"

Dobbs sighs and begins to stir. He is resigned to the fact that he needs to do something or else people are going to get pissed off with him and after all, he thinks, it will probably be not much more than a motor-taxi ride there and back and it wouldn't hurt to show willing.

"I'll go and get it but you might need to give the exact directions to the driver or I'll probably end up at the local swimming baths with my Spanish," he begins, then looking at all the supplies to be loaded, changes his tack.

"Then again maybe you might want to come with me while they're loading up all this stuff; there's sure to be something else you've forgotten."

Agent6 takes a look at the stack of supplies waiting to be loaded,

"Yeah, ok," he nods, "Let's go. Can you guys get all this loaded whilst we go off and get the water?"

Dobbs drags his sorry ass out of the boat and clambers back over the other fishing boats to walk up the quay with Agent6, who is shaking his head and rubbing his brow with a look of worry.

"Fuck man, every time we bought one thing we realised we needed another. If I get a team of workers for what, five days, we're going to need loads of stuff for them."

Dobbs had already considered this to be the most likely outcome. Now he can't help thinking he could be lying in the warm embrace of Gatita, but he chooses not to mention that,

"Really?" he says instead, trying to sound surprised.

He's been finding the humidity of the tropical morning nearly unbearable, especially with the effects of the hangover, so to be flying along in a motor taxi and feeling the wind cool his body is now deliciously refreshing. They don't have to go too far to find the shop though, and Dobbs can more or less just watch as the shopkeeper loads the motor-taxi up with refillable twenty-litre water bottles.

The motor-taxis can really take some weight, but because they have two independently suspended rear wheels - effectively the rear end of two motorbikes - the whole structure seems to twist a little and distort with the load. Observing the old, knackered tires fitted over the top of relatively new ones to squeeze a bit more life

208

out of them, he shakes his head to think that, though, they are stamped 'Made in China', the rubber probably came from here in the first place.

By the time they get back to Belen, the boat is loaded and there's a sense of calm amongst everyone, even Swifty, who's looking more than relaxed and almost a little smug with himself. It's a job well done, and an exciting mission to be a part of although Dobbs is a little concerned about the volume of water that is now being loaded into the already packed boat. He frowns at Swifty,

"I don't suppose roof racks are the way forward with narrow boats like this are they?"

The work crew seem completely unfazed however, which is reassuring. Dobbs has heard that one of them has seriously advanced cancer, but he's unsure who it is, and doesn't want to bring attention to the subject. Possibly it is an older man, whose eyes are almost laughing, but Dobbs knows cancer has no respect for either age or creed; it takes whoever it chooses. Suddenly, he feels acutely aware of how minor his feeling of being under the weather is in comparison, and tries to look a bit sharper.

The crew all look very Indigenous; not so much because of their clothes or their facial features as their eyes, which are dark and mysterious with a gentleness and a subtle sense of humour about them as if they know something Dobbs doesn't, and they're constantly close to pissing themselves laughing. It's not just with him though, it's with everyone. Their humble presence somehow inspires a sense of reverence.

Juan has remained calm throughout the whole affair so far, and now he has taken his place at the rear of the boat. He seems very settled. He's smoking a *mapacho*, which looks similar to a tailor-made cigarette but has no filter and is locally handmade with pure unrefined tobacco -a key part of ceremonies in this neck of the woods. They're a harsh and heavy smoke to say the least: one toke hits your chest like a club hammer, but Juan seems to savour them and smokes smoothly, his little flock of Westerners gathered closely around him.

Dobbs wonders what draws them. It must be those *curandero* eyes: the knowing eyes of a shaman. That look is something Juan could never hide, but maybe not all can see the depth beneath the mundane veneer of his cool Jeep and the baseball cap he wears back-to-front, which almost seem to act as a disguise, although both are actually tools of mere practicality. The way he manoeuvres himself with his gentle ways says so much about his manner and the pace at which he deals with his universe.

Finally it seems everyone's on board except Agent6 and an older-looking Indigenous guy, Elder. Both stood on another boat, to which the *Christina* is moored. It's exactly the time Dobbs figured they'd be setting off, although he didn't need to be a fortune teller to work it out as some things are absolutely inevitable. Agent6 nods at everyone, then indicates to Elder to jump on board the boat, which is now sitting stupidly low in the water, and casts off.

"*Vamanos!*" he cries, jumping across the rapidly widening strip of water, and they're away.

On the River

At last, it's all starting to look like an expedition. Dobbs has bought himself a full-length machete, and feels all set for hacking through the thick forest like some wild explorer. One of the older Indigenous men looks at the machete and then at Dobbs and smiles. He looks down at himself in his hot pants and then at the machete and then back at the man, and has to chuckle. As he does so all the workmen burst out laughing in unison that he can see how funny he must look to them.

How totally impenetrable the jungle is to a man like him, machete or no; in the hands of the Indigenous such a tool is the ultimate in jungle survival kit, whereas to Dobbs it is almost a toy. He feels slightly embarrassed, but there's no sense of belittlement, rather a feeling of understanding that he knows something of their window on the world and that they can laugh with him, rather than at him. Their idea of work is far removed from his - not that he hasn't worked in his time - but Dobbs can imagine how he looks to them, and he has to admit that their rather comical assessment of his capabilities in such an environment is probably not that far removed from the truth.

Looking over at Agent6, Dobbs attempts to redirect the attention.

"I can't believe we've got all this on board," he says.

Agent6 just raises his eyebrows and shakes his head.

"There still a lot more to load on up the river," he says. "Three more lumberjacks and all their supplies and chainsaws."

Looking round at the crammed boat, Dobbs shakes his head.

"You've got to be joking."

Peering down at the bottom of the hull, he sees water trickling over the dark planks in all directions and then glances at Bolivar.

"Apparently all boats leak a bit," he says, more to reassure himself than anything else

Bolivar just nods his head, grinning.

"Yeah, and this one quite a lot!"

One of the work crew at the stern pulls the starter cord of the little *pecki-pecki* and she fires up, driving the propeller through a long pole that enables the boat to be propelled through some of the shallowest water and can be easily lifted free of obstacles such as reeds which will become much more common as the river narrows, further up stream.

No one says much, but it's exciting to be moving, and as the noisy motor takes the load, its anxious whine dropping to a duller, more content tone as it begins to drive the *Christina* through the water, there's feelings that at last the fundamental purpose of the whole journey is beginning to be realised. The excitement soon overshadows his headache and rising body temperature and now, looking at the tiny port from the water, it is like seeing the place anew: A tiny port with no sense of grandeur other than its sweet simplicity that is laid bare.

Now, turning his attention back to the river, Dobbs notices that though there's many mooring pontoons, there's not nearly so many big vessels as he remembers. Apparently they're mostly moored further down river, the opposite way from which they're sailing, which is a relief, but they still have to be careful as there's quite a few of the little, gunboat-like high-speed ferries darting around, and the wake they leave is enough to capsize their small, overloaded vessel.

It's a magnificent day, and though the sun is blisteringly hot, the breeze off the water is very cooling. The river seems to lack the intensity of flow that Dobbs remembers from his last trip, but as the boat slowly moves up stream, Agent6 points out a line of contrast in the water up ahead.

"*Nappa*," he shouts across the noise of the motor

Dobbs hasn't a clue what the word means, but now he re calls the odd phenomenon from before and remembers that it marks an entry point into one of the main arteries of the Amazon, and the true power of its fast moving flow. On the Negra, where they are now, the water is so dark it is almost black, and its flow is just a meander until it hits up against the direct flow. The layout of the river system they've just left is a little complicated as Iquitos is effectively an Island, but with the benefit of distance and perspective, Dobbs now gets more of a picture of just how stranded it really is.

When it comes to exotic travel, Dobbs has been lucky to say the least, but still the might of the Amazon blows his mind every time he sees it. Now, as they enter the powerful currents of the main artery, the boat is shunted to one side and for a moment the bow begins to rapidly swing in the wrong direction. The acting skipper soon has it under control however, charting a course to cut as directly into the flow as possible to prevent the strong flow from broadsiding the little boat. Despite the thrust of the labouring engine, they're only moving forward very slowly now, so the helmsman swings the tiller over and brings them in closer to the bank, where the water travels slower. The river is easily a kilometre wide, and Dobbs marvels at it's incredible speed and the immense volume of water being drained from the jungle. They're going to be pushing against it all the way up to the land project, although as soon as they turn off from the main artery it will slow significantly.

Once the excitement of being underway begins to fade, Dobbs's hangover returns with a vengeance. The glare of the sunlight bouncing off the water feels like it is burning into his retinas, intensifying the pounding in his head, and he can feel a fever coming on, as if his body is fighting an infection. He wishes he could cocoon himself up in something and fall asleep, and finds himself thinking how good it would be to drop a Valium about now and drift off to the sound of the little *pecki-pecki* gnawing away at the water. Unfortunately, Valium is just one of the myriad of things he's forgotten to bring.

He lies down across a tiny piece of bench and a pile of supplies and tries to relax and enjoy the view but the intense light is too much to bear, so he closes his eyes and focuses on the subtle melange of scents carried upon the air, the sensation of the wind flowing over his body, the rocking of the boat, the rumble of the engine and the sound of the water gently slapping against the wooden hull. As he does so, he realises that the next few days are going to be a reluctant discovery of all the things he's forgotten to bring.

Not so for Bolivar; he's an experiential marketing manager and wouldn't go anywhere without the proper gear. He's got on a pair of properly sleek safari pants, a grey safari shirt and a decent pair of boots. With his cool shades, and a *Che* beret similar to Agent6's only in plain green rather than camo, he looks well set for a big Amazonian adventure, and a stallion compared to Dobbs in his girly hot pants and contradicting trilby and plain brown shirt. Despite his hangover however, he's happy enough though. Now, lying there in a kind of feverish bliss, he glances over at Bolivar all dressed for the part.

"Did you remember to bring the polo stick?" he says, unable to resist a little dig.

"Fuck off. Did you bring another can of spray-on hot pants?"

213

Dobbs chuckles; 'touché!' and as he does so, the helmsman steers into the bank and cuts the motor as the boat slides to a gentle halt and Elder jumps ashore and ties her off against a shrub. If all goes to plan, this will be their penultimate stop, where the last of the workers and their equipment will be loaded, although, they've not come far at all yet, and still have a long way to go before they'll reach the land project.

There's another shanty diner set on stilts where they've docked and a small Indigenous village of wooden huts, also on stilts, although set much further back than in Iquitos. They all disembark and take seats while Agent6 negotiates with the waiting workmen. Dobbs is impressed with how organised he seems, as if he is now totally back in his element. Whilst the workers load monster chainsaws with what appear to be metre-long blades and hessian bags full of more supplies onto the boat, some of the Westerners experiment with the food being offered in the diner, which seems to be very simple offerings all cooked over charcoal. Dobbs isn't hungry in the slightest though; even the thought of food is an anticlimax.

Negotiations concluded and bills paid, they climb back on board but as one of the workers clears some space at the back of the boat and lifts the duckboards to get underneath and bale the water that has accumulated on the way, a huge tarantula runs for safety. Dobbs doesn't see how, but somehow it gets clear of the boat into the river. To his complete surprise, it doesn't splash down but instead just spreads out its legs and then runs across the water like Jesus in a hurry. He looks at Bolivar, exchanging a look of amazement at the sight.

"I didn't know they could walk – well, run - on water. It reminds me of when I was a kid and my father had a bonfire in the garden and this huge spider crawled out of a burning box and ran to the top of the flame. That one didn't make it I'm afraid, so I guess they're not heat retardant, but this one's got some moves, hasn't he?"

Agent6 isn't at all fazed by the appearance of the huge, hairy arachnid.

"They live under the floorboards of the boats," he says. "Well, actually they live everywhere in the jungle but they're hunting spiders and there's good pickings to be had in boats. That ain't nothing to what we're going to find tonight though; you'll not find a square millimetre that's not teeming with life."

Dobbs nods and then Bolivar adds,

214

"It's ok though Dobbs, not all of it wants to suck your blood or harvest its loving offspring under your skin or in the warmth of your liver."

"Or crawl up your dick and make a nice nest in your kidneys!" Swifty shouts across.

Dobbs looks up.

"I'm not in the mood for that type of conversation right now," he says. "If they're under the floorboards and I'm above them, then its happy days. Notice that he ran for cover. He could so easily have run for blood but he didn't."

The pecki-pecki is soon fired up, and once they're under way again Dobbs is pleasantly surprised to find that despite the increase in the amount of gear, somehow the redistribution means there's a little more space to lie out flat. He's feeling very feverish now, so he greedily gulps back some water then, taking one last glance at the spectacular view, he rests his head back, closes his eyes and promptly falls fast asleep

When he awakes, much later, the scene is very different. They've turned off the main branch of the river onto a much narrower tributary and it's a lot cooler, although by no stretch of the imagination cold. There's the occasional lodge and a few *malokas* to be seen on the banks, but in the main it's covered with thick jungle which overhangs the water on either side. The water is very calm, getting on for a glass finish that perfectly reflects the tangle of trees and vines and the few slivers of blue sky overhead. It creates the impression of floating down some floral portal into another world. It's a mystical sight, and the felt reality of taking off to the depths of the jungle is spectacularly present; they may not exactly be going where no man has gone before, but it's certainly enough for Dobbs, equipped as he is with little more than a very large chopper and a very small pair of hot pants.

The boat is just purring along at low revs now, meandering up the winding river of glass, and when he closes his eyes he realises the sense of serenity and the overwhelming beauty is so much more than just visual. It's as though the jungle has sent forth tentacles that have somehow penetrated beyond the density of his physical matter and are almost feeling into him, as if the Amazon is a single conscious form, a collective mind that is systematically surveying him, analysing his intent.

Now and then children can be seen playing in the water in dugout canoes, and sometimes whole families go past, their tiny vessels loaded down to the gunwales yet still floating perfectly, the calmness of their occupants a mirror for the calmness of the river. It's pure serenity, and exactly what The Brigadier most fears. Pestilence runs in complete contradiction to all this, although ultimately, Dobbs muses, this is the final place it dumps you when it's done with you and had your all - and it will have your *all* if you're willing to give it up so easily.

They've been on the river for ages, but the speed at which they're travelling seems to that they're close to their destination now. It's about fifteen minutes before dark, and the light's starting to wane considerably so it seems Dobbs's was not far off in his estimation that they wouldn't arrive until after nightfall. There's quite a lot of water in the bottom of the boat, but it's difficult to reach down and scoop it because of all the gear in the way, but no one seems too bothered though and the little *pecki-pecki* is still going like a trooper, and that's all that matters now.

Though the hustle and bustle of Iquitos has been left far behind, Dobbs is missing Gatita. Even the thought of her seems to amplify the beauty of his surroundings, and now he can't help wondering why he didn't just bundle her into the boat with him. That would've been a proper jungle treat, he thinks to himself. He's soon distracted from such thoughts once the helmsman powers down to half-cock and the sounds emanating from the twilit jungle begin to take precedence over the chug of the engine.

It sounds like a hundred trillion grasshoppers on speed, plus a cacophony of random squawks, yelps and other unidentifiable noises, intermingled with the shrieks and shrills of monkeys and birds, and whatever else is lurking in the thick forest running either side of them. Some must be warning signals, but some must surely be just for the sake that they *can* make those wonderful sounds. Surely it's too late in the day for mating signals he muses, but then he grins to himself: no, it's never too late for mating signals.

There's other distant sounds too - woodpeckers maybe, although Dobbs has no idea if they are native to this part of the world, but something out there is tapping away. What he's hearing more than everything else, however, is the collective hum of the mass of insects buzzing about in their trillions. It's the sound of enthusiasm turning into regret.

As they continue their slow journey against the current, which now offers so little resistance that its flow is virtually undetectable, Agent6 is telling the workers not to kill the monkeys. Apparently last time they killed one and ate it, but it turned out to be a friendly pet from a reserve just down river. No doubt the monkey was just being curious, but someone thought, 'ah, here comes dinner'. The incident caused some problems apparently, but the reality is that the Indigenous around here are expert fishermen and hunters, so food is abundant in the Amazon and it shouldn't be a problem to find whatever they want without eating their neighbours cuddly friends.

The river is very narrow now, and everyone on board seems a lot more awake. Although he's still feels like he's fighting something, Dobbs feels a lot better than he did and it's clear a good sleep has done him the world of good. The boat is going even slower now, and as the light properly fades and the day gives way to night, the noise of the jungle changes with it. There's the occasional squawk and other distant sounds of larger animals, but it's that electric hum that occupies the airways more than anything now. It's a sound Dobbs knows only too well and it's uncomfortably close and intense.

When you leave the jungle behind you soon forget what that sound means but right now, as it intensifies with every moment of fading light, everyone starts grabbing long sleeved tops and rummaging for bottles of insect repellent. Dobbs knows that his rich Western diet makes him a banquet fit for a king; to the mosquito he is like a walking chocolate bar - just hold an index finger up and the hungry hordes will cover it in seconds.

Now the boat is going so slow that the motor is barely above idle. Before when they've hit patches of aquatic life the boat has just punched through but now, with the motor so slow, they hit huge swathes of algae, massive water lilies and thick lattices of smaller aquatic plant life that brings the boat to a standstill. It's all dealt with in a relaxed fashion though, and with a poke around with the oar they're clear again.

They're now moving at such a slow pace that despite the darkness Dobbs knows they must be very close. Then, suddenly, a patch of bank protrudes a little further out with a tree that bends over the river in a fashion that would suggest they should navigate round it, but instead they head directly for it. Agent6 makes a squawk like some exotic Amazonian bird.

"Hi Honey, I'm home!" he shouts out.

The boat glides under the overhanging tree branches and into a recess beyond, but as her bow noses into the bank they are greeted by a storm of mosquitoes.

"Holy fucking shit!" Dobbs screams out. "Why aren't I prepared for this?"

Swifty just laughs: this is going to be tough for all of them, and from now on every moment will be a test of endurance. Dobbs knows he probably won't enjoy much of it until it's all over, but hopefully then he'll love it, and at least the memory of it will seem all so romantic.

An English Phonebox

The main lodge is literally ten feet from the river's edge, and Dobbs can't help wondering how much further the water will rise, as the rainy season has now begun. It's probably not the best time to be coming to the Amazon but Dobbs doesn't know if there really is a particularly good time to be here. Apparently there's a lot of leeches in the rainy season though, and he's never been keen on them.

Although the main lodge is probably forty feet in diameter it has quite a thin-looking thatch on its roof and in the last of the fading light, seeing this hideaway tucked tightly into the surrounding jungle amplifies its almost eerie seclusion. From the bank, Dobbs can see two other circular structures beyond, similar to the main *maloka* though not nearly as large.

Gathering all their bags from the boat, they ferry them up the bank and into the raised space that sits on stilts. As they ascend the stairway, Dobbs can see a thatched walkway that extends off at the rear running up to a 'T' junction ahead, and connecting to the two smaller *malokas* about fifty metres back. The layout immediately makes him think of the *SS Enterprise* from Star Trek, and it feels like they're entering the bridge, a command centre equipped with a complex jungle cloaking system. It reminds him of exactly what he's really here to do and sends shivers darting through his body that trigger greater, almost involuntary energetic judders at the thought.

"It looks like a camouflaged spaceship," Dobbs says, glancing over at Agent6.

"Well, that's exactly what it is my friend," Agent6 replies, although a little distractedly as he and Swifty seem more preoccupied with the terrible state of the place. Swifty is cursing all he observes, but the jungle consumes anything that's idle in days and weeks rather than months or years, and much of the sense of disrepair is probably due to the fact that they're viewing it in the darker part of dusk, which amplifies the feeling of being engulfed by overgrowth.

The jungle always seems so alien to Dobbs that it feels like he's in a sci-fi movie, although maybe that has more to do with the experiences he's had here. Mind you, none of his golden rings of protection or sci-fi defences are currently offering any shield against the incoming squadrons of mosquitoes. Dobbs knew this moment would come and he's already stuck on some DEET, but the jungle is basically hard work, especially on the irritating insect front, and it's not doing much. It's all just part of the ride though, and what it boils down to is the sweet nectar of simple surrender.

Let the fuckers feed, Dobbs thinks, but then again he has little other choice, and even with his best efforts at equanimity he can feel a state of panic rising with the ever increasing hum, which is now bordering a scream.

As well as the three *malokas* there are two more tiny round huts, and looking around it's clear that Agent6 and his troop of merry men were indeed busy the last time they were here, although everything seems completely overgrown now. By the looks of the clothes hanging out and other miscellaneous artefacts of habitation, the small *maloka* off to the left is perhaps someone's home. The other one, which is slightly back and to the right, looks as if the roof has half collapsed although it is still a functional, if somewhat wonky.

Juan, his students and all the workers are hanging their hammocks in Swifty's *maloka*, which seems to be drier on account of the much newer roof.

Agent6 pulls his mosquito net from his pack.

"Come on," he says, "let's get these nets up and get some cover from these things. In an hour they'll all be gone."

Bolivar shakes his head with disbelief

"Gone?" he chuckles.

"They're never gone!" Swifty shouts back bluntly.

"What d'you reckon then Dobbs? You like the lay out?"Agent6 says, tying off one side of his hammock. "It's got an odd sort of feeling about it -not that that was in the plan – but it's home."

Dobbs is attempting to tie up his hammock with some lame piece of nylon rope, but it's a bit of a makeshift operation, which of course was always destined to take place at the most muzzy-abundant hour of the day. If they'd arrived twenty minutes before, it would have been a whole different story. He looks back at the *malokas* for a moment, taking in the whole sight.

"It's 'cause it's raised off the ground," he says after a moment's consideration. "It looks like it's just floating with those thatched walkways all connecting it together. Like it's just waiting to take off. Which one's yours anyway?"

"That one," Agent6 says, pointing to the hut on the left.

"So what are they then - yours and Swifty's?" Dobbs says, glancing around and trying to get his bearings a bit before the last of the light completely goes.

Swifty's seemingly lost in tying up his hammock and rummaging through bags, but Bolivar says loudly,

"His and hers," which gets a marginal grunt from him.

It's no surprise he doesn't want to be distracted with small talk though; the aerial assault is instilling a definite sense of urgency, and everyone is trying to move in such a way as to constantly scare the horrid little vampires off.

Dobbs is still looking for a place to tie the other end of his hammock which is secure enough to hold the weight and traverses the least amount of wet floor in the hope of avoiding leakage from the roof, but with the extent of the rot that has consumed the central supporting upright it's proving quite a task. None of it's made any easier by his poor supplies and crap net, however, and the mosquitoes are by now reaching biblical proportions.

"Oh my God, I'm being completely annihilated!" he wails, vainly swiping at the invisible cloud of biting insects.

Swifty and Agent6 are piling on the *Deet* and Dobbs, who was under some illusion that he'd be able to get away without using such toxic repellents reluctantly, pulls his own bottle from his bag and begins splashing it all over, like a teenager with cheap aftershave. The chemical stench of the stuff is scary, but the hum of the onslaught is literally creating a feeling of hysteria in him, and his hands are covered with the blighters.

In sharp contrast to the unfortunate and ill-prepared Dobbs, Bolivar is unbelievably organised. He has his all-in-one camouflaged mosquito net and hammock thrown up and is inside, all zipped up and cocooned away from the humming menacing seconds. Dobbs stops for a moment.

"Look at you, you ergonomic git," he says, shaking his head ruefully.

He's somehow shocked at his own stupidity. How could he have forgotten all this? The impact of the humidity and the intensity of the heat, even in the darkness, the maddening high-pitched whine of swarming mosquitoes – an onslaught that actually comes with its own air raid warning!

Nonetheless he gets to work finishing the last details of his makeshift mosquito net, which appears more like a huge collapsed spider's web. He's had to cut holes in each end for the hammock to pass through, which has not done much for it cosmetically, but it reaches the floor all the way around, which is the main thing. There's some gaps in the floorboards which he guesses the accursed little blood suckers will discover quick enough, but at least now he has somewhere to duck under and get a little respite from the full scale invasion.

By the time they've brought up the last load from the boat, stashed the motor and got all the hammocks erected, the light has completely disappeared and the drone of intense mosquito bombardment finally begins to subside, revealing a completely different spectrum of audible irregularities that softly saturate the airways. Each one, Dobbs has no doubt, is some form of mating signal, yet at the same time it is attracting a mate it is giving vital information about its location away to predators. Sex in the jungle is, he's sure, a risky business. Beyond the harmonious chatter of what is probably mostly insects, and the occasional shrill shriek from an unidentified nocturnal creature, there's a feeling of vast space in a world beyond, which he cannot enter.

Even under the net he's still being bitten, though it's not as extreme as before, and finally he can start to relax a little, trying to ignore the intense irritation developing all over his body and his rapidly swelling, furiously itchy knuckles.Agent6's net is a large, green, rectangular military number that completely encapsulates the whole hammock but can easily be pulled back during the day when there's not much biting going on. It's a neat little setup.

Swifty has the same rectangular zip-up net, only he's hung it with huge lengths of climbing rope, trussing it to the central support and the outer uprights as though it normally gets hooked up in the canopy of the forest, high above in the darkness. It's a complex web of zips and chunky climbing carabineers and all looks a bit overkill, but if there's an emergency at least he could abseil out of it relatively easily.

Peering inside, Dobbs can see that despite the fact it's only been up a few minutes, he's already laid out a smorgasbord of jungle survival accessories.

"You ain't got any spare dog tags have ya Swifty?" he jests.

For a moment Swifty tries to be serious and ignores the comment. Then he turns to Dobbs as if about to release some poignant pearls of wisdom,

"Fuck off Dobbs," he fires back genially.

Not to be so easily brushed off, Dobbs inspects the rope Swifty's used to suspend his hammock

"Blimey O'Reilly," he says, "What are you expecting to share this hammock with?"

Agent6 laughs.

"Who you expecting, more like?" he adds.

"I should have got a decent net man," Dobbs says looking back at his odd structure. Then, looking back at Bolivar he bursts out laughing.

"I mean, you can't seriously call that thing a hammock, can you? It's an Experiential Regeneration Pod!"

Bolivar's lying in there with his tiny head torch on. Beyond the two main supporting ties at each end there's one last, thin, supporting string pulling the net up above his head and creating what looks like a netted shield, stretched taut. It creates a cockpit-like effect, and the torchlight illuminates the sleek, pod-like military green hammock and its adjoining net so that it glows eerily in the stark white LED light, contrasting sharply with the darkness of his skin.

"Fuck me man, I'm scared: you look like some kind of space age chrysalis, about to hatch a one-eyed trouser snake into an experiential butterfly. If I shine a torch on you after midnight, you might have completely liquidated in the transmutation."

Dobbs can see by his head torch that Bolivar's now casting a disparaging eye at his own setup.

"Let's have a look at *your* house then shall we Dobbs?" he says, inspecting the flaccid state of the net covering Dobbs's hammock,

"Nice net," he says eventually. You obviously like sharing your space – *with* mosquitoes."

"Well, it's a *double* hammock actually so where the net falls short, the hammock makes up for the shortfall. Plus, if some fine looking lady wanders through in the night, I can happily oblige her," Dobbs retorts, although now he's also observing how he's placed his hammock above a distinctly wet patch, and just hoping it doesn't rain.

Bolivar is still looking at Dobbs's mosquito net with a bit of concern though.

"Yeah, well by the looks of things you might be expecting a bit of a *short* fall! Dobbs, why don't you put your bags round the bottom? Then the mozzies definitely won't come in."

"What, you reckon they're going to pull the sides up?"

As he speaks, the first pitter-patter of a cloudburst can be heard falling on the roof above.

"Oh, fucking great. It's raining," Swifty says, sounding like he's already at the end of his tether. He's been cursing at the sight of the place and the way everything is falling apart since they arrived.

"Yeah, but we've got everything in haven't we? And the hammocks and everything are up aren't they?" Dobbs says, attempting to quell his moody moans.

"Ten out of ten for optimism Dobbs," Agent6 says, observing the roof, "but considering we've taken the only space that leaks like a teabag, that sound might not be good news at all,"

Dobbs crawls into his hammock and does his best to make himself comfortable. He's tired, and the sense of excitement at coming to the jungle has subsided considerably, especially in light of the fact that he's covered with bites and he can still feel his body fighting off some sort of infection. The temperature has dropped with the sudden rain and dampness, so now, cocooned in his hammock, he pulls his sheet over himself to lock in the heat, and waits to see if the rain will come pissing through. Sure enough, the drip-drip-drip of water can be felt impacting against his hammock, but it's nothing that would warrant relocation and after a while, lying there listening to the orchestral harmony of the nocturnal jungle and the occasional mosquito buzzing round his ears, he slowly nods off.

***

When he awakes, the rain has stopped and it's another gloriously bright sunny day, but despite the fact that he's had more than enough sleep and should feel recharged, he's feeling both damp, yet dehydrated. He's been dreaming – something about a British *phonebox* that was super modern and about double the size of the normal classic red *phonebox* - but it was a disturbing dream and as he opens his eyes he's relieved to see the bright sunlight bursting through the trees all round the *Maloka*, and realise with a refreshed sense of excitement that he's out in the jungle.

He'd woken several times in the night feeling feverish, and can feel that whatever he's fighting has still not shifted, but he feels rested at least. Now, lying in his hammock and looking up at the roof, he can see the extent of the rot that has set in almost everywhere; it seems as soon as the rain gets in the life expectancy of the structure is drastically reduced as there's so much insect life that is ready to come and consume the place.

Even from here he can see just how thick the forest is in the immediate vicinity and now, looking down at his machete, he realises that to a man like him, other than digging holes for a shit, it's pretty useless. Suddenly he wonders again what hope he has of finding a story out here - other than charting a record of his lame survival techniques, that is. Realistically, he's never going to get much further than about twenty metres through that growth, and the outside of his net is already covered with mosquitoes, waiting to feast on his rich blood the moment he steps beyond its thin veil of protection.

Dobbs looks enviously over at Bolivar's hammock. It really does look like a vegetative life pod or some kind of weird chrysalis.

"How do we know the real Bolivar's in there, and not some body-snatched reproduction?" he calls out.

Bolivar just grunts.

"Sounds like a *replicant*," Dobbs continues, not to be deterred.

"I'm still asleep!"

"A moody *replicant!*"

But then Bolivar pulls himself up a bit and notices the view that Dobbs is taking in.

"My God, this place really is in the bloody jungle isn't it?" he exclaims. We're not going to able to get ten metres through that."

"Yeah, that's what I was thinking," Dobbs muses, then, changing the subject, "You know, I read some *twatty* psychology report or something - years ago, when I did my Access Course maybe - that we only dream in black and white."

"Maybe we do." Bolivar says.

"No, definitely not,"

"How do you know?"

"'Cause I just saw a bright red British *phonebox* in my dream. It was all getting very weird, and I actually thought to myself, in the dream, 'that's funny; I thought I was only supposed to be able to dream in black and white.' I was so surprised, I bloody woke myself up, just when it was getting interesting."

Bolivar says nothing while Dobbs ponders on the dream, trying to remember as much as possible.

"It was an odd dream," he continues after a while. "I was so chuffed that Agent6 had picked this space - it was next to a river, and just outside an industrial compound that looked like an airport or, no, a railway perhaps. There were all these warehouse-like things, but there was a railway track that ended there too, with a train; a huge train, with a massive engine at the front."

"This man was watching me from behind a fence. At first I thought he was a worker or something - he was wearing an orange boiler suit - but then I saw how he clung to the fence and I suddenly realised he was actually a prisoner. He was staring at me, like he wanted to talk, but he was kind of across the way - whatever the way was - so I just stared back at him and the train beyond him, and the eerie track. It sent a shudder through me." And he stops to consider the notion, "Maybe it wasn't good to be on that train; maybe it led into prison - or worse - and that's when I saw the *phonebox*, and I wanted to ring this bloke but I didn't know whether to tell him to get on the train or not. I wanted to talk to him and so I took a look in this *phonebox*. It was twice the size of a normal box, and red, exactly the same red as the old British style *phoneboxes*, only this one was very modern and spacious with a huge, vandal-proof brushed stainless steel box and a complex-looking inbuilt keyboard with a large flat screen above, like something I could imagine they'll have in airports in the very near future."

Bolivar just grunts, but it's a thoughtful grunt.

"And then I woke, all sweaty and covered in mosquito bites in my wet hammock, but so pleased to be here with all of you."

"Ahhh!" Bolivar responds.

"I was so happy to be here; it was like a feeling of joy that I wasn't in that other space - that I was somehow beyond the prison and this odd man, just staring at me, wanting to be free. It was like a concentration camp Bolivar, and there was something about this big train and the railway line into the camp that just made my heart sink. I felt like I was seeing the trains that led off to the concentration camps in Germany during the war.

I wish I could remember more; I'm sure there was a girl right at the beginning who I thought was coming with me and then she went with someone else and I was sad. I wish I could remember it all; I just can't see how it all fitted in the dream now."

"Maybe the prisoner was you," Bolivar offers.

"Maybe. But maybe the *phonebox* was me. Like a high tech communication device."

"What?"

Dobbs looks at Bolivar and shrugs.

"Who knows?" he says. "When I dream of cars and boats, and things like that my mum always tells me that the vehicle represents me. So maybe the *phonebox* could also represent me as well."
"My God Dobbs, who needs *Ayahuasca* when dreams like that are coming through?"

Smoke is emanating from the *maloka* built off from the three main structures, the wonky one, which is not sitting on stilts but rather a raised circle of mud and earth that looks as though it has been patted down to slow the growth of vegetation rooting into it. It acts as a dam Dobbs guesses for the abundant water that's moving through the land when it rains. It is the only structure that has a place for a central fire and is obviously the kitchen and he's now he's also wondering where the ceremonies will be conducted. There are signs of life and activity all around and the smell of fish barbequing. A small Indigenous girl in a sweet little stained and worn out dress appears. She has obviously noticed the signs of consciousness coming from the main lodge and come to have a look. She's probably only about four years old and has the most beautiful little face. After a few moments a little boy appears too. He's older, but he seems shyer. They both just stand staring at the two men in their hammocks with a look of intense curiosity.
"*Hola!*" Dobbs says, waving.
The little girl looks at the boy to see how he deals with situations like this, but he's clearly not too sure either, and after a few moments they both turn and run off towards the area where food is being prepared.
Dobbs begins getting up and pulls on some clothes, but as soon as he ventures out of his protective net he is immediately met by a torrent of mosquitoes. He's noticed they seem to avoid the light though, so he makes a dash for the door and, once outside, stands blinking in the bright sunlight on the stairs leading up to the main lodge.
"Is that an orange tree?" he says, staring at a tree right next to the steps.
Bolivar, who's now also climbing free of his hammock looks over.
"No Dobbs, that's a lemon tree," he says sarcastically. "You see those rugby ball-shaped things with skin a bit like an orange only bright yellow? They're called lemons Dobbs. The jungle's amazing isn't it?"
"You can't get lemons that big. It's not possible."

"Well what are they then, other than large lemons?"

"Well it's obvious isn't it? They're yellow, rugby ball-shaped oranges."

Agent6 and Swifty, who've been up a while already, now enter the lodge with a couple of the workers to take a closer look at the roof. They both seem disappointed at the way things have deteriorated and all the weaknesses that have developed in such a short space of time. The outline of dark lines left by massive armies of termites can still be seen all over the roof beams and it's easy to detect the now obvious design faults.

Many of the horizontal, load-bearing supports have snapped directly above the uprights, which have 'T's on the top to carry the weight of the roof. These have been secured by a single, fat nail straight through the horizontal - splitting it in two, and obviously weakening the supporting beams at the point they need to be strongest. The error has been repeated over and over again, and totally works against the longevity of the structure. Swifty's cursing the short-sightedness of the design.

"Fuckin' hell. It's fuckin' had it. Look at it - it's in fuckin' pieces. The whole thing's gonna have to fuckin' go."

"You could quite easily take the weight off where it's snapped, replace the broken beams and maybe grease the supporting uprights. It might be cheap to replace the whole roof but come back next year and, one way or another, it's going to be the same story. Don't go crazy replacing everything, it's not worth it: you don't see Building Regs coming round this way too often do you Swifty?" Dobbs jests to calm the situation.

"Nahh. That roof's been knackered for a while really; we should have replaced it last year. It needs to be higher so the water deflects off more than sort of impacting. You wait until you see the fucking rain here Dobbs. When it rains, it fucking rains. It needs to be a thick thatch too," Swifty says. Agent6 is nodding approvingly, but he doesn't look so present really.

With all this talk of work, and fingers being pointed this way and that Dobbs and Bolivar decide to exit the space. It's still too early for all that, and they both descend the *maloka* stairs and head down towards the riverbank to stand in the sun.

The scene is so overwhelmingly vibrant it's almost impossible to take it all in. Light is radiating off the saturated ground, sending glistening shards of sunshine in all directions. All around them are countless varieties of plant life, still wet from the rain and covered with tiny globules of water that deflect the light like a billion tiny suns. Trees tower above them to the forest canopy far above, and the whole place is just crawling with life. It's still early, and the day feels fresh - unlike Dobbs, who feels sweaty and dirty after his feverish night.

Below the *maloka*, the *Christina* is moored up on the riverbank next to few dugouts. With her gorgeous thatched roof, she makes a heavenly scene and except for the tiniest ripples, which send yet more shimmering sparkles shooting off in all directions, the water is like a mirror, adding to the sense of divine serenity. The root systems of the trees look like massive bony fingers, reaching clear of the banks and disappearing into the depths of the river below, and looking at them helps Dobbs appreciate the sheer size of the trees, some of which are at least two or even three metres wide. It's all so green and bright he has to squint to take it in.

"Wow," he says, looking over at Bolivar. "This place is just too fucking much."

Walking down to the water's edge, Dobbs turns around to get a better look at the *maloka* and its conical roof structure, which blends so perfectly with the jungle. Agent6 and Swifty's *malokas* have the same conical roofs but the thatching is thicker, with a far steeper gradient. They both have an added thatched gable too that will possibly become a sheltered porch, or tiny patio area. Neither of them are fully completed, however, and the main lodge has obviously fallen into a terrible state of disrepair. It's unlikely that it will be a great expense to put things right, but what's immediately apparent is that if Agent6 was only out here building these structures the previous year, then the level of maintenance needed to keep them in tiptop condition is obviously quite high.

Bolivar pulls out his phone.

"Can we get satellite GPRS signal here?"

"You fucking joking with me man?" Dobbs immediately fires back. "You might find a Virgin with a nice pair of Nokia's but I reckon GPRS is off the service list!"

"Err, that would be a better reception than I'm getting."

"Fuck Bolivar, you know what?" Dobbs says suddenly, off on his own track again,

"What?"

"That train I saw; massive it was. But maybe it hadn't just arrived: maybe it was about to leave…"

Fetching Techo

The small *maloka* with the half-collapsed roof has now become the main cooking area and is a hive of activity. Small fish, wrapped in leaves, are slowly cooking on a charcoal fire around which almost everyone has gathered as the smoke is definitely warding off the mosquitoes. Now, in the daylight, it's easy to see the whole place is an overgrown building site. It's totally incomplete and needs, at the very least, one finished space that has an area screened off with mosquito netting for guests. There's nowhere to sit other than the cramped kitchen area and even this is half collapsed and looks more like a kids camp.

The food is very basic and the small fish are crammed with tiny, sharp bones. Each mouthful involves such a labour of love to extract them that it almost seems easier just to suck the scarce meat off the skeleton. Dobbs notices that the workers have a technique to pull out the bones but when he tries to do the same he fails miserably. He doesn't much care though as he's still on the tail end of whatever he's been fighting and not really hungry at all.

Swifty's getting all fired up for work by stomping round the camp to survey the extent of the rot, and distant *'Fuckin' 'ell!s'* can be heard echoing out from the location of each new horror he discovers. Agent6, meanwhile, has retreated to a hammock he's put up between two outer supporting uprights in the main lodge, as near to the smoke as is comfortable but at an appropriate distance from all the activity. Apparently he's not feeling so well, so for now he's just lying back and observing the goings on, but he's clearly having trouble taking in the abominable state of things.

He seems to have come down with the same bug as Dobbs, which is not so bad really, but the sight of all that needs to be done has knocked the wind clean out of his sails and he seems to have temporarily disengaged from the unfolding process, being little more than a witness to affairs right now. Not only is the project no longer such a novelty to him as to everyone else but when he originally built the place - especially his own *maloka* - it was with his daughter and partner in mind. Clearly, the implication that she's maybe with another man now is sinking in, and that's taking its toll on his enthusiasm no doubt. It seems there's so much to rebuild and make good and this retreat represents only a tiny part of the work he will have to undertake to sort his life out.

Fortunately Swifty has a bunch of workers following him around who are surely taking mental notes of all the things that he's pointing at and uttering obscenities. Not that they understand a word of what he's saying, but they're nodding a lot, which is a good start, and having someone else around to at least shout out all the work that needs to be done is giving Agent6 the opportunity to relax and take in the bigger picture.

Right now he looks exactly as Dobbs pictured him in his mind's eye back in Iquitos; lying back in his hammock with lots of people running about looking busy. Maybe he's going to have to rebuild his relationship as much as his *maloka*, but whichever way it pans out, Dobbs at least, is sure all three of them are going to be fine. He needs to just carry on regardless, using the project to stay focussed, forget about all his expectations and just offer the space up to the gods. And after all he is a shaman - a *curandero* in his own right – so maybe he's already done that anyway.

Agent6's sails may be sagging but one thing's for sure; Swifty's here, and he's on the case. He's got his moody head on, which is not a pretty sight, though it is very effective for getting a bunch of workers to pull their weight and it's clear that, whatever energetic deficiencies Agent6 may be experiencing, Swifty's more than making up the shortfall. Agent6 invited him here as he needs the help Swifty's offering and all he can offer in exchange is the opportunity for Swifty to build his own *maloka*, a home to last as long as it lasts - with an accompanying slice of the unfolding adventure of course.

Dobbs is not sure of the details of the land negotiations. He knows Agent6 doesn't own it, but just has a standing agreement with the Jaguar tribe who does. He employs the tribesmen to carry out most of the work which is obviously appreciated, as earning hard cash in the jungle is not easy. Besides the business though it's clear they like him personally; he's *tranquillo* - proper *tranquillo* - like them. He *sees* them, and he has made the effort to learn their ways - and they know it. Basically, he is always careful to bring the appropriate gifts and he's straight talking; he says what he does, and he does what he says he'll do, unlike most gringos. You can see they all look at him with respect.

His tour completed, Swifty finally marches back to the kitchen area.

"Fucking hell!" he grumbles, shaking his head in utter disappointment. "Everything's rotten. We should have completed the roofs before we left last time."

"I know. I said that last year," Agent6 replies, sighing.

"That whole walkway has rotted; the uprights have turned to shit, and we've got no preserver for the wood even if we put new posts in."

He turns to Dobbs and Bolivar.

"Fucking hell, you wait, you're going to see hail stones out here – maybe soon...Size of fucking golf balls when those fuckers come! It's not just heavy rain that fucks these roofs."

"Look," says Agent6 with an air of diligence to mask his apathy, "I'm not feeling that well really, so the best thing we can do today is to get one team on the chainsaws and another to go off and get *techo* for the roof. Also, I'll organise to buy as much sawn timber as we can from the local villages and leave some guys here on a clean-up mission whilst we go off and get it all."

Swifty nods.

"Aladdin's getting ready now," he says, pointing to one of the workers assembling the parts of his chainsaw, "And there a few guys already out there cutting fresh tracks and looking for suitable trees."

"To be honest Swifty, whether we buy sawn timber out here or prepare our own, it's not going to make much difference price-wise either way," Agent6 sighs.

"Yeah, I suppose" Swifty concurs, "but we need a fucking generator man, and we need some fucking power tools or we'll only be able to tickle this place."

Dobbs looks across at Aladdin. He's not particularly tall, but now he has his top off it's clear to see the man's built like a brick shit house. His whole upper body looks like one massive muscle and, observing him wielding the metre-long chainsaw blade, Dobbs can't help musing that he's certainly not a man to be messed with.

"How many can go on this *techo* mission?" he says, looking across at the remaining Westerners in Swifty's *maloka*.

"As many as you like. We'll just lie on it on the way back."

"Let's get that lot out on a boat trip," Dobbs says. "They're all looking a bit lost."

Agent6 glances over at them as if he's not bothered either way.

232

"I still feel fucked, you're feeling fucked and Bolivar's got a fucking toothache; the more hands for loading the better I reckon," Dobbs continues.

Agent6 observes Bolivar with a look of concern for a moment.

"Toothache?"

"Not that bad," he shrugs it off. "My gums"

The cook has just got the coffee ready and it seems the chickens have discovered where the food is being prepared and are busy just out the back. They're not nearly as friendly as the huge cockerel that is wandering about systematically trying to shag them all however. He seems totally unaffected by the humans, which is perhaps not surprising as it's clear from his monstrous size no one has ever attempted to eat him.

"Anyone fancy a trip up the river?" Agent6 shouts across to where the few other westerners are now gathered. Distracted with other things, however, nobody seems to hear so Dobbs wanders over to speak with them. Nobody says much as he joins them, and it's obvious there's a sense of discomfort. It feels almost as if the mosquitoes are dividing everyone up into their own little camps as there's no collective space in which to take shelter from them.

"You guys going to come for a boat trip?" Dobbs asks.

Most people nod, obviously keen to get some respite from the rigours of the jungle. He can see that the Israeli in particular is covered with bites, the swelling blemishes highlighted by the paleness of his skin. Dobbs is about to say something but then decides against conversation as his Spanish is too crap and speaking English just seems to accentuate the sense of separation between them. Instead he gives him a sympathetic look, pointing to his own bites, but the response he gets is still standoffish; he's not part of their little clan. Dobbs just shrugs; a cup of *Ayahuasca* will bring them back to the heart and break down those barriers quickly enough when the time comes.

One of the Indigenous guys helping Aladdin has seen Dobbs pointing at the bites, and now he laughs and points out at the jungle, speaking rapidly in Quechuan. Dobbs can't make out what he's saying, but from his gestures he seems to be describing some kind of insect to be found out there. He holds his thumb and index finger a good two inches apart and then, in the posture of cutting with a chainsaw, darts his index finger at his arm before showing the size of whatever is out there again just for good measure.

"*Es muy grande mosquito, uh?*" Dobbs asks.

The man nods,

"Si. Grande!"

Casting his eye over the dilapidated mess all around him, Dobbs gives a little sigh. He feels dirty, sweaty and groggy from the long journey, illness and exertion of the last few days. Some of the guys are talking with Juan about the possibility of drinking the brew tonight, but he can sense the idea is being met with some resistance; in light of the lack of facilities it seems they're un-keen to stay any longer than necessary. In his present state he can empathise with their sentiment as personally he doesn't feel ready to drink himself; he would have to mentally prepare for that. Tomorrow would be better or perhaps even the day after, but no one will want to stay if things are not better organised and the reality is that that's just not going to happen in the next few days.

"Fuck me, look at that. We only put those lower steps on last year and they're completely rotten!" Swifty moans, kicking the rotten stairs.

Dobbs nods.

"Imagine if you didn't touch this place and came back here in ten years time. There'd be absolutely no trace of its existence whatsoever."

Three Indigenous men are standing round Swifty as he kicks the stairs and mutters curses, and Dobbs notices one of the Westerners from Swifty's maloka looking down at the ground as he does so, obviously embarrassed by Swifty's rude tone. As he looks up again Dobbs catches his eye.

"Don't worry, he's all bark and no bite mate," he says reassuringly. "He's just getting back into work mode. He may sound like a slave driver, but he's a pussy cat really."

Swifty just chuckles sheepishly.

"Man, that's one *rough* toilet," Bolivar says, shaking his head as he makes his way back to the maloka after a trip to the toilet lost on all the growth somewhere further back. "It needs some serious work. The steps are rotten, the ground's drenched and it's seriously full of mosquitoes - my arse is bitten to fuck. Worst of all though there's a spider in there that's literally the size of my hand."

"It's wet season. Welcome to the jungle, man," Agent6 declares. "No one said it was going to be easy."

Dobbs squats down to inspect the ground around him.

"Fuck, you can see how the water gets to the river. It's not flowing in little streams but just moving through the ground around you.

234

I'm dreading taking a crap: stop moving and you start sinking! And every step you take, there's snakes above and spiders below and creepy crawlies everywhere. It's like the jungle is saying 'no entry'. As soon as you leave the smoke haze, it's all just coming at you."

Agent6 just laughs.

"You know what though Dobbs, as soon as you're back in Iquitos you'll be missing it and forget all the hard parts. They'll just make you long for the adventure of being back here."

"Well, I suppose that's true as here I am, back in the jungle. We should start making a list of all the things we need to bring with us next time to make it more comfortable though," Dobbs suggests.

Agent6 catches Swifty's eye.

"You're on that aren't you Swifty?"

"I know what's on the top of *your* list, Dobbs -" Swifty shouts with a cheeky grin "- Gatita!"

Then he marches off. Nothing's stopping him from getting down in the dirt. He's just carrying on regardless, shirt soaked with more DEET than sweat. That stuff smells horribly toxic, and Dobbs can't believe it's not harming his system in some way, but it doesn't bother Swifty one little bit. Out here in the jungle he's as happy as a pig in shit.

Dobbs looks at Bolivar and then at the other foreigners and starts to ponder as to what his mission here really is. He came not only with the grand idea of presenting a series of questions to the *Ayahuasca*, but also of writing a book on the wonders of the Amazon. Now he's realising things are going to be a lot harder than he'd bargained for. He's feeling despondent, and can't help noticing that everyone around him is in a similar state.

He'd thought the jungle would be a lot more accessible and he could trek through, discovering wonderful new plants and animals as he went. Now he's faced with the reality that he can barely face going to the bog, let alone get past the first line of trees, and apparently he's even having trouble identifying a lemon. How can he ever begin to describe this sacred place, with its impenetrable gateways seemingly policed by mosquitoes, snakes and spiders - oh and some other terrifying thing about two inches long with a chainsaw for a nose that Dobbs has yet to witness?

Apart from what he learned on his last trip he basically knows nothing about the jungle and he's stupidly forgotten his most important lesson from back then; that it's an unfathomable mystery to a city boy like him. So where's the story? - *Man goes to the jungle and finds pestilence* - What the fuck am I doing here? he thinks to himself.

It seems the jungle is a bit of an anticlimax. He can see that, apart from Swifty, everyone else is in the doldrums too, and thinking about it now their whole little gander through Peru has really been nothing more than a pestilence binge. Nothing so far has really gone to plan, and even the hope of getting The Brigadier on side is failing too. Maybe this is why writers turn to fiction; to bend a story into something more interesting and adventurous than the author's ability to actually live a truly adventurous life themselves? he ponders anxiously. 'Maybe there's no fucking story at all. Maybe this is where I have to just start making it all up because I'm a coward who's scared to live his life.

It's also clear to see that Juan has brought the other foreigners out on the grounds believing that there would be a fully functional facility. Now the reality that the whole place is still only half built and what little there is falling apart because of design issues and poor maintenance is all too evident. Dobbs realises his whole trip has been loaded with expectation and the reality is just not matching up, but then he stops and thinks again: Maybe this fever is just bringing me down - that and the state of the place. It should have been in far better condition than it is now!

Some of that responsibility, if not all, must fall on the Indigenous family which Agent6 has been paying to look after the place. Basically, that should mean a little bit of basic roof maintenance perhaps and at the very least, stopping termites building nests in and around the site, none of which has been done on any level whatsoever. Juan is clearly as disappointed as Agent6 and Swifty. For the workers, it's happy days, as there's lots to do, but for everyone else it's a tragic discovery to find the place in such a terrible state of disrepair.

Dobbs's lack of Spanish, though he's making an effort, is really separating him from the others, who aren't up for speaking English. None more so than Juan, who expects his students to understand basic Spanish - as they all do, it appears. Dobbs isn't one of his students, so there's a bit of a separation there and he can feel a degree of isolation developing. The anxiety of the situation is making him feel nervous about other things too - namely his situation with his girlfriend back home and Gatita. All in all, he's having a bit of a reality check.

236

He wishes he could go back and sit in his hammock to get some respite from the mozzies, but he knows that would deliver him, alone, right into the centre of his whole paranoia about the trip being a farce. He can see that Bolivar is in a similar state, except he has a toothache now as well. Not that any of that's affecting Agent6 who's still just lying in his hammock watching the world go by.

Soon enough the workers all have jobs and are either cleaning up the place or working with the lumberjacks cutting trees. Everyone else jumps in the boat. Dobbs takes the helm first, which is perhaps not the best idea; manoeuvering the boat is difficult with the motor driving through a prop shaft over a metre long and even the tiniest movement alters the course considerably. Agent6 and Swifty have sat closer to the back, perhaps in anticipation of the inevitable learning curve before Dobbs gets the hang of it, but those sitting at the bow have to duck for cover several times. After a while though he works out that you have to negotiate turns way in advance of the bends and curves of the river and though he still makes some mistakes it's not long before he's become a dab hand at helming the vessel, which helps take his mind off the affairs weighing him down.

As the boat moves slowly down the river, Dobbs begins to realise that rather than attempting to escape the fear that he might have made a mistake coming to the Amazon he should do the opposite and enter the space within him like a warrior entering a battleground. He begins to consider all the terrible fears and thoughts that come to him, one by one, and deal with them as best he can: hold each one in his heart and breathe with it and just feel it. It doesn't matter if he has no answers right now. After a short period of retrospection he arrives back to the dumbfounding beauty of the river and the water that is now like absolute sheet glass.

He feels open, and his fears seem so silly as, whatever his worries, he's here now. This isn't something he wants to do; it's something he's doing. He's not living in fear, he's moving through fear. Maybe he won't find his story but he'll never have to regret not trying. And as the dancing sun beams scatter and shatter off a hundred trillion shiny droplets deposited in the sprawling growth he finally starts to feel his fear: not hear his fears as some wordless rant in his head but actually feel the physical sensations of his anxiety.

It's as if his surroundings are so perfect that they highlight all his own imperfections, and he suddenly realises there is a massive part of him that is terrified of beauty. His mind just cannot handle it, as it shows the rest of the world how inept and lowly he is in contrast to its magnificence. He feels a little shocked at the realisation, and decides that he must make more effort with his creativity, to maybe let the story take care of itself and focus on his intentions. Breathing in this wisdom soothes him.

It's so beautiful he can barely contain the feelings it brings up and now his eyes are watering slightly as he feels the jungle again; the moist, fresh smell of the abundance of life, the cooling breeze in his face and the sound of all the unseen life competing for the loudest squawk or hum or tweet; all suddenly fully audible, like someone has just flicked off a *mute* button in his head as he realigns with the now again. It's like a magician pulling a rabbit from his hat. All the birds and animals begin to appear. Bright parrots and toucans can be seen in the trees above, squawking at the sight of the boat coming up the river. Sloths are slowly crawling up trees while agile monkeys jump from branch to branch, apparently in playful pursuit games. The whole jungle seems to come to life for him in this awakening moment.

Maybe that's what this book should be about, Dobbs ponders momentarily: Playful Pursuits. Isn't that the story of my life? But somehow none of this seems like a game anymore. It actually feels like a real mission, it's just he doesn't know what the mission is anymore. Then again, did I ever know what the mission was about - my mission on Earth?' he wonders. 'Was there ever really a mission? Is there a purpose to life other than to amass experience, pay off karma or something like that?

He hates the notion that souls come to Earth to pay off Karma; it implies they arrive with a debt of sin, and the thought of that makes him cringe with the bitter taste of Catholicism. Pulling out his voice recorder, he begins to rattle off his thoughts and feelings, even though in truth he feels lost as to how to begin to capture the magnificence of so much as the water splashing up as the bow cuts through the still surface, creating shimmering crests of ripples like sea horses swimming in formation as they cut through the leafy tunnel. The others observe him, including the young boy who's come along for the trip, but he's getting used to being observed making his recordings now.

And then he suddenly just relaxes, realising that it doesn't matter; just do the work of making the recordings and finish the mission. Even though he doesn't know what the mission is, that doesn't mean he should stop now. Instead he should gather as much information as possible: good experiences, bad experiences, love, lust and whatever else goes to make up the heady cocktail of his adventure. 'Stay focused and stay optimistic - miracles happen all the time. It doesn't help seeing Bolivar down in the doldrums with his toothache but he's enjoying the river a little more now and the break from mosquitoes attacking them is making things a little easier,' he voices into his voice recorder.

Suddenly he has a brainwave: 'Ah! Maybe I just don't know yet because it's so exciting that it's not *given*, as I just wouldn't be ready for it until right up to the very last minute. Maybe if I knew what the mission was it would detract from *everything else*, and the *everything else* is probably the hardest work. I'm here and I'm up for it though: I'll say a prayer!'

'Dear God, I'm here and I'm up for it,' he begins, and as he says it, a tear runs down his face. 'God, I don't know quite what I'm up for, but you know me better than I know myself. You know I'm here to find out if there's a way to stop what I saw on that blast of laughing gas. My country seems to be obsessed with war, but actually I don't believe that: I think it's so few that are obsessed with war that I've never met a single person myself who says they want this killing. But in my name, and in the name of Britain, my government is dumping Depleted Uranium on innocent women, men and children, and I am of a mind to believe that this is all the agenda of Ego. In fact, that all this warring is actually a psychic attack - just like I saw happen to The Brigadier when he opened himself to the lower astral. If it doesn't stop, and what I saw happen on that fated day has to happen to stop these atrocities it will be a dreadful loss, as so few are with this murderous agenda.'

And he stops to consider what he wants to happen. 'So I'm asking you to spill the beans, please. I have devoted much of my life to anti-war demos and to promoting peaceful awareness, and have carried the pain of what I saw for long enough without understanding why all this is happening and what this nuclear obsession really is. Humanity needs a break. I need a break. Surely Soul itself needs a break from this needless suffering? Surely even *You* need a break? I know there's a reason for me to be here on this Earth at this time. You've got to spill the beans. You've got to put the cards on the table!'As soon as he has said this more tears run down his face, and as they do so the light seems to become so much brighter he has to squint his eyes against the radiance.

The boat potters on. He's been observing the carburettor as they go and now he sees how it has a little sprung regulator on the side that has no direct link to the throttle than a tiny spring. He immediately realises that if he pulls the main throttle butterfly it will probably give a burst of power over and above what appears to be full throttle. He realises that the universe has just answered his question in the way he it knows he'll best understand. That indeed, he has more powerful resources available to him, whenever he wants and whenever he's ready. He leans back just as they hit a perfect straight, and pulls the tiny lever. Sure enough the little *pecki-pecki* roars like a lion - well, more like a big kitten really, but nonetheless the boat surges forward slightly with the acceleration.

Agent6 is suddenly curious.

"How do you do that?" he asks.

"Just squeezing a little more juice out of her," Dobbs replies.

Agent6 is not taking that as an answer though, and now he stares at the motor, working out for himself what Dobbs has just done. He quickly figures it out, then reaches over and flicks the butterfly and the engine surges forward again.

"Nice to know there's a bit tucked away for emergencies."

"Ain't it just."

Everyone looks so content now as the boat travels up the river. Occasionally there's little clearings with lodges and tiny malokas but they are very few and far between. A boat maker can be seen hammering fresh white wood to the side of his latest creation, with a haze of smoke running off from the small fire on which he cooks up his bitumen for sealing the hull.

Dobbs has had enough of fast - not that fast quite describes the speed the boat travels at full throttle, but he slows the engine down now to take in the glass finish of the water. There's something so space-age about the jungle, something so *breathtakingly* beautiful that you have to separate yourself from yourself to see it. As the boat cuts through the water gracefully Dobbs can see how brown and completely opaque it actually is; not dirty, just crammed with microscopic life. Everywhere in the jungle is crammed with life co-inhabiting. Quite how aquatic life navigates though that thick pea soup is totally miraculous though.

Finally they arrive at a tiny village made up mostly of thatched huts except for a more modern-looking building which is probably a government funded school. Dobbs would normally have expected locals to be coming in droves to seek potential business but nothing of the sort is occurring, which seems a bit weird. Nonetheless they all disembark and make their way to the other end of the village, which despite its tiny size seems a strenuous stroll for Dobbs, who's feeling wiped out by the intense humidity and burning sun. His temperature is still a little high, and he really just wants to lie down and sleep in an open area free of mozzies.

At first a few children emerge to have a look at the visitors, but they keep at a safe distance until some of the adults also come out of their huts. Agent6 finds the woodsman, who has a good range of sawn timber, neatly stacked in a shaded area away from direct sunlight so that the air can evenly dry it and prevent it from warping as it contracts. It rapidly becomes clear that Agent6 is not so impressed with the prices, though he doesn't push his dissatisfaction as he seems to know other places that sell timber a lot cheaper, but makes it clear they're only looking for techo now. That's fine by Dobbs, as timber is heavier than techo and he's in no mood to haul heavy weights right now.

Juan is taking his troop up a track that runs up behind the village and leads off into the jungle. Dobbs and Bolivar follow, but as soon as they enter the shade of the canopy they're met with a torrent of mosquitoes and huge horse fly like things whose bite is particularly nasty. It's a beaten track, but all the foreigners except Carlos, who's coping with it slightly better than the others, are struggling with the onslaught. It's as if the jungle knows they're intruders and is warding them off, like a barking dog to a stranger.

Dobbs still doesn't know if they are going to drink tonight, but Juan is collecting *shacarp*a leaves from the jungle and these are commonly used by *curanderos* to clear a space of unwanted energy and raise the vibration in ceremonies. Even within the first fifteen metres of jungle he's pointing to countless different plants and showing their uses including one plant with thick spikes. They're tough, gnarly little blighters that look like rusted iron barbs and Dobbs remembers them lining the river banks on his last trip in the Amazon. Just one of those little bastards can put you out of action as, although they're so tough they're also very brittle so they snap off once they've penetrated deep into your flesh, and tend to hold an array of nasty infection. The only thing to be done is to dig

241

them out with a blade to make sure nothing's left inside. If you step on one you haven't got long to act; it's boots off and bam! Whack the blade in and dig the fucker out.

Juan mentions *Ayahuasca* when he talks of the barbs, and 'dolor', which Dobbs understands to mean pain. Then he motions like he's blowing a blow pipe with his mouth and fingers, clearly more for Dobbs's understanding than the others. Dobbs looks at him with shock.

"*Ayahuasca* can be used as a poisonous *dart*?"

Juan's face is calm, his energy very gentle, and when he looks across he speaks almost with humour in his face.

"Not to kill but to create pain; a warning to stop with your intention."

Dobbs just nods. He can't imagine *Ayahuasca* used in any fighting context; his experiences with it have been so otherworldly and beautiful. Juan can see he's struggling with the concept.

"Sometimes we need a warning," he grins and yet his eyes do not carry the humour expressed with his smiling features.

"Yeah," Dobb says, nodding and remembering the old witch he'd met on his first mission to the jungle.

Suddenly he realises Juan's English is better than he lets on, though he doesn't like speaking it. All those years in the US Army have obviously both helped and hindered his grip of the language in different ways. He never talks of those times, but Dobbs can't help wondering what it takes to make a man turn from total war to the path of complete peace. Maybe he has to experience both poles of the equation before he can truly grasp the fundamental logic that war is not an eternal technique.

Dobbs is looking into those knowing eyes now.

"We're drinking tonight aren't we?" he whispers.

Juan says nothing, almost like he doesn't know himself, but considering the state of play back at the camp there's clearly no way they're going to stay, and that can only mean one thing: that jungle juice is going down tonight.

Preparing the Space

Dobbs peers further down the dense jungle track, through the cloud of mosquitoes that is swarming about him and rapidly covering his exposed arms. Juan is casually pointing at several plants which he apparently uses as medicines, but as he speaks Dobbs realises he just can't handle it anymore. The huge swarm of insects is completely encircling him in a feasting frenzy and suddenly he's experiencing a desperate feeling of panic that he has to get out – like Right Now. Juan, on the other hand, seems quite unaffected and just nods at him with a knowing half grin across his face. It's as if, for whatever reason, the jungle just says 'No' to Dobbs and 'Yes' to him.

Dobbs just turns tail and runs towards the bright sunlight beyond the shadowy jungle canopy, Bolivar close on his heels. Once out in the open he shakes his arms furiously as he doesn't want to brush any feeding creatures away with their spikes still stuck in his skin.

"Man, this is impossible!" he says, dancing from foot to foot. "If we're going to stay in this environment we'll have to completely eliminate all the sugar from our diets so they don't recognise us; this shit's just too much for me!"

"Me too, man," Bolivar agrees reluctantly.

"Yeah, but you've been in Africa and done all that. You're hardcore…had malaria and all sorts."

"Well, to be honest Dobbs, they say it's the worst thing you can have - a full week of terrible fevers and pain, but the truth is I don't remember any of it. It's like I was on acid or something, and that whole week only seemed to last about an hour. You wake up and everyone tells you how terrible it was and gives you loads of sympathy, but all you know is that a week of your life is unaccounted for really."

"Sounds great!" Dobbs says with a bemused chuckle.

Catching sight of Agent6 and Swifty walking up to the other end of the village Dobbs and Bolivar follow behind, crossing an old iron bridge with a quaint techo roof that must have been there for many years. The tiny village is sparsely spread out over about half a kilometre or so along the riverbank and the scene is simply heavenly, with kids playing in the fields and locals peering leisurely from the windows of their wooden huts. Most of them have techo roofs, although there is the occasional, less attractive corrugated tin one to be seen here and there. Apart from a single power cable running along the track, they are the only identifiable attributes of the modern world.

They join Agent6 and Swifty right at the end of the village, in a shack with techo roofing combined with odd bits of rusting corrugated steel sections. It's a large space, completely open on the upper floor, whilst out the front literally hundreds of sections of prepared techo are drying in the sun. These consist of long strips of split bamboo with leaves - or perhaps reeds - tied whilst green and fresh by their stringy stems. The knot is a simple one done in such a fashion that it goes round and under, and where the end of the stem comes out another leaf ties over the top of it, stopping it coming undone. Each thin strip of bamboo is about two metres long, and crammed with leaves. They have to be the most effective and sustainable roofing system Dobbs has ever seen as they're dirt cheap, and it's an easy job to replace broken and leaking patches in minutes.

Beside the pile of *techo*, looking distinctly worse for wear, is an old single cylinder engine block with a large thresher wheel that's all been disassembled. It's quite a big thing, and judging by the size of the hole smashed in the crank case has clearly shot the big-end out of the side of the block. Dobbs, ever the undercover mechanic, is curious to know whether repairing the machine is a necessity, as replacing it might be financially impossible. He finds himself pondering the possibility of plating the hole, but eventually he gives up on the idea and clambers up a rickety wooden ladder to the living area whereAgent6 is discussing prices for the techo with a mature, very simply dressed Indigenous woman. He seems to be on very good terms with the lady, and he obviously knows her quite well, as she seems genuinely pleased to see him.

She is working with her children preparing some kind of pulse, or bean stew, and when Dobbs asks what it is she says something that sounds like '*Yaka*'. Its bright yellow colour looks wonderfully fresh and vibrant, but it's rancid smell makes Dobbs feel nauseous. Supposedly it's very nutritious, but to Dobbs the aroma is just like *Ayahuasca* which, apart from the psychedelic San Pedro cactus, is the most acrid, foul taste he knows. Apparently the *Yaka* must first be properly ground with water then left to ferment, which gives it it's bitter taste.

It reminds Dobbs of when he went to China and smelled all the Chinese herbs. At first he found them quite repugnant but then, on his second trip to the region, the same things seemed really quite romantic and nostalgic. It seems good taste revolves largely around association, so maybe the same will be true for this stuff; if it brings good results and harbours no negative reactions, you come round to the good side of it and eventually grow to love it.

Deciding to risk it for a biscuit, Dobbs takes a swig and does his best to hold it down but it immediately makes him want to retch, and for a few moments he's expecting everything to go horribly wrong. Even once the acrid aftertaste has subsided he's still waiting for the violent projectile evacuation of his guts, but to his immense relief things settle surprisingly well. He breathes out a sigh of relief when he's passed the emergency and the woman bursts out laughing and her kids immediately join in - as does Agent6, who's been sipping away quite happily.

"Do you seriously like this stuff?" asks Dobbs, still making strange faces. Agent6 nods in approval.

"Yeah, I love it!"

Once the business is concluded they all spend some time lazing around in the shade of the hut. There are still a few mosquitoes, but it's far enough from the jungle not to be completely dominated by the evil little blighters. Finally it's time to leave and they all make their way back down the rickety step ladder.

Dobbs is not feeling like loading the boat one little bit. He knows it has to happen though, and is pleasantly surprised to find that, by forming a chain, the job is done in less than fifteen minutes. Once aboard, the rustling pile of techo is like a huge floating mattress and, lying there with the others, he soon falls fast asleep.

***

As they approach the lodge the engine revs drop down low and the change in tone wakes Dobbs out of his slumber. Looking around, he sees that everyone seems much fresher, probably because, like him, most passed out on the boat ride back and managed to get some much needed sleep. Bolivar, though, is still cradling his mouth a bit, and wondering if drinking is the best idea in such a state.

"It might help," Dobbs suggests.

"Yeah, and it might not."

"Look, last time I came to the jungle I was with this girl who was adamant she wasn't going to drink, but she wanted to come and meet the shaman. And you know what he said when he met her? 'You've come a long way, just to tell me you don't want to drink!' It's a medicine, man; people use it to cure all sorts of illness and disease. It might be just what the doctor ordered."

"Pressure!" Bolivar says, shaking his head and looking stressed.

"I'm not pressuring you, just saying what I would hope a friend would say to me if the situation was reversed. If you don't drink, you might regret it."

"And if I do drink, I won't regret it?"

"I'll be putting a big golden ring round you man."

"*Thanks.*"

Personally, Dobbs feels ready to drink now. A few hours on the river, a bit of exercise, some sleep and a prayer has set him to rights. Now all he needs is to get in the water, bathe himself clean, and stay with his intention.

He and Agent6 head down to the river but as it turns out it's not such an easy process getting in the water, and once he does he's a bit freaked out to find little fish biting him all over his body. It's only like a pinch though, and whilst it's a little unnerving at first, considering what else lurks below the surface and *could* bite you, it come as a bit of a relief. Once he's all the way in and has swum out a bit though he soon loses himself in a playful splash about, forgetting his fears as to what may lurk below the surface of the thick brown water. He'd envisaged himself swimming with a blade strapped to him in the event of an alligator attack and yet here he is, armed only with his underpants.

Agent6, like Dobbs, looks much refreshed after his dip. Now, observing Bolivar and Swifty looking decidedly fed up as he gets out of the water, he shouts across to them.

"Get in and wash! The medicine will work better if you're feeling clean and mentally prepared."

Swifty just grunts and continues running about cursing. Bolivar doesn't respond at all.

Meanwhile Juan is preparing the kitchen area for the ceremony. His three students are with him and he's discussing his preparations and their individual intention, but Dobbs gets the feeling that the discussion is closed off to him. He understands that these are Juan's students, and respects his reluctance to speak English though; it's him that should be making more effort, as

246

effort in anything, with an intention in mind, is a powerful combination.

Whatever it is that Juan is saying at least sounds very focused and intellectual, and the students all look very attentive. For his part, Dobbs wants to tell them just to go and wash themselves, but it's almost like they're not talking to him at all. No doubt there's a lesson in there somewhere, but still he feels it's important for them to cleanse themselves and mentally prepare - to wind their whole thought process back to the here-and-now, and the issues that truly rule their lives. They need to quiet themselves now and to attempt to become aware of the underlying frequency of their own being, but that is not always the nicest picture to see, so sometimes it can seem difficult. As far as he's concerned though, there can be no change until there is awareness of what needs changing: how can you heal yourself if you don't even know you're sick?

To Dobbs it seems they are trying to intellectualise their process right now, keeping it up in the head, whereas he feels it all needs to come back to the heart. Of course that's just his intuition, as he doesn't really understand much of what is being said, but the troop seems heavy to him and he feels disconnected from them. Maybe they don't like him, or maybe they're just struggling with the jungle like everyone else. The Israeli certainly is; Dobbs has been watching him trying to get these little tiny red bloodsuckers off the skin around his legs. They are almost impossible to see apart from the tiniest red dot, but cause terrible irritation.

Dobbs wants to take all that intellectual activity and let it dissipate into the heart; recycle it into awareness and let it break free from the restrictive confinement of the head. He appreciates that sometimes we need to intellectualise a process in order to be able to clearly describe it but though it's fascinating to discuss the latest scientific data about *Ayahuasca* the reality is it's not something to be intellectualised as, to a large extent, it appears to work *beyond* the analytical mind. What *Ayahuasca* offers is gifts - offerings from another dimension - and it is difficult to understand and intellectualise a gift, an insight, that has not necessarily yet been given.

The whole atmosphere of the group - apart from Agent6, who is just pottering about clearing the space - is very *heady*, and Dobbs can't help thinking they would be better off emptying their heads rather than filling them even further with expectations, science and rules. This is not a time to be heaping up 'knowledge' about *things;* it is a time to turn inwards and tap into the divine wisdom of their own heart song. It is time to disengage from the thinking mind, to surrender to the Mystery, and accept the blessings that flow forth from the portal that *Ayahuasca* opens without expectation, but only a honed and processed intention.

He accepts that drinking is always a daunting prospect; even to those who do know a little of the Other Side, it represents such a massive unknown, and can sometimes seem totally unbelievable. How does someone surrender to something they do not know, he ponders? But then he realises it's just a process - a pathway. *Ayahuasca* is certainly not the key: his mother has never taken it, and she goes further than anyone he has ever known. It seems there are many pathways, but these guys are clever enough by the looks of things, so he just has to trust they'll work it all out themselves - even if they *are* too nervous to wash themselves in the river!

Shrugging his shoulders and still feeling that energetically the group is somehow divided and knows that Swifty's attitude with work and the way he gets things done has had an abrasive edge on some of the others, and can sense Swifty has his shields up a little. He's still has his work head on. Dobbs senses that if Swifty and Bolivar do a cleanse it might calm the energy and in turn, make him less anxious also.

"Listen," he says, "You're not going to get much from it if you don't mentally prepare for it: It's like a door, but a door to a higher space, so you have to raise your whole vibration a little - not much, but sufficiently to at least knock on the door. Even then that don't necessarily mean the door will open, but if you never even make the effort to bloody knock, then it definitely won't open. You have to align yourself a little."

"The head has no control over this whatsoever; all the head will do is process what happens and feed that back into your state of being. It will always only be on the tail end of it. So both of you need to go and wash in the river, regardless of whether you plan to drink or not. You need to feel clean and then make your decision. Go on - you'll feel refreshed at least. Just forget *Ayahuasca* for the time being, and think about the issues within yourselves."

"It never does anything to me anyway," Swifty grunts despondently.

"Do you have any bad intentions for anyone in the world, to bring about suffering to other beings, and pose a threat to their being, to their peace?"

"No," he says bluntly.

"Then if you're not going to bathe fully, at the very least focus on that and just wash your hands and face. And remember - you are a being of peace by the accordance of your actions, if nothing else."

"I don't know if I want to do it anyway," Bolivar adds.

Dobbs wants to tell them to clear off from the space where the ceremony is about to occur, as they are both carrying doubt and uncertainty. It's a heavy attitude, and Dobbs can sense that it's annoying Juan, but he can also see that Swifty is tired and agitated after all his hard work, and Bolivar is in pain, so he says nothing and resigns himself to the fact that neither of them can seem to raise themselves above their negativity.

The odd energy conflict in the group is still unsettling him a little; like two separate clans and somehow, despite the shared adventure of the trip, they remain divided. It is not a circle, as his mother would say, which means, as a group they amount to nothing. But then he thinks, after this, we will all have shared a little adventure, and through adventure, circles can be made.

As nightfall draws ever closer it's clear that Swifty and Bolivar still haven't prepared themselves to drink. It's not that they're filthy blighters or anything, but it is a bit of a process wading through the muddy river bed with all the mosquitoes and other sorts of creatures that are said to lurk in the water just waiting to nip your knob off. The simple fact is they've only been in the jungle twenty-four hours so far and it's proving to be much harder work than most of them expected, even though they've all been here before. It's almost as if they've been in a state of collective amnesia about the difficulties awaiting them. A little more pre-planning could have made all the difference.

Perhaps now this journey into the jungle will engrave a little more on their mental faculty that the Amazon is hard work unless you're properly prepared, and even then it's no easy ride. One thing's for sure though: they're all going to chip in to buy a huge mosquito net as a communal space to hang out in when they go back to Iquitos tomorrow. As it is, everyone disappears to their own muzzy nets at dusk until the major mosquito squadrons have gone. It's actually a lovely feeling to be inside the net when it reaches its peak hum but as soon as it subsides they all pile on the repellent and cover themselves with long sleeve tops, socks, thick trousers and a blanket to hide in.

Finally there they all are, sitting round a few candles in the kitchen area, which has been cleaned and prepared for the ceremony by Juan and Agent6. Dobbs is pleased to see Bolivar and Swifty are present. They still haven't washed, but perhaps they have tried to mentally prepare. Dobbs hopes so, but he knows also that, like most Westerners, they have become all too practiced in the art of paying the money and then expecting to just watch the show. The only trouble is that *Ayahuasca* is not a show to just sit and watch; once you drink, and you open that door, you *are* the show. If you're not happening, the show's not happening.

That said, Dobbs is still confused as to exactly what his own intentions are for this journey. He's thinking of the prayer he said previously, but his intention feels somehow bigger than himself now but he still hasn't connected with any of Juan's students apart from Carlos and here he is, about to do a sacred ceremony with them.

Closing his eyes, he tries to empty his mind of thought, and focus on the feelings in his heart. Immediately he feels the loving embrace of Gatita, but then he thinks of his partner and suddenly that warmth transforms into a melancholy sadness. For a while he just sits in that space, letting the sorrow sink in. It occurs to him that perhaps he can't send anymore intention up to the Universe right now, but still he feels he needs to be clearer. After all, to sit in a ceremony and not know your own intentions is surely a little like standing at the ticket office and not knowing where you want to buy a ticket to, he ponders. For now he finds himself teetering on the cusp of indecision. Sure, he wants to write a book - but about what exactly? Yet, simply asking for some insight into what the hell is happening on the Earth right now all seems a little vague, especially whilst trying to ignore the pain and sorrow of his failing relationship which has all been brought to the surface by his involvement with Gatita.

Suddenly, he feels nervous. He knows only too well that the *Ayahuasca* can tear him to pieces if it wants, as he's already had some full-on experiences - though thankfully those have been few and far between. Mostly his journeys have been very beautiful - well, the truth is they've all been beautiful - in hindsight - but sometimes when he's had to release something really deep the process of letting go has sometimes been simply horrific. And, he remembers now, he's been bingeing on booze and pestilence and all kinds of other shit. 'Oh, please, go easy on me!' he finds himself praying, but then he reconsiders. 'No. Do as You will: in your great hands I place myself.'

Juan begins the process of blowing smoke over his concoction, which he has prepared in his own special way, cooking up the leaves and bark of the *Ayahuasca* vine with, no doubt, a few special added plants to help soothe the nauseous affect it has on the body and maximise the time it can be held down. It's not called *La Purgativa* without reason, as it can cause abrupt evacuation of the guts, to say the *very* least.

In Dobbs's experience Peruvian ceremonies are generally extremely simple compared to those he's been to in the West, which can sometimes become too focused on the external trappings of the ceremony to the detriment of being present with oneself. That said, the more effort one makes in the ceremony, the more likely it seems that something will happen as the spirits respond well to focused intention, which ultimately is the true point of ceremony and ritual.

Dobbs pretty much knows the routine by now. Juan will no doubt start singing the *icaros* later, but that will be at the point when he feels everyone needs to be pulled from their slumbering nausea, way after they've all thrown up and rid their bodies of all it's unnecessary baggage, like a rocket discharging its fuel tanks once its broken free of the atmosphere. First they have to drink though, and for Dobbs that has always been the hardest part; getting that potion down his neck is a feat in itself. It tastes so repulsive it's quite unbelievable. First-timers often say 'Oh, it's not that bad,' but once your body has run it through its system and finally realises that, actually, this stuff's bloody horrific, it pulls the rip-cord and just sort of says no after that. For Dobbs, just the smell of it brings about spasms now.

This time he's unfortunate in that he's last to drink and so he has to watch as the rest of the group have their names called out. One after the other, they approach the little temple Juan's erected, take the glass and knock it back, then return to their places and begin to go through the agonizing process of digestion. It's an agonising process to watch, although to be fair, they all handle it very well.

Finally Juan looks at him.

"Dobbs," he whispers.

Dobbs gets up and takes the glass, nodding at Juan.

"Gracias," he whispers in reply, closing his eyes for a second and holding the glass to his brow as he clears his mind. With his free hand he holds his nose, like a child jumping into deep water for the first time: anything to stop that smell hitting his nostrils. There's not much, and it's easy enough to take the whole mixture in one mouthful, but he just can't seem to swallow and is gagging straight away. Eventually he steadies himself though and manages to send it down, grabbing his water straight after and swigging some back to clean his mouth of the residue.

The DMT is pungent and he can feel it burning in his mouth as he shudders and shakes like a leaf at the feeling of having that intense potion suddenly within him. It's an exciting and scary feeling all at the same time, but he's done it; now all he has to do is breathe and regulate his body, as the more awake you are in this period the more aware you are of just how difficult it is to keep down.

"Gracias Juan," he manages to whisper once more, and then returns to his seat.

For the first half an hour or so there's silence as they sit in the now near-total darkness. Then, as the discomfort starts to develop, the sound of movement can be heard as people shift around, restlessly trying to find some respite from the creeping nausea. Dobbs feels sick, sick to his stomach. Rolling up into a ball on his bench, he tries to sleep through the hardest part as he knows the longer he can hold it down, the more effect it will have. Meanwhile Juan is making noises like he's softly whistling *icaros*, although the highest peaks of the pitch are carefully omitted.

Dobbs pulls himself back up to a sitting position, trying to establish his body in an upright position. His head is whirling round and round and behind his lidded eyes a fairground of colours is beginning to bloom in the darkness. It's like a kaleidoscope of ever-expanding imagery, and every now and then almost as if reaching some critical mass, the colours seem to merge into a central point before oozing back out again like some kind of fluoro-coloured toothpaste spiralling out from the tube.

This is the signal that the *Ayahuasca* is telling him to prepare to evacuate his system, and he's carefully placed everything of vital importance, like his torch, water, lighter and some *mopachos* to smoke nearby, ready for this time of total disorientation. He fumbles for his head torch, although he doesn't switch it on yet, and begins the process of standing up, which thankfully isn't too hard.

Slowly he walks out of the maloka and makes his way to an open area just far enough so those in the ceremony don't have to listen to him vomiting then, kneeling down on the ground, he tells his system that he's ready to let go, and waits. He can feel his solar plexus going into periodic spasm but he wants a clear, flowing motion, as he knows it's easy for the body to panic now and go into wild, painful convulsions. Eventually he feels completely ready. He knows that the next contraction will probably be the one, so he tries to relax himself in readiness. At last, like a wave, it comes, and in one fluid motion and then a couple more smaller heaves he expels the remains of the *Ayahuasca* from his system. He continues to sit there for a while, but though he's still a little nauseous, he now feels completely present. Everything is clear, and though he knows his body will be a quivering mess, his mind is in that special state.

Standing up once more, he makes his way back to his bench in the darkness with ease. He feels completely clear, perfectly calm, and in the exact space he knows he needs to be in. He doesn't know if he will have to travel or the experience will occur here, but he's ready.

'Come on Dobbs, you can do this' he says to himself, taking a couple of deep breaths like he's going to dive into a lake.

Then he closes his eyes.

'Ready when You are.'

Cat Suits and Whips

It's completely dark with his eyes closed, but even when he opens them and looks around at everyone in their positions he can only make them out very slightly. Still, there seems to be some other kind of luminance in the room, as before it was pitch black. Nothing is really happening yet, so he lies down on his side and cocoons himself under the blanket. Just as he's getting comfortable though he suddenly finds himself sitting up again, looking down at his hands resting on his lap.

'That's odd' he thinks to himself, 'I thought I was lying down.' Then he looks again and sees that his hot pants are different. They're like his old hot pants, only in green camo instead. He runs his hand over his legs and then peers back at his hands. His nails are perfect and not gnawed away with stress. Then he notices his new sexy camo pants are slightly flared, with a laced gap up the sides. He likes his taste! 'This is new', he voices in his mind; 'I've never had a body beyond my own Earthly body - well, not one I've known about before, anyway.' He's always just been a sort of floating consciousness before but now, looking at his hands once more they seem so beautiful; almost manicured.

'Is this my light body?' he asks. 'Wow. I've got better taste up there than down here! So where am I?' But he knows where he is, and no answer is given. He's in the dream world. He's been several times before to this space. In fact, the first time he was in this world was the first time he drank in the jungle on his last trip. It had been quite a journey, and since then he's been back a few times, but to see his own body - and, have control over it - is a great surprise to him.

He looks up to take in the view of this world in which all that exists is illuminated by its own inner light, and painted in colours he's never seen in the waking world. But instead of the rolling hills he was expecting to see, he is shocked to find, standing in front of him, a woman with her legs slightly akimbo and a whip made of long strands of light dangling from her right hand.

She's literally right in front of him but though he's getting a full frontal of her gorgeous body, when he tries to look at her face he can never seem to see beyond her neckline. She's wearing a tight, latex cat suit that is sexier than Dobbs can quite get his little head around, an all-in-one number that covers her shoulders and drops down at the front to reveal a truly impressive cleavage. By the looks of things, the only thing preventing her gorgeous, gargantuan globes of pleasure from exploding free of it is the brightly coloured cord that binds the low, sensual cut together.

It's all an impeccable fusion of indefinable colour and light. Sparkling, psychedelic rainbows of luminosity arc off the exquisite curvature of her voluptuous hips and backside, all of which is perfectly defined by the elastic armature of the skin-tight suit. She is nothing short of spectacular, and Dobbs finds himself completely mesmerised by the curve of her crotch and the way it meets her buttocks. Every detail is perfect, even the fine stitching of her outfit, which seems to be made from many small patches, all over-locked together, like some kind of luminous latex mosaic, with the seam-work all of a similar thread to the lacing containing her cleavage, only much finer, and the sleeves opened out to frame her slender hands with even finer detail still. In short, and not to put too fine a point on it, she's sex on a stick.

Dimly, Dobbs begins to become aware that he has all but forgotten about the wonders of his own new body and is completely overwhelmed by hers, but then she raises her arm and flicks the whip. As she does so the strands of coloured light curl over his head and seem to split off almost like tentacles. One strand snakes down behind him, lashing his lower back, and immediately he feels an immense blast of sexual energy flash through him as he leans back in sensual delight. A tidal wave of tingles goes juddering straight down to his crotch, and now all he wants is to put his hands between her legs and slide them up to the curvaceous conch shell between her thighs, every fine contour of which can be seen in glorious detail just beneath her sheer rubber garb to, pull her close to him and grab two fat handfuls of that tight, sexy arse.

She's luring him in, and he can feel himself going with her, willingly, but as the intensity of his attraction increases he hears a voice speaking to him, almost imperceptibly, from the furthest reaches of his mind.

'I don't know if I'm here for this,' it seems to be saying. He feels powerless to resist her seductive sexual energy, which is now reaching an almost agonising intensity, but he knows it's not love, it's just lust, and as inexorably she takes him he begins to feel something else; a sad feeling, like he's descending into darkness, dropping into an abyss.

'Something's not right,' he thinks to himself, but the siren song is singing so sweetly,

'It's ok, just go. It's OK.' But it doesn't feel OK.

'I'm not here for this,' he suddenly realises, and then he repeats it in his mind to clarify his thoughts. 'I'm not here for this!'

He's descending faster and faster now though. As he does so, darkness surrounds him, and now he feels the shudder of fear. He tries to open his eyes but she has him; he's not in his body anymore, he's just a naked spirit, falling into an ever-deepening abyss, to a space beyond his control. He knows now, with a cold certainty, that he does not want to go with this woman.

'Please, I'm not here for this!' he shouts out, but his words are worthless, and still he's descending.

Finally he cries out, in his mind or however one cries out in that space,

'I cannot go with you; I am not here for this. I am here for another purpose. Thank you for what you offer me, but I am not here for that.'

He searches for the light, for a way out, but he cannot see it, and the fear is starting to seriously set in.

'Don't go into fear!' he reminds himself. 'I need to find the light; I need to find the light!'

And then a voice replies, apparently from somewhere else,

'Does it matter where the light is, so long as you're looking for the light?' And no sooner has he heard these words than he sees a black hole; a tunnel running off right in front of him, which he's just about to fall pass, like a lift dropping down past the floor it's supposed to stop on. He doesn't wait around. 'The light's down there,' he says to himself, and then shoots towards the black hole, diving deep into it.

No sooner has he disappeared into the depths of the black hole though, than he reappears - now with his head suddenly poking up through the kitchen floor, back home in England, watching his partner serving up the kids' dinner. She looks so beautiful, but also somehow so lonely, although the kids seem happy, and totally unaware that she's feeling so alone. Their sweet little faces are shining as they look at her. The house seems such a warm little homestead, and he sees what a beautiful symbol mother she has become. It's a truly honest and simple scene.

256

He loved her and her kids; it felt like they'd become a proper family, and never more so than when they sat together at the table and ate. Even if their time was over now he knew that she would always be a symbol of love in his heart, and this symbol was now his saving grace. Now he had to just watch them from a distance, longing to be there in that moment, sitting at the table with them. He knew she felt she was missing out on all the fun of being in the jungle and yet here he is in the jungle with her and the kids. It was their sweet shining grace that now seemed to save him from being taken off to the lower realms by a siren that could perhaps exploit his spirit and take his Earthly body. For a few moments more he savours the wholesomeness of this heavenly scene, seeing his little family just being their beautiful selves, and then the image becomes blurry and starts to fade until, at last, all that remains is the softly scented darkness of the tropical night.

Coming back to himself, he feels so light and free, but when he tries to move his body, nothing seems to be responding. It's not until he attempts to move his head that he realises his body is still well and truly unconscious. Slowly, fingers by finger, he begins to regain sensation, returning by degrees into his physical form, which, it appears has half fallen off the bench and he finds his face is flat against the dry muddy floor of the *maloka*.

Slowly he pulls himself up to a sitting position, and as he does so Juan begins to softly sing his *icaros*, gently pulling the group back together as he energetically senses it is time for them to return from the Dreaming and remember that they are in a ceremony. In that world, it is all too easy to slip into bliss and out of consciousness, especially if you leave your body.

Dobbs pulls himself up and, stretching his body, looks around at everyone else, wondering if they've all had an experience too. It's still early in the ceremony but, though his head has not yet stopped whirling from the effects of the *Ayahuasca*, he knows his ride is over. Whether he can make any sense of it is something else however; he feels like it was a test - but for what purpose? Whatever it was, it seems he's passed, but as soon as he has that thought he feels a pang of ego take him and has to pull himself back. 'You're not there yet,' he reminds himself.

For a while he lies back, pondering the wonders he has witnessed, and wondering at the weirdness while he waits for the others to fully return. Finally, when everybody seems to be back in the room and back in their bodies, Juan lights a small candle and everyone just sits together, quietly contemplating. There are a few nods and smiles exchanged as they all come round, but nothing is spoken, and no one else is really looking as though they've just returned from some mad adventure.

Eventually Dobbs is ready to depart, and gets to his feet.

"Gracias Juan," he says, bowing his head and placing his hands together in thanks.

"*Como estas...bien?*" Juan enquires, his gentle eyes searching Dobbs's face.

"I think I saw the body I have on the other side...oh and I fended off a siren," Dobbs shrugs, a little flatly; he's ready for bed, and doesn't really feel much like dissecting the whole experience right now, but Juan suddenly looks concerned.

"Oh, it's OK," Dobbs reassures, "It was, like, a lesson in finding the light and staying with the love and navigating through fear, I think."

Juan looks him up and down once more as if somehow still concerned and then their eyes meet again and he smiles warmly. He says nothing for a while, then just nods as if finally satisfied Dobbs has emerged from his experience on the sunny side and hasn't got a lower astral attachment hooked up to his being.

"I will do a ceremony at my home in a few days. You are welcome to join us," he says eventually. Then, looking across at Swifty, "All are welcome."

"Gracias Juan," Dobbs says gratefully, inclining his head. Then he takes his leave.

His mind is in a blissful state, but his body feels heavy and tired, still sluggish from the drug's effects. Disinclined to go and chat with the others, he decides to retreat back to his hammock so he can relax in a muzzy-free zone. After drinking some water he lies down as if to sleep but refrains from letting himself quite drop off for a while. He feels so beautiful and happy he just doesn't want to waste the appreciation of this feeling of awe he has in his heart, but eventually he can resist no longer, and surrenders himself to the sweet arms of oblivion.

In the morning, after breakfast, they are all sitting around the fire and Dobbs asks the rest of the group how things had gone for them. Bolivar, it seems, had bordered on something but felt nervous to go further.

"It felt like acid to me," he says, shaking his head, "And I just didn't feel I needed to go to wherever that leads."

258

"Were you in fear?" Dobbs presses him.

"I don't know. I just didn't feel I wanted to go wherever that leads. I don't need that right now," he whispers in a slightly defensive tone.

"What about you Swifty?" Dobbs asks.

"I never get any effect from it. Don't reckon it's very strong," Swifty states bluntly. He's clearly disappointed and, by the sounds of it, a little angry that's he's wasted his time again.

Juan is standing right there, and though Swifty's voice has what could be construed as a rude tone to it Dobbs - and Juan also - clearly appreciate his candidness. Whatever else you might say about Swifty, you always know exactly where you stand with him, and that is a commodity all can respect. He's not one for talking about people behind their backs.

When it comes to Agent6's turn however, Dobbs gets little more than a sigh and a shake of his head, as though he'd been challenged by the whole experience and doesn't want to speak about it. He looks so weighed down with all the work to be done on the lodge and the state of his relationship that it was obviously difficult for him to let go into the light. None of the other Westerners really comment much, although the Israeli is now making eye contact with the group a little more, which Dobbs finds encouraging.

By midday the whole group have gathered their belongings and are in the boat, making their way back to Iquitos. It seems no one else has really had a major experience and the others are all a little curious as to what happened for Dobbs. Agent6 normally gets strong experiences, but he didn't get so much out of it this time it seems. Then again the effects of *Ayahuasca* can be very subtle; sometimes, even when Dobbs thinks he's got absolutely nothing by way of a journey, he still feels unaccountably euphoric afterwards.

Now, as they make their return voyage, he would have thought that he'd be thinking about the realms beyond the waking reality, or his new body in the dream world or about the woman he managed to escape from. Or perhaps, his partner back home. But actually all he's thinking about Gatita.

Doors and Knockers

As the boat pulls in to Belen a feeling of relief washes over Dobbs and no sooner has he stepped down on dry land the first than he's thinking of Gatita again - which seems odd as, after last night's experience, he would have expected to be thinking about his partner back home.

The journey back from the lodge had gone by in a flash as this time they were going with the current, but Dobbs had been lost in his vision and much was still coming through. It felt as if a door had been left open deep in his heart and information was still flooding in. He had to keep taking deep breaths as if trying to contain something bigger than himself that was struggling to get out, and every now and then he would have to wipe away the odd tear as his emotions overcame him.

He'd seen his body! It was a different body, in a different space, but it moved just like this body - except it looked far better maintained and had a better sense of taste -although that part, he has to accept, isn't actually too hard to believe.

Out on the dockside lots of arrangements are being made but Dobbs just sits out the whole process until a huge American pickup turns up and everything is loaded into the back. Then it's straight off to Juan's. At last the truck is unloaded and Dobbs is back down to just his small rucksack and a few odds and sods, ready to head back to the Hotel. He's just about to go, but as he turns to leave he catches Juan's eye and nods a smile as thanks for holding the ceremony.

"So, you had a good experience; a challenge?" Juan says. It sounds like a question, but it could just as easily be an acknowledgement of something he already knows, as those deep, gentle eyes are almost laughing at him.

"Unbelievable Juan. I feel I was...tested, but I don't know what for."

"Maybe you will find out," Juan says mysteriously, looking at him with the subtlest hint of a grin.

There's a silence then as Dobbs realises the *curandero* is not going to be forthcoming about the opportunity to drink again unless he actually makes the effort to enquire.

"So, when are you doing this ceremony?" he offers eventually, suddenly feeling slightly uncomfortable.

"Tomorrow night."

"That soon?" Dobbs says bluntly as he mentally calculates how long that will be since the last dose.

"It's OK if I come along?" he asks a little sheepishly.

"Si, is open ceremony."

"What time?"

"Before nightfall."

He nods, but decides to think it over; for now all any of them can think about is a massive meal.

"Shower and the hugest, finest salad on the market, methinks!" Dobbs suggests.

An hour or so later, and they're all sitting round a table on the sidewalk outside the *Yellow Rose of Texas*, a café just off the main square, lost in white noise and bliss, just taking it all in. The busy street of a late-evening Iquitos fast slipping into night conjures a scene that's amplified by the flirtatious waitresses in their seductive frilly gingham retro aprons and short skirts, all vying to get the men's attention. The whole place is just rammed with the most eclectic collection of American memorabilia and relics to the sorts of things dragged back from the jungle by wild-eyed explorers. It is such a cornucopia it is almost a little overwhelming for Dobbs to investigate in his present state and yet creates a fusion with the backdrop of the Caso de Fierro with it archaic sections of cast iron panels, imperial uprights and juicy fat rivets holding the whole place together.

The café and the location are exactly what Dobbs is looking for. A large portion of the seating is situated out on the sidewalk, offering a fantastic opportunity for people watching, which is exactly what they all need after the jungle; the hustle and bustle, the noise, the pretty ladies. Even the TV in the background, blaring out CNN propaganda seems like perfect escapism, a saturation of the airways that makes it easier to unhook from the internal dialogue and just allow the world to be whatever it wants; to be in it but not of it.

The Brigadier has joined them but he has no money left at all and is looking a bit nervous. At least he's looking alive though. He's in the kind of situation most people are terrified of finding themselves in, although one that is often easier to deal with than the actual fear of being plain old broke. Dobbs is secretly quite pleased that The Brigadier has struggled a bit in just the few days they've been away. It would make him think twice about coming to the jungle with them when they return, in a few days. If he can get a week without pestilence it might be enough to break the cycle he's in. Certainly, no one in the group would mind helping him out if it didn't all have to go up his nose.

Dobbs takes pity on him and offers to pick up his tab though, so now he's sat with the others, waiting for his salad to arrive. The café is actually quite busy but they all seem very preoccupied and though they're all sat at the same table there's an odd space between them and little is said until finally the food is brought out.

"What's this stuff?" Dobbs asks, picking up what looks like pasta strips with his fork and eyeing them suspiciously. He's really not feeling like anything wheat-based.

The Brigadier points across.

"*Chonta*, err...Palm heart," he says. "It's delicious, and really good for you. They have to chop the whole tree down just to get the centre of it out so it's a bit unsustainable like, but at least they're a fast growing tree. They cut it off in long strips like that."

Dobbs coils a load of it round his fork and is amazed just how fresh and wholesome it actually tastes. "That's delicious!"

The street running next to the café is a hive of activity and the feeling of being back in the city, even after less than forty-eight hours in the jungle, is refreshing to say the very least. The response from the others is not exactly one of booming excitement however. Swifty especially is distinctly moody about the lack of effect he got from the *Ayahuasca*.

Dobbs looks across at him.

"Come and drink tomorrow Swifty," he offers, but Swifty's shaking his head with a look of total disappointment,

"Nah, his mixture don't do anything for me. It ain't strong enough."

"I promise you Swifty, it's way strong enough," Dobbs declares.

"Then why don't it work then?"

Dobbs goes to give his most obvious line, but Agent6 beats him to it.

"It's only a doorway Swifty. *You've* got to do the work," he says. Dobbs just nods.

"Oh fine, so it's all me is it?" he grunts in a tone of denial.

"It won't just come to you like that Swifty," Dobbs says, snapping his fingers. "You're here in this body, having the opportunity to be in the jungle with the *curandero* and drink the juice, but that's still only the base of the ladder. I told you before; you've got to climb

262

up to where that door is. And sometimes you have to climb up several times to prove you really want to open that door, that you really intend to align with that frequency - and that takes effort."

"What - you saying I'm bad or something?" he retorts defensively.

"No Swifty, but your whole approach is that you feel it should just work if you knock it back, like you expect the worlds beyond should be completely in service to you. Why? Why should they. What are you trying to achieve? It's like jumping in your car and being surprised when the thing doesn't start up, select a gear and start taking you where you don't even know where you want to go. We do it all the time. Meet a nice woman and not say what we want to do or ask for what we want to experience. Or like wanting to build a house in the jungle and just wanting the house but not make the effort to make it come together. Just drinking the *Ayahuasca* is like having the money in the bank to build the house. It won't just happen - unless *you* happen."

"I'm fucking trying," he moans abjectly.

"Look, try this. Think of your daughter. Just close your eyes and think of her and how beautiful she is, and how lucky you are to have such a lovely little girl in your life."

Swifty doesn't seem to take the advice, but he nods at the idea.

"Well go on then!" Dobbs urges.

Eventually Swifty gives in and closes his eyes. As he does so his face take on a calmer aspect, his breathing deepens and a slight smile appears at the corners of his normally tight lips. When he finally opens his eyes again he looks at Dobbs with an endearingly sheepish smile.

"That's the doorway Swifty. It's that simple and that beautiful. It's a feeling, not a knowing or an expectation. You can't study your way through, you can't think your way through, you can't blame your way through, and you certainly can't just buy your way through. Even doubling the dose just to bust your way through is simply futile. When the *curanderos* drink they sometimes barely touch the potion with their lips.

"You have to enter your heart and feel your way through, man. Your head will process the data that comes back as you go through but your head cannot negotiate the terms and the sooner you accept that, the sooner you'll begin the process of understanding that there's a door here in your heart that is only going to open through feeling - not thought."

Dobbs pauses, tapping his heart.

263

"But I'd like you to come though Swifty. Sit next to me next time and we'll do a bit of preparation before, to let go of expectation and all that heavy intellectual shite that weighs on our minds and just enter into the heart space a little more."

Swifty takes a deep breath and holds it for a moment. Then he slowly releases it, forcing it out against his sealed lips before just sitting quietly, biting his lower lip in contemplation.

"You need to think about some questions you might have as well Swifty," Dobbs says gently after a few moments.

"I haven't got any questions," Swifty replies.

Dobbs is stymied there for a moment.

"Maybe you should ask it why you haven't got any questions when the world we live in is in such a mess and being torn apart by war, disease, famine, pollution, greed, and hatred?"

"Yeah, alright," Swifty concedes, "I've got a few."

"I can assure you; just one answer makes one hell of a lot of questions."

"What about you Bolivar?" Dobbs asks.

"I don't want it Dobbs."

Dobbs is confused that someone can make all the effort to come to the jungle and then refuse the opportunity to enter into the spirit of it.

"If you stay in town tomorrow night you're going to be taking something for sure," he says eventually.

"Oh come off it," Bolivar retorts. "You guys have all come out here and done all that. I want to do more of that before I do more of *that*. You know what I mean Dobbs?"

Dobbs sighs. Perhaps he's right - for him, at any rate. He instinctively performs one of those Indian head waggles that is neither a yes or a no.

"You know, I've never turned down an opportunity to drink in the jungle, though I've come close once or twice. And I've done more pestilence here with you guys than I've ever done in my life. But it's never been my drug of choice on any level. Not because I'm above it - God knows, I've tried it a fair few times, but I just never got that thing from it - whatever that thing is."

"Yeah, OK. I might still drink again, but out in the jungle. And for fuck's sake, we only did it last night. Fucking hell, Dobbs. It's a rough experience. It's not nice trying to get that stuff down, is it, really?"

264

Dobbs looks at Bolivar. He's got his straight-talking head on tonight.

"You know, you might think you've got this stuff covered and it's just like a blast on acid, but it's not `Bro. Sure, acid is a door that changes the perception of the brain, which makes it a bit like *Ayahuasca* I suppose, but it's different - very different. This is all about lucid dreaming, and about trust, and focus. Maybe acid's about that as well, but every time you approach a doorway you don't say: 'oh I've been through a door before so I know what's on the other side,' do you? There are many doorways leading to many places. Some lead into dentist's surgeries, others into brothels, banks, restaurants, homes, secret gardens and who knows where else"

"You had to mention dentists didn't you?"

"Well, there's an opportunity to move through fear right there. You've got good teeth and you know why your gums are suffering at the moment, don't you? You know pestilence fucks your gums right up."

"I'd almost managed to forget about my teeth. Anyway, it's different for you. I don't know if I want to go through those doors; I don't know if I need those types of experiences in my life."

Dobbs shrugs his shoulders, although he's not quite believing what he's hearing. He looks at Agent6.

"You going to drink?"

Agent6 looks out at nothing and nods slowly. He seems to be making his mind up as he nods.

"Yeah," he says eventually, then drops his attention back to his phone, and in doing so somehow brings everyone's attention down to the communication device that has got him so absorbed.

"Talking of phones, where's Gatita then Dobbs? You ring her?" Swifty asks.

Dobbs lets out a long, slow breath, like a punctured beach ball.

"I keep thinking about her."

Agent6 nods assertively.

"Give her a ring," he says. "You've got her number."

"I have already but I got no reply. It's like her phone's off or something."

Agent6 looks decidedly bored with the goings on.

"Shall we go to *Niko's Bar* and get a drink?" he says.

"What, the place looking over the waterfront?" Dobbs says in a disguised tone, as he knows that Gatita's mate runs the place and if there's anywhere she's be having a drink, it will probably be there.

In the end they decide to wander round to the bar, which sits right on the waterfront on stilts embedded into what appears to be a raised embankment. Its epic views, sprawling plant life and bamboo-structural simplicity all seem so perfect, but it's closed. Dobbs peers down the raised walkway that hangs over the river embankment between the thick bushes which flank the entrance to the place, almost concealing the walkway.

"Can you even drink after *Ayahuasca*?" he says.

"What, you really have to ask?" Agent6 replies.

Dobbs chuckles and looks at the others. The truth is, he doesn't really feel like drinking alcohol tonight.

"Maybe it's a sign," he says. "We *are* supposed to be doing a ceremony tomorrow after all. Let's blow it out. Well, I'm going to blow it out." Then, contemplating the notion of returning back to his bed, "Yeah, I think I'm gonna head back to the hotel, roll up a fat one and get a decent night's kip then have a fine breakfast in the morning and make that my last meal of the day before I drink"

As they turn to head back Agent6 frowns at Dobbs.

"When did you ever play by the 'before and after *Ayahuasca* rules and regs' anyway?" he quips.

"What, you think I'm a rule-breaker!"

"You're either a rule-maker or a rule-breaker."

It's fair to say that Dobbs has not always taken all the rules associated with *Ayahuasca* too seriously. They're mostly dietary rules, as there's a chemical called a Monoamine Oxidase Inhibitor - MAOI for short -in the *Ayahuasca*, which prevents the metabolic breakdown of the psychedelic DMT component of the potion, which is identical to the neurotransmitter the pineal gland produces to induce dreaming. NormallyDMT would be completely broken down by an oxidising enzyme in the body called Monoamine Oxidase (MAO) within fifteen minutes but the MAO Inhibitor stops this breakdown and thusmakes the trip last more like four to six hours. However, the MAOI can also stop the bodyfrom metabolizing toxic elements in certain foods like cheese and red wine so it's avoid such foods before and after drinking.

On the whole Dobbs does obey the rules but as with most things every little clan has its own particular set of superstitions that goes alongside the sensible precautions and some of these can be a bit overkill at times. Much of that is about the ceremonious side of preparation and implemented to make people make some sort of effort - to show willing for the gods almost - rather than for any really objective reason. But then, maybe not. He did have to just fight off a siren. Perhaps he is taking it all a little too lightly. Whatever it always seems to Dobbs that the most important factor is the degree of focus and peaceful intention the master of ceremony can bring to bear.

They wander back up the cul-de-sac that leads down to *Niko's* from the waterfront and back up to the main road running parallel with the waterfront and, to Dobbs's surprise, as they turn the corner there is Gatita, just sitting on a step looking a bit frazzled, like she's having a good night out. But then he sees she has a young, European-looking guy with her. His eyes look fervent with desire and yet half rolling in drunken stupor. He's a little shorter than Dobbs but he has a stockier build that amplifies his fit, toned physique. Seeing them together immediately has a profound effect on Dobbs and he suddenly remembers what a small town Iquitos really is. Just then Gatita catches sight of Dobbs and immediately looks away to Agent6 and the others. All of a sudden everything feels a little tricky.

Agent6 begins chatting fast with her, using his Iquitos dialect as though trying to fill the void but finally they're finished and she looks at Dobbs.

"How was the jungle?" she says.

"Hard work, and we were only there for a couple of days! Very tired now though, really need some sleep," he replies, a little too hurriedly.

She looks at him, then shoots a glance over her shoulder in the young man's direction who, though he is clearly drunk, is also looking a little uncomfortable as he observes her surreptitiously positioning herself almost between the two of them. Dobbs brings his attention back to Gatita but she says nothing. It's an awkward moment. He doesn't know what to say, and he certainly doesn't want to make her feel like he's caught her out or something. They'd made no promises to one another - in fact he'd made it clear he has a girlfriend, so he doesn't have a leg to stand on even if he did object. He feels like he has to say something though as, whatever their arrangement, it's obviously an awkward moment for her.

267

"I had an interesting ceremony last night," he mumbles eventually, but he can't manage much more. "Maybe I'll ring you tomorrow or something," he says, although as soon as the words have left his mouth he's regretting them.

"OK," she says.

Her tone is giving absolutely nothing away, but as he turns to walk away she looks into his eyes. He returns the gaze, and it is as if they are both looking for something. They hold the moment and just for a second a keen observer might have been able to detect the faintest glimmerings of what could be construed as a smile surfacing from deep, deep below the frozen surfaces of their faces. Then Dobbs turns and takes off.

"Looks like you got some competition," Swifty says conspiratorially as they get clear of the corner.

"Oh, that's so not my game right now," Dobbs replies. All the same, he's aware he's tight-lipped. Swifty just looks down at the floor and cocks his head to one side.

"I wonder?" he says, but leaves it at that.

Bolivar just shrugs his shoulders as they come to the next junction.

"You don't know what that means Dobbs," he offers philosophically. "And if nothing else it probably did you a world of good to have a good shag!"

"We didn't actually have sex."

"What?" Bolivar almost chokes, looking at Swifty in shock.

"You didn't have sex?" Swifty immediately follows.

"No. I know it sounds crazy. I kind of asked her if we could make love without having sex."

"What the fuck did she say to that?" Bolivar enquires while Swifty is half chuckling, shaking his head.

"It was a bit weird at first, and then it just went off the scale. It was like doing everything you can imagine only without actually doing 'it'. It went off the scale man. I properly made love with her. It was...intimate."

"Fucking hell Dobbs. No wonder she's gone off with another bloke; you must have left her gagging."

"Maybe. But my head just couldn't deal with having sex with another woman at that point; it would have just fucked me right up."

"Did you tell her you had a girlfriend?"

"Yeah."

"Fucking hell! Ahhh… It's very sweet Dobbs," Bolivar bellows out, laughing.

"Fuck off!" Dobbs replies, half jesting but half testy. "No, seriously…I just told her I wanted to hug, squeeze, kiss and…well, you know."

Bolivar and Swifty are both shaking their heads with astonishment.

"It was one of the most beautiful nights of my life I think."

Swifty just glances back at Dobbs.

"It might not be over yet Dobbs!"

Ponte las Pilas

It's still light when they arrive and though there are people about - a mix of the local Indigenous who Juan mostly works with plus a few Westerners - but there is no sign of Juan. It seems everyone is in their own mental space preparing themselves to drink and there's not much in the way of conversation which Dobbs appreciates. His preparation process needs a lot of quiet. He has no real expectations for this journey as he feels like he's at this door, as he describes, but doesn't know how to open it and yet, also understands that it is not him who *can* open it. It's an anxious, almost unnerving feeling, almost like he's about to have a major operation or something mad. He decides to take a walk out to the back yard and roll a small spliff to calm him down a little.

There seems something very beautiful about the back yard in the deep sepia half-light of the dying day. Perhaps it's because it's such a simple, un-manicured space. The bare earth around him has been trodden to a shiny, dry finish but the little stands of shrubs, bushes and trees appear almost like statues in the deep golden glow. A solitary chicken is making its way to roost for the night, where just beyond, a little, rickety wooden shed, which Dobbs figures is the loo, stands silhouetted at the back. He wanders over to check it out - just to be sure, in case of emergency. His assumption proves correct, although only just; it offers the most basic amenities possible to qualify as a bathroom, yet in truth it is all that is needed.

Just then, his old friend the hairless mutt materialises out of the shadows and puts its head against his leg, hoping for the tiniest bit of affection. Dobbs was once told by someone that you shouldn't touch animals before you do a ceremony and it has stuck in his head, but as he looks at the poor, scabby mammal, bald from chronic mange, he can't help but feel moved by how satisfied it seems just to hold its head against his leg, snorting a comfortable sigh as if in acceptance that even this little morsel of contact is sufficient.

Dobbs has no choice but to put his hand on the crusty old creature's head, and suddenly thinks to himself what an absurd rule that is. He'd broken almost every other *Ayahuasca* 'rule' for far less reward than the humbling affection of such a beautiful soul as this old fellow.

'Sorry,' he voices in his head to the *Ayahuasca* Police. 'I do seem to break all the rules, don't I? But I can't really see what's wrong with giving a beautiful creature like this a little affection. I know the Vine won't mind.'

Kneeling down, he can see how horribly mangy the poor old mongrel has become, and how much a little bit of affection now means to him - affection that was probably once lavished upon him all the time when he was young, fluffy and feisty.

"Do you think I'll get in trouble with the gods if I give you a little love, old friend?" Dobbs whispers to the ancient-looking animal, which has now become so floppy that it's dropped right to the ground and is now almost asleep with its head resting on his foot.

"Will you guard the house tonight, and keep away all the horrible things that might want to disturb us? Will you be one of our guardian angels?"

Darkness descends, and now the atmosphere in the back yard becomes almost a little eerie. It feels as if he's already tripping, and somehow the energy of the space suddenly seems enormous.

'Where would be the best place to throw up?' he thinks to himself.

It's a dilemma he often experiences when doing a ceremony in such a natural environment. When the *Ayahuasca* takes effect, rising up inside of him, everywhere seems to become a huge temple, and it feels somehow wrong to urinate or throw up in an unprepared space. Decisions like that are difficult to make when the urge to purge becomes overwhelming. So mentally sanitizing your process is always important, as he knows there's a good chance he won't be able to make it all the way to the loo.

Dobbs finishes rolling his little spliff, enjoying breaking yet another little *Ayahuasca* rule and then sparks it up, smiling to himself, as he savours each and every toke. Personally, though, he has only one rule for himself when it comes to drinking *Ayahuasca*: navigate your intention, and where possible help others to navigate theirs. Well, in Dobbs's mind, they are the same thing.

'Is that two rules or one rule with several components – like 1 and 1(a)?' he briefly ponders.

The simple fact is, though, that without intention it's difficult to navigate! To Dobbs it's like sitting in a dark room, waiting patiently for yourself to happen, and that seems to be the unfortunate story of so many people; sitting, hoping, waiting for something exciting to occur in their lives, but never having the balls to take the bull by the horns, state their intention clearly and just make it bloody happen.

Unexpectedly, a man walks through the door that he does not recognise at first, and then he realises that it's Yahu, the Israeli man he'd met on his last trip to the jungle but his head is now shaved and though he looks almost naked without his long locks, its his energy that is most startlingly different. They smile at one another. No words are spoken but the energy between them is different somehow. He's clearly been going through some massive process. They both have it seems.

He feels disappointed that Bolivar did not come along. He knows he's apprehensive and he can't blame him for that. No way would The Brigadier go near it. It would likely tear him apart in his state. For the better no doubt. And then he thinks, shit, it might tear me apart. But where Bolivar has opted out, Swifty has come along and his energy is much lighter tonight. And he's done a cleanse and properly prepared and is looking like a gentleman.

Finally, Dobbs Returns to the ceremonial space where he finds more people have gathered and are starting to form a circle, sat with their backs against the wall. Swifty is sitting over in the corner with a free space to his right, which Dobbs figures has been left for him. Walking over now, he sits down on one of the blankets which have been provided to create seating. A few of the more Indigenous-looking men have opted to sit on the plastic chairs against the wall near the far door closer to the end of the room. Other than that the room is almost bare except, oddly, for a faded poster of *Arnie* in his twenties, flexing his pecs, which seems delightfully out of place.Agent6 is sat to the left-hand side of the spot where Juan will no doubt be sitting.

An American, or perhaps Canadian man is sat to Dobbs's right. The man nods at him with a sense of enthused and almost animated, bright-eyed curiosity, which Dobbs finds oddly jarring to his somewhat sombre head space. Nevertheless he smiles politely and nods back.

"You feel good?" He asks the man.

"Yeah," the man whispers back calmly, and somehow Dobbs suddenly feels more comfortable.

Closing his eyes, he can feel instinctively that the place has been used for many ceremonies. He also senses something else though, like that door is still open within him, or perhaps that many doors are open around him. The thought makes him a little anxious, and he has to calm his breathing a little; he has a sneaky suspicion that this is going to be an unusually intense ceremony. Remembering his golden rings, he begins places one around himself, then Swifty and Agent6, then around everyone else in the room, bringing them all into an area of warmth and protection. Then he places a huge ring right around the house and finally one around Juan, who is still nowhere to be seen.

Time seems to slow as they all sit, expectantly waiting for the *curandero* to appear. Light is seeping in from the kitchen, but it is now fully dark outside and after a while there seems to come a point when everyone emerges from a collective mental silence all at the same time. There is no talking, just a sudden sense of alertness, as if they all know something is about to happen.

Right then Juan appears from a door opposite to where Dobbs is sitting, that no doubt leads upstairs. He has a bottle full of a dark, almost rusty coloured, acrid liquid in his hand, but his energy is uncharacteristically brash, as if he's been deeply annoyed by something. Dobbs observes apprehensively as Juan takes his seat next to Agent6 and just sits there, twiddling with the bottle of *Ayahuasca* and his packet of *mapachos*, arranging his things. At last, though, it seems he has placed everything where it needs to be for the ceremony, and now he just sits calmly, his dark eyes staring straight ahead into nowhere as he takes one deep breath after another, the out breath slower and much noisier than the in. It's just like Dobbs's stepfather would breathe before he channelled.

Suddenly, to Dobbs's amazement, he begins to shout something out in Spanish in what almost seems like anger. The outburst does not seem directed at anyone in particular, but it's venting is duly noted by all. Finally he seems to have finished but then, after a brief pause, he exclaims with full power:

"*Pon'e la' pilas!*" He suddenly commands, whilst almost simultaneously, pouring the thick, bloody-looking brew into a glass, then taking a long drag on his *mapacho,* blasts out a rapid jet of smoke in a slightly staggered exhalation - his lips pouted so as to direct it over the oily red surface of the *Ayahuasca*. Then immediately shouts, "Swifty!" in a voice so angry-sounding it almost makes Dobbs shudder.

Swifty doesn't understand what's been said anymore than Dobbs, but he's clearly got the message that Juan's not messing about tonight, and promptly jumps up to go and take the proffered glass. He knocks it back with what seems like relative ease, but as he does so the shudder of shudders runs through Dobbs's body, knowing that it's his turn next.

"Dobbs!" Juan calls out, although this time in a slightly softer tone that makes him feel a little less in the line of fire.

Being first - or nearly first - is sometimes easier, he thinks, as you don't have to endure watching something like the show Dobbs is about to put on whilst waiting for your turn. It's like loitering outside the headmaster's office, waiting for him to summons you and administer the punishment. Mind you, Dobbs used to love that when he was a kid! On the other hand, having that noxious potion working away inside of you whilst you watch other people gag and spew is not so favourable either. To Dobbs this is the part of the ceremony that separates the whole process from being a recreational experience, as it seems so far removed from anything you might do for fun purely on account of the purgatory you have to endure in getting it down.

Dobbs rises to his feet, walks over to Juan and takes the glass. It's a big glass, but it doesn't seem overly filled and so he tries to knock the whole thing back in one, but he can't quite manage it. Clenching his fists, he contorts his whole body trying to control the shudder and immediately begins to tremble all over with a harsh, feverish shiver.

Bloody hell, that smells strong, he thinks. Smell is a big part of taste, and though he's tried to take a big breath and completely seal his nasal passage from the back of his mouth that first gulp, though it goes down smoothly enough, is crashing around in him like an angry rhino trapped in a tin can. He manages to hold it down but he knows all eyes are on him, and the scene he's now acting out is unlikely to be making things easier for those still awaiting their turn.

He still has to get the last swig down, but he's trembling so much he can barely hold the glass.

'That's fucking strong!' he voices in his head then, absurdly, finds himself apologising for swearing. 'Come on, do it, get it down. Be a man about it!' he chides himself. But then, as he puts the glass to his mouth again he accidently takes a big sniff of the smell coming off the venomous-looking red liquid and the acrid stench hits his olfactory senses like a cricket ball smashing full force into his nose. He gags, but somehow manages to literally chuck the rest of

274

the concoction down his throat whilst simultaneously blocking the threatened upsurge from his guts as if arm wrestling with his stomach muscles. Ignoring the alarming sensation of the DMT burning his mouth and gums, the moment he experiences the first sign of a respite he swallows forcefully and vaults his system closed, blocking his shell-shocked oesophagus like an impenetrable iron door resisting a ram raider. Finally he feels a modicum of calm returning; it's down now - all he has to do is keep it down.

Pouring himself a glass of water, he swishes it round his mouth and swallows once more. Almost immediately he feels a distinct tingle running right though his being. At this stage it's normally psychological, like you've just moved through a fear barrier - you've committed yourself - but this feels ominously different, and he's almost swaying with an instant sense of delirium.

When he feels he has gained enough control over his body's reaction to the concoction to open his mouth again he thanks Juan and returns to his place to sit in lotus position with his back up against the wall, breathing deeply and feeling very odd. Swifty can see he's struggling.

"You OK?" he asks under his breath.

Dobbs performs the Indian head waggle, then closes his eyes, breathing out slowly.

"Oh my God, I think it might be quite strong. Does that feel intense for you?" he whispers back, but Swifty just shrugs, observing him with a blank expression.

Dobbs is still adjusting himself, trying to get more comfortable and master the volatile energy now coursing through his system when Agent6 speaks out; his voice uncharacteristically soft:

"I don't know if everyone understood what Juan just said then, so if you didn't, I'll translate. He said that tonight we will do real and proper spiritual work together, and that no one can blame anyone else other than themselves if they are not prepared to do the work to achieve this goal."

Then he raises his voice a little.

"*Ponte las pilas*: 'Put in the batteries!'"

Dobbs looks at Swifty, who clearly knows that, after his previous complaints, the message is mostly meant for him. He looks down and nods ever so slightly, as if accepting that he has to make the effort this time. Then he glances up at Dobbs with a naughty schoolboy grin, who's looking like he's holding on to the last

275

threads of reality by his fingernails now and can only whisper, as much for his own sanity as Swifty's,

"Golden rings of love and light Swifty - around yourself and all in the ceremony, and extended to all you feel need that loving light. To give is to receive. Hold the space of love and compassion and leave all expectation behind. We are nothing but little children to this gargantuan greatness. This thing we sometimes describe as God."

He smiles at Swifty and relaxes, relinquishing his hold on those last, tattered threads of the cognitive workings of his mind. Then he closes his eyes and buckles up for the ride. Holding this concoction down, it feels like wrestling with the angry thought of a psychic attack, and it will have to be dealt with as such: moment by moment.

Death

Dobbs knows it should take a while for the DMT to permeate into his system enough for anything to happen, but something feels wrong. Normally he has ample time to sit and get comfortable before it kicks in and often, once the pressure of drinking's off, people can quite happily communicate for half an hour or so -not actually chatting, but just tuning into each other's space a little with a bit of facial recognition and eye contact, all in the calm before the storm.

This time it's different and Juan has still only dosed about a quarter of the people in the room and already he can barely regulate his breathing. The initial queasiness of getting the brew down should have subsided by now, but still he feels like he wants to expel his entire system, organs and all, and a jarring kaleidoscope of colours has appeared behind his eyes which is way too intense for having only just drunk. Had Juan mixed up a super strength brew this time? Has he over done it?

He starts the process of placing a golden ring around his being, attempting to picture it clearly in his mind, but waves of energy are moving through his body in hot and cold flushes and when he closes his eyes he feels like he's being bombarded with bright shards and streams of colour, sharply defined and shockingly three dimensional. He can't even begin to see his golden ring, but at least he knows he's rigged up his intention of doing it and intention, powered by choice, is the focal point of Will. To simply *want* protection without actively bringing it in is weakness but, for lack of training, that is what the greater mass of humanity does. They don't *bring* in, they *want* in, and wanting to be in on something you're *already* in on has the opposite effect, as it is buying into the illusion of lack: It is, in fact, pure self pity – and poison to the potency of the Will, which is ultimately your most powerful magical ally.

That said, although Dobbs knows he *has* the power to set up the sophisticated protective shield his mother had taught him, he's worried that his delirium has compromised that ability – and, defenceless, he could very easily lose all the discipline he'll need to navigate through this nauseating pea soup of kaleidoscopic mental mayhem. He needs to keep focused if he is to stay the course and hold the potion down, as if he gives in to the notion that it's time to pull the rip cord he'll be up in a shot (if his legs work that is) and spewing his guts - and that just can't happen. Not yet.

'Hold it down. Relax!' he keeps trying to command himself. 'Think of golden shards of sunlight, daffodils, sunflowers,' but all he can see is a mad circus of whirling and contorting colours and shapes constantly converging in upon themselves then oozing out towards him. Normally this phase is like a screen in front of him, but this time the fusion of colour has somehow formed a spike-like tentacle that seems to be heading straight between his eyes, flowing and fusing into his head, squishing his thoughts and turning his brain to jelly while the illuminated colours whirl so brightly·it almost feels they are burning away his mind. The nausea is also stupidly intense, and the effort of having to hold it down against vaulted muscles is making his body go into sharp judders and spasms.

'Relax,' he tells himself again, 'and hold on.'

Finally the last person in the circle has drunk and, almost as if preparing an altar, Juan spends a few moments positioning his *Shacarpe* leaves and *mapachos* before extinguishing the candle with his fingertips. The room is plunged into pitch black, and Dobbs can see absolutely nothing apart from the bright kaleidoscope burrowing into his mind's eye, but at least everything is silent - and he likes the silence.

Still he can't relax though, as by now it feels like the automated process of his breathing has become completely defunct and he will suffocate if he doesn't consciously control it. His life itself feels strangely, like it's hanging by a thread and he's constantly one step away from complete panic, as though his whole system is on some sort of manual override. His fingertips have long since gone numb and he's lying there just waiting to die, but he can't fall into the realms of death yet - not carrying this heavy load within him. He feels too filthy to face death- too wretched to make the return- so instead he just does his best to stay conscious and wait until it feels absolutely right to evacuate his guts. In his mind, he knows, there will come a critical turning point, calculated far from the realms of his Earthly body, and he just has to hope that whoever's doing the maths has got their figures correct, because right now it's all just an agonising waiting game.

He lies there on his side, shivering and breathing in rapid, shallow breaths for what seems an age, his hands clenched together between his thighs and all the muscles of his body locked solid,

278

and finally he can hold out no longer; he has to release this torment from his system and somehow get up and navigate himself through the darkened house to his chosen spot. As he mentally prepares himself for the journey, periodically gagging but still just about managing not to spew, he keeps running the map of it through his mind. Eventually though he's ready and, donning the shoes that he'd carefully positioned prior to drinking, he shakily rises to his feet and casts himself off, like a child on its first bike ride. He knows that if he slows too much it will all get too wobbly and he'll likely lose his bearings, but somehow he manages to successfully traverse the room and feel his way through the kitchen to the back door.

Outside in the back yard the dim glow of distant lights and the sparkle of the stars above offers some marginal sense of orientation, but it all looks so different now - twisted and distorted, like his mind. The whole place has, indeed, become a huge temple, and he feels filthy in its presence. His ankles feel like they are fettered by heavy chains, but taking small steps, he finally comes to a stop at the special spot he'd previously decided upon. Looking down towards the earth, he stands waiting for the convulsions to move through his body, but nothing happens.

'Come on Dobbs, you can do it. Let it go,' he chides himself.

His head is a total mess, and the utter hugeness of the task ahead of him is now almost overwhelming but still nothing happens. Finally he shouts out, in desperation,

"I'm ready!"

To his complete surprise, the moment the words have left his mouth, he feels a blow at the back of his knees and his legs are literally kicked out from under him, and he falls to the ground on his hands and knees. The same thing happened to him once before - on his final *Ayahuasca* ceremony in the jungle, ten years back, and then, as now, no visible source of the force could be detected, although he distinctly *felt* the blow to the back of his legs. Thinking back to that night, he knows that whatever is about to emerge is going to be drawn from the very base of his being, as if his very core is being ripped out, and suddenly, somehow, in the periphery of awareness, he knows what's going to happen. He's waited all his life to see what he's about to see, but there is only one way that he can see it and there is only one door left now: Death.

"So, it's going to be like that is it?" he says to the crowd of spirits gathering round him. "OK. You do your half, and I'll do mine."

This is going to hurt – of that he is sure. He could easily pass out with the pain, and suffocate from the intense convulsions of vomiting he knows are about to follow, so it's vital to keep as many breaths going as long as he can before the first wave kicks in. He's been through this little process before: The Cleaners are here, and they're as harsh as fuck. Then again, he *had* chucked all that filthy pestilence in there, and he knew from the outset there was always going to be a price for that.

"Just think of all those bastards back home, thinking what a lucky cunt I am travelling the world, huh," he whispers with gallows humour, but the tears are running down his cheeks now, and the sweat springing out in beads on his brow as he knows that on one of these breaths the purging will begin. This is what he's been waiting for; this is his date with destiny. The truth is that drinking *Ayahuasca* is a wonderful experience, but once you've had your fun and seen a few things you need to get to grips with what your life is really about; that you are an agent of Soul: an ambassador to a higher being. That's kind of where the fun stops, and the work really starts.

Bam! The first convulsion kicks him, and the acrid aroma of *Ayahuasca* and bile bites into the back of his throat, immediately triggering a greater convulsion, and then another and another. More and more keeps coming, but finally there's a break and he can catch his breath for a few short seconds.

'So this is all the shit coming up is it? You gonna clean me out, ah? Is that all there is? Somehow I don't think so!' he voices in his head.

There's no point getting cocky with The Cleaners though; tolerance and small talk are not their fancy, and no sooner has he had his little outburst the next convulsion comes ripping through him. By now there's nothing left in his system, and every tiny bit of fluid he brings up is like squeezing a football through a garden hose.

'Poor Swifty,' Dobbs suddenly finds himself thinking. 'He's come to the ceremony hoping for a bit of *psychedelic breakthrough* and now he's seeing people having experiences like this.' For a moment he grins inwardly at the thought, but then another convulsion racks his body, and another, and another until finally he can no longer support himself and rolls onto his side, periodically going into spasms.

At last the agony begins to subside, but it seems he's still not through to the other side and ready to fly with the eagles. Normally after such a powerful purge he would expect to feel healthy and vibrant. Instead he still feels sick, weak and broken. Surely there can be nothing left to throw up now, though? Surely he's done?

'I'm going to get up and go back inside now. OK?' he articulates internally. 'Am I done? Are we finished?'

Looking around the yard, he can barely recognise anything. The dream-world has somehow morphed into the matrix of what existed, and the two previously separate planes are now overlapping. It seems lighter now, and all the plants and shrubs are gently swaying in time with the ripples of light surging through his mind. The house and everything around it has transformed into a huge temple with and the once barren-looking back yard has become the rolling landscape of another world, with each and every bush and tree now a majestic, flowing entity, and yet nothing is clear and he's barely holding on to consciousness.

'I'm going to get up and go inside,' he voices tentatively. 'Is that OK?'

He's developed such a relationship with the potion that he sometimes seems to be able to address the spirits almost as if they are old friends, but this time there's no answer and he has the uncomfortable feeling that The Cleaners aren't done with him yet – in fact that the fun hasn't even started. He feels battered, as if he's been beaten to a pulp from the inside out, but nonetheless he gets to his feet and starts to limp towards the back door. As soon as his foot touches the concrete track however another convulsion, stronger than all the others, comes writhing through him. He manages to stagger a couple more steps before collapsing on the shiny, trodden-down mud and surrendering to another seeming endless wave of huge, shuddering convulsions, none of which produces anything more than a trickle of bile. Eventually the pain becomes so severe he feels like he's ruptured something. And then suddenly the feeling of yet another judder goes through him.

"Stop!! There's nothing left," he screams out loud, struggling desperately to reign in the spasms.

Suddenly, he's terrified.

"Please help me!" he begs, sobbing. "I can't do anymore. I'll die!"

281

Tears are running freely down his cheeks now, but at last it stops and he's able to breathe deep again and catch his breath. As he lies there, gasping on the ground, directly in front of him, he can see a wooden house, more of a shack, the veranda to which was mostly blocked by a thin veil of bushes where an indigenous family with the sweetest faces are standing on the veranda waving at him. In his heart he could hear them shouting out to him; Good luck.

"Do I need luck?" He asks the family of indigenous waving at him. "Why do I need luck?" He whispers to them. No sooner had he asked, the house disappears. The cogs in his head are working again at last and his breathing is starting to automate again. His thought process are clearer and cognitive again but one of pure clarity and that strange feeling of being unfathomably present, without any interference that is the first, most unusual experience *Ayahuasca* brings about: Pristine consciousness. It's like everything changes but you can't work out what has changed and then you realize that the noise in your head has gone; whatever that noise is.

And he's clean out of the circus realm now. He's in the launch pad state. He is ready to blast off, anywhere in the universe now. In this state, he'd travelled to far distant worlds but he'd never really seen the world he'd always longed to see. The one that's all around us but we cannot see or touch. Not that the cleaners can do that or open that door. They're just abrupt and harsh. Or at least turn up when you're really experiencing abrupt and harsh conditions really. They just help facilitate the process. And everything has its price right? We all know that don't we? That odd spliff here and the odd line there and the one last toot that won't matter. It's all got its price, just like everything else.

He gets to his feet but his body is going into a totally internal process. His breathing and other processes are all coming back on line. Whilst on the other hand, his limbs and eyes are now starting to experience complete shutdown. And his ability to define direction and bearings has almost completely vanished. One step after the next, he makes his way to the kitchen door. And he manages to completely open the door and raises a foot, placing it through, calculating the distance between the two uprights and using them to triangulate his position whilst drawing the map in his mind. It seemed so simple on one hand and yet so complex without a functional body. But he has one foot through the door.

And so came the next journey as he made his way into the main room. Once he was in, he decides the best thing to do would be crawl to the corner and feel his way with his hands but it was a mistake and he rolled to his side not being able to calculate which way was up or down, let alone the geographics of his location anymore. Now he could only fumble around like a blind man, finding random feet here and there, and other barely definable objects that gave little clue as to his orientation.

"I'm lost." He whispers in desperation.

Finally he feels a hand reach out to him that guides him to the corner.

"Thanks," he says not knowing as to whom the hand belongs. He's surprised at the clarity in his head compared to his heavy body which he literally feels he is dragging behind himself. Like a pristine state locked in a slug.

Then he realizes that it is Swifty that is guiding him to his place and on arriving back, crawls into a ball, fumbles for his blanket and pulls it over himself. His stomach feels rough. Maybe I can control it, he thinks. Ah, but maybe not. It didn't matter anymore. It was beyond all of that now.

Dobbs could feel Agent6's presence. It was like he was there for him. Like he is his wing man. He loves Dobbs so much. He's a brother and true soul mate, and as he feels his presence more tears run down his cheeks, "You're a beautiful friend. Thank you for being who you are," He says under his breath. But he feels so sick. So very wrong. And then he did what he knew he could do no more; he gagged. I can't throw up anymore. Not in here with all these people, please. We're done now.

The cleaners didn't listen. The convulsions come again and he buckles. His breathing becomes shallow and erratic again. It is so painful now. He lies on his side in foetal position with my hands between his legs half shivering but more shuddering.

"You OK Dobbs?" Swifty whispers.

"Yeah," he says surprisingly rapidly without emitting any tones that would cause worry.

And then he gags again but it's noisy and he knows it will be disturbing to everyone in the room but there is nothing he can do and as he reaches, the noise that comes from him is nothing short of disgusting.

"*Peredone*," he says, hopefully loud enough that people can understand there is nothing he can do. For all the ceremonies that he'd sat through and had to listen to someone go through a terrible noisy process; letting go of something massive. And he never gets angry, always just puts a golden ring around them and tries to soothe their pain.

But as he retched he knew he had nothing left and a trickle evacuated from the core of his being, trickled out the corner of his mouth. He felt cold now and he could barely move his body. No way could he stand up. He had to accept that this was going to happen here. And then a calming feeling of control comes over him but he knew it's only a respite.

'Are you prepared to do this?' a voice suddenly asks from inside his core. A man's voice, not loud but not quiet, with neither tones of doubt or persuasion. But it at least offered him a choice. In every journey he'd ever undertaken on *Ayahuasca* it always asked him in its funny way.

He barely has a moment to think of his answer, though he immediately knows his answer booming through him but has not the time to say even just a yes before he's interrupted with the words, spoken as clear a bell; 'I will do whatever it takes to complete my mission here on Earth.' It stalled him completely. He wasn't expecting that. Whose voice was that, that just so blatantly used the word I? How can that be me? Are there like two me's? And then he thought, no; that was just me actually hearing what my divine soul's intention before my human state translates the feeling of those divine words into thought. That's me hearing my soul driving me, beyond the filter of humanity's thought and feeling based operating system. And then he suddenly realizes that there must be two I's. As he had to agree. How the fuck does that work? And as the thought and realization came to him he realizes that it's all down to him now; his humanity. Tears run down his cheeks as he knows now he has to answer that question. He has to make a life changing choice. He has to surrender to this. Fucking hell, he thinks to himself. Nothing will ever be the same again after this. This was his story: The death of Dobbs. To step away from himself, to step out of I and to abandon me. Immediately he feels loneliness at the thought.

I am the just the echo of that aren't I? He says in his head and more tears run down his cheeks. He never imagined he could do it and now here he is at the door. He'd taken worse risks in his life. He'd regret it for the rest of his life if he said no now. And is it worth the risk? His intentions were solid, he wanted to know who the fabled *them* really were. Who were the *depleted gang* that run the system of financially inflicted pain. There must be a way to stop this atrocity if he can pose the question to the creator, itself. Direct, so he absolutely knows, beyond the doubt of his interference – his doubt.

'Yeah, I'll do it. I was always in - always.' Tears run down his face but he quickly consolidates himself. 'Yes I am prepared to do it.'

And as soon as the last syllable is uttered in his mind, like a dagger thrusting into his core, that felt football haemorrhaging up inside him just explodes and a whole spew of shit that he wasn't expecting, the taste of which is utterly foul haemorrhaged from within him. A whole load of shit buried way below the long since spewed pestilence. And then another convulsion and then another and so on and so forth, whilst tears ran down his cheeks. Now it feels so different, like his whole stomach has contracted into a long tube and it has stretched down deep inside of him and opened a tiny little area in his core. The whole thing, contorted tight and this little orifice right at the bottom is just contracting and convulsing right down at the very base of his being. And each convulsion brought up the tiniest amount of fluid, which just oozes out of his mouth unabated. There was nothing he could do other than just lie in his own vomit.

The sound he's making is so awful and such a terrible thing to put other people through but there's absolutely nothing he could do. And on it went; not heavy convulsions but putrid sounding evacuations that sounded like an animal being killed within him and finally there was nothing left that could be evacuated and yet still it went on.

The poor man next to him had clearly had enough and says courteously, "If you're going to be sick. Maybe you should go outside."

Dobbs nearly bursts out laughing at the impossible thought. "I'm OK," Dobbs replies and says nothing more. What could he say?

And then it came again, heavy convulsions but a light appeared around him now or at least, light from a source, as though the lights had been switched on but when he opens his eyes it is dark, so he closes his eyes and goes back into the light. It feels like he's trying to push his heart through his abdomen when the next convulsion hits and in the light, just like before, he is surrounded by indigenous shaman brushing him down with *shakarpe* leaves stirring up all the light around him.

And then as the last of his energy shifts into a state of surrender, no more convulsive waves of energy could move through him, all his energy was gone, even his breath was failing him and he felt the fear of what he was approaching. Come on Dobbs you can do this. And then the light got brighter and his body felt so much lighter. And right then, someone in the room starts talking as though sparking up a casual conversation. It is nothing to the noises he'd been making but he found it offensive and disturbing. He couldn't understand how someone could even bend their head around a conversation in the middle of a ceremony – especially, right at the moment of his death.

And on his dying breath managed to utter, "Please…be...quiet.". The conversation terminated along with his life. Into the light he went. And as he passed, the words, crystal clear: Everyone will have to do this to enter.

Butterfly Kiss

When Dobbs opens his eyes he finds himself lying in a foetal position, his arms huddled between his legs as he was when he was lying in Juan's. But now he's nowhere of the sort. He's on a rolling, grassy embankment. Looking down, he can see he's wearing those same sexy camo hot pants that have the look of romp about them.

'Ah, so this is where this new body's for,' he thinks to himself. 'A new body...and a new world.'

Looking up, he sees Agent6, lying a few feet in front of him wearing some sort of safari trousers, the kind that Bolivar often wears, and a lumberjack shirt. He looks so very relaxed, sprawled out on a straw bale with his head resting on his hand, calmly chewing a length of straw.

The whole scene is simply breathtaking. A whole landscape stretching out forever. He's seems to be at a reasonable height can see right down into the rolling embankment, where he sits. It's a luscious green, gentle valley. And lower down where it gradually swings to the left, he can see children playing and people putting up tents. And then he notices the forest walling off the top of the valley and running towards him to his right. He can't make out much of the detail of what the men are wearing, but the women are all in beautifully coloured dresses that look, at a distance, like ribbons gently blowing in the breeze. It all seems strangely old fashioned - especially the tents, which appear to be made of canvas in an almost Bedouin style - and yet the scene is more, one of a modern festival than some kind of desert nomad settlement. It looks like a beautiful festival, too; not a corporate Babylon affair but something much more alternative and wholesome like the *Big Green Gathering* he remembers from home. He can only see a little bit of it, but somehow he gets the impression that it sprawls out to a vast expanse beyond where the line of the valley is blocking his view.

Maybe it's a the party that's being prepared when I finally make it through for real. Maybe that's the reason for the sense of union he feels when he sets his eyes on the scene, only it's more than that; it's like a totally blissful feeling of peaceful convergence mixed with something approaching an awe that engulfs him as he just stares down in perplexity at the beautiful scene filling his awe. His grandfathers are down there, he can feel them. He remembers

287

flying, high in the clouds over this world when he was a small child. He would get so excited when he went to bed. Back then, he could just close his eyes and bust through, as easy as that. He'd forgotten all about that, but now it all seems so vivid, like he dreamt it yesterday.

"Fuckin' 'ell. What *is* this place? This is it, isn't it?" he exclaims.

Agent6 looks at him with a proud grin across his face, then cocks his head to one side and winks before directing his eyes to a old fashioned suitcase that sits on the grass between him and a massive oak tree, the trunk of which must be five or six feet wide and towers above him. He realises he's neatly tucked in the forest on top of the hill having a peep from the distance.

The suitcase is lying open, and Dobbs is shocked to see that it's laden full of bombs and crazy looking missiles; the detonator caps of which are all poking out the sides. As he stares, bemused by the sight, it suddenly lifts up and snaps closed in front of him - it's a leather like skin now hovers in the air, struggling with all its might to snap closed, The clasps suddenly meet one another and click together and the gut like fabric seems to stretch and squeeze the bombs inside with only the brightly coloured nose caps poking out the sides. And suddenly pop and it completely snaps closed, like a leathery gut bulging full. Then, still hovering right in front of him, it begins to bend in the middle as if something of incredible strength is forcing down upon it, until it folds completely in half, and then in half again, like a car being crushed. By now it's seems almost like plasticine in the hands of whatever is bending it over and then forcing it down and into itself until it is half the size again. Again and again it folds until at last, it's a tiny dot which, for a moment, hovers in front of him, and then pings off to a nearby tree where a flower immediately just pops up, as if by magic. It's a daffodil. He was just spoken to by a daffodil. Wow, he thinks.

As he looks at the flower a tiny butterfly flies over and hovers above its delicate petals and then, as if it's just spotted an old friend, it comes flying over to him. It's such a tiny thing with wings the colour of bluebells but it hovers, completely unafraid, right next to his face, almost as if it's trying to tell him something, or at least just making sure he knows it's visiting him personally. Its presence is so beautiful that he struggles to stay focused as it bathes him in the most exquisite bliss. Then, drawing in closer still until it's tiny, gossamer wings are literally fluttering against his cheek, it shows him what a butterfly's kiss is really like. The sensation is so gentle, yet so intense that he feels as if he's being gently battened into sleep by the tiny, silken fluctuations. Resting his head on his arm, he takes one last glance at Agent6.

"I'm going now. Thank you," he yawns.

It seems to go on forever, as if his lungs have somehow become as big as a whale's, and then suddenly he finds himself taking one massive breath after another, greedily gulping the air down like he's just surfacing after a deep dive. And just like that, he's back, lying on the floor in a little puddle of his own puke, in Juan's house. Despite the slightly rude awakening, he simply memorized.

"Thank you. Thank you so much," he sighs again.

Slowly, still lying there lost in bliss, Dobbs pulls himself back together as the last of the strange light that sometimes appears around him. And then, lost in bliss where he feels his body drift in and out of consciousness, he is woken when Juan lights a candle.

Dobbs looks at the man sitting to his right a little sheepishly.

"I'm so sorry," he says, shaking his head, "I couldn't do anything. I'd completely lost control of my body."

"Wow man, you look a lot better than you sounded. At least you're alive!"

Dobbs laughs at the comment and tears run down his cheeks at the thought of what he's just been through.

"Cheers man. Next time someone asks me if I want to give death a blast, I'm definitely going to say no."

"Was that you, Dobbs - making all that noise?" Agent6 pipes up.

"Yeah," Dobbs sighs. I'm so sorry. Honestly, there was nothing I could do. It seems last night I was destined to die."

"If I'd known it was you I would have dragged you out *me sen'*," He says in his cocky Yorkshire accent.

"Lucky you didn't know it was me then! Actually you were too busy with other stuff anyway," Dobbs shouts back.

"How was it Swifty?" Dobbs asks, turning to Swifty who's looking very calm, almost like he'd just woke from a deep, well deserved sleep.

"Interesting. Very interesting," he says eventually.

"More interesting?" Dobbs enquires.

"Yeah. I mean it was a bit distracting sitting next to you mind," he jokes, but all the same he looks softer and more relaxed perhaps than Dobbs has ever seen him.

Juan's energy is also different: indeed the whole energy dynamic in the room has changed. Dobbs can't work out too much of what's going on, and not just because of the obvious linguistic restrictions. As he stares at the enigmatic *curandero* though he can see he really knew something big was going to happen in this ceremony. He can only wonder, with a sense of apprehension, at the change that each and every experience brings into our lives. Perhaps it's the fear of loss of control amidst the inevitability of change, which is sometimes nothing more than a gentle breeze and at others a terrifying tornado that seemingly blows everything we were clean away. A refusal to recognise the logic that creation and destruction are born from the same womb – that permanently impermanent state of being where all continually rises and fades away in a Universe of perpetual change.

Finally people start to get up to leave, and it's clear that the ceremony is over. As they start readying themselves to exit the property though Dobbs catches Juan's eye.

"Sorry for making all that noise Juan," he begins, "I had another unbelievable experience: I died and – well, I went *through*. There was no real mess luckily, but I just couldn't move."

Juan clearly isn't offended in the slightest though; no doubt such things happen relatively frequently.

"We're planning to go back to the jungle in a few days and I was wondering, would it be possible to come and get some prepared brew from you to take with us?"

Now Juan looks at him more intently. "You will do the ceremony?" he asks.

Dobbs looks over at Agent6, who just gives a noncommittal shrug of his shoulders, and then he looks back at Juan.

"*Si, con* Agent6," he says.

He looks over at Agent6 and then ponders for a moment,

"For how many?"

"I don't know. About four maybe? Actually, make it five – just in case there's an unexpected guest."

Juan observes Dobbs a long moment then nods his assent.

"It will be ready tomorrow evening," he whispers, looking at him a little closer, "*Y tu? Como estas?*" he whispers with a half-restrained grin that radiates through his eyes.

"*Muy bien,*" Dobbs says with a chuckle. He can feel bruising in his abdomen and he knows that tomorrow it's going to really ache, but right now any thoughts beyond this moment are overshadowed by a feeling of total euphoria.

Dollar

Dobbs is awake, and yet lying there feeling so comfortable and relaxed in his bed that he looks half asleep. It's another perfect day and despite the fact that his insides are feeling very bruised, as he glances once more through the cracked window at the astonishing view over the Amazon. He is still in such complete bliss that the radiance of the sun beaming through somehow seems to make even the blemishes and dirty marks just add to the glory of the whole scene.

This is beyond anything imaginable, he wonders, staring out in awe. I'm actually in heaven.

Lying there, totally blown open, his mind whirling through the events of the previous night, he somehow feels that an All-Seeing Eye has turned its gaze upon him and is now just watching, scrutinising the absolute truth of who he really is and how he's faced the adversities life had thrown at him. His actions, scribed into the fabric of history, have been laid bare - the good, the bad, the right and the wrong - everything.

Just before he'd opened his eyes, in that special state between waking and dreaming, he'd seen the symbol that's printed on the dollar bill in his mind's eye. Now, slowly coming back to full consciousness, he finds himself considering the wall - or gap - that he'd had to traverse through his death to get into that other world. The word 'dollar' keeps circling in his head: 'dollar, *dolor*, dollar, *dolor*' – 'money, pain...' Somehow the coincidence is too appropriate to ignore and, as he stays with the word, the All-Seeing Eye appears clearly in his mind again, peering from the upper, separated crest of the pyramid, the base isolated below.

Just then Bolivar jumps out of bed and makes his way to the bathroom, stepping by Dobbs's bed and bending forward with one arm out in front of his crotch as if he's taking a lady from behind, the other held high like he's riding a wild horse.

"High five, Hans; *dame cinco!*" he shouts, striking his best Seventies porn pose.

Dobbs chuckles at the jest, then turns his attention back to the world outside his window; the endless jungle, the broad, meandering river, and the birdcage with the lady inside, hanging up more washing.

"Where are you Dobbs?" Bolivar calls over his shoulder as he's disappearing into the bathroom.

Dobbs doesn't answer. The truth is he's not so sure himself. He'd expected to wake feeling so fresh following last night's blow out and though, in one way, he is, but in another way, he's just blown wide open, like a flower head ready to shed its payload of cotton candy thought seeds to the first strong puff of wind. More than anything he wishes he could just disappear off with Gatita and talk to her about what he's experienced these last few days. Like his mum, she feels like someone who can understand where he's coming from without all the long, analytical explanation seemingly required by those whose heads are full of doubt. It doesn't much matter to him right now if she's with someone else; she's beautiful, and he craves her presence. And he didn't know what the story was with the Frenchman. He takes his phone from his shoulder bag before his mind has the chance to turn it into a drama and sends her a text. As soon as he has done so, he feels his anxious mind relaxing and knows it's all just down to the gods now how things pan out and he lies back down pondering on the strange dream that he seems only to really remember the All Seeing Eye.

It seems so strange to him now to think of its image on the dollar bill and what it represents. He'd innocently been thinking it was printed on the dollar bill to illustrate the bright shining power of controlling forces that bring order to the world and use these ancient symbols to big themselves up. Now he realises that it is actually the Establishment showing the people the precise formula by which they perpetuate the tyranny of wage slavery: to separate, divide and thus conquer.

They use money to create pain, he thinks to himself; to separate us from ourselves. And thus they are neither the base of the pyramid nor the raised crest. In fact they are only the gap in-between: *the gap that separates us from our True Self - from our Divinity*. What puzzles him more, though, is why they have to make that so absolutely clear? Is it some kind of licensing deal with the real gods; that it has to have the absolute truth written on the packet? And, even odder, that it is called a 'dollar *bill*'; normally you think of money as something you sort of own and a bill as something you owe. He still finds the whole money thing so perplexing that it rules his mind, endlessly circling around like a bird trapped in a cage.

Now he has so many questions. Is death the only thing that can open that door? It seems to him that this Earthly plane, the plane of pain, the Kingdom of Dollar, is like a cross between a prison and a

293

crystal palace - a prism, perhaps. Each soul is like a beam of light, trapped in an invisible cage, a karmic reflection of Divinity destined to endlessly bounce off the mirrored karmic walls of cell walls until its rotation increases as it gets ever closer to its central core as its vibration slowly rises until it eventually arrives at the centre of its being, where it finally passes through the centre of itself to discover a whole new dimension.

So what about that door then – the door between the divide? Dobbs has always considered himself more a man of science than some fluffy hippie, and he's long suspected that science lies at the core of it all – but a science on a level far from his current comprehension. In light of his experiences in last night's ceremony, what opens the door now seems suddenly obvious – death! The real question is what grants passage *through* that door rather than a one way ticket back to Earth in yet another body; another prism?

Suddenly he sees what it is. Of course! It's plain old invitation, just like an invitation to a birthday party. It must be: what else can it be? He muses in his head; how silly; it's as plain as the nose on my face! he thinks to himself.

For a moment he feels a bit big headed that he got invited in, but then he remembers that he did have to die and he only really had a quick glance, so perhaps he was merely a gatecrasher after all. Agent6, on the other hand, looked pretty at home in there - like a long term resident. So how *does* this big old thing actually all hold together?

Somehow it seems that the gap, represented on the dollar bill, dividing the pyramid is similar to the wall that divides the realms he traversed with his death. Is Earth really being ruled over by a lower dimension that can only do so if all is laid bare to so; with humanities consent? Is it that crazy? Almost every supermarket uses the same symbol in its architecture. A Pyramid with a separated peak that's divided off, invariable by a clock. Huge corporations that come into towns and cities and funnel off all the potential business and leave the people with nothing other than *convenience*. Institutions that break all the monopoly laws set down to protect society from unchecked, rampant profiteering: Institutions that buy Government policy.

It sometimes seems to Dobbs that the Government is used to perpetuate the endless suffering of humanity just to keep us tuned in to anger and resentment by the perpetuation of war and economic wage slavery - all in the people's name. As so often, the clue is in the word: *govern* - to rule over - *ment*, or*mente* from the Greek for *mind*. 'The Rulers of Mind' that inhibit free thought, free speech and free will.

Why like this? he wonders. Why, exactly do they go by the name; Govern – Ments. As in exactly what they are: Thought Police?

More to the point where, exactly, are these Policemen? Where do they really reside? What is the ego in absolute reality and in realm? Who and where is the ego? It seems to him that all too often, when the world of spirit is being discussed, it's as if it exists only as some metaphysical concept rather than the complete, if fantastic, world it really is: As though it's just comforting fantasy or perhaps some invisible spirit world that hangs in the clouds and ether alone. A gaseous floating nothingness from which everything rises and into which all disappears, just some big nowhere where everybody finally goes to live happily, in love and peace forever and ever, after death, only ever thereafter to exist in the wind perhaps. An unutterable realm, something's to be accompanied by a throat-clearing harrumph and followed with deeper tones that invariably isolate the subject like an infectious disease that needs to be incubated in some intellectualised prison, far from any properly cognitive analytical thought process, there to rest in peace. That has never cut it for Dobbs.

If the ego isn't here and exists only in the gap, then the ego must be somewhere else; i.e., not here and certainly not that place I went last night. It has to be somewhere; somewhere it doesn't really want to be, as it can lull about all day in our heads if we let it. Something tells me that this isn't simply humanities story unfolding here, this is as much, the story of the ego unfolding here - what and whoever they are.

Bolivar emerges from the bathroom, breaking his reverie.

"So, how was it then? Where are you at?" he enquires.

"I'm in a pretty mad space, man."

"Still worrying about the collapse of the world?"

Dobbs just tuts; he's feeling too sensitive to be mocked this morning.

"I'm only fooling with you man," Bolivar says in a more conciliatory tone. "At least you're out here trying to work it all out with the intention of trying to find a solution, and writing this bloody book. It's cool man. You're fucking mad - but you're a cool mad."

295

"Cheers."

"What happened, was it a good ceremony."

"Un-fucking-believable man. I...died."

"You died?"

"Yeah. Wasn't so bad actually, although it fucking hurts when I cough. Feels like my belly's been beaten to a pulp."

"Fucking hell Dobbs! What the fuck are you doing this shit for man? Death's not really that good for you," Bolivar says, shaking his head in total disbelief.

Just then the door bursts open and in marches Swifty.

"Morning boys!" he says, sounding sickeningly chipper. "Off to the jungle again tomorrow. Don't forget!"

"Have you heard this? Dobbs reckons he died in a ceremony last night," Bolivar says, ignoring the comment.

"I know. I had the pleasant task of sitting next to him for the whole horrible ordeal," Swifty states, then turns and disappears off again, leaving the door open behind him so that he can periodically pop in and out ferrying bits and bobs of kit. Meanwhile Dobbs relates the tale of the previous night to Bolivar who for the most part is just frowning really, and clearly unsure what to say.

"So where are you now with it Dobbs; like where the fuck's this book going man?"

"Well, it seems I had a one to one with a daffodil last night, man. I saw what a daffodil is becoming through its physical incarnation here on Earth."

"You reckon that the bombs in the case were the daffodil?"

"Yeah. Think of a daffodil pushing through a tarmac road. The constant pressure of absolute determination to break through to the light, all focused in one place. We have to find our focus on the elements that are controlling us and dividing us from our own divine light – as hippie as it sounds. We have to begin to understand the nature of how money operates so we can see it, perhaps in only definition, even if we never end up with the cash we need that all just goes to the *depleted gang*. We have to make the effort to understand the method of their strength that thrives only on our weakness that we do not attempt to understand the nature of the chains that bind us. Only if we can all understand the nature of its flaws can we can upgrade them or even supercede them with something better."

"Understand the world of banking? You're having a laugh," Bolivar shouts out making his way to his bed and instinctively going for the weed and skins.

"Our pestilence excursion in Lima was the best education into the banking world we'll ever get man. Pestilence crazed lust followed by a massive comedown. Boom and bust man. You just can't jump off until it goes bang.

"It's the lack of consciousness that exists there and how it's implemented, that we could facilitate a system that allows unchecked, *free* trade. It can only exist in the *absence* of the understanding how the powers that be can place us in the economic stranglehold we find ourselves. If we can understand the mechanism we can begin to understand, like the daffodil, where to apply our focus. We all have to attempt to understand the way in which the monetary system - in the form of debt -,seems to be designed to act like a black hole and wildly consume beyond its own value. I mean, I know I'm not exactly the first to be shouting out about this; just watch *Zeitgeist*- or any one of a dozen other documentaries for that matter - but somehow, after last night, it just got *personal*. You know what I mean?"

"Fucking hell Dobbs, your head. I can't see any link between what happened last night and the fucking world economy." Bolivar sighs, exasperated.

"Look man, you see the waterfront out there? That's like the last bastion of the People's Front. For the Indigenous, the jungle and the river is their livelihood. I bet there are not many bankers lining up to offer *them* much in the line of credit because they cannot see the value of all of that," Dobbs explain as he stares out across the vast, organic emerald carpet steaming in the morning sun.

"Well, hopefully that's their good fortune," Agent6 says, following Dobbs's gaze and tuning into the conversation. "It's the jungle that keeps them intouch with their native roots."

"I agree. And if the shit hits the fan with a full scale depression moving in, who is likely to be least affected by that?"

"Them probably," Agent6 answers.

"Exactly. They have the least exposure to credit, right? But for the rest of the *developed* world, who have come to rely on the savage economic slavery that feeds them, it would be a drop kick like nothing they've ever known."

"Fucking hell Dobbs, you're certainly charged at the moment," Bolivar chuckles, 'but I *still* don't see the link between anything you've just said and the world fucking economy."

"You see it's the money, isn't it? That's what really fascinates me because that's the medium by which we enact our *will* here on Earth, especially if we don't have the support from friends and our communities which is exactly what big corporations like supermarkets attempt to break down. No wonder they build them like churches. But what happens when money becomes debt. That for everyone that you buy or sell, they can immediately buy or sell ten with credit artificially created through your one. That the value of money is not built on a lie but on the deception of *self imposed*, mass stupidity where the bankers tempt you to borrow what you think is *value* when, in actual fact, it's merely selling you your own wealth as debt with interest and tax. And the more debt you buy to secure your future, the more it chains you. Like a mortgage."

"*Mort gage*: That's French for 'death grip,'" Agent6 throws in as he fumbles with his iPod and speaker system.

"Exactly," Dobbs says. "'Death grip,' Have you ever wondered why it's called that? It's all hidden in plain sight man."

"You certainly have a strange window on it Dobbs. It seems like there are going to be banks going down."

"There *is* banks going down. They're merely the tentacles of the credit machine being harvested."

"All I know is that when I first met you, just over a year ago now, you told me the banks were about to go down after that blast of nitrous. I thought it was quite mad but your whole take was also quite funny. No way did I think that would happen, but the way things are sounding, it's getting closer by the day. So I reckon you can't be *all* wrong about this. Something is happening right now and although I don't understand it myself and I think you're bat-shit crazy, the truth is I don't know anyone else who saw that coming as clear as you did."

"Well..."

"You did though Dobbs, you absolutely knew they were going to go down. You were convinced. Still, even if that stuff does make you psychic I don't know if I can drink it man. I mean, I wouldn't mind knowing the lottery results but, fuck ..."

"No man, you've got it all wrong. It wasn't *Ayahuasca* that told me the banks were going down: it was gold! Or, to be more precise, it was the impact on the gold price of Iran switching its oil trading from US dollars to euros in March 2006 that told me. It's that simple. And it wasn't just me; so many people were talking about the impact on the US and global economies if that ever happened. Rob Newman, that comedian from *Newman and Baddiel*, was the man of the moment there. He had it sussed; kick the fucking legs out from under the table, and the table falls. Check him out online man: that dude tells it how it is.

"There were endless blogs going up saying that Iran would make the switch and that it would kick off if they did and they did it and everything inside me screamed out to check the gold prices to see if this thing really did have the density I was assuming it really had. That graph spells it out. And all the complex bullshit that will be thrown at you by economists, there it is, written in fucking gold - rocketing at exactly the same time as Iran switched. It suddenly became blindingly clear what the big boys up top were really thinking. Not what they were saying mind, or more specifically for the British newspapers, what they weren't saying, other than the normal, 'and the weather; it's gonna be shit.' I'm not sure of the percentage of Britain that actually believe that if it's not in the papers than it's not true. But that was the iceberg. Well, this is a big iceberg but what was really going on in their heads. It was going off the fucking Richter scale man; they were shitting bricks. The single most important thing propping up the US economy - the thing that America and Britain had fought so hard to maintain for nearly a century - was in danger of falling apart; the monopoly on the sale of oil in US dollars – the fabled petrodollar.

"Germany tried to fuck with it and paid the ultimate price – twice - and then it was Iraq's turn, and we all know what happened there. What most people *don't know* is that that was the real reason for the dumping of all our nuclear waste on Iraq – it was *punishment* for Saddam's attempt to thwart the supremacy of the US dollar. But then, in March 2006, just when George Dubya thought he'd finally shown those pesky 'ragheads' who was boss, suddenly the Iranians do the same thing - legally and legitimately - right under the noses of UK PLC and the US of A.

"You see Europe was finally muscling in on the business as Iran was sharing the wealth and saying 'fuck you' to Britain and America, where up until that point oil could only be traded in US dollars via New York or London. And why not? Think about it; nearly thirty billion barrels of oil being burnt every year, all of it traded in US dollars, just to offset America's debt repayments. So along comes the latest threat that Iran couldn't be trusted with nuclear energy, right after we'd just dumped loads of depleted uranium along its borders!

"Personally, I think that was the last straw - the ultimate insult that caused the Iranians to pull the rip cord. What else but a desert storm of depleted uranium dust from all our armaments would make a business partner terminate relations so catastrophically? Come on man, it's the lowest form of racial cleansing ever used in the history of genocide. There has never been a worse crime committed on the face of the globe. *Never*.

"To the masses, it's just another conspiracy tale that they cannot allow themselves to believe, that the British Government couldn't have done that, even though the evidence is utterly staggering with birth defects and radiation-related disease going off the radar. No man, that weren't shamanism, *Ayahuasca* or clairvoyance Bolivar; that was good old fashioned common sense man. Iran dumping the Petrodollar was the equivalent to the gash down the side of the Titanic, twisting the myth of the unsinkable ship into a million broken tales. But the truth was right there, *written* in gold. Just look at the gold prices at the in March 2006 and how they've rise from that point like never before.

"Just the fundamental stories of it and how history repeats itself, over and over again. You see, the greatest threat to the US dollar and the FED is not just Iran, it's *any* large enough currency that can challenge the FED."

"Like the Euro?" Agent6 replies.

"Exactly. Two birds that the FED wants gone forever and which it can take out with one stone if it can get its war off the ground. But it needs a Trojan horse to get into Europe and smash it."

"Britain, right?"

"Yeah. People have actually started to think that Britain could be independent. The last time we experienced that was in the Second World War when we distanced ourselves from Europe with our alliance with the US. That's when we launched the whole 'Dig For Victory' allotment campaign, when Heathrow was still the main market garden area for London and most houses had veg growing gardens. If we do that again, most of the country would be starving to death in less than a month. I reckon we need Europe more than they need us."

Bolivar passes Dobbs a spliff and wanders over to stare out of the open window on the far side of the room.

300

"Yeah, I can get my head around that, Dobbs, but would the masses want to get their heads around that? Aren't you telling them their money is worthless?"

"Well, it's not that it's worthless, it's just seeing where the value really lies. The value is all around us. Yet when we question a system that sucks up value with unchecked, and unfairly distributed debt, we seem to operate in the manner of any other addiction and it seems to terrify something deep within us that twangs the doubt strings governed by, I don't know, our ego I reckon. Whatever it is that screams at you shouting, 'you're not a fucking economist.' It is tough to consider, quite scary in fact, that the money's got no value anymore. Britain lost its sterling silver pound back in the early Seventies when we traded it, effectively, for the IPE - the International Petroleum Exchange. No one really understood it at the time and the people just knew it as decimalisation, but in practice what it meant was that oil could now be traded through London as well as New York. So now everything the entire globe consumes all has to go via those two stock exchanges. However, the IPE was always an American consortium though, and thus had the pound on strings. Which effectively meant America had Britain on strings. Well, not America to be more precise, but the Federal Reserve. And since the Fed - counter to what you might think from its name - is not owned by the US government at all but is in fact a privately owned corporation that *funds* the government's schemes. So the FED actually had America - and thus the world - on strings.

"So, long gone is the sterling pound along with the gold indexed US dollar - and any remaining *sense* it had with it. These days it's only speculation that gives money its value; trade moving one way or the other, hedge funds that trade both ways, corporations that bet on demise as much as success simply because the money moves. You have to properly get that Bolivar, that it's the *movement* of money that drives the wheels of credit; it doesn't even matter whether it moves up or down.

"So even if all the wealth of the middle classes just gets harvested by the corporations and nothing really comes back down to the people, even whilst most businesses are showing drastic losses; as long as the wealth is siphoned out, it's still moving and the bankers make their killings - often quite literally- well, just so long as there's a regulated supply of pestilence to ease the guilt. You can see why pestilence is the number one commodity used by the CIA and other even more shadowy agencies to fund their Black Ops and pull the strings behind the scenes that make sure what the money men *want*, the money men *get*. And whereas oil once drove the cogs of the economy, what works equally well is also Fear. One flick of the switch and off goes *lend*, on comes *repay*, and the whole thing goes into reverse, like a massive vacuum cleaner sucking up anything and everything which is over-exposed to credit - which these days means most of the globe."

"Shit man. You really do think it's going to hit the fan."

"You can't have war without a fundamental lack of basic amenities and rights."

"A hungry man is an angry man," Agent6 whispers.

"Totally. And those that collapse pave the way, driving the cogs of the credit given to the banks to buy all those debt foreclosed acquisitions – in real terms our businesses, our houses - and our mum and dad's pension. It's just a black hole of debt, sucking up all the wealth of the middle classes. The politicians do their part of the bargain and pass it all off as the fault of the greedy benefit claimants, or the thieving gypsies, or the work shy Travellers, and all the while the bankers - the henchmen of debt - are just pissing themselves laughing whilst snorting rails of pestilence as long as Pinnochio's nose to celebrate humanity's doubt that it is really happening right under everyone's noses.

"Like I say history does tend to repeat itself. It was onlyin the late Sixties, early Seventies the French demanded all their gold back because they didn't believe the US had as much in reserve as they were making out. That was the last time the whole workings of the currency system were remodelled."

Bolivar looks somehow doubtful.

"Have I lost you or are you doubtful?"

"Well, people who were sat on big piles of dollars must have known that their money was being devalued."

"Yeah and it was a completely different system then; but most could not understand the change simply because they couldn't comprehend the credit Britain and America had unleashed by moving into a speculative currency. You see, technically, America was bust. So what they did was just move the 'gold posts' as it were - which meant that everyone who owned huge volumes of US dollars would suddenly see a substantial rise in their value. It's like,if you can't dig yourself out of a hole, dig it bigger one so everyone else falls in too."

"Think about the whole ENRON story man. The whole collapse all due to over speculation. Claims that the wells had more than they really had, thus pushing up the amount of oil they could legally take in one year. That then directly pushed up the value of the dollar which pushed up the credit status of anyone who had their savings in dollars. Like the very OPEC countries that were selling the oil.

"That's when the design flaw was fully implemented and given the 'gold seal' of approval by the Middle East through the creation of OPEC – the Organisation of Petroleum Exporting Companies - which swore allegiance to the US dollar and backed the move to a system based only on the speculative value, i.e. what goes through the banks. In practice what that's meant is that the more cash that goes through American and British banks, the greater the credit that can be advanced on it. All the gold was basically exchanged for borrowing power.

"This thing had a bit of a ceiling before – you know, like 'all the gold in Fort Knox' kind of story. Then it was suddenly all the wealth of the obliging world. It's like taking a formula one racing car, dropping it into neutral and then putting the pedal to the metal and just holding it down. It was never going to be long before something went bang, except this is debt – so it's actually more like a black hole powered vacuum cleaner that seems to be sucking up more gold than ever before. These fuckers seriously want to clean up."

Dobbs's take on all this obviously fascinates Bolivar and he seems to be making an effort to understand.

"So that would mean that, say China makes stuff and uses oil to make it, which it bought only in dollars then America can print bills of credit (i.e. more dollars) to buy China's stuff - manufactured with the oil they first bought."

"Exactly. Welcome to economic wage slavery man. But as soon as China started buying Iranian oil, outside of the US dollar, the main cog in the gearbox of credit got *yanked* out – if you'll pardon the pun.

"In some way, I could almost believe the banks would deliberately direct more of the now limited line of credit to the banks and corporations because those really in control of the FED are almost embarrassed to admit that the money in people's pockets and bank accounts is backed by no real value and the governments' fear that the masses will do the most stupid thing possible and hoard their

303

savings, actually killing the cash cow because there's no movement. It's just a *bill*, remember? *'I promise to pay the bearer on demand the sum of...* 'Interest rates are gone mate. They have to force every bit of speculation they can and get everyone to put their cash on the table. We're being driven into the dirt.

"It's like a game of poker where you try to flush out of all the wealth on the table. But this is obviously more than just a flush - it's a fucking sweepstake - because the value of the dollar and the pound have been allowed to exceed way beyond anything close to their original sterling silver and gold indexes. The moment that you move, say a billion dollars of wealth in the form of say stocks and shares, which represents a financial transaction, which might likely be carried out because of fear generated in the market. Not necessarily a profiteering move but a safety strategy. But profit or not, with the movement of that billion dollars, the FED rolls off near ten billion dollars in credit, that's lent at a near zero percent to their buddies in arms.

"And is it an irony that it all seems to mirror the state of the world on so many other fronts? I mean we just seem to be piling into so many walls at the moment: the seas are like cesspits, the air's polluted, the forests are dying, and the atmosphere's thinning so we are getting over exposure to solar radiation on one end of the spectrum and insufficient heat retention in areas with least solar exposure. It's as though our thermal homeostasis is going out the window. Too hot and then too cold with horrendous storms like *El Nino* dividing the two extremes. Species after species are becoming extinct, and meanwhile the people are just sitting staring at this ever unfolding catastrophe whilst the military industrial complex continues to perfect the ability to wage all-out war and dump depleted uranium on anyone and everyone who refuses to surrender their sovereignty to the profiteering greed of the bankers.

"Think about it," he continues, shaking his head in despair. "It was barely more than a hundred years ago that the Maxim machine gun was first invented and five thousand African warriors were massacred in the First Matabele War in South Africa using just four of those guns. Four! Then there was the invasion of Tibet when we enticed their rickety soldiers, armed only with antique muskets, out for negotiation and just opened up on them with our shiny new Maxims. Overall we must have killed probably half of every able bodied young man in Tibet.

"A hundred years later and look where we are; depleted uranium and nuclear missiles. *Daisy Cutters* - so called 'conventional weapons' with the explosive force of the Hiroshima bomb, and now *mini* nukes – just one of which will give you about ten times more bang for your buck than that pathetic little party popper. We've reached a wall on every front. We've reached the wall man."

"Shit man. Fuck."

"We're not just running out of financial credit, we're running out of *karmic credit*. There's no place to offset negative karma in the future anymore – it's all piling into a 'something' that absolutely will not budge."

Dobbs pauses, turning his attention back to the vastness of the vista outside the window. It's achingly beautiful magnitude almost feels like it is crushing him now.

"I mean, imagine if that was the *real* message of Christ? What if he wasn't here to save us; dying for our sins – that saving ourselves was our job. And actually he came to warn us that Earth really does have a Super Soul Highway scheduled to come through; that right now the planet's coming back on line. It's like don't look busy 'cause Jesus is coming; look fucking busy because God's coming - and He's The Daddy."

"So what do you think the end game of all this is then Dobbs?" Agent6 ruefully enquires.

"Well, we all hear and read the prognosis in conspiracy websites and most anyone who's slightly clued up is saying a similar sort of play out, right? That this isn't a credit crisis; it isn't even a currency war. That it's the end game in a strategy for total global domination: a cyber-linked, solid state military dictatorship. That's the obvious prognosis right?"

"Well Yeah. Surely *you* can't disagree with that Dobbs?" Agent6 follows.

"It's not that I disagree. But I'm not so sure that it's the true prognosis. Personally, I think that's merely the carrot on the end of the string. The reward for carrying out the Sweepstake and genetic cleansing. It's no different to Proslairo's multi million pound house in payment for his part in massively degrading the Muslim gene codes. Has he not received his part payment for his part in the plan for a New World Order, which is just the redistribution of the wealth back to the *Depleted Gang* right? But what if the whole plan always revolved around, not simply ruling over, but

305

dominating. As in, deliberately making people suffer. That pain *is* the sole prognosis. You see it's a wall on every front that we're fast approaching. It's unchartered time. They don't know what will happen. No one knows what will happen. It's a blank canvas – a new age and a whole new start. They're terrified."

"Sounds..."

"...unbelievable?"

"Well...yeah. Why though, Dobbs?"

"Well. It has the makings of a gold robbery really, by the looks of things but of course, that doesn't really mistake as it would be a robbery that's taken centuries and even millenniums. I really don't know. This is really what I'm trying to work out. All I know is that whatever's going on at the moment man, it's gargantuan; bigger than we can ever perceive and the only thing that stands in its way of us seeing all that is laid utterly bare in front of us...is doubt. But then we doubt everything, unfortunately, that includes ourselves. How can we believe in absolutely anything if we cannot fundamentally believe in ourselves? If you do not believe that you are truly happening then how can you believe anything is happening? It's our doubt that we have to question because it seems to me that our doubt is all that we are not. Whatever it is, is living off our doubt or actually is our doubt."

"What?" Bolivar shouts in protest.

"It's crazier than we can ever believe I suspect but humanity is about to find out who the big ugly *they* really is or are. This is a psychic invasion. That's what the vine is trying to tell me or at least allow me to see beyond my doubt."

"Shit man," he sighs glumly. "I hope none of this shit happens in my life."

"I'm sorry to alarm you man, but I think it's happening right now," Dobbs shakes his head, "and people need to adjust to the reality of that. Fast. There's going to be serious food and energy shortages soon, especially if we hit hyperinflation, and it's all because we're in denial that the party's over and the planet will no longer sustain a parasite species that refuses to own its power and use it wisely, for the benefit of *all* beings, human or otherwise.

"But then who knows, maybe we can beat Iran and wipe them out because they have the intelligence to create the nuclear technology we created and prove to be as irresponsible as us. I mean, if our governments can just go and do that in our names...well, just the logic that if we can do it than they might do it too. Guilty by potential alone. So maybe our Government will give it a go. But Iran is armed to the teeth and they're ready to go. They've got the biggest reserves of oil of anyone in the world, they've got a massive, well-trained army led by generals seasoned by ten years of trench warfare with Iraq. They've been preparing for this ever since the Islamic Revolution back in the Seventies. This is not some piss-pot dictatorship weakened by sanctions and civil war but a modern military machine backed up by some of the most advanced Russian and Chinese technology available and motivated by a fundamentalist religious mindset that makes even the Vietcong look like a bunch of soft soap quitters.

"Are the masses really so blind, with our heads in the sand, that we're too distracted by all the media scaremongering to realise that outside forces have taken Britain over and are using it as a machine to wage war without end - in our names, but against our will. The fact is we're not equipped for this, and we're sleepwalking our way into Armageddon. But then, what the fuck; you're the ones building a bolt hole in the jungle."

"It's an Amazonian rainforest retreat, *actually,*" Agent6 states, putting on his posh tone.

"Yeah, right, of course it is."

Swifty's nodding with a grin of satisfaction across his face though.

"If the shit hits the fan I know where *I'm* gonna be: sitting in the back of a dugout with a fishing rod somewhere out there mate."

Dobbs has to chuckle at the notion. He finds the thought of such a simplistic solution to the challenges ahead of humanity almost touching in its childlike naivety. Not that Swifty won't be there in his dugout. It just seems so out of reach to the masses that seem to be stuck in some non-present stasis.

"You think it's negative to think that times are going to get tough and to start telling people to make provisions for that time? It doesn't necessarily mean running off to a bolt hole or climbing the nearest tree only to discover that you forgot a pot to piss in you know.

"What I'm talking about is food programmes and grass roots activism, like the creation of vast numbers of new allotments and taking back control of our communities. I mean you don't wait until you need a shit to build a toilet into your house, do you? But, on the same hand it would seem quite silly to flush nitrate rich fertiliser - which is what shit effectively is - away with drinking water! If there's no credit then we have to reinstate the monopoly

307

laws, base our currency on real value with a clear transparency and become the butchers and bakers and candlestick makers all over again – become the true communities we were destined to become. There are incredible technologies that we've discovered out there, advancing all the time. We have nearly all the answers we need except the fundamental question. Who and where is the subversive? What and where does the element exist that is driving war.

"England would go into civil unrest if the shit properly hit the fan," whistles Swifty, who's now sitting on the corner of Agent6's bed. "It would be a fucking famine. It will be a famine. Well…,"

But before he can finish his sentence Agent6 cuts in.

"It already is a famine – if you're on the wrong side of the dollar divide"

"Exactly. Green famines in Africa as we speak. Fields full of crops, already bought and paid for by an overzealous credit system that buys the common people's pummelled sovereignty that they can only watch and weep as their children go hungry while their government forces them to grow flowers to pay for that loan they got from the IMF, the money from which all got paid to foreign corporations to build infrastructure designed to benefit the super rich few at the expense of the starving many. I don't know man; perhaps the size of the famine might not change that much once the credit system is stuck in reverse ready for the next big pay out, but the geographical location certainly will, and all that wealth has just been distributed into the chubby, grubby little hands of the CEOs of those super rich corporations, ready for resale. It's like the snake that circles the Wheel of Samsara, consuming its own tail."

"Bloody hell Dobbs, you so need a shag," Bolivar suddenly shouts out.

Dobbs is suddenly acutely embarrassed by the notion.

"Have you rung Gatita back yet?" Swifty says, in a more humoured than curious tone.

"No…I sent her a text though."

"Ring her. You don't know what that was about with that guy. That's doing your head in - must be. Fucking ring her man. I know what you need."

"Well, I did text her earlier."

"Switch that fucking voice recorder off Dobbs and ring her, for God's sake man," Bolivar commands.

308

As much as Dobbs hates to admit it they can read him like a book. He takes his phone from his shoulder bag and selects Gatita's number.

"Maybe you're right," he says with a grin.

"Don't forget we've all got to get a lot of shit done today," Swifty says, wagging his finger in mock disapproval and then starts laughing at what seems the impossible task of leaving tomorrow.

Dobbs nods in affirmation and is just about to key in the number when Agent6 raises his hand.

"Dobbs!" he says with a cheeky wink, "Tell her we'll all do something together; no pressure!"

Dobbs pauses for a moment longer, just staring at the green button on his handset and wondering what the hell he's doing.

'Fuck it, what have I got to lose?' he thinks. Then he presses the keypad and waits.

Blown Open

Peering from the shaded recess of the ground floor of the hotel, Dobbs can make out kids playing in the sun splashed street. Their figures, bathed in the bright morning light seem to be just happy sparkles; such a gleaming radiant that he almost has to squint to make out any physical form at all. From his present perspective, the only thing that truly distinguishes them from the angels they appear to be are their sharp, playful shrieks as they chase each other this way and that, cavorting in the golden rays without a care in the world.

The rest of the extended family that run the hotel are all crammed, their faces blank and expressionless, in the downstairs lounge, glued to a seemingly endless stream of American sitcoms. The picture on the decrepit TV set is being partially hijacked by another channel which, at first glance, makes it somewhat difficult to decipher but something about it makes him do a double take. Looking again, this time letting his eyes relax and tuning into his peripheral vision like he does when he's being slightly clairvoyant, he has to smile to himself; very faintly he can make out the bobbing silhouette of a woman giving a blow job. For a moment he wonders if his subconscious is playing games with him but just then Gatita, who's been idly watching the screen whilst he checks he's got everything before they leave, peers over her glasses at him and raises her brows with the suggestion of a smirk. If he is merely having a salacious daydream then at least he's in good company.

Everything accounted for they set off an excursion but just as they're walking out of the hotel the youngest daughter – a child on the cusp of womanhood - comes running over. She's in total awe of Gatita, as is Gatita of her, and both stare at one another for a long moment before launching into a quick fire exchange of conversation that Dobbs shamefully doesn't understand at all. Whatever the girl's saying it's clear that she regards Gatita as something akin to a rock star, but it seems the excitement of being in her presence is all a bit overwhelming as once she's had a few of her questions answered she just turns and runs off back to her little girl's world of playing in the street, happy to feel she's been acknowledged.

Agent6 had been right of course; asking Gatita to come for a random wander through the town with them all had been a lot easier than asking for what he really wants - which is just to hold her and, given a half a chance, probably cry his eyes out in her arms. Now that she's here though, standing in front of him, he can barely stop staring at her. Even in the temple of his memory he had forgotten how beautiful she truly is.

She's clearly curious as to what's going through his head, but she's asking no questions and he's telling no lies. Instead he just stands there, letting the smile he feels in his soul radiate out through his eyes and soaking up the feeling of freedom she instils in him with the sunbeams dancing in her hair and the mighty river sliding silently by behind her. Even the air smells so fresh and rich it's as if he's still in that other world, the outer environment morphing with the vast space within.

'Perhaps this is nothing but a trip induced by a glass of jungle juice,' he thinks, 'a mere experience generated by psychotropic ingredients, but it feels more like a looking glass left by the gods until their return. Then again, maybe they never really left?'

Either way, everything is reversed for him now. Standing here, so close to his Goddess, he feels as naked and needy as Juan's old mutt, just grateful to bask in the warmth of her presence. He can see somehow that the affection she needs right now is not to be bound by conditions though.

"You've been having some strong experiences haven't you?" she begins.

He nods but the others are all coming down the stairs, so he refrains from elaborating. For now all he wants is to spend some quality time with her, go for a mellow stroll and see where they all end up.

Judging by the state of the street it must be a bank holiday or something as clearly some pretty wild been partying has been happening overnight and a big crowd is lazing around watching a football on the black and white TV outside the sandwich bar on the corner, which is normally pretty empty until after the working day's done. Once again the reception is terrible but in this case it's the commentary that fills in the grainy picture rather than some lusty subliminal blow job, and all eyes are glued firmly to the aging tube.

The whole world just feels so crushingly beautiful that somehow Dobbs feels as if his consciousness is in multiple places, both present in the here-and-now yet subdued by a million thoughts whirling through his mind, all projected on a backdrop of total bliss.

"You certainly look like you've had an experience," Gatita presses again, searching his gaze.

"It's been quite full on Gatita," Dobbs concedes eventually. "Look, I kind of... died in the ceremony last night," he goes on eventually, slightly unsure how to phrase such a statement.

"You died?"

"Well, yeah... And the mad thing is, I actually agreed to do it - and to go where I went."

"Where did you go?"

Dobbs shakes his head. He's unsure what to call that place. Heaven' is way too loaded with Christian connotations of Good and Evil. Maybe he should call it 'Nirvana,' he thinks, or perhaps 'Shambhala?' In the end he settles for the word the Chinese use to describe their hidden 'City of the Immortals.'

"I don't know Gatita. Shangri La maybe? Either way, a proper 'nother world like," he says, half turning away from her and looking up the promenade as if edging towards the centre of town and it's many temptations but he turns back to face the water, all too aware what madness lies that way.

The thing that still flummoxes him more than what to call it though is where it's *located*. Many of the places he'd visited on *Ayahuasca* had seemed light years away, and he'd actually experienced the sights, sounds and sensations of travelling at high speed to get there. The first time you astral travel is always a bit of a shocker; it blows your to mind to find you can just shoot off to the Milky Way like that. It's only happened to him *twice*; once on acid and once on *Ayahuasca*, but both times he'd left his body and felt his spirit or whatever travelling away from his body. The first was the most shocking of course, especially as he'd seen himself standing with a woman, the two of them holding each other's hands, eyes locked as if deep in trance. He'd always wondered after that when he was going to find the woman whose hand he's holding in that other world.

Yet, of all the wonderful worlds he's glimpsed it's this Other Earth that fascinates him the most, this other world that we build with our toils in this world. The true Spiritual Work his mother and father talk of, the same Spiritual Work that Juan demanded in his ceremony when he told the group to *put in the batteries*. And to think it was right here, tucked right into this world somehow, right under everyone's noses. He could scientifically get his head around the concept that another world could so easily hide itself in the vast space that exists between the protons and neutrons at the centre of an atom, and its electrons that orbit far-far away, like planets orbiting the sun, leaving the atom being mostly just a vast vacuous hole containing the realms untouchable by the orchestrations of the thought, it seems to Dobbs.

"What do you actually *do* back in England? Same as Agent6; working festivals?" Gatita says, before turning and walking in the direction of Belen Market, the opposite direction to the promenade. It's as though she's almost defusing the question as she turns.

"Yeah, kind of the same thing really."

Bolivar, who has just emerged from the hotel and has just caught them up overhears the comment bursts out laughing.

"That, and crashing and burning on TVs all over Britain."

"Well, I do seem to have a regular slot with destiny to make a total fool of myself at every convenient juncture," Dobbs shoots back.

"TV?" Gatita says, attempting to look impressed but looking more confused.

"Reality TV; it's kind of the opposite of being famous. Or, as Ben Elton would say: 'Whereas stars are special, reality TV stars are equally special; 'special needs.' It's terrifying; you know that you're going down in the ring, especially if you've completely set yourself up for it, which was the only logical way of getting in front of six million people. The masses love crash and burn. It helps people feel better about their own bleak lives to watch someone making a total fool of themselves. It doesn't really look terrifying until you're there, like I was, in front of some panel that basically wants to tear you to bits.

"The show's called *Lions Lair,* and the idea is you present your business idea and try and get a bunch of hatchet faced fat cats to invest in it. Bolivar was a massive help actually; he's an experimental marketing guru, aren't you Bolivar?"

"*Dobbs* is taking the piss Gatita. Suffice to say, no one got rich off it though – ay Dobbs?"

"What were you doing?" Gatita asks.

"Well, we were presenting a new marketing paradigm. Well, that's what we told the TV channel: An alternative digital self that's powered through electronic sensors that tracks your body's movement that in turn drives a digital puppet on a screen. It's a cartoon that does and says whatever you do and say. It's a digital puppet, basically Gatita."

"Oh shit, here comes Shakespeare Gatita." Bolivar bellows.

"It's true I guess. The TV stuff was always about Shakespeare but I just knew there was no way I would get that on the BBC with the political implications of what I was really up to. I was never going to get the *Dragons'* money. Crash and burn was all that was on the table. I didn't have any choice, as I didn't own any of the technology or have any intellectual property rights over it - no previous business, no nothing. I was always going down in the ring.

"What it was *really* all about was the publicity I could harness as a result of getting the system on the show which, in turn, was me getting some footing in a very costly industry. I didn't have the money, so I just had to work around that. Well, I'm still working around that. It all started with attempting to build Prospero - or 'Proslairo' as Hicksy calls him. I didn't even know there was this all seeing and all knowing powerful spirit that Prospero had at his command and bidding; the fabled Ariel. Many directors of the play capture Ariel in far-out ways apparently. Ariel; he or she, is the vengeful spirit that creates the great storm, the Tempest, that blows all that have wronged Prospero upon his Island where he enacts his redemption upon them.

"I mean, I've only read a couple of the plays myself, and *I* had to read the children's versions to get my head around the stories before I attempted to read the original script. If you can understand it, there's a message of love and forgiveness in there."

Gatita smiles. And Dobbs can only lose himself in her sweet face that harmonises with the shanty town and the forest beyond the watery expanse of the Amazon River.

"Wow, I feel as beautiful as you look."

Gatita cocks her head to one side as trying to read him then turns and gestures towards the market area and the shanty side of the city, completely in the opposite direction from where he'd thought they'd end up walking.

"So you wrote this..."

"...parody?"

"No. It was written by my mate, Hicksy, but he'd helped me write a play along with the guy who's kind of with my..."

"...girlfriend?"

Dobbs immediately catches Gatita's eye and then looks away and just nods, giving no indication of what his feelings on the matter are – primarily because it all suddenly seems so far away that if anything he just wants to laugh about it right now.

314

"But, anyway, Hicksy had written this play and I loved it," he continues, not even allowing his mind to let that massive other story even close to this experience now. "Well, I loved the idea of it. It made the story accessible beyond the crazy text that it's written. It probably needs updating a bit now, but Tony Blair will always be Proslairo in my head with his magic manifesto; that's timeless. So after me crashing and burning on TV everything just dried up a bit. The thousands of prospective offers and whatever else I was expecting actually amounted to about two vague emails and everything else just stopped dead. I guess that was when I got the big idea of turning the whole thing into a book, and bring enough attention to it so perhaps I might be able to link up with any and all that could help me get this show on the road in the proportions I saw it in my mind's eye. Now I just don't where any of this is going, to be honest. It's all suddenly bigger than me now."

"Do you actually have a story?"

Dobbs busts out laughing at the statement. As does Bolivar, who's wondering just beyond observing what seem mostly empty stalls closed shops but is somehow just comfortably being there.

"Well, I was trying to think of something big for 2012 but I don't know what it will be anymore. I was trying to work it round the memoir's of a hash fudge salesman before my mate suddenly came up with that bloody Tempest parody. You know, trying to capture the definition of someone whose only way to deal with this invasion of his land that has entered through the corporate loopholes and that is now attempting to take his country from right under nose. That the only thing the Fudgeman can do is to break the law with honourable, victimless crime, thousands of times a day, right under *their* noses but without a shred of fear and not a trace of guilt."

"Is this what you do at festivals?"

"Well…"

"He can't break the law Gatita. He's technically a politician," Bolivar shouts across to Gatita who's wondering just behind as they slowly walk, more waiting for the others.

"Are you?"

"Well, technically, I guess I am. But Gatita, do I honestly look like a man that gets off breaking the law hundreds of time a day just for kicks?"

"I don't know."

315

"That was never the story though. It's the tale of a coward. Well, it's the tail of a hash fudge salesman who thought he could diminish the risk of getting busted selling illegal cakes by selling laughing gas instead. The only thing he knew that sold like hash fudge. But - of course - as he sails from one near miss, he sails straight into another storm, by blowing his mind on a blast of nitrous. It's the story of a man who loses his bottle selling the cakes he knows everyone wants; the story of a man who was scared to do the best job in the world and..."

"Well, what happens?"

"Well, it's a *fictional* tale attempting to create the perfect template for the ultimate Shamanic training ground. I mean, imagine what it's like smuggling illegal cakes into a festival, knowing that you're absolutely right and just in what you do and then breaking the law hundreds of time each and every day of the festival, right under the noses of those that wish to bust you? Tracking your intentions back to absolute to your highest grace and hiding in that alone. Hiding in the sun beams. The problem is that..."

"What?"

"Well, I told you what happened in the vision. It's not exactly a happy ending is it? I wanted to call it Laughing Gas. It's about festivals, sunny days and all the colours of the rainbow, happiness, bright pinks and yellows, about brotherhood and sisterhood - *compadres* in real life, not the action adventure *shite* that caters for the six year old mind alone. I just need...a..."

"...a happy ending?"

"Well, Yeah, except that my character kind of dies half way through. That's not so sensible is it?" He says giggling at the notion.

"Is that what you're looking for; a happy ending?"

"Well...isn't that what we all want in the end?"

Gatita says nothing and just observes him again with a seduction that causes Dobbs to experience a hot flush that he can barely look into those whirlpools. And he breaks away from the intensity, "I mean...I don't know where it's going anymore." He splutters. "I seem to have started a whirlwind that's turned into a Tempest itself. Like I thought I was writing a story about how the powers that be catch a monkey with his own fucking nuts, only to find I'm the monkey caught by the nuts. But if I do find my happy ending, I'll definitely tell the story of the Fudgeman that I suppose bit off more than he could chew. I mean, what does a Fudgeman do when

316

the odds are finally too stacked against him and he can't do anymore, what he's born to do?"

"Am I going to be in your book?" Gatita asks with a look of touching curiosity.

"I don't know Gatita. What do you reckon?"

Gatita says nothing though. Instead she just keeps on moving.

In no time, they're at the shanty, indigenous market by the water just a few hundred metres down from the hotel which is still in view. He'd expected to see lots of people about by the sound of the music still blasting out but to his surprise it's virtually all shut up and everyone's gone but a few last stragglers.

Gatita spots one of the vendors who's still trading and, wandering over to the simple stall, selects a fruit drink for Dobbs to try. Its dark, chocolate brown colour is in vast contrast to its peculiarly bland flavour, which seems to be buffered only by a sickeningly sweet saturation of sugar. Dobbs is not at all sure he likes it, but he sips politely whilst waiting for an opportune moment to discard it.

Dobbs is walking side by side with Gatita now whilst Bolivar lags behind, waiting for the others. For a few more precious moments they're alone, and Dobbs can't help it; he has to express his feelings. "You're very beautiful Gatita," he says, looking closer at her face. "I don't know what meeting you is all about you but you are; you're beautiful."

Gatita smiles modestly then spins round on one foot, still sucking on the straw sticking out of the top of the plastic bag like a little girl.

"Negrita!" she breathes, in the lowest most seductive tone that makes his knees tremble.

"Negrita?" Dobbs repeats and lets out a short breath. She looks so adorable he doesn't quite know where to put his eyes.

"I like it. Not as much as Gatita, but…it's a cute nickname."

"You just want me to purr like a cat to you?"

Dobbs has to look away as when she glances at him. It's as though she can peer right into him. She's absolutely right. Glancing back, he can see the others finally exiting the hotel. To his surprise The Brigadier, who they've been seeing less and less of is with them. He waves them, even though he's half regretting not just taking off on his own with her, but at least they've had these few moments together, and he knows it will be good for them all to have an outing together as a group.

"I saw Agent6 last night in that other world you know," he says, looking at his friend pacing towards them, clearly engaged in some logistical discussion with Swifty. "It was weird; he just seemed to be calmly waiting for me to arrive. He looked so beautiful and at peace. How the hell does that work?"

"In the dream world?" Gatita asks.

"I'm not sure. I've seen what I know as the dream world many times but this was different. Somehow it just didn't really feel psychedelic. It was a real world Gatita. Like a second Earth almost - and not, like, 'up here' or 'down there' or over the hill and round the fucking bend but *right here* - like a parallel dimension or something that we just can't see. He says he doesn't remember meeting me but it was *him*. I mean yes it was his face, but it was also more than that. It was his eyes, his *warmth*."

Just then Agent6 catches up to them.

"He's saying nice things about you," Gatita whispers in greeting.

"About bloody time," he grins wolfishly.

Agent6 takes a sweeping look around. Whatever festivities had been occurring are pretty much over and though loud Latin beats can still be heard blaring out from some unseen sound system with some of the last remaining stragglers and waning die-hards, still busting salsa moves - the men moving their hips as fluidly as the women. Normally, on market days, you can barely move a foot in front of you in this place but now, by comparison, it seems so deserted it's almost eerie. The stalls are all empty apart from a few vendors selling snacks and fruit drinks and as they walk through, all side by side- apart from The Brigadier, who's lagging behind looking a bit twitchy - the sense of somehow having just missed the party seems to mirror Dobbs's own feelings about the events of the last couple of nights.

"It's so weird, walking through this place and seeing it so deserted," he says. "Especially with the music still blaring. It's like they're all still here but I just can't see them, like they've all gone to some special place...beyond. Perhaps the party's still happening there?"

"It all seems so odd Gatita, I've spent the last six months learning how to build a virtual avatar and incorporate it a live, virtual theatre and then I come out here and find another avatar that extends from me into another world - except it doesn't look digital and, oddly, it doesn't quite look real either. It's like it's me, but it's made of some more energetic form of matter. My mum channelled

318

my guide once and he told me that I was here for my words and that I would become like one of my puppets on strings. I never imagined I'd see that so clearly as I do now."

Gatita doesn't respond immediately, just looking at him with a kind of perplexed wonder. Personally he's not sure if he's going to burst out laughing or burst into tears. Walking through the barren market, shoulder to shoulder with his compadres like a cowboy in a crazy spaghetti Western, he's suddenly struck by the comedy of the situation as well as the pathos. It feels like he's stalking through a battlefield in the eerie silence of the aftermath of some big clash with the Indians, the music still blaring like an echo of something missed by a moment and yet the saturation of sound somehow making it seem as if they're all still there, hiding behind the bright shards of sunlight breaking through between the stalls and now dancing all around him.

Looking around, he suddenly realises someone else has also disappeared.

"Where's The Brigadier?" he asks.

Nobody attempts to answer, but Agent6 looks at the ground as if in momentary contemplation before slightly shrugging his shoulders. Nothing more is said; nothing more needs to be said. They all just keep on walking, up and through the sea of shanty wooden stalls covered with tatty pieces of tarp and rusting corrugated roof panels, all looking as if they've been handed down generation after generation.

"It's like they're still here, dancing," Dobbs whispers to Gatita. She turns around as if in contemplation. "And then all that's left is the music, right?"

"Yeah, I guess," Dobbs nods.

She stares at him for a moment with an expression half of an almost intimidating sense of pride, and half just very tranquillo. This place is her roots, and she loves and respects it and its people.

"So then we dance, right?"

Taking her hand he pulls her close to him then twirls her round. He is surprised to feel how elegantly she moves and the hidden strength behind her calm façade, and even though the exchange only lasts a moment it's immediately clear that she can properly dance.

"So what do you do here then Gatita? You always look like you're doing OK," he says, more to hide the sudden thumping in his heart he feels when he holds her close.

"I make trees."

"Trees?"

"Si. Out of copper wire and beads."

The answer is so simple, he really doesn't know what to say.

"I'd like to see one of your trees Gatita," he finally whispers. "I bet they're as beautiful as you.

They are approaching the end of the main market thoroughfare before it disperses into a narrower section of smaller roads, all of which look very quiet. Agent6 just shrugs his shoulders as he peers down into the barren streets.

"Come on," he says, "this is well over. Let's take a boat round to the main harbour."

Dobbs likes the idea immediately.

"A leisurely boat ride on the river, Sir? Yes please! But how?"

Turning around, Agent6 delivers the exact wink he did the night before, in that Other Earth.

"I'm sure we can cross someone's palm with silver," he says with a conspiratorial grin.

Shakespeare

Meandering through the small back routes it's not long before they're at the river where Agent6 negotiates with a fisherman to take them on a trip around the harbour. A few minutes later, and they're all on board a vessel similar in design to the *Christina* only with an open top and a slimmer, slightly smaller hull.

"*Despacio por favor!*" Dobbs shouts out to the pilot who, once they'd cleared the river bank, had cranked up the engine speed thinking perhaps that his cargo might be in a rush. Immediately the revs drop obligingly.

Gatita nods, smiling in acknowledgment at this unusually bold attempt at Spanish. He hasn't had much call to practice since they met as her English is so perfect and she's clearly enjoying every bit of practice she can get. Her voice is deep and her words so calmly accentuated that talking to her is like seduction on a stick. Dobbs feels as if he could listen to her for a year non-stop, and still not get bored.

After a while the fisherman drops the revs down even lower to a slowest potter more in synch with the sedate pace of the river as they sit on one of the benches traverses the hull. Somehow, with his friends present along with the captain he'd expected it to feel too crowded for him but it makes the perfect, most un-intensive space.

The sight is mesmerising. The homesteads of the Indigenous living along the banks can be seen in their most spectacular aspect from this perspective. Though very basic they are beautifully kept and Dobbs is gratified to note that there's barely a single piece of rubbish to be seen anywhere. From here the harshness of life in the shanty town is hidden and instead it seems joyful, honest and unassuming.

As they round a bend in the river he sees a sight he'd been half expecting but which brings memories flooding back - a boat exactly the same as the *Claudia,* a fine old vessel on which he'd travelled down from *Urimagnus* to *Iquitos* on his last trip. It's a battered old flat-bottomed steel dinosaur from an era long since passed with only two long rails from which to string a hammock - and those rails hold a lot of hammocks! Some are set high and some low and others tied off in between in a multi-level system that crams a hundred or so people into the tiniest space - comfortably.

He'd spent days just lying in his hammock looking out watching the Amazon go by on that delightful trip, but the nostalgia evoked by the ship runs deeper than that. Shopping in Columbia on his way down through the continent, he'd met a girl who was running a shanty bar out in the sticks. He'd sort of caught her eye a few times and not much more but on one occasion as he was wandering past down the old dirt track on which it sat, he'd thought he'd glimpsed her in there and popped in to say hello. Once inside he was disappointed to find she was nowhere to be seen but then, noticing a flight of steps, he'd called out, thinking she might be upstairs. No one had answered and he was just about to give up but then the word 'upstairs' started rattling around in his head and he couldn't resist the temptation to have a peep. There she was, just lying on the floor, staring at him. He didn't even try and talk – there had been no need - and when he finally went to leave, he'd asked her name, half giggling that he hadn't done so yet.

"Claudia" she'd breathed at him as she'd just lain there, naked, on the floorboards, watching him watch her with a slow, knowing smile.

A few days later they'd taken off on some horses up to the mountains and he'd made love with her again, under the stars on some pasture outside an old abandoned farmhouse. She was a wild little thing, but it was before the time of wall-to-wall email and mobile phones as standard and he never saw her again, something that almost added to the romance of the encounter. After that, when he'd seen this old vessel, the *Claudia*, in all her battered magnificence, he'd known it was going to be a beautiful journey.

Now, as he takes in the sight of the ancient tin cans sparsely lining the harbour, he is transported up and away to the mountains with Claudia for a moment. Then he looks back at Gatita, appreciating the simplicity of her uncontrived beauty against the epic backdrop, and it burns his heart.

"It's hard to believe you can sail all the way through this continent for the price of your weekly shopping bill in Tesco's," he says, half to himself.

"Tesco's?" Gatita smiles, and her half questioning expression perfectly captures the total irrelevance of the remark. Then she just turns and stares back out at the vessels that have so clearly moved Dobbs.

The truth is, love stories apart, he's always had a thing about ships. The thought of sailing out in the open sea scared him too much to call it an obsession, but the superstructure of ships fascinates him nonetheless. With their flat hulls these cargo ships look as though they probably draw less than three feet of water, which seems unfeasibly little for such big vessels. He'd sailed all the way down from where the jungle starts in North Peru to Manaus, in the centre of Brazil, on a variety of these battered old ladies, most of them well in excess of a hundred feet long and many probably over a century old and plated and welded more times than anyone could remember.

The vessels had particularly come to represent something of an enigma to him ever since he heard the story of a crazy Irishman, Brian Sweeney Fitzgerald, who'd come to Iquitos and acquired one back in the days of the *Caucheros* and then proceeded to haul all 340 tons of her over a mountain in order to gain access to some new 'virgin' land that supposedly belonged to no one - apart from the natives of course. Fitzgerald had become immortalised in the Werner Herzog film *Fitzcarraldo*, which tells the story of how he attempted to muscle in on the rubber boom and woo the natives into working for him with little more than balls and blarney, driven not by mere greed for gold but the desire to build a theatre and bring opera to Iquitos.

It's all true, apparently. Well, except for the fact his father was American, not Irish, and his real name was Carlos Fermin Fitzcarrald. The rest is true though, apart from his soft, cultured charm that actually involved the execution of any native who didn't agree to slave for a pittance in appalling conditions in order to make the White Man's dream come true. Carlos did at least drag his ship over the mountain – well, actually a high dividing ridge between two estuaries - but sensibly, if less romantically, he dismantled the thing first.

Not so for Werner Herzog however, who was besieged with failure and calamity all the way through the film. First the young actor playing Fitzcarraldo's assistant left to go off touring as lead singer with a new band called *The Rolling Stones,* instead. Needless to say, Mick Jagger never made it back. Then, when the film was already half finished, the main character got so sick that the whole thing had to be completely reshot.

Eschewing the convenience of special effects, Herzog actually dragged his 340-ton steam ship *intact* over the mountain, which was and probably remains the single hardest feat ever undertaken in filmmaking. He went on to win the Best Director Award at the

323

Cannes Film Festival for his efforts, but the most interesting point of the whole story for Dobbs is that there never was a Fitzcarraldo. Or at least there was, but his real name was Werner Herzog - a man who came to Iquitos with the crazy dream of living out something that only existed as a true story in his head. But then, to attempt to rewrite history and elevate a *Cauchero* into a saint was always going to be an uphill struggle.

The small fishing boat labours slowly on whilst this rush of thoughts is racing through Dobbs's head. He wants to put his arm around Gatita but he realises perhaps that's not appropriate, That old feeling of restriction is back within him again, making him feel like the daft Englishman he is, trapped in his frustrating little thought cage. Then he remembers that he *is* a daft Englishman and relaxes into the bliss of that for a moment.

'Just enjoy the ride kid,' says the feeling inside, and he allows the little harbour to elevate itself into the temple it truly is.

It's times like these, when Dobbs touches beauty, that his mind often plays its most terrible tricks to lure him away.

What is that process and why am I so infected by it? Is this just what happens to a man when he suddenly wants a woman so badly - or am I, actually, a bit fucked up? he ponders.

He focuses on his immediate surroundings again, and though he still wants to embrace Gatita he decides it's just inappropriate. He's not sure if it's just him, or he's picking up on some bigger picture that she's glossing over - some complication that she's hiding behind her huge sunglasses. Is she somehow compromised? Isn't everyone? Dobbs knows it's possible – probable in fact - that someone else is on the scene. After all, he thinks to himself, what are the chances of finding the most gorgeous girl in Iquitos with no strings attached? Whatever the complication, there's nothing to do right now but keep breathing and just take in the bright shafts of light deflecting off the ripples, the gentle purr of the engine and the soft, scented breeze in his face.

"Are you still happy here in Iquitos? You look like you belong here at least," he says.

She doesn't look at him, but just keeps staring out over the water.

"I've been here most of my life...all of my life. I want to leave Iquitos."

"To go where?"

"Somewhere exciting. I want to go to Europe...to France I think."

"You have friends there?"

324

"A few."

"Where?"

"Down in the south. Have you been to France?"

"Yeah, Brighton's just across the water. On a good day you can skim pebbles across the water to France and hit the ankles of Frenchmen."

"It's that close to England?"

"Well, not quite that close maybe, but you could try."

"You can see France?"

"Well, no."

"Hmmm."

"It's close though. People swim it! Thirty, forty kilometres maybe."

But just then he finds himself observing a house without quite believing what he's actually seeing.

"My God Gatita," he exclaims, "look at that. That's the house I saw in my vision. Exactly that house."

"What house?" Gatita asks.

"Last night. Before I had the main sort of vision. Fuck, I nearly died throwing up and then I saw that very house; I'm sure it was that little house - exactly that house - with an Indigenous couple and their children standing out on that little veranda, waving to me and wishing me good luck. Even that bush in front looks the same!"

Gatita looks at the house and then back at Dobbs but says nothing.

"Can the mind *really* just fabricate such things? I saw a huge snake in a vision I had here in Iquitos - the first time I came here actually - and every detail of its visible structure was absolute perfection, from the shimmering, emerald pearlescent glaze of the scales to the crystal clear contour of its nose. Can a mind fabricate stuff like that? Fuck, it was the size of jet plane."

"You have such strong, clear visions. Was this the first time you drank here?"

"No. The first time was in Columbia when I was just on the regular Gringo trail. Here was the second time. It kind of changed all my plans a bit. It was beautiful though; my first time in the dream world - seeing it, I mean. It's kind of like this other place I visited last night except everything is illuminated by its own light, it own aura with colours you just can't describe and rolling landscapes and things that just float in the air, like giant seahorses. It's almost like an underwater world without any water.

325

"I mean, I did have this story of a huge snake in my mind as I'd travelled down through Columbia and Ecuador. A huge serpent that is said to live deep within the jungle and is so vast in size and has been sleeping for so long that most of its huge body is covered with earth and foliage. It's so well hidden in fact that even the finest hunters cannot discover its exact whereabouts but, if they do, it will be the last thing they ever see on this Earth. It is said that this snake emits a frequency- the very same frequency the hunter hones in on to find his prey. It's not fear - it's the pure serenity of True Freedom. The hunter must tune into the utter freedom and abundant beauty of nature in order to find his prey, but in the process he becomes the hunted because the greater the gift, the greater the risk; if his sense is *too* acute the hunter will walk right into the snake's mouth."

"*Sachamama*," Gatita says. "It's a Quechuan tale - from here. Did you drink on the reserve at *Sachamama*? I don't even know if it's still there now."

"Yeah - with Fernando and Francisco. So there I am, drinking the brew, and I'm just gob smacked at the size of this snake that appears to be just a few feet in front of me, just calmly staring at me through an eye easily over a metre wide. I could feel it observing me, and then it asked if I wanted to come on a journey with it - I'm always asked by whatever *Ayahuasca* is if I want to have the experience it's offering. I mean I was scared but I'd come all that way and shamanism is all about overcoming fear and developing trust in the Divine, isn't it? So I was like, 'yeah, let's go.' I wanted to see.

"Oh Gatita, each shiny scale on its vast body was bigger than both my hands splayed out," he says holding his hands up. "Like fiery, pearlescent emerald slates of natural body armour, each so perfectly formed and immaculate. And the contour of its nose and its nostrils and the way the scales meshed together - even the tiny translucent scales just round the very edge of its eyes - was surely all just too perfect for my mind to fabricate? It was immaculate. It was absolutely massive and not much more than a few feet away, just looking at me, waiting for my reply. Nothing could be hidden from its vision; my entire process was laid bare to it.

"Even just knowing that I had a choice was just so empowering - that I could actually say 'yes' or 'no' to this Being and it could offer such unconditional passage. As soon as I had acknowledged that I was up for it, I found myself approaching the snake's eye.

Disappearing through it, I dived down into a winding tunnel that looped round and round and was full of bright streaking colours. It was somehow just like the way the *Ayahuasca* vine itself grows, winding along the floor of the jungle and randomly looping a few times, apparently for no other purpose than sheer beauty alone before it shoots up again, curling and spiralling around trees as it makes its way up to the canopy."

"And that's how you found the dream world?"

"Well, everything just came to a stop and I found myself just staring at what looked almost like a wall made of a fusion of colours in front of me, and as I stared at the wall I realised it was an image. I recognised random things and was almost sure amongst it all I could see my red Doc Martens. And then, as I looked closer, I saw other bits of my life; odd artefacts, most of which I couldn't remember after, but I remember it was like this bizarre, eclectic collage of my life - all woven into a single tapestry. And the oddest thing I noticed - more than the boots, more than anything else, was a knife. It was a dagger, with a curved blade and jewels in the handle, totally fairytale-like. And I knew this dagger."

He twists slightly in his seat, dropping his hand into the water as if suddenly needing to touch the mirror-like surface and reassure himself of its reality.

"Years before, when I was about fourteen or fifteen, still just a boy really, I'd had a dream that I was being chased on all fours down an earthy, winding tunnel matrix underground by someone or something I couldn't see. I was in a state of panic, crawling as fast as I could go to escape, and then, in front of me, I saw what I thought was an opening. It was a place where a number of tunnels all converged, and bright light was bursting through from above the muddy, walled junction ahead. So I race for the junction and I'm nearly there, but my hips get stuck and I just can't get through, no matter how much I wriggle, and whoever's following me is now right on my tail. Just when I feel I can do nothing, that I can't break free and I'm done for, whoever it is behind seems to take another route, and I just catch a glimpse of my pursuer as they dart across a tunnel running off to the right. Then I get another glimpse of the man down another tunnel running off the previous one, and I realise whoever's chasing me is now racing round to cut me off."

"Suddenly, there he is - directly opposite me. He's like an Indian, but more of Columbian *Arawaku* descent than *Quechuan* perhaps, and his eyes are wild, like an animal's. He's got this dagger in his hand – up, like he's going to throw it at me with all his might and then he throws it at me, like full on. Instinctively I put my arms up to block it but nothing happens, and when I open my eyes the knife is just sat there, in the palm of my hand."

"I just throw the knife down on the ground in shock, literally terrified of the man, but he immediately grabs it off the ground and throws it back at me. Again I try to block it and the same thing happens, but this time I take a proper look at the dagger and I see not just the curved blade, but the leather bound handle and the stone, shining like a bright star with a colour I've never seen. A dream world colour, like an emerald translucence that has analluring depth, like the texture of a butterfly's wing."

Taking a deep breath, he drops his hands by his sides again and looks into Gatita's eyes.

"This place stirs up such intense emotions," he whispers before continuing. "And then I opened my eyes to wake in my bedroom and no sooner had I opened my eyes, I heard the words: 'cut away,' as clear as a bell in my head. I always wondered exactly what those words meant. I had so many interpretations running through my head but I'd never really known."

He nods at Gatita, checking she's still with him. "My crazy stories Gatita, sorry," he says.

"I like them. Not everyone experiences *Ayahuasca* through visions. You're very lucky. So you saw this same dagger in the vision here when you first drank?"

"Well, immediately I see this same dagger, I recollect the dream from when I was a kid, only as clear as if it had occurred the night before, and suddenly the knife jumps free from this collage and is just hovering in front of me. It was just like a cartoon, but so real, just floating there in front of me in the air. But no sooner do I try to get my head around the knife's meaning. it shoots over to the corner of the collage and starts cutting in the most animated fashion around the sides of the image that was just hanging loosely in the air. The collage sagged slightly in the middle, although still taking up my entire field of vision, and then I see these huge, but soft and gentle hands holding each side of the partially draping collage.

"I was nervous as to who was on the other side; like just suddenly noticing them sent shivers through me, and then one hand just let go and beyond was this huge man, and beyond him, this landscape, this...new dimension: the dream world. I'd seen pictures of it in Pablo Amaringo's book, *Ayahuasca Visions* but had never thought that such a world actually existed, that the dream world was a *real* world, full of conscious beings."

"So who was he do you think?"

"I couldn't see the face of the man as it wasn't possible to look up, but he was dressed like the wood cutter out of a fairytale and had an absolutely massive build. In fact everything about him was like a fairytale; from his boots that were well-worn soft leather and his trousers of translucent velvet and this huge white shirt covering his massive shoulders, tucked under his belt with this slightly bulging belly protruding just over the top. And these beautiful embroidered cuffs, perfectly encircling and framing his massive gentle hands. He was a gentleman Gatita, a genuine gentleman."

"Wow."

"Over the top of his shirt he wore a tight waistcoat of dark green velvet that was open at the front and that would probably struggle to stretch round his barrel chest. But then he gently takes the collage, the tapestry of my life, and places it over his arm like a waiter with a tablecloth, and I watch as the fabric gently slides through his fingertips. Then he pulls open his waistcoat and I can see that inside are many, many other fabrics like mine, all stashed in the inner lining. He leans closer so they are directly in front of me and I can watch as he gently thumbs through them, like the pages of a book.

"One in particular was very thick and had such a compact weave, with what looked like gold thread set deep into the warp and weft of the fabric and he knows that I'm looking at it, as when his thumb stops on that particular layer, which seems so soft and richly woven, he pulls it out ever so slightly so I can see the full splendour of the soft richness and warmth of the fabric. And then, ever so gently, he caresses it between his thumb and forefinger before pushing it back into his waistcoat and then tapping the huge buckle of his belt. Suddenly I realise that this is probably me, and that these might actually be lives - under my belt so to speak - and in that very same moment I conceived the thought that this life I am living now could be something of that great splendour."

As he says it, he wipes a tear away from his eye.

"It was a thought that came crashing down when I glanced upon my cloth, still folded over the man's arm. Suddenly I was devastated, because whereas before I'd seen the artefacts and experiences from this life woven into a single cloth of magnificence, now all that remained were dirty stains, and in places it was so threadbare it seemed to be worn right through. And I realised that in fact my life was nothing more than a dirty dishcloth, like the thinnest piece of fabric you can imagine.

"The universe has such a lovely way of asking you to clean up your act, doesn't it?"he says, wiping more tears away from his eyes. "To do better, to be better than what you thought you were. I felt my energy dropping with a feeling that things weren't quite as good as I'd kind of hoped. That this life was more of a mess than I'd realised and I was being asked, politely, to clean up my act. And as I started to have a serious word with myself I noticed that the cloth had gone. And then I followed the man's arm to see that in his right hand he now held a spear and there was my cloth. He'd tied it around the shaft of the spear, just below the blade that was spliced with cord into the wooden shaft. It looked so magnificent and I was overjoyed and I could feel tears running down my face. And as this feeling of victory coursed through me as he pulled me back from the brink of despair, he literally shook the spear and then just held it high with his arm fully outstretched. And then I woke up to find myself face down in the mud again, as I so often do after an intense ceremony."

"You really do have intense ceremonies."

"It's weird. I know that someone can go off to university and study for three or four years and come to me and give their synopsis, but academia sometimes makes me cringe with its basic lack of belief in the wonder of the universe. The realm of academia denies the existence of all that is scientifically unproven – a mind stuffed full of knowledge feels insulted by wisdom that is beyond it. It's all too easy to become so full of knowledge that there is no place *left* for Wisdom. And all because everything has to be placed into a box and labelled as 'known' and therefore understood. It sometimes seems science has become a full scale invasion on all that cannot be proved - like an invasion on God, if there really is such a thing as a God."

Gatita raises her eyes as if to question the concept herself and smiles.

"You make me want to drink it again."

"Maybe you should Gatita. But I guess nothing's such a big deal when it's right on your doorstep. What you have to remember is that every ceremony in Britain is like a covert mission, where those who hold the ceremonies risk losing their liberty. It's outlawed, along with everything else now. Our shamans are just common criminals and all those who stand for peace are locked away. Only the D. U. dumping Christian crusaders are allowed to speak the word of peace – even as they pursue their relentless war."

As he speaks, he suddenly notices her posture.

"You sit so straight Gatita," Dobbs says, suddenly aware that there's pain there.

"My back is always a bit of a problem. I had an accident years ago and now I have to keep it straight or it gets bad."

"It makes you look very proud Gatita, and it keeps your whole posture perfect. It might have been a bit of a gift. What did you do?"

"It didn't feel like a gift. I fell and broke my coccyx."

"Iyah!!! I sat on a shard of glass in a broken window years ago and it went straight into my coccyx. I thought at the time that I'd busted through into a whole new realm of pain, but to break your coccyx? that must have been unbelievable. Do you get any back massage for it?"

"Si, and I learnt massage; deep tissue massage. That's what I love. When everything that holds everything together all softens and goes back to its natural position and I can relax."

"Sounds beautiful." He whispers, knowing that the boat rides nearly over and wants more time her. "Can I take you out somewhere for dinner Gatita?"

She looks at him like she's wondering what he really wants, or perhaps weighing up some other complication, but then she just smiles.

 "OK."

"Cool. I've got to go to Juan's and grab some more potion. But we can meet after'"

"You're going to drink again?"

"Yeah, we're going to the jungle again, tomorrow. Last time I came here to sort out my knee, this time it seems I've come to sort out my head."

"Is it working - or are you just blowing your mind?"

"I think I asked too many questions early on, Gatita. I don't know if there's a road back now. I know something big is about to happen; I can feel it. Something massive is going down on Earth right now but it's like we're all missing the elephant in the room.

331

We're all too scared to look at it, but the real truth is just staring us in the face."

"Which is what?"

Turning away from Gatita, Dobbs just casts his gaze over to the tiny shanty houses on stilts.

"Shit, if I knew that, I probably wouldn't have bothered coming here. I'm just starting to get a picture of the size of this thing - the real dimensions of this miracle we call Earth. You see I've been searching for this thing all my life and it seems that it might have been searching for me."

The bow of the boat suddenly hits land and the ride is over.

She turns almost abruptly and observes his face again, staring into his eyes.

"Your happy ending."

The Dancing Frenchman

The downstairs of the *Yellow Rose of Texas* diner is a bizarre space, and as they wait for their food to arrive Dobbs casts his eyes around the assorted artefacts and arcane knick-knacks lining the walls with a slightly bewildered sense of curiosity. Every surface is crammed with an eclectic cornucopia of exotic ornamentations not just from the jungle but, it seems, all over the world. It's such a strange collection in fact that despite the decided oddity of each individual item the overall effect is that they all cancel each other out and nothing in particular has the power to hold the attention.

The thirteen-ringed knot of the hangman's noose – 'illegal to own in the states' - is almost lost amongst the vast array of indigenous face masks which seem in turn to harmoniously blend with the camouflage cover of wall-to-wall snake skins, crocodile heads, animal pelts and enormous tortoise shells. Even the seats around the bar are riding saddles from World War I, and the normally flirtatious waitresses are all dressed in traditional Texas gingham - although they seem to be guarding their smiles a little now Gatita's about.

Dobbs had thought *The Rose,* one of Iquitos' main tourist hubs, might be the perfect place to finish the day, but as soon as they sit down he knows he's made a mistake. He can sense Gatita's uncomfortable and this place, in the spotlight of the tiny town, isn't somewhere she would normally come to. He taps his knuckles nervously on the table.

"What *is* this wood then?" he says, trying to distract her and making a show of inspecting the solid grain of the surface, which seems to have the density of iron.

Gatita's mind is elsewhere though, and she seems barely even to notice he's spoken at first. After a moment she focuses on the huge chunk that's been chopped off square at the top, fine sanded and then polished and just shrugs her shoulders.

"Not sure," she says.

"It looks almost like a cancerous growth; you know, those huge knuckles or knots that grow from the side of trees. They're too tough to do anything with; the grain's all twisted as it grows. Can't be used as firewood - you'd never chop it or split it. A dinner table seems to be the only option left on the, well, the table ..." he trails off lamely.

"You're not comfortable here are you Gatita?" he says, searching her face. "Look, we can just swig this back - shit, we could take it with us and chip off somewhere more tranquillo - find another restaurant somewhere in the backstreets, away from prying eyes."

"No, it's OK. It's just Iquitos is such a small town and people have…opinions."

"It probably ain't going to change in your lifetime or mine Gatita. And we're only having dinner."

"You know I'm half kind of thinking I'd like to drink again," she says, obviously keen to change the subject.

"What - the brew?"

"Si."

"Well if you're looking for an invitation to come out to the land you know you've always got that - I'd love to do a ceremony with you. You could come to the jungle with us tomorrow if you like. There's enough potion - I've got more than we need. I'd love to have you there."

"Maybe next time. There's still much to do there, huh? Swifty said you've just torn it all apart."

Dobbs holds his wine glass as though it were a morning coffee, warming it with his palms to bring out the woody taste and observing how Gatita hides her insecurities.

"Yeah, but it'll be a functional space with shelter and a main net this time I reckon, at least."

He can tell that the connotations of it are all too loaded for her at the moment though, so he doesn't press the issue.

"I'm determined to find out just how deep this thing goes and find, well…" he begins instead.

"Shakespeare?" Gatita says, shaking her head slightly. She clearly finds the whole thing a little amusing.

"It seems a little odd that Shakespeare, whoever he really was, is having such an odd influence in my life now. Maybe it's an age thing. Seems almost silly; I left school at fifteen and became a mechanic. I innocently thought you had to be intelligent to write a book, when all that's really needed is a story I guess."

"Look, thanks for coming out with me today Gatita, and sorry for bringing you here. Where do you normally prefer to eat?"

"I guess I just prefer the simple places. But this is OK."

"Will you take me to some simple places Gatita? They're probably more fun - and I bet they're a lot cheaper!"

"Sure."

For all that, Dobbs can see there's nothing sure about anything Gatita's saying and as soon as they've finished eating he gets the bill.

"Come on, let's get out of here and work on some other plan," he says as they're leaving. "What do you want to do - other than splitting from here?"

"What do *you* want to do now?" she says, half smiling with a naughty expression across her face,

The thought going through his head is; take you to my bed and make love with you all night long, but there's no way his inner Englishman is going to let him say that. Instead he settles for something a little more conservative.

"I don't know Gatita. This is your town. What do you think?"

"You want to play?"

"Play?" he gulps, not quite knowing where this is going and not daring to hope. Maybe I should just kiss her and get the formalities over and done with? he thinks as he looks into her deep brown eyes. 'Play?' he toys with the word in his head. Play? Like playing cards... And no sooner do cards pop into his head than the words, 'strip poker' come slouching in behind like some lewd baggage handler shuffling along behind his gentleman master. What a fool, I should have seen that coming, he thinks to himself. It will definitely have popped into her head too now but she won't know if it was her idea or mine. Shit, I don't know either. Say nothing. Just hold the space. She doesn't know what to think right now and, thank God, nor do I.

"Like a dance maybe?"

"Oh yeah...dancing. Of course. That sort of play...yeah."

Right then the last thing he's expecting happens; the young Frenchman he'd seen her with the night before just pops out of nowhere - with another woman on his arm. Gatita and he immediately start speaking rapidly in Spanish, leaving Dobbs feeling very left out. He may not understand the language, but he can certainly sense the stickiness of the web of complications though –as, clearly, can the Frenchman's young, European-looking companion. Dobbs turns to her now, hoping to ease the embarrassment.

"*Como estas!*" he says cheerily, offering his hand.

"*Hola,*" she replies, and then stands silent, clearly waiting for him to go on.

Suddenly all the pressure is back on Dobbs, whose creaking Spanish is already almost at its limit.

"*Donde...eres?*" he ventures, the grin now becoming more fixed.

"Barcelona."

"*Bueno! Hablas Ingles?*"

"No."

Shit. Now he's in trouble.

"*Peruvian henti ablas Espanol muy dispasio, pero henti de nationalidad de espanyol ablas muy-muy rapido. Peredone, me Espanyol is no bueno...*" he gabbles out with a slight air of desperation.

The Spanish girl's expression says it all; she's only really concerned with one situation right now, and trying to decipher the lost language of the Ancients is not it. In truth, Dobbs is in the same boat and the situation seems as hopeless as his Spanish. He's just starting to think that a solo stroll along the river and a fat spliff before bed is probably the best bet all round when Gatita turns around and says brightly;

"Shall we all go and have a drink together then?"

"Sure," Dobbs replies, nodding in agreement and not quite believing the word just popped out so casually.

A short motor taxi ride to another small port later and they're all sitting in a floating restaurant drinking beer. Gatita is lost deep in conversation with the Frenchman, which leaves Dobbs in the same awkward situation with the Spanish girl. Not being English, she clearly doesn't appreciate the stoic virtues of hanging on in silent desperation though and after finishing her drink she stands and with a simple 'ciao' takes off. Now they're sat as an uncomfortable trio. It's all too weird for Dobbs, and clearly not cricket, but stiffening his upper lip he soldiers on.

"What are you doing in Iquitos?" he says, hoping the Frenchman understands plain old English.

"I'm installing solar panels into villages in the jungle that have no power," he instantly relays with barely an accent.

Dobbs is totally taken aback, and feels his spirits droop a little further as he realises the drunk kid he'd seen sitting on the step that night with Gatitais actually a super cool young man who speaks at least three languages and is doing seriously admirable stuff for the local population.

"Wow! What a fantastic thing to be doing," he replies, trying not to look too green and deciding that his best option now is just to be

336

friendly and accept the situation as it is. He doesn't know anything about the Frenchman's relationship with Gatita - other than that he's really very cool - and he doesn't even know if he wants to know much more.

None of this seems to be part of his story, although he can't help noticing that whenever he's with almost anybody from anywhere in Europe outside of Britain they can understand him but he can't understand them. Plus they're normally super cool, highly sophisticated, and rooted in their culture in a way that the Brits just seem to have lost in their headlong rush to become the fifty first state of the burger munching brain-dead.

Perhaps, he's starting to realise, his personal shortfall might not be entirely his own fault. The concept of left and right wing politics for Britain is just meaningless; Britain is stuck in the middle between Europe and America. There is no left or right, only East or West - and as things stand at the moment Britain has become America's Trojan Horse, with the intention of crippling the euro and destroying the European alliance that is the most important legacy of all those who fought and died in the last World War. The British Government has chosen the wrong side as far as Dobbs is concerned.

Entente cordiale aside though, it's clear the Frenchman is there to talk with Gatita, and Dobbs feels like a spare wheel. He's just at the point of getting up to bid farewell and put an end to the agony when the Frenchman suddenly turns to him and says;

"Come on, let's all go dancing!"

Gatita immediately nods her approval before looking at Dobbs, who once again feels he has no choice but to agree. The situation can surely can get no more uncomfortable he reasons, and so they all jump into another motor taxi and go to a club on the outskirts of the city. Lines of motorbikes are parked up outside and, glancing through the windows; Dobbs can see the place is rammed. The deep bass of Latin salsa tunes and the cheer of vibrant commotion can be clearly heard from within, but he so doesn't feel in the space for dancing.

It's too late now though, so swallowing his pride and stiffening his lip an extra notch he holds the door for Gatita then heads to the bar to buy drinks. By the time he gets back she and the Frenchman are dancing to a salsa tune and, to Dobbs's despair the Frenchman can dance like Dobbs could only dream of; not throwing her around, but counting every step with perfection, twisting and twirling her

337

with an incredible sense of grace. He's only eighteen but he's so mature beyond his years it's unbelievable. Dobbs doesn't really know what to do with himself, other than leave them to it and use the opportunity to chat to people and practice speaking what little Spanish he has. Luckily just then he catches sight of Julio, the pyramid builder

"Hi Julio, how's the Great Pyramid going?"He says, wandering over for a chat.

"It's OK. I mean the whole thing is a logistical nightmare to keep afloat - in terms of buoyancy anyway."

"I know that feeling only too well, "Dobbs says with a sigh. "But you know what? It's such a crazy plan that it might just work - and what an adventure to attempt something so ambitious! I mean people will talk about it long after you're gone from here, you know that don't you? It seems Iquitos attracts people with crazy plans."

It's pretty relaxed just hanging out with Julio, chatting with his friends and meeting other people in the bar, and after a while Dobbs starts to get over the feeling of awkwardness. In between dances Gatita wanders over with the Frenchman and he has to let go into the fact that things are just the way they are. He still doesn't know what's going on but by now he doesn't much care either. Julio is a gentleman, and a comfortable companion, and in surrendering to the situation he's found some inner peace.

Eventually it's time to leave and, after saying farewell to Julio, Dobbs jumps into a motor-taxi with Gatita and the Frenchman and they head back towards the promenade, bombing along the dark empty streets. When they finally come to a stop Dobbs, who is expecting Gatita to leave with the Frenchman prepares himself for the pain. But then...no, he thinks; this isn't something to fear - the truth is just the truth. It is the fear of the truth which is most scary.

It's all cool, he reassures himself; live and let live. Not that he has a clue what's really going on anyway. Perhaps if his Spanish had been better things would have been a lot easier, but there's no point beating himself up. He's not looking forward to saying goodbye and watching her walk off with First Prize, but he figures he can handle that; he's handled much worse in the past and there's nothing really happening with him and Gatita anyway. Sure, there'd been intimacy but that was a gift; it doesn't mean he has the right to demand the keys to the cookie cupboard. Maybe, after all, it was just Spirit giving him a little helping hand to raise his vibration so he could achieve what he had achieved in ceremony. Well that's what his mother would have told him, anyway. She always used to say that we find love when we need to raise our vibration for whatever lies ahead.

Right now this has become a case of respecting other people's choices. The Frenchman obviously feels a little threatened by Dobbs's presence, which is understandable, but he's a decent enough guy and he's clearly giving his life the absolute all. He's a walking advert for everything that's cool about the French (even though he is a bit brash), and Dobbs can only take his hat off to him and wish him the best of British.

The Frenchman offers his hand, and Dobbs arranges his face.

"Mucho gusto," he says.

."Very nice to meet you," Dobbs says, genuinely amazed by the bloke really. "You really are doing amazing things here in the jungle you know man. As hippy as it sounds I think you're one of these old souls that is incarnating on the Earth right now. Life is precious to you: I can see that by all the effort you make."

"Gracias," the Frenchman says and then, just like that, he kisses Gatita on the cheek, jumps out, and the machine motors forward. Now Dobbs doesn't know what to think. That was all a little bit intense and he's suddenly in unknown territory unsure where things go from here. He looks at Gatita, wondering what to say. The evening has been quite hard work for him and now, heading along the last stretch to where he will jump out, he doesn't much care what happens anymore. In fact he really just wants to go to bed and sleep.

As he looks over at Gatita she reaches across and kisses him, just once, her eyes searching his. He just doesn't know what she wants though and when she moves closer and tries to cuddle him he finds himself strangely stiff – and in all the wrong places. But then she properly kisses him, and whatever apprehension he had is suddenly just blasted away by the intensity of her affection and they just melt into each other's arms.

"You're going back to the jungle, right?" she says once they disengage.

"Yeah. You want to come?" he says, half afraid to ask.

"I have to work."

"I'd like to stay here with you Gatita" he says, looking down at his hands then back at her face. "But something tells me there's a book waiting for me in the jungle. Then again maybe *you're* my book.

When I come back, in four or five days, I'll come and find you -if you want me to that is?"

Gatita's silent for a moment, obviously thinking. Dobbs doesn't want the complications of going off to find a hotel room with her - or even assuming that's what she wants. His head is spinning and he doesn't want to force things or make her feel like he's just using her. She's way too lovely for that.

"If you get bored, come and find me in the jungle. Otherwise I'll come and find you," he says, a little lamely as the motor-taxi jolts to a halt outside his hotel.

And then, all of a sudden, he's standing on the sidewalk watching her take off into the distance and wondering to himself once again, what the fuck have I just gone and done?

The Hundredth Monkey Dilemma

If possible the boat journey seems even more serene this time than before although an odd cloud of separation seems to have settled around all on board. Each man seems closeted in the cocoon of his own thoughts now and the overall air is neither happy nor sad, but just *there* – present, yet almost devoid of passion. There is an unexpected passenger too; The Brigadier. Perhaps unsurprisingly he seems pretty distant, sat on his own at the stern just staring into the slick surface of the water as if trying to divine his destiny. All things considered though just to have him there is a miracle - especially as only the night before he'd still been emphatic that he wasn't coming. Then, this morning, there he was, sitting down in the hotel lobby looking well rested, if a little lost. When Dobbs had told him what had happened the night before with Gatita - or, more to the point - what hadn't happened with Gatita he'd seemed genuinely shocked; he just couldn't get it through his head that he'd turned down the chance to take her to bed.

For Dobbs's part, he feels Rome wasn't built in a day and if they're destined to be together then Destiny, being the sensual beast that she is, will take it nice and easy, savouring each day at a time as every tiny moment is extracted, unwrapped from past and future and presented, with perfect timing, as the divine gift that it truly is. There's no rush, he thinks to himself; for so many reasons he had just felt uncomfortable to make his move last night. That said, he *had* walked away from the most sensual woman he's had the good fortune to meet in years - dare he say it, in his life - and now he's wondering if perhaps it's just fear that prevents him from being more forward? It would not be absolutely incorrect to say so, but for now he prefers to think it's just that the moment wasn't right.

The fact is, he's still trying to get his head around the realisation that Ruby is most likely in love with someone else – and that actually he's OK with that. Thinking back now he can't help recalling how, whenever Flaco phoned, she'd jump about like she was dancing barefoot on a hot tin roof, tingling with excitement just to hear his voice– just like she used to with him. At the time he'd just let it go, reasoning that Flaco's just one of those amazing guys who *everyone* loves. He'd certainly helped Dobbs plenty but now the question gnaws at him; was he helping himself too?

If it *is* true it certainly hasn't come from nowhere; Ruby had told him over and over that if he didn't give her more *attention* she'd go elsewhere. He'd listened, but he just hadn't heard her or, more truthfully, he had but such demands didn't make him want her – quite the opposite in fact. He'd found the whole tone of it ugly.

Looking back, the real truth was that he'd lost her respect the moment he started going on about the banks. Now it felt like she just sneered at him – just like her father had when he'd confided his fears in him. The sad thing was, he loved Ruby's father too. He's an amazing man; probably the *most* amazing man Dobbs has ever met. He had achieved so many great things in the arena of what Dobbs defined as Great, but when Dobbs had told him the global economy was about to crash he'd just told him, with a cold and almost snobby sense of self-certainty that he was a fool. Sometimes even the wise see only what they want to see and miss what's right there, on the end of the fork, it seems. The simple fact was, he hadn't *wanted* to see, and his blunt response left no angle of discussion open. Personally, Dobbs had been shocked by his pompousness.

In a sense he could understand his point of view; things were going well for him so why rock the boat unnecessarily - especially when you've got a family to provide for? He loved Dobbs - or so he believed, anyway - but his cold response, no doubt designed to steer him away from 'dangerous notions' had taught Dobbs something else - something he still found hard to accept. Namely, you can be as intelligent as you like but it is virtually impossible to fully take something on board that threatens to shatter your comfort zone unless you are forced to do so by the unshakeable conviction of an inner vision which bypasses all the filters of the mind and hammers straight through to your core like a spear thrust to the heart.

He'd only ever told one other person the full horror of what he'd seen that fateful day, and that was The Brigadier - who'd utterly dismissed the whole thing and bluntly pointed out that there'd never been so much cash knocking around. As long as it's summertime and the livin's still easy why would anyone want to entertain the notion of an all-out economic crash - unless, like Dobbs, you'd glimpsed the future with your own eyes? He understands only too well the natural desire to bury your head in the kitty litter and hope the horrible truth goes away as, personally, the burden of that knowledge had left him feeling like he'd had a prolapse, just haemorrhaging pain and sorrow.

Dobbs had shared that gruesome vision with The Brigadier because, on some level he didn't fully understand what he had seen, he was the only person he knew who he truly felt had the *capacity* to cope with it. Now he finds it significant that, after the previous evening's conversation, his friend has suddenly decided to come to the jungle and reassert what has been so lost in all the emotion and extremes of his addiction: the power his own choice. It is Dobbs's hope that, with his friends around to help when the withdrawal kicks in, perhaps it will be possible to get The Brigadier clean again – at least long enough so he can get some sort of perspective on his life again. Otherwise, if he's left to face this terrible addiction on his own in Iquitos - which is a scenario Dobbs can see unfolding - the shit is so clearly going to hit the fan and he will truly experience the type of hardship that Dobbs wouldn't wish on his worst enemy. Dobbs can't help wondering why he allows this hold over him to endure. From his point of view it seems almost like he feels guilty and somehow believes he needs to be punished for his sins - as if he's mortgaged his human state of being and the devil holds the deeds. But then the currency of the soul is nothing more than choice and experience though and it seems to him that it is neither God nor Godlessness that drives the mechanism of this mundane world – but only our God-given right to choose.

Leaving the city and heading back to the land is the best hope The Brigadier has to break away from the black hole of compulsion that is consuming all his light. For now at least, with the cooling breeze buffeting his sleeveless shirt and ruffling his hair as if airing the dark attic of his soul he seems happy to be cocooned once more in the company of the people who truly love him. The Monster is still palpably present though; it is something truly sinister of which The Brigadier himself has no real awareness. It's a sickness. When he surrenders his sovereignty to that and allows himself to become a channel for that entity he is simply no longer present.

Observing him now, sitting calmly in his own space at the stern, it seems to Dobbs that, above and beyond mere empty hope, some window of opportunity to separate himself from the knowledge of what he has become and allow himself to dream what he can still be has opened. This is real; he is here, in the boat, with the active intention of dealing with his problems. Hope was never going to be

343

enough to make change possible, and holding him against his will is not an option. His only salvation now lies in active choice. Just hoping the shit won't hit the fan simply is not an option now. Too much power has now been given over to this monster.

Hope is the death knell of change and the lifeblood of tyranny; humanity must throw it out with the garbage and replace it with choice. To choose change and to be change is the absolute nemesis of hoping and waiting for change. Hope is the cotton candy of the soul; a saccharine pill offered by politicians to kill change, quell action and render the masses helpless. Hope on its own is the most pitiful of all illusions, purely because it is so anodyne. As regards his own process Dobbs is pondering what question to pose this time - and how should he ask it? His mind feels so different from before; larger and more complex and yet, at the same time, much simpler. He's made his choice, and he's carrying the shaman's potion in his bag like a doctor carrying a precious antidote.

A passing steamer, just like the one Fitzcarraldo never dragged over the mountain, sweeps him away with the fairies and carries him off to a calmer stream of thought. Where has it come from, he wonders? Leticia perhaps? Or maybe right up from Manaus? Perhaps even as far back as the Brazilian coast. Pulling out his voice recorder he clambers onto the bow, where he can sit without disturbing anyone as he waffles away into the device, which now seems almost to be becoming his therapist. Beneath the bliss he can't help but feel pangs of frustration. Perhaps it's not going off with Gatita? Perhaps the whole idea is as absurd as Herzog trying to rewrite history through a crazy story that attempts to make a saint out of a sinner.

He's become obsessed with this idea that Francis Bacon had, if not written, then at least orchestrated the writing of the works of Shakespeare. Somehow he feels as certain of the fact as he was that the banks were about to go down. *Why* it matters so much to him, just like why he's so fixated on the global economy remains unclear however. He can only think of his vision, all those years back, of that gentleman shaking his spear.

But surely, just knowing Shakespeare was created to unite a country that was under a full scale Roman attack by a newly evolved means of policing belief, using the last gasp of the empire to hijack the teachings of the prophet they had executed by adding their own spin to it. Of course, those who wrote the bible hid arcane knowledge in the form of metaphors and parables that speak to all, each unto his understanding; a lifeline thrown by the gods to cling to amidst the rapids of the river of life. Was the Shakespeare Project a resurrection of the real teachings of Christ? Was Francis Bacon - the Spear Shaker - a prophet himself? What was the fascination about Shakespeare? Was it all about taking the awe away from Shakespeare and simply passing it over to another?

I wouldn't be the first to put such notions forward, he thinks to himself. It all just somehow seems a bit *American Super Hero* again; who is the masked man; '*look not upon the name, but upon the words.*' sort of thing. Perhaps it was meant to lure the reader into a peaceful sense of security with all his country's kin, and united against a common enemy that wishes only to have control of our thoughts: To reduce us to believing we are nothing more than what we think we are and bound by the restrictions of only want and hope.

Mind you, even if it was Bacon who done the deed' he suddenly thinks, 'it still leaves so many flaws in the story. I mean, first off, it must have been so blindingly obvious even at the time that William Shakespeare, the actor, was not the author of those plays that the whole notion of presenting him as such seems absurd. Not a single piece of correspondence to or from the man who supposedly wrote the most powerful and most performed piece of programming in modern history has ever been found. A man, who supposedly, single-handedly, systematised the rules of English grammar, invented hundreds of new words, possessed the fluency to pen puns and write poesy in half a dozen different languages, and was familiar with the legal systems and regal wranglings of half the monarchs in Europe. Yet this man did not even take the time and effort to teach his own children to read and write?'

No, William Shakespeare, the actor, was definitely not the writer of those works, and yet why would Bacon make so much effort to conceal the true identity of the man - or women - that did? Even odder still, why, having gone to such effort, would he have tried to pass off such sublime pearls of wisdom as the work of such an obvious impostor? It was like forcing the eye to view two separate images at the same time, as though looking through 3-D goggles in order to see the bigger picture. The question now is: what *is* that hidden image?

Even more obscure to Dobbs is why some of the early plays are in different handwriting. Even the name is spelt differently sometimes. Could he not spell his name or was that simply because

345

there were no printing presses and the early reproductions of his plays were penned. Certainly feasible although that kind of implies Sir Francis Bacon was out and about dishing out his plays willy-nilly, whilst on the same hand, covertly structuring a whole new language, through a secret literary think tank, hidden away in Canonbury Tower in Islington perhaps. Dobbs had the pleasure of living right next door to Canonbury Tower in his early twenties which was when he'd first heard of the conspiracy tales that Bacon had ran a literary think tank from that location. It made sense on the level that he was supposedly the prodigy of England's last wizard, John Dee. The Tempest itself must have been inspired by the Spanish Armada tale. Surely the whole Armada story is a tale of God's retribution on those who were intent on murder on a scale that had, nautically, never been known; those who themselves suffered cold, famine and terrible disease by virtue of their own intentions alone.

Dobbs had once spent ages looking at an ancient image of John Dee passing a lantern to Francis Bacon. John Dee was Elizabeth's astrological adviser –and, some say, an enlightened Master. It was he who had advised Elizabeth to turn a large proportion of her fleet into fire ships and then unleash them before the winds of fate alone, trusting in God alone that they would be carried into the midst of the anchored Armada. It is a David and Goliath story and as far as he is concerned the resulting destruction of the Spanish fleet was nothing short of a miracle.

Maybe it's the name: *Shakespeare*- and how that resonates with the figure from his visions. Since ancient times the sword or spear has represented both the power of speech and the courage to cut through the bullshit; whomsoever shook the spear in the circle of Elders was claiming the right to speak, uninterrupted - and to be heard. The wisdom of the Word backed by the strength of the Sword grants the true right of freedom of speech - a right and freedom that the Holy Roman Emperors and latterly the Catholic Church had sought to suppress on every level.

The image of Elizabeth, waiting on the mercy of such is a crystalline image in his mind now; she must have been at her wits end waiting for Mary to give birth. The moment the Catholics had an heir to the throne a mandate would have been drawn up for her immediate execution. Everything Henry VIII had implemented to break England from the Catholic Church's genocidal policies would have been reversed and the inquisition would have swept across the land. Every doctor, every herbalist, every writer, painter, lover - anyone who dared to proudly display the spirit of *human* beauty would have run the risk of being tried for any one of a million victimless man-made crimes against their Jealous God and then tortured, humiliated, starved and raped, and then mutilated until nearly dead before being burned alive. And then, miraculously – again! – she dies, and the Catholic's golden hour, the birth they thought would give them the green light to bathe themselves in the blood of the English heretics, in fact sounded the death knell for their dream of total domination.

It's all so perfect in Dobbs's head; so romantic and so noble. But something is not quite right. He is haunted by the image of this man locking himself away, working with his undercover literary think-tank to disseminate a code to crack the prism cell of polarity yet casually distributing his excerpts willy-nilly. It still doesn't hold together in his head. Why did he do it? Could the *Ayahuasca* answer such a question?

"Do you ever put that thing down, Dobbs?"

"I'm just rattling off some ideas, man," Dobbs replies to Bolivar.

"I think you might have to be a bit creative with the action adventure parts now because you're kind of moving away from any ideas of romance, aren't you?"

Dobbs chuckles at the comment but knows that he had to let Gatita go then. He was near burnt out after the previous night.

"Right then, it just wasn't man. I was just too blown open. Just sitting on the boat was so intense. It's all opening up for me on one hand but it's all loaded with so much weighted emotion and I'm not sure where it's going, man. It's like trying to boil things down to the sweetest nectar. Kind of helps if you know where you're trying to get, I guess. This is my process to meet whatever *Ayahuasca* opens in me half way I suppose. And how can we meet that which lies at the borders of our understanding if we do not go to the very breadth of ourselves and map it out."

"Do you know anything about the story you're writing Dobbs - really?"

"Not really. It's a totally eclectic collage of things that somehow I want to weave together into a single picture. Except I still can't see the picture. It's doing my head in actually."

Agent6 glances back at the riverbank and then immediately turns his attention to The Brigadier who's sitting with Elder at the stern.

"You want to check out the monkey reserve?" he says, catching his eye.

The Brigadier gives a swift nod and relays some flamboyant Spanish translation on to Elder, who laughs and pushes the stick hard over. The boat banks hard over to the left and suddenly they're heading for what appears to be a large opening in the forest wall with a few huts scattered amongst the trees.

Observing the energy between The Brigadier and Agent6 has been interesting. Agent6 is clearly apprehensive to be around him at the moment; he's a liability, and despite his thick skin the hidden shame of his addiction is wearing so thin in places that their relationship has been almost irreparably compromised. Even The Brigadier would probably admit he's a fraction of himself at the moment; the slave of some low vibrational astral entity. Dobbs just wants to pick him up, wash the dirt off him, and give him the entire treatment, but he's just too feral and he won't, on any level, acknowledge he's got a problem. To push it would become a violent situation.

Agent6 was the last person who'd had enough balls to take him to task, and that had ended with the battle of the wood burner. These days though he won't rise to The Brigadier's antics at all, especially when he goes into free fall after a massive session. He's there for him on one level but he's just letting him go on another. What else can he do? It seems to Dobbs that pestilence is one good way to really meet your ego. Perhaps, before we can accept who we truly are, we need to see who we truly are not. From that perspective pestilence has the potential to be a shamanic drug rather than the hedonistic thing it usually appears as. The Brigadier may be hiding behind a mask of cool oblivion right now but things are going to get a lot tougher if he's really determined to go cold turkey and take on the monster that lurks just below the surface.

Everyone is quiet now as the *Christina* pulls in to the bank. Sure enough there's a monkey, just sitting there, waiting. The boat's not as heavily laden with supplies as on the last mission – but nonetheless that little monkey has eyes for only one thing and as they moor he climbs aboard and gingerly attempts to make his way past Dobbs, who's still sat on the bow. He's seen a fair few monkeys in his travels but this little fellow is a new one for him. He's small with thick, almost straw-like grey hair and a very animated little red face. He looks exactly like his Uncle Harold.

"You think he's friendly?" he asks, looking back for reassurance.

"It's a monkey sanctuary, so maybe. Chance your luck," Agent6 replies.

"Fuck that man. He'll have my hand off. They can kill dogs, monkeys can, you know."

"He's tiny!" Swifty retorts.

"So are tarantulas and I didn't see you going to tickle that furry little beast under the chin that jumped out from under the floorboards. He does sort of look friendly, but I just don't know…" Dobbs says as the thing gets uncomfortably close to him, still edging its way towards the pile of bags and sacks in the centre of the boat.

Just then a young woman appears, giggling at Dobbs's apprehensive expression.

"Es amigo?" he says, then, looking more closely at the monkey's face "Amiga?"

"Si," she says giggling, and then rattles off something too fast for Dobbs to understand.

He reaches out his hand and as soon as he shows some attention the cute little creature laps it up clambering up to cling to his shirt and all the while glancing to and from the cargo and back to Dobbs's face.

"Oh wow, he's amazing; so friendly!" he coos as the monkey cuddles up to him.

Once on dry land another attractive girl appears, plus a few of the local men. They all seem very friendly. There's many monkeys playing and noisily competing for attention; Dobbs recognises a howler monkey and a spider monkey but most of the others are new to him and there's quite a few different species all seemingly getting along fine.

Lost in play with the animals, The Brigadier seems to forget himself, and for a few precious moments that devious, calculating presence seems a million miles away. The girls are warming to his energy and natural charm too - as they are to Agent6.

"Donde piace?" Dobbs asks one of the girls.

"Costa Rica," The girl replies.

"Oy!" The Brigadier chirps with a cheeky grin across his face.

"Don't go changing lanes, Dobbs!" Agent6 shouts out and suddenly the two of them seem to be the inseparable double act they once were, all attitude and cool Latin slang.

Dobbs just watches The Brigadier and the happiness that radiates across his face as the inquisitive animals clamber all over him. The old Brigadier is so still there, Dobbs thinks to himself, and a warm feeling of optimism spreads throughout him as he watches him, in his element, without the interference of the pestilence. Suddenly, Dobbs realises with a stab of shame, he is no less a tortured soul than The Brigadier himself at the moment. All the noise in his head just seems like such nonsense; he's become so obsessed with this book story that the real story is just passing him by. Perhaps The Brigadier is really his story and then perhaps it's Gatita. Maybe it's somehow all of them.

And then in slams the doubt: He can no more write a book than he can stop The Brigadier baling out as soon as the first rattle kicks in. What the fuck are they going to do then? That rattle's already in the post; why the fuck should the jungle give him any reason not to just jump in the boat and head straight back. It was like expecting the jungle to just off load a story onto him.

Surely you should learn to write before you just decide to write a book? Have a fucking story you want to write before you start out? Am I just wasting my time with all these stupid questions? he hears the voice in his head hectoring him again. So far he hasn't found one answer - apart from some half-baked utopian notions of a hidden heaven on Earth which only serves to clarify what everyone has already worked out; that he's completely fucking cuckoo.

Shit, Dobbs thinks to himself. Where the fuck is this journey actually going?

What is the Question?

They've taken off on the branch of the river that leads to the land project now and Dobbs is sat on the bow again, taking in all the beauty around him. Physically, he's feeling a whole lot better than he was the first time he'd made the journey, and yet he's just sitting there biting his nails, wondering how on Earth he's ever going to be able to capture any of this. This is another Earth entirely – an almost alien landscape. He feels anxious in the presence of its incomparable beauty, trapped by this burning need to somehow *capture* this beauty which makes his eyes well up with tears. He suddenly feels like a trophy hunter, intent only on capturing the beauty and terrified what will happen if he can't find the answers to the world's woes here. The Brigadier is not looking so relaxed anymore either, but Dobbs can't help but wonder who is making who twitchy. They're both lacking something; crippled inside by need.

Still mulling over the whole Ruby dilemma, he casts his mind back to the first time he met Flaco. It had been a highly unusual meeting but, as he was soon to find out, that was par for the course with Flaco. The setting was a massive WTO protest in Seattle at which a small but highly disorganised cell of some of Britain's grittiest political activists had gathered to balance out the banker's plans for a New World Order with a little bit of good old fashioned Chaos. Dobbs had gone along for the ride really but there were writers, film makers and photographers present. Flaco himself specialised in writing incendiary pieces for anarchist mags, mostly in the 'garden triangle' of Brighton, London and Bristol.

Hicksy, who wrote the Tempest parody, was obviously there as he's at all of them. He was the one who had first got Dobbs into the whole scene after he'd taken him to a road protest - *Reclaim The Streets* - back in 1995. He'd first met Hicksy in Hong Kong in '92 when they'd illegally hawked Big Bird puppets together on the streets. One thing Dobbs always respected him for was how he didn't force his radical views on you. At the time Dobbs used to eat in *McDonald's* all the time and though Hicksy was already switched on to the evils of the Golden Arches he never tried to make Dobbs feel guilty for eating there. He would just sit quietly whilst Dobbs munched processed crap from a Styrofoam box, politely declining Dobbs's offers to help himself to even the *Freedom Fries* or what would have been *French Fries* back in '92

351

as it was before *McDonald's* withdrew the name, 'French' from their glorious fries because of France's opposition to the 2003 *illegal* invasion of Iraq. The French must have been gutted. But then, maybe not. Considering José Bosé, who was atop podiums in Seattle during the massive WTO protest talking of the terrible woes of capitalism amidst his cheering fans who just wanted to see the French farmer come urban legend who blatantly destroyed a *McDonald's* restaurant with a bulldozer in France. Everyone kind of thought they'd bang him up and throw away the keys, and indeed, the French Government did try for a conviction but it was before the days of Nicolas Sarcozy. Thus America had to watch with dismay as José Bosé openly claimed proudly, that he did the deed but that he was not guilty. The jury agreed.

"Nahh, don't touch the stuff really, Dobbs," Hicksy would say.

Everyone was there in Seattle - even Agent6, who was making a film - and everyone seemed to be doing something or part of something; trying to make a difference and bring some awareness, but Dobbs wasn't doing anything. He'd watched the whole free party scene morph into *Reclaim The Streets* and the Anti Capitalist demos and he loved the parties but he'd never really understood the issues as everyone seemed to have a different take on why they were there and if you sat anyone down for any length of time and asked them to explain, their arguments would fall apart. Everyone knew bits of the picture but on a *feeling* level it all seemed pretty obvious; more than half the world is starving whilst the other half is obese. Go Figure! When talk of the *WTO* protest in Seattle had spread it was like 'battle stations' had been sounded. After considerable persuasion from Agent6 and Hicksy, Dobbs had finally thought, what the hell.

There were seven of them in all, most either writers or part of some crew. Agent6 would make his first of three films there. He'd originally wanted to make the Seattle film with Dobbs but he barely knew what the WTO did, and in between the IMF, the G8, The World Bank, Free Trade, Fair Trade and all the other jargon he felt completely unable to get a take on it. In Dobbs's head a protest was basically a free party that, with a little help from the riot police, usually went off like fire cracker. Not that he ever went to a protest looking for a riot. He'd dressed in a fluffy Dalmatian top to make sure everyone knew he was a big softy, well, not even big. And at later protests, always wore something pink to eliminate any sign of anger or aggression.

The WTO protest was unusual to Dobbs, though. It was much larger than he could ever have conceived it would be. It was a proper protest. Contrary to all the bullshit propaganda being spewed out by the mainstream US butt licking media channels the Yanks really did fucking care – much more than the Brits it seemed, and they were clued up. Hundreds of thousands of people had come from all over America and countries far beyond, and they really seemed to understand – many of them from firsthand experience – why what the corporations call 'Free Trade' is really the nemesis of fair trade and common decency.

Unlike all the rest of his crew, who each seemed to have their own complex take, it was all over Dobbs's head really. He'd gone out there with next to nothing and what little money he did have was supposed to be for getting a room for the winter or buying a ticket to India, as it was the end of summer – time to leave the UK to the wet weather moaners again. Seattle meant that he'd be back in *Blighty* about a week later, broke, with nowhere to live apart from a truck that was not properly fitted out and that had no wood burner.

He went anyway. To Dobbs, it was such a star studded cast of activists and anarchists that as much as he couldn't afford to go, he couldn't afford to miss it either. In the end it was an incredible protest. He heard a great deal of much more informed opinion and he got to see how independent news channels like *Indymedia* work to counterbalance the highly processed output of the establishment, streaming everything real-time and putting up every contribution unedited. Everyone he was with was either taking pictures, shooting a film, interviewing people or being interviewed and it all made little sense to him. It was like a million different names and a million different departments, all being shouted at the same time; five minutes of listening to anyone waffle on and he was lost. He felt like a twat, totally ashamed that he had so little knowledge of what was really happening in the world when others seemed to have made such efforts to educate themselves. And he did not want to attempt to talk about something he didn't understand just to fill the gaps. He genuinely wanted to understand.

Predictably the whole thing just went into full-scale police brutality, with *kettling* and every scare tactic in the book being used before the cops finally brought out their ultimate crowd control weapon: The euphemistically named *Peace Keeper*, a huge, tank-like armoured vehicle with ninja turtles manning its turrets. In a perfect example of Orwellian Doublespeak, really it was just another riot making war machine, with guns firing rubber bullets, pepper spray, gas canisters and paintballs that stain your clothes for easy identification and arrests later. It was a terrorising riot making machine.

Just when it seemed it couldn't get any worse, the Mayor declared Martial Law and pandemonium set in. People were just running in all directions, desperate to get away from all the tear gas and pepper spray. Dobbs, his eyes burning had ran too, gagging on the acrid gas until eventually he found himself on his own on some boring suburban road. It was a cold September night and he had barely a penny to his name.

'What the fuck am I doing in this place?' he remembers thinking to himself. 'Did I really spend all my cash just to come to a protest that the cops were always going to force into a fucking riot? Against a system I don't even understand?' He tore himself apart in those few moments, feeling like a total coward. He felt like he had absolutely nothing new to offer the world and even when it had come down to merely making up the numbers he'd ran like a twat. A steady flow of other protesters were tearing their way past him as he just stood there cold. He'd lost all his friends and he felt like a total idiot. This was not his protest. But he'd inadvertently asked the fundamental question.

And in that; in the bleakest moment of self, his answer arrived from nowhere. It was in that moment that he understood the difference between destiny and fate. He'd argued the toss in allsorts of ways over the years but suddenly it was clear. Destiny was what had brought him to this place; a place where he had no choice but to ask that all so precious question we so rarely ask: 'What the fuck am I doing here - on this planet, in this place, at this time?'

If you don't know the answer to those questions then you are there by destiny. Those times when it all seems bigger than you, more fantastic than you, more switched on than you, more happening than you, more talented and more alive than you, and more brave and more beautiful then you. More sophisticated and more shiny than you. And you almost want to drop to your knees and cry, because it seems there was nothing left for you. No purpose on this Earth and no way to change the injustice of this world that you have to ask that question. That's the moment, when destiny turns to fate.

354

Destiny was what had brought him to ask the question, but his fate; that hung upon what he was or was not going to do now. He'd always thought that one's inevitable fate was death but death is not fated - it is guaranteed. All those who are or will or have ever have fought for peace are dead, or will die, and thus death can never be one's fate. To Dobbs, fate is what lies at the end of destiny and Humanity's fate is what it will choose now; whether to just hope that our governments stops dumping depleted uranium, or choosing to try and actually stop them doing so.

Standing there on that cold September night in Seattle he got his answer, and as crazy as it was it sent tears of joy down his cheeks. It was such a silly answer. The words spoken in his heart, crystal clear: 'Because you're up for it.' On one hand, it might not seem like much of a reason or answer, but it was enough. And right then he realised he wasn't just there to dip his toe in to this whole peace movement, he was all in. He always had been. So fucking what if he didn't understand how the structuring of the countless different government departments hides the tracks of war, slavery and human suffering. He didn't need to know how the *IMF* or the *WTO* worked to understand that a ten year old girl sold to a factory to work twenty hours a day for nothing was wrong, and he didn't need a degree in politics to understand that 'freeing the world from trade laws' in order to legalise the sale of depleted uranium was a crime comparable to any ever committed in Earth's history and worse still.

Suddenly he realised why he was in Seattle in the biggest uprising since the protests that stopped the Vietnam War. Ultimately that war was ended when the US army itself became the biggest source of conscientious objectors; one soldier passing on to another the terrible truth they had seen with their own eyes: 'American soldiers are killing women and children in Vietnam.' The last thing the government was expecting was their own troops to say, 'No; not in my name' but eventually it was the soldiers themselves that woke up to the hypocrisy of the war and just threw down their weapons.

With the dawning of that realisation he'd found himself running, joyfully, back into the riot. All around him it was properly going off with people running for their lives, and then he'd seen this punk with short, spiky bleached blond hair who was just pissing himself laughing as the world went mental around him. He was standing outside a tattoo shop, and obviously a mad dog of an Englishman. Meanwhile the woman who looked like she ran the

355

place was bordering hysterical. Her expression just said 'Now's the time to be panicking you fucking idiot,' and the sight of this crazy punk just laughing his head off and loving every minute of the madness was clearly freaking her out.

Dobbs had made his way through to where Flaco stood and hung out with him, just watching. Whereas before he had felt terrified, now he seemed to be beyond the whole thing, like it was a show, a film set in action, almost like they were in some kind of protective bubble. Then, just as it all seemed nothing could get more surreal, some big redneck guy had come out of the tattoo joint and seeing Flaco pissing himself laughing, had just lamped him, knocking him flat on his back in the street and instead of pain or fear he had just stared up at this man and laughed even more hysterically. Suddenly, it was like a contagious disease and Dobbs knees suddenly went out from him when couldn't stand, let alone get a breath as he fell into hysterical laughter.

It was a lesson to Dobbs to see someone stand their ground amidst the chaos and refuse to stop demanding justice on behalf of those who were being exploited, the silent billions that in their short, brutal lives would probably never otherwise have a voice. As he stood, shoulder to shoulder with this man who seemed so fearless in the face of those that wished to smash him for his defiance against their narrow mindedness and the bonds of a powerful friendship had been formed in that moment.

Dobbs loved Flaco. He encouraged people to express their anger with words and not their fists and taught them that when you have vision and courage you don't need violence. He was cleverer than violence. Now, it seems, Ruby had fallen in love with him and out of love with Dobbs. He'd gone off the radar and they'd gone in separate directions. Something had basically entered Dobbs from another space and almost taken him over; not a demon, but a *conviction* that bound him in some intangible way to take hold of which somehow meant also, to let her go.

Strangely though, of all the people he'd most like to bump into now, Flaco would probably be top of the list as he feels like he's back in that same space he'd found himself in on that cold September night in Seattle. He's all out of questions now and feels as if it is now only destiny that brings him here and he still does not know his fate in all this and has only that one question left now; what the fuck am I doing here - on this planet, in this place, at this time?

356

No answer comes but he's up for it and he's here and he's wide awake. And he's not just along for the ride; he's all in.

"Fucking hell Dobbs. Will you put that fucking voice recorder down! Look at you; we're in the Garden of Eden and there *you* are biting your nails," Bolivar breaks in on his monologue. His tone is joking but he's clearly genuinely concerned.

"I don't know man. I've kind of hit a wall with it all." Dobbs says with a chuckle. "I'm lucky to have you as a friend man. I must sound like a fucking mad man. I feel like a mad man at the moment. Being here and having this opportunity you know… just to be here, living this life. But Ruby's right; I'm no fucking economist and I'm certainly not a historian. I'm obsessed with this thing and it's all just a wall. All I can see is economic collapse because of a credit machine with the needle moving right through the deepest red until it's bending like a fishing rod battling with a killer whale."

"Back on that one, eh?" Bolivar sighs. "It's torture for you, isn't it?"

"Yeah, I'm afraid it is. Our governments will never come clean; they never *can* come clean about the atrocities they've inflicted in 'God's' name. They believe that God rules through fear, through suffering and, more than anything, through sacrifice."

Bolivar just shrugs.

"It's a bit heavy though isn't it Dobbs - especially here? It's almost sensationalism to think of such a collapse. I mean what did you actually see on that blast of nitrous? Like, you just saw the banks going down, right?"

Dobbs shakes his head, not knowing quite what to say.

"In a word Dobbs," he persists.

"Destruction caused by illegal and unjust war. But destruction in a way I don't understand. Perhaps it was like cause and effect. I saw the banks go down which seemed bad but it was only the precursor to a far bigger crash engineered through war. That causes the reaction and the crushing pain of the reaction is beyond all imagination. The truth is, I don't truly know what I saw. Plus, what I saw just drives fear. It was what I felt that crushed me. The feeling of utter, devastating loss that crushed me. I mean nobody can avoid death, can they? Not you, and certainly not me. That's not negative or positive; it's just a fact. What I think I saw was quite simply *Proslairo*, probably unknowingly, leading Britain into a trap. He's running around America uniting the Christians under

357

one common banner in the name of this apocalyptic crusade but when the shit hits the fan all America will want is a scapegoat, and that's what Britain will be; a sacrificial anode to absorb the shockwave of what the Fed is reaping. They'll need that scapegoat, to offload the blame."

"*Proslairo?*"

"No. If only it were that simple."

"Then what?"

"Britain: the banking enemy of the world. People all over the world have waited a long time for this inquisition. The bankers and those in control of Britain are now saddled up to the sweaty crack of America's back side simply to hold on to their international banking rights, but The New World Order is nothing more than *Americanisation* peddled through war and suffering.

"Think about it; Gordon Brown kept underfunding the war in Afghanistan and was totally pro Europe so they lump him with all the blame for *Proslairo's* woes. He was always a Tory plant from the beginning and in the States at least he's been made something of a hero. 'The International Ambassador of Peace'- just watch him go as he promotes the dumping of depleted uranium whilst at the same time giving sermons in the name of God. I mean what the fuck? It's like I want to shake the world and shout: 'Wake the fuck up! We've got a bunch of Zionists on one side, running a credit system via the Federal Reserve that has the dollar on strings and is using it to drain all the wealth of the world with just a printing press and then depleted uranium dumping religious fanatics ready for anyone who questions their God. And both are promoting a self-serving policy of warfare and division at every juncture.

"What has *Proslairo* finally allowed to land on the shores of Britain? Corporations so powerful they can buy the government lock, stock and barrel then sit back and rub their hands while they drive our communities into the dirt. All legal and above board just so long as it's done with a hollow smile followed by a 'have a nice day!' served as greasy as their burgers. But until people can comprehend that under the present crooked system supermarkets will always be able to out-price small businesses simply because they can make massive profits just from the movement of money. You think, just *cash-back,* offered by most big supermarkets. When technically there is no profit at all. But that money goes via the supermarket's own bank and thus can be used to generate massive amounts of credit through the fractional reserve system.

358

How can any small business compete against a corporation that does not even need to make a profit on goods because their turnover *is* their profit?

"As long as they can sell that ninety bucks worth of potential debt generated by the technically profitless movement of the customer's ten *goldless* dollars or *silverless* sterling pounds of *money movement*. The Big Boys don't care, as the governments are lending it out to the corporations and banks at stupidly low interest anyway. Supermarkets are nothing more than leeches, destroying our communities. Britain is being torn to shreds and then being used as the Fed's Trojan Horse to break what our grandparents fought and died for; the only thing that could have stopped the Fed's intention of all out war; a unified Europe. Once the euro is broken the shit will really hit the fan for Britain because *we* will get the blame for it, and the rest of Europe will ostracise us."

"I thought you said that the euro would go up?"

"Yeah, sure. As soon as Iran realised that Britain and America were spoiling for a fight they switched from dollar sales to Euros; what else could they do? But America had long since tagged that, as the European banks had unwisely invested in America's subprime lending portfolios. The people running the Fed are blood thirsty fascists I'm afraid; literally."

"I think this will take years to happen Dobbs. As far as I can see the economy's still in good shape."

"I think you might change your views on that Bolivar. Nothing can stand in the way of that printing press that's just reeling off the power to buy wars, and depleted uranium and the complicity of greedy, frightened people. Nothing except the courage to stand up and say 'fuck that shit!' and demand that the monetary system revert back to something with a direct link to the value of a sustainable existence can work. The idea that whatever actually increases the value of currency *has* to operate through the betterment of the natural environment so that sustainable policy becomes the backbone of the credit system."

Bolivar pulls his cap off. Staring down into the murky water he allows the tips of his fingers to drag through it.

"If it gets as bad as you reckon it's going to get there'll be riots in the street and people will know it's the bankers and then they're going to get it, aren't they?"

"Yeah, but that's just more scapegoats again. You see it's not the bankers; it's the design of the banking system itself. Money is not

359

the problem and the bankers are not actually the problem either. It's the *motive* of what drives the people up top to run the mechanism like that. Forcing the entire wealth of the world into unbalanced monstrous piles of cash, like huge dams hoarding the wealth through dirty tricks and blatantly biased funding; smoke and mirrors techniques to throw the blame off and complex departments that hide information away so that it takes decades to follow the paper trail – by which time the world has moved on and nobody's interested anymore because they're too busy dealing with the fallout of whatever the next big scam is."

Even The Brigadier seems to be attentive to what Dobbs is saying from the far end of the boat now.

"And even stranger is that the thing humanity's most terrified will collapse around them is the very system that enslaves them; the dollar - the pain. Humanity has somehow become trapped between our higher, divine souls and this other influencing factor from somewhere else - The Ego, or whatever you want to call it- and something has to shift.

The Earth just cannot take another World War. It's like humanity is either on the verge of all out destruction or waking up and walking out of the prison. We're standing at the crossroads and each and every one of us has to make that choice: to walk free of a millennia of mental slavery or just grab the remote, bang on *Deadenders* and drift back into the *X-and-why-even-bother-Factor* while the world goes to hell in a hand basket."

"Fucking hell, Dobbs, you're on one, you know that?"

"Just think for a moment; what was it that made Ken Livingston famous?"

"Dunno. You're older than me Dobbs!"

"Just a banner Bolivar - a fucking banner, man. He stuck the real figure of Britain's unemployment on a banner and hung it from the GLC building opposite the House of Commons. Margaret Thatcher went crazy. One banner really. That was always why Hicksy kind of liked him - because he bucked the trend with just one fucking banner. His career was forged out of that one expression over everything else. He became Mayor of London, years later, largely because of that banner. We all know that the truth is staring us in the face but Livingstone had the balls to speak out even if it meant alienating himself from the corporate cock sucking media.

People have been brainwashed by the likes of *Proslairo* to believe that it's beyond them to comprehend the intricacies of international politics, but what's so hard about understanding the morality of deliberately contaminating an entire country with nuclear waste?"

"You're so angry about it. And I am angry about it but I can't touch it like you, right now, here."

"Sorry man, it's just I can't see a fundamental purpose to any of it. *Why like this?* Therefore, if this huge cog has been removed from the credit gearbox by the Iranian switch, perhaps it's really a gift from *God?*

Something has to stop this madness; the American war machine and its wanker-banker poodle Britain, the backstabbing murderer of the European dream cannot be allowed to succeed. Why the fucking hell do I see this so clearly? Why does it rule me so? Why must the world be run on a system that's *sole* purpose is War and the basic commodity of which is Fear."

"Whoa, Dobbs. Man! chill out! You're just going to snap if you keep going on like this man. You need to just breathe deep and check out all the beauty that's right here, all around you man!"

"It's this beauty that makes me see it though Bolivar, believe it or not. The Earth is so overwhelmingly beautiful, and yet the atrocities I see going on in it just keep tearing down my belief in the fundamental goodness of *human* nature. I thought I could come here and cure myself of the nightmare I saw on that blast of nitrous but all I'm doing is chartering a course straight into the centre of the Tempest that is tearing our beautiful Earth to bits.

"This thing's got me by the fucking balls man, and it just takes me wherever it wants to take me. It's like that Siren that was dragging me down is trapped in my heart and I want to be free of it, but every day I do nothing about it I feel like I'm guilty of murder by my silent consent."

"It's not insane what you're saying Dobbs; you're just trying to carry too much of the weight of it. If you want to spend your whole life focussing on that then I guess that's OK, man but I just can't see what you're getting out of it - other than tortured."

"What do you want to happen?" asks Agent6, who had seemed to be lost in chat with Swifty.

Oh come on man, the concept of a monetary system based on real sustainable value, a proportionately run voting system and reinstating the monopoly laws would be a great start but try relating that to the totally dispensable thugs who are about to replace the British Police Force.

"I don't know man. It seems I've got nothing new to say; no refreshing ray of *hope* for this little planet. In fact, if anything what I'm coming to realise is that humanity doesn't need hope; we need a little more than that. Humanity's stuck with the same *Blairites* after thousands of years of tyranny – if not more - but why do they do it? Why do they have to make people suffer?" He stops and looks at his voice recorder, almost as if hoping *it* might give him the answers he craves.

"I'll be honest with you; I'm haunted by this overwhelming feeling of sadness that there's absolutely no logical reason for any of this suffering. I mean, are we doing all this just to learn hope? Is that all we have? Is that what we're here to develop and understand? There doesn't seems to be much else left..."

Dobbs looks at Agent6, shaking his head woefully.

"Who knows?" he says, "Maybe Obama's right and it's all just about hope - but that doesn't seem to be much of an answer to me. Maybe his book of hope will get him in power and we can all hope as hard as we can that he doesn't continue the warring ways. Where does hope really exist anyway? What is it? Because it's like I haven't got a question or an intention for the *Ayahuasca* anymore other than 'what the fucking hell am I doing here? What is my *purpose*here on this Earth?'

"We need more than fucking hope to stop what the architects of war have attempted to mastermind; they're so obviously eyeing up Iran, man, and if we pick a fight with them we're all fucking dead. Ten million people died in the Eighties in trench warfare between Iran and Iraq. That's more people than died in the whole of the First World War – 'The War to end all wars'.

"Whilst I was at home discovering *George Michael, The Skids* and *Bananarama,* a rerun of World War One was being instigated by Britain by getting Iraq to attack Iran. Ten million died and I didn't even know man. We need a whole lot more than just hope to stop this madness: we need an all-out miracle."

Agent6 nods.

"Maybe you're right."

"Why *does* humanity operate an economy that is set to self destruct? Why is there so much suffering? Why is there so much pain? I'm not the only one that sees it? The economic structure is literally rigged by design to produce debt, wars are bought and sold, famine is economic theft, disease is nothing more than a business model and governments are simply cartels offering wealth they do not own in exchange for debt. And just to see it, to jot it down in a book, to redefine the monster again and again is not enough. It's the same old monster that won't leave us alone, that brings us back to just one thing, the only real thing man has ever had: HOPE. Sweet, basic empty fucking hope man: The disease of perpetuated war.

"That's all we have. That's all we've ever had. And you know what? It's just not enough anymore. We need more than hope now. We need a miracle. Earth needs a fucking miracle to stop these *wankers* because although *Proslairo* has probably never taken a life, directly, with his own lily white hands, he's been responsible for instructing kids straight out of school to kill millions. We are defenseless against his intentions and the intentions of those that bankrolled him."

Bolivar, who usually plays devil's advocate, doesn't rise to it this time.

"That's a pretty heavy thought to be carrying round in your head Dobbs," he shakes his head.

"Is it not possible to run an evenly distributed credit system throughout the world that's fair? To have rich and not so rich without all the incorporated suffering, and for everyone to be in on the show? You get what I'm trying to say; that surely money, on its own, is not evil? I mean there's many wealthy businessmen who are not necessarily bad just because they want to make it big. To make the big time it is not necessary to want to willingly make other people suffer - is it?"

"Expensive dreams; nothing wrong with that," Agent6 says with a chuckle.

"Exactly, so why would there be the need to create suffering by design then? If it was just that, we, as a race, would be nothing better than savages - so why would we be given all this? Just to destroy it in the name of profit when, in actual fact, it is in the name of fear and suffering. Suffering is the driving force behind fear - the mechanism that empowers it, and the product of war, debt, famine and disease. But is profit wrong? To want to make a buck, to feed your kids, to buy your woman a necklace? Is it wrong to follow your dreams and find your fortune, whether man and woman, if the endeavours exist in the bracket of the fair and sustainable? Profiting from our endeavours is not wrong in my book."

Nobody says anything. They are all lost in their own thoughts. Dobbs knows he's intense at the moment; this whole obsession rules him like an illness now. He can neither forget nor forge a passage through the wall that is blocking any further discovery.

"I mean, fuck, what is it? What part of humanity is actually subverting us? I mean, maybe we're being duped? Supposing the need for suffering is actually so distant from human consciousness because it isn't actually here at all. Supposing it's somewhere else completely: background interference resonating from a bygone era of our – or someone else's- past maybe. Something beyond this world, from somewhere so far away that when we attempt to follow its source through all the elite clubs and corporations that the trail just disappears and all we can see at the trail's ends are the stacks of cash and piles of gold.

What we *see* is the 'greed' - the pay-off, but not the purpose. Perhaps there is no fundamental purpose for creating suffering through profiteering that we can understand. And what if the trail doesn't stop there but just keeps on going, clean out of this world. Then where does it go? Into another world?"

"That's pretty out there Dobbs," Bolivar says, now looking seriously doubtful.

"Yeah, definitely out there. But absolutely no more insane than to believe that humanity is nothing more than deluded savagery motivated by only blind greed and *sin*."

"Juan talked of aliens once. Is that what you mean?" Agent6 asks.

"I truly don't know; maybe I'm talking about The Ego. I mean, no one actually knows what The Ego actually is, do they? What is it that actually *wants* others to suffer? I mean even if there was some kind of outside intervention what would they get out of us suffering?"

"It's just all lies peddled by fat-cats with blood blatantly dripping from their hands," Swifty grunts with a look of distaste across his face.

"Yeah, but for what purpose Swifty?"

"Greed! What else?" Swifty declares, "What else can it be? It's just greed."

"No. I don't believe it anymore. That's where the payoff comes in to play. But supposing that's not the motive. What if we can't see the motive for suffering? Do you see what I'm saying? So we dupe ourselves that we understand. But actually, we, as the masses that is, perhaps don't actually understand the motive."

364

Swifty shakes his head.

"I don't understand that."

"Well, what if it all comes down to a standoff between Iran and the West in the end? That's the end game scenario I saw on the nitrous and I just feel so powerless to stop it" he says despairingly.

"You think: most of us have been going to all the protests; anti-war demos, *Reclaim The Streets*, *Anti Capitalism, IMF, G8, WTO, World Bank* right down to the Newhaven Incinerator. I mean I was in East London at an arms fair demo on the day the Twin Towers came down – an event which probably caused the largest proliferation of arms sales in the history of the planet.

"We've all been doing our damnedest but we just can't stop them it seems; not so much as put a dent in the war machine; they are absolutely relentless. And yet one person can ring up and stop a party or get a Gypsy chucked off some land or a Traveller moved on. Virtually every person in Newhaven along with the whole of Brighton, Lewes, Hove and Kemptown combined cannot stop an incinerator and all the people cannot stop our government dumping depleted uranium on a country that had about as much to do with 9/11 as Bugs Bunny.

Everyone knows what's going on, but everyone feels powerless. I mean what have I changed, in going to all those protests? Sure I met a lot of very wonderful people; fantastic. But have I, you, or anyone ever changed anything?" he sobs, tears running down his face.

"You. You changed *you* Dobbs. Didn't *we* change? Aren't *we* different for that? Wiser for that?"

The boat is moving even slower now, drifting dreamlike through the glassy water and the soaring canopy above is replicated in plunging perspective below, as if the silver surface upon which they sail is the dividing line between the worlds - a line which, Dobbs senses, is now so thin he can almost touch the other side.

The Mosquito is Indeed a Marvel

The mosquito is indeed a marvel. Not the most auspicious marvel perhaps, but a marvel nonetheless. As the daylight begins to diminish, the sonic saturation produced by hundreds if not thousands of different species of life begins to pipe down just as, at some other very low level the pitch of the night shift begins to kick in. Birds are singing and shrieking, insects are buzzing and tapping. Some of them even seem to be vibrating like miniature *kangos*, boring and munching into the *maloka's* roof beams. Quite suddenly, the shrills and shrieks, the squawks and howling subside as one side of Earth's solar cycle shuts up shop for the day and the other begins its wake up process. At some point there comes a tiny, intermediate gap that could almost be described as silence. No sooner does Dobbs's ear attempt to adjust to this unaccustomed luxury, however, than he detects a subtle hum. Its harmonic is set so acutely high as to be barely audible but suddenly it swells from every direction until its pitch is almost a scream that blankets the senses so completely as to seem almost internal in origin.

The sound of a trillion mosquitoes swarming is like a siren that consumes everything else into a single, all-encompassing shriek. No matter what man does to attempt to quell these tiny beasts, their lust for blood will always keep them one evolutionary step ahead. From the more environmentally friendly options of citronella, mozzy coils and incense sticks to the most toxic of chemicals, all attempts to repel the onslaught seem, in the jungle, to be merely a joke to tickle the humour of those voracious little vampires.

For the natives, too, it must be an odd spectacle. They watch the outsiders plaster themselves with repellents and yet seem completely unaffected by the ridiculous volumes as they begin to swarm.

Here, right by the river, anything that stops moving is instantly engulfed and consumed. Like hearing a German doodlebug somewhere above and hoping that it keeps on going and doesn't run out of fuel over your head. It's when that high-pitched hum stops - the tiny zzzzz... followed by an abrupt ...zzzp - that you know the little bloodsucker has landed and is probably already administering its tiny anaesthetic, all ready to drop its drill bit through your skin and into your system as easy as lowering a straw into a lime soda. A thrust of flailing arms and legs seem appropriate in the panic but it only serves to advertise your presence further, wafting out an olfactory welcome-mat of pheromones - the equivalent to the smell of a kebab shop to a drunk. Your position completely triangulated, vast squadrons move in like tiny biplanes dive-bombing King Kong. They sense you as clearly as a dog senses an intruder and the more you fear them, the fiercer they become.

Dobbs endures for as long as he can, making the most of the last light to clean out the kitchen space in the small *maloka*. This time there's even more crew, so the collection of pots and pans, cups and plates, buckets and wash basins is getting out of hand. It's not exactly total disorder, just the workings of a busy kitchen, but tonight its vibration will be raised from kitchen status into temple again: tonight they'll drink.

Dobbs doesn't know what to expect anymore. Not that he ever really did, but he nearly always has an intention in mind; some clear focus of what he wants to do, or perhaps heal, and what he wants to know or understand. He sees it like walking into a library, and not just any old library; this quantum connected archive serves not just this world but the whole universe. It is a wizard's tabernacle, a magician's spell book, a witch's lair, and the nemesis of those who wish to control thought. It can wake a mind.

In order to operate this library though it's almost as if you need to have your answer before you ask your question - or perhaps have a rendition cast of faith alone - as if it expects that one can prove they are of sturdy enough material to handle the truth they want to carry away with them. Truth, like anything, has a gravity - the emotional mass attached to it. It is as though daring to understand in your head what you truly already know in your heart is a kind of sacrifice in itself.

Ultimately, *Ayahuasca* can only offer confirmation; we are staring at the answers all the time, laid bare for all to see. The questions are the gifts as the truth is so utterly fantastic we can only carry a tiny part; tiny questions that serve as peep holes upon the Infinite. Yet now he has no questions and so many new answers it seems like synapses are firing off throughout his head and the whole edifice of his world view is crumbling like a collapsing cliff face, taking all the notions of everything he thought he was or hoped he could ever become along with it. The very supporting pillar of what was him, or what he had always thought he was, has been exposed as bare and irrelevant: nothing more than background interference. The lie that you are only what you think you are

367

which drives humanity from its heart core, its vector equilibrium; away from being and doing what it truly is that keeps us imprisoned in the prism of hoping and wanting that one day you will achieve becoming what you hope you will become.

For Dobbs, hope has become the language of thought, and the walls of hope are fear. He sees now that it is not our hopes or desires that define us but our *actions*. What we do and what we say, what we create and what we destroy are what and who we truly are. *Being* is the conduit of life, not thinking. The measure of that is nothing less than the frequency of one's intention, and his intention can no longer be sated by just one answer. The wall has to come down. He sees now that his whole life has just been a pilgrimage and now he wants only for the veil to be removed and the holy of holies to be laid bare. It's time to let go of all the old answers and give up this attachment to the 'me' and 'mine'.

He'd always thought you went to heaven when you die but if that's so, then how is it possible that Agent6 lives in heaven already? He's not died. He wasn't, like, in terrible shock to be there. He was cool, calm and collected. So who else lives there in that oh-so-beautiful world?

I always thought I went somewhere when I sleep, he thinks to himself. Maybe life is just the soul's work-in-progress and after a hard day's work it goes off to wherever that place is but after all the big song-and-dance that he'd seen heaven, so what? It's not exactly a brand new concept. It's nothing new; no revelation, no resolution, just business as usual.

He crouches closer to the smoke of the cooking fire, which seems to be offering a good shield against the torrent of collective humming that saturates the space about him. He's on his own.

"So is that where God lives?" he says under his breath. "It seems to be where *I* live perhaps, and *this* body is what is used to create that higher identity. But where does any of this actually get me? I'm right back to the same question: what the bloody hell am I actually doing here? Am I just a tourist who's come to meet some pretty girls and drink *Ayahuasca* so that over dinner with friends I can say, 'been there and done that?' Is that it? So that I can say, 'I'm a cool, mad motherfucker livin' the motherfucking dream?' Is that the big revelation? So what? So fucking what? Lucky cunt! It's all just pathetic ego again. Total shit."

Tears run down his cheeks and suddenly he's crashing, and everything feels impossible again.

"Maybe it's the *quest* for the purpose that is where the fault lies? Maybe I shouldn't have questioned and just learnt to be a good mechanic."

And he *was* a good mechanic, right from the onset. If anything, he'd trained himself in the ability of opening a bonnet and *not* understanding how anything works. It had taken him more than twenty years to arrive at the point where he could finally pop the hood and genuinely shake his head clueless to the goings on. Well, inbuilt obsolescence and the determination of motor manufacturers to make it impossible for even a mechanic to fix a vehicle without expensive diagnostic tools had perhaps helped - that and an economy in which it's just cheaper to replace than repair due to a credit system set on insane.

He can feel himself trembling as the whine of the mosquitoes intensifies though the thick, sweet-scented smoke of the *Paulo Santos* chippings he is burning to cleanse the space offers some respite from their assault, buying him a little more time before the panic sets in. He still doesn't know how to solve the crazy conundrum which has somehow entered his core like a tiny, once free, robin redbreast, trapped in a cage not much bigger than a human heart. Trapped pain, like the point of a spear lodged deep within. Is he scared of asking the question he so wants to ask because he's so scared of the answer? Is it all just another wall for his tears to run down? Can he - can anyone - handle the truth of what this world really is? Is the truth so big and fantastic that he would be crushed by its utter vastness? What part of him is so scared of whatever the bigger picture really is? What is this invisible pane of separation?

Dobbs finally has to accept that he's way out of his depth. He's always been out of his depth, but now he's scared to go forward and there seems no way back. That scene of Ruby serving up the kids' supper in their little house - that is the top of his little mountain. That's as high as it gets; his loving family. He may not be their father but they'll always be his kids. And she's a good mother too - as good as they get. Ah, she likes a party but that's what *makes* her a good mother. She lives her life and makes her kids part of that, adamantly refusing to give up her life for them. They're learning, just like her, to make the most of it, and in being true to what they are they are bound by a love that exists beyond this world. Now they have become a symbol of salvation in his mind; captured forever in that image of her serving them up their supper. Even as he saw that image of her, though, he knew that somehow in this mad process he has lost her, and as he digests that more tears run down his cheeks.

"So here I am, for whatever purpose that is," he whispers just under his breath, crouching in the smoke as though hiding from his fate, the glowing embers of the burning *Paulo Santos* at his feet. He has spoken this last almost like a prayer and is almost annoyed that no response is forthcoming; all he can sense is a vacuous silence.

'Maybe I should just pack up and go home,' he thinks to himself, and then he stops and lets the idea sink in for a long moment. But there is no way back home; only onward now.

If I don't knock that shit back tonight, even though I'm in this crazy fucking state, I'll regret it for the rest of my fucking life, won't I? Fuck knows what's going on at the moment but it's fucking big. It's like a wave's coming in and when I see it, I'm gonna start paddling and I'm gonna catch that fucker and ride it all the way in. That's what I'm gonna do; I'm gonna ride that fucker all the way in.

Then he chuckles to himself.

"This shit really is insanity on a fucking stick, isn't it?It's properly pushing the boundaries." He whispers down to the burning embers. And then, as though they completely agree, "And yeah, so fucking what? Yeah, billions upon billions of people in the course of history have shared his crazy dream, this dream of true love and true freedom for all beings, of liberation from all the pain and suffering of this fucked up world. So fucking what? He voices. "So fucking what if I want to surrender my sword in that temple, to lay down my arms and kneel at the feet of whatever you are and place my spear before the greatness of you? How do I give allegiance to whatever you are, to whatever this thing is which can no longer only live in fairytales? It's like I'm here to pull that dagger out of my heart and place it on the altar of whatever you truly are. To surrender something, to surrender all my pain and completely abandon the sword of I at the altar of your unfathomable greatness. I know that you're there; I know you hear my words, so I'll put all my cards on the table:

"I am at your service, as is the code by which I have attempted to live my life, so judge me however you choose for my actions on this plane. And whatever is going on and however big this zeppelin really is, I'm here, laid bare, stripped of what feels like everything.

370

My dagger, my sword, my spear, I place at your feet. Just tell me; what do you *want*? Because whatever you are, you're the biggest part of me and so I ask you only this: what would you ask of me? For I have nothing more to ask of you. My enquiry is complete and my investigation is over. The weakness of this world I lay at the altar of you and ask only what would you ask of me? I'll do anything to be in service to this Earth, to be in service to you."

By now the tears are running down his cheeks in such torrents that he can hear them sizzling on the burning embers.

"It's not the most sustainable means of having a conversation is it? Kind of a long way to come you know?" he adds with a half chuckle.

Is it really so mad to actually knock on the door of whatever the source truly is? So what if billions before him have knocked? Maybe that is the whole plight? Unwittingly and often unwillingly to arrive at this great wall, like the Wailing Wall itself and be nothing less than Joshua, circling round and round and bringing it down by intention alone. He's failed, technically, in so much he's attempted to achieve in life, but what a life it's been. Someone has to ask these questions so surely someone - or something - has to answer them too, sometimes?

For want of a better way of putting it, he has come here to cure his whole state of being, to find relief for the pain in his heart and translate the vision that tore his life apart. The vision that no man would ever want to see and the story no one would ever want to tell. No, what he saw does not and will never compute for he knows, through the channelling of his parents, that no one knows when a soul will exit this world other than that soul. So what was that then that he saw? An order to come here, the only place he knows that deals with this type of conundrum? Was he actually summoned here simply because there is nowhere else he can go? Well, regardless. Here he is: Dobbs, in the flesh, and, as always, absolutely bang up for it. And as he allows himself to move through that the words that come back to him are Juan's:

'Pon'e la' pilas' – 'put in the batteries!'

Now is the time to build his fortress, to consolidate the armoury of his physical state of being, and as he wipes away the tears he knows that he's said his prayer and however warped and confused it might sound to whoever truly listens, it is done. It is time to prep the protection and prime the interstellar quantum transit lounge and so he pictures his rings of golden light around himself.

'So what,' he thinks, 'if it's just too big, too fantastic and too abundantly obvious and simple for our complex doubting minds? So what if it's too affiliated to another type of intelligence we've not harmonised with as of yet. Maybe this whole age has been about calibrating the human race ready for the quantum leap in consciousness it will take to clear this wall – for the wall will not budge. Maybe we needed to understand war while we were still relatively scientifically underdeveloped so that we were the only one that could go under the wheels of our killing ways?'

And he bows one last time to the *Paulo Santos*.

"Great Spirits, I ask you now for your help and to send the highest beings of light and love to work with me tonight. This is all of me laid bare. I wish only to save my country from this terrible fate I have been shown."

He clears the last utensils from the work surfaces and as he drags out the large washing basin his mind is spinning round and round. All these years he's wondered where Sister Anna, White Cloud, Running Water, John, and the many other beings his parents channel actually reside. They identify themselves by lives they've lived here on Earth which they feel are the most appropriate platforms to deliver their messages but they all talk of Earth as a place which they now only visit. Their words are so beautiful, so concise. They talk of such love and such compassion - qualities that his father and himself would struggle to comprehend with their enormous grace. Could their world and that Other Earth he'd seen be one and the same?

"Stop," he suddenly says under his breath. "You're torturing yourself. No more questions."

Being alone with his thoughts now is almost like standing naked outside in the midst of the swarming mosquitoes. He doesn't know what will happen anymore. The game has become bigger than him and he now feels he is just a puppet in this. That's all we ever are really; puppets to our souls - or to our egos, whatever the ego truly is.

The intensity of the mosquitoes is now becoming unbearable, and he is desperate to get under cover. First he carries out the final act of wiping the two low lying benches circumnavigating half of the little *maloka*. As he does so he sees a huge, hairy spider sat right next to the furthest bench, at the rear where the walls rise, and not much more than the span of his hand to where he'll probably place his head. The notion of having the huge spider right there for the whole ceremony brings him back abruptly from all his crazed thoughts.

"Hi," he says, deciding to make friends

The huge, hairy beast remains motionless, and just seems to be staring back at him. It is a proper hunter and he knows it is pointless to kick it out. Instead he kneels down in front of it.

"We're going to do a ceremony in here if that's alright with you. You're welcome to stay, but we've kind of *baggsy'd* the benches. You cool with that?"

The spider doesn't answer.

"From your silence I will assume we have an accord. Don't be offended if we don't shake on it though. Thank you."

Happy that the first part of the preparation is complete, Dobbs makes his way back to the large rectangular mosquito net they've rigged up in the main structure which is easily three metres square and is making a world of difference to the comfort of all concerned. As he climbs the stairs up into the main lodge, he glances back at the *maloka* one last time before the darkness fully consumes it. It all has to be absolutely right in his mind, and at last he feels ready.

"Sonic BOOOOM!" Bolivar shouts out, hammering two dice down on the table and peering at them under the light of the oil lamp.

"There you go you see; that always works." He says, fixing Agent6 with a smarmy expression and moving his pieces on the backgammon board.

Agent6 looks at Bolivar, holding his space steady and calm. Then, staring at Bolivar and nodding ever so slightly, he throws the dice.

"Double six. You bastard!" Bolivar cries out.

Swifty's sitting in the same sweaty clothes he's toiled in all day, making a note of who has worked, what they've used, what they need, how much they've spent and so on in his note pad. All day long he's been shouting and screaming obscenities from various locations all around the site, nearly always in a rage and having to always demonstrate by example what he wants done as his Spanish is not up to the job of explaining. Every time Dobbs has looked over at him there always seemed to be about three Indigenous workers standing round him watching, quite relaxed, as he toils away, soaked to the bone with sweat and *deet* but absolutely in his element. It doesn't seem to bother him in the slightest that Agent6 kicks back and watches the show with his feet up. Swifty's like a

373

proper old fashioned foreman and he'd not think twice to dock the worker's wages if any tried to skive off.

Having entered the net, Dobbs seals it back up behind him and is gratified to discover the space is almost totally clear of mozzies. He picks up his ukulele and starts strumming but Agent6 puts on a look of mock distaste.

"Bloody hell Dobbs," he says, "It's great you're learning an instrument and all that but can't you at least try and learn more than two chords? We'll go crazy if we have to listen to that for the next week."

"Get over it. Three chords is just showing off," Dobbs protests.

"'erey'are, pass it here. What chords are you playing?" Agent6 asks.

"Don't know," Dobbs shrugs before demonstrating the two chords he's been practicing again. Agent6 takes the ukulele and works the same chords with a more rhythmic strumming pattern.

"Do it a bit more rhythmic like. It's all a bit too just sort of up and down. Looks like you're..."

"Yes, thank you for your positive encouragement." Dobbs says shaking his head and cutting him off before the climax.

"That fucking chainsaw," Swifty moans staring at his notepad. "It could be days before he comes back you know. You do know we've basically given someone who's got what is now rapidly approaching a very, very bad pestilence habit quite a bit of cash, don't you? I should have fucking gone back myself."

The lumberjacks had gone out this morning with the chainsaw Swifty had bought just two days before only to discover that the central casing threads had rounded out and it was shaking itself to bits after barely a few minutes running. He'd bought a duff chainsaw, and it was essential to the project. "Fucking hell. Fuck me. We've fucked it. I've fucked it. I've bought a total piece of shit," he'd said, staring at the machine. The main casing had come apart and the screws that held it together had all fallen out. It needed a complete overhaul and the threads needed be re-tapping. It was an old machine. "Fucking mutton dressed up as lamb," he'd screamed.

It had been a perfect trip up the river and a perfect set up in the afternoon followed by a relatively early night but by the morning The Brigadier was already looking decidedly twitchy. He'd been pottering about beyond the safety of the net, away from Agent6's silent treatment, not really doing anything but unable to keep still even for a moment and at the first talk of going back and sorting out the chainsaw his ears had sprung up like a Yorkshire terrier's.

"I'll do it," he'd immediately volunteered.

"Come on man, you've just got here. We're trying to get you away from that place, trying to get you away from you know what," Dobbs had said, hoping to persuade him not to fall at the first fence.

"No, I ain't going back for that. But I'll go and I'll get it fixed by them that sold it ya," The Brigadier said, sweeping away any connotation that he was even vaguely interested in anything other than fixing the machine.

"Someone's got to go, and I'm quite happy to do it. We seriously need wood, and we seriously need at the very least two chainsaws on site. We'll be here for decades otherwise," Agent6 had stated.

"I'm goin'," The Brigadier had said again, a determined look on his face.

"Sure?"Agent6 had said, clearly thinking, like everyone else, that it was an absurd idea to pack him off to town on his own with money given the way he was clucking.

"Yeah."

Agent6 had just given him a long look then, and nodded.

"We need a few other bits and pieces as well. You definitely coming back?"

"Just write down all what thou needs and I'm out of here."

"Take ya man along to help carry stuff. He knows where the saw comes from as well," Agent6 had said.

The Brigadier nodded to the youngest worker who, though he didn't understand English, had already guessed what was being said.

Agent6 knew he'd have to pass money over to The Brigadier and Dobbs could see exactly where his mind was at. If The Brigadier blew the cash and fucked it all off it would give him the perfect excuse to end their long relationship, but if he didn't perhaps it meant it was worth giving him another chance. In the end he'd passed the money over totally casually apart from a momentary point when their eyes met, and then just nodded his gratitude. If he had his doubts he kept them well hidden. And then The Brigadier was gone, leaving a massive space. Everyone knew exactly the risk Agent6 had taken giving him the money but this was all about his choices, his pathway and more than anything, his free will. In truth Agent6 couldn't handle any of it anymore. The project had been laid open to anyone who wanted to get involved but The Brigadier had become a terrible liability. If this money was to be the rope he hung himself with, then so be it.

Looking up from the backgammon board, Agent6 glances at Swifty.

"It's done now," he says, "If he fucks up, he fucks up. But whoever went back he'd have jumped in with them. And his Spanish is perfect. Plus, can you imagine if they refuse to repair it? He ain't exactly going to let it be easy money for them is he? He'd sooner spend a night in jail before he'd let them get away with that."

"Yeah, that's very true," Swifty nods. "And I suppose it was me that bought the stupid bit of fucking crap. It sounded alright in the shop," he says, shaking his head glumly.

"Well," Dobbs says, taking advantage of a momentary respite from the chainsaw woes, "the space is clear and nearly ready. Got to do a bit of a *pooja* in there maybe, get some more mosquito coils going and what have you. But there's enough if you all want to drink you know. You still up for it Agent6?" Dobbs asks, not applying any pressure. He will drink on his own if need be, but Agent6 *is* the best wing man he ever had.

"Yeah," Agent6 says, absolutely matter of fact, without breaking his attention from the game.

"What about you Swifty? You want to drink?" Dobbs asks.

"Don't fucking work on me. And I know, 'bla-bla-bla.' But no. Don't want to really. Another time maybe."

Dobbs looks at Bolivar lastly. His facial features are amplified by the flickering contrasts brought about by the flame of the oil lamp.

"What about you Bolivar?"

But he'd known what both their answers would be when he'd washed in the river just before the light had started to fade. Agent6 had grabbed some soap and gone off to swim and wash, but when the other two didn't follow it was clear that they had decided not to drink. Maybe it was for the best.

Pulling off his cap, Bolivar runs his hands through the bristles of his shaved head.

"I'm pleased I tried it and all that but it's just not my thing right now, Dobbs. It's too much like acid or something. I want to do more of the adventurous thing here than the psychedelic thing really. That's what you guys did when you all came here first time. Well that's my excuse anyway. And I'm sticking to it."

376

Agent6 glances up at Dobbs. "Just you and me Cowboy."

"There's going to be loads of mosquitoes in there anyway. Why don't you drink in here," Bolivar says glancing up at the net.

Agent6 pulls his attention away from the backgammon board.

"Yeah, we could drink in here Dobbs."

"I kind of like that space now though."

"Yeah, I know what you mean,"Agent6 nods.

"Aren't you nervous drinking without Juan or a...Shaman?" Bolivar asks.

"A *curandero*?" Agent6 offers, shaking his head without a care in the world. "Nohhh."

"I am a little bit. That's why I've spent some time preparing the space."

After another hour or so has passed all the workers have retreated to Swifty's *maloka* and Dobbs can sense that the time is getting close. The area is now quiet enough and free of activity and the drone of mosquitoes has subsided sufficiently for him to start gathering together the bits and pieces they'll need for the ceremony.

"Shit, we've got no *shakarpe* leaves," Dobbs says to Agent6.

"I picked some earlier. They're growing all around us. We're in the middle of the Amazon."

"Oh yeah!" Dobbs answers with a chuckle as he gathers *mapachos* and mosquito coils and walks over to the smaller *maloka* to do a bit of more of a *pooja* or cleansing ritual. Lighting a *mapacho*, he draws smoke into his mouth and blows it over the spaces where they will sit and then around the entrances and then the walls. When he's done, he visualises a golden ring round the whole *maloka* again. Then, finally, he closes his eyes and, sitting in the space, asks once again for all his guides and spirits and beings of light to work with them, and requests that only help from the lightest sources be involved with the ceremony. No sooner has he finished than Agent6 appears.

"You want to sort out the *Ayahuasca*?" Dobbs asks him.

"No. You do it. This is your show."

Dobbs feels nervous at the sudden thought of the brew itself. Oddly, until now it's hardly gone through his mind but now that it does he suddenly gets that incredible shudder all the way through his body and right to his core.

"Shall we dust each other down then? You ready to do this?" Dobbs asks.

"Yeah. Let's do it." Agent6 is so casual about the whole thing but Dobbs, in contrast, is suddenly fraught with apprehensiveness. He can feel almost seismic juddering shifts jolting through him as he takes the *shakarpe* leaves and a *mapacho* and begins brushing agent6 with the leaves from head to toe and front to back with a rapid shaking motion before blowing smoke from his mouth at the location of the leaves. When he's finished Agent6 does the same for him.

Finally they sit. Dobbs sits on the bench next to the spider, who's still right there, his tiny eyes shining brighter than stars. He knows he's being watched through those eyes.

"Remember our little agreement, right?" he says.

"What's that?" Agent6 asks.

"Oh, nothing, I'm just sort of sharing the space with a spider of the very large and hairy variety."

Agent6 looks over at the creature but is not bothered by him at all. Dobbs goes to pass the concoction over to him.

"No. This is your ceremony remember? You prepared the space for something. You do it."

Dobbs can barely hold the bottle though. The shudder going through his body is so difficult to suppress that he has to put it down on the mud floor and shake his whole body. He can taste the *Ayahuasca* in his mouth already but, steadying himself, he opens the bottle before lighting a *mapacho* and blowing the smoke first into the top and then into the glass. Then he pours out a glass and again blows smoke across the top of it before passing it to Agent6, who closes his eyes, takes a moment, then necks it.

Now it's Dobbs's turn again. He pours himself a glass, blows smoke over the top and then holds it in front of himself, between his palms. It feels like jumping off a high rock into freezing water far below and he knows the longer he waits the harder it will be. He takes three large breaths, downs it in one and then immediately gags but manages to suppress the spasm it until it passes.

As his face returns to an expression of calmness again, he looks up to see Agent6 smiling at him.

"Let's go down that rabbit hole," he says.

Where Would You Rather Be?

Dobbs has dug his hole. He knew, before he started, that there was no way he could brave the journey to the mosquito-ridden crapper out the back with its huge, forbidding spiders and rotting, man-trap floorboards. Now he's just lying, trying to sleep and doing his best to ignore the immense sense of nausea building up inside him. When it's time, he will wake - or Agent6 will wake him - but that time feels a long way away right now and so, secure in the knowledge that all is exactly as it is meant to be, he drifts.

An indeterminate amount of time passes, and when he awakes from his sickly slumber it is to find himself fully immersed in a funfair of colours something like a collision between a sweet shop and a circus sideshow. Behind his eyes everything is merging and swirling whilst an obscure, twitchy hum, seemingly more a product of the strangeness of the vision than something actually audible seems is resonating deep within his back-brain. His stomach feels uncomfortable and volatile; the urge to purge is strong now, and the time to let go of what lies below is nigh.

OK, I'm going to go, he says to himself, pulling himself up to a sitting position. Sure enough, there is Agent6, his wingman, just sitting quietly on the bench at his right-hand side. The normal chatter of his monkey mind seems to have stopped and he feels completely present. It's very dark in the hut but he can clearly detect Agent6's form, traced out in that other luminescence; the light beyond light that exists beyond the veil of absolute darkness. It is that same strange luminosity that occurs around the sun during a total solar eclipse, as if some other type of light is concealed behind the brilliance of the sunbeams; a sort of shining Void.

Returning to the matter in hand – or rather in his belly - he peers out of the large opening of the *maloka* in readiness for the next big manoeuvre and sees what looks like a giant wolf, peering in at them from the deep darkness of the forest beyond. Glancing at Agent6, who seems close, by the looks of things, to pulling the rip cord himself, he catches his eye and points to the image. Its two huge eyes are set in the blackest of blackness and its shaggy head is made entirely of leaves and branches. It seems to be just staring at them, so close that its nose is almost inside the *maloka*.

Agent6 peers out and nods.

"It's watching," he says. Then he gets up, steadies himself for a moment, and moves slowly outside of the thatched hut to stand, swaying a little and looking like he might vomit, a few feet away. Dobbs is tempted to look away, but he gets the sense that Agent6 is struggling to let go of something and then sure enough he just drops down and sits on his backside his legs outstretched, like he just can't do it. Dobbs senses he's about to release something big, he pictures a big golden ring round him.

Finally, when it comes, it is a strange sight indeed. It looks to Dobbs almost as if not just Agent6's mouth but his whole face opens up as if his body is releasing something from deep down in its very core, almost like the base of his being has reached up through the centre of himself. It is so strange it seems almost like a painfully impossible, utterly animated spew. And then he does it again and again. It is harsh even just to watch, almost like he is turning himself inside out, and it seems to be going on and on. He is clearly letting go of some serious shit but eventually it is over and just sits for a while, in peace at last, before getting to his feet again and making his way back inside.

Personally, Dobbs feels a lot clearer than he did last time, but he knows his time is coming and he is determined to allow whatever needs to come up, regardless of the consequences. Before beginning, he communicates his immediate agenda to his body:

Get up, walk out to the hole, throw up, have a shit if necessary, and then return - as simple as that. Then, getting to his feet, he walks out with precision manoeuvring of his legs and body mass finds the hole he'd dug, and stands over it, waiting. So far, so good. Now he brings all his attention to the discomfort of the nausea, allowing it to grow and develop until he can almost taste the brew in the back of his throat.

"Please don't let it be like last time unless it's really, really necessary," he prays.

OK, here we go, he thinks as he feels the first little flutter starting in his stomach. Then he kneels down and, in one fluid motion, it all comes up. A couple more heaves, and he's clear.

"I won't count my chickens," he says aloud, "but that seemed a lot easier. Just like the old days: thank you." Then he gets back to his feet and starts to walk back to the *maloka*.

As he approaches, the whole *maloka* has been transformed into the compartment of a huge Ferris wheel.

It's gonna be a ride ah? Well, I'm bang up for it – all in, Let me sit and get comfortable,' he says in his head as tears run down his cheeks. I'll buckle up first if that cool.

380

Making his way through the door into the lightly illuminated space he finds Agent6 sitting up, but with his head just hanging forward from his frame. He's gone already, but Dobbs knows exactly where he is. Taking a deep breath, he rubs his hands together, barely able to contain the tingling energy he can feel coursing through his fingertips. His mind is absolutely clear and he is completely beyond the reach of doubt now, in a totally egoless space. He is crystalline consciousness now.

Wow, he thinks. Every light on the flight panel is flashing green; All systems are Go.

First perching himself on the bench, he lies out flat. Sometimes when he really goes his body collapses in the dirt, so when he senses he's going off on a proper voyage he lies out flat and then cocoons and cuddles himself up as expectation won't fire these engines; bliss is the only thing that drives this vehicle. Bliss or sadness: it's the same thing really. If you track it all back, it's the only door that Dobbs knows which traverses straight through the heart and clean out of this world. You've only got to do it a few times and then it kind of gets easier until they've kind of got your number; the structure of your intention - the vehicle within which we *all* fly, consciously or unconsciously.

Some people say you can never tell when a big wave is coming, but you can, and as he cuddles himself up into that bliss space, like he's going to fly off in his dream, he brings his attention to the trembling excitement now ringing through him. He's ready now, right at the doorway, but opening his eyes one last time, he pushes his body up to check his shawl is not interfering with the spider. Sure enough, there's his lucky mascot, completely unaffected by the proceedings.

"Might see you soon," he says, "I'm leaving you in charge by the way."

He's not sure, but it seems to him that the two little stars wink their acknowledgement back at him. Then, satisfied, he drops his head down next to the creature and closes his eyes.

'OK. Ready when you are,' he says, bringing his attention to the eclectic imagery hovering in the forefront of his vision. Feeling the excitement of all his anticipation in his breath, he draws it deep into him and as he does so he sees his father, working the bellows of his great barrel chest, and he remembers the sound of that last final breath he takes before he channels. It sounds almost like a death rattle, like an echo just dissipating into peace, and then he

381

releases his own breath and as he does so he passes straight through the wall.

Agent6 is lying on the straw bale, exactly where Dobbs was expecting him to be, chewing on a blade of grass. He winks at Dobbs just like before, and nods a greeting. Dobbs glances down at his hands and then flicks them out as if doing a magic trick and locks his sight on them. Just like before they seem almost elegant with a supernatural beauty. He's pleased to see he's still wearing the camo hot pants with their laced bottoms too; lookin' good on the Other Side.

Looking around, he becomes aware of the huge oak tree with its massive roots reaching out far from the main trunk. Once again, it seems absolutely real, exact in every detail and yet almost so perfect that it seems like a digital animation. Suddenly The Brigadier just pops out from the side, looking like he's stepped straight out of a Robin Hood movie, but no sooner has Dobbs clocked him than he disappears back behind the tree again. Dobbs peers round, trying to catch a glimpse of him but The Brigadier shoots round the other way and grabs something from his back pocket. It's the compass he'd found when he was a kid, hidden behind a log, although quite how he knows that, he's not sure. His father had confiscated it because he was sure it was ill-gotten gains but a year later, he'd relented and taught Dobbs and his brother orienteering.

Dobbs spins round to catch The Brigadier but he's gone again in the blink of an eye, and as he peers round to the right of the tree, he pops round from the other side again and slips the compass back in his other back pocket. As Dobbs spins back to the left The Brigadier disappears like a shot but as he disappears, he hears the words, 'Don't worry, there'll be mischief,' spoken in The Brigadier's voice resonating through him. And then, just like that, The Brigadier is gone.

Looking back down at his hands again he suddenly realises he's not actually standing up anymore; he's actually sitting on a long log in a small clearing that opens out to afford a view of the valley below with all the tents. As his eyes follow the log away from him to his right, he nearly falls out of his tree with surprise. There, with a leg on either side of the log, just sitting facing him and staring right at him with the most captivating gaze, is Ruby's father, Doddi. His face is warm and friendly but his expression focused, like he wants Dobbs's absolute undivided attention.

382

"What is this place, Doddi?" he tries to ask, but the words don't come out.

"Why can't I speak?" he tries again, but Doddi just puts his index finger up to his lips and nearly smiles, except his face is full of concentration as if he's saying, 'no kidding about.' In fact something approaching fear seems to be the overriding expression, or grave concern at least. Dobbs is so excited that he feels almost like a little child, but Doddi clearly cannot accommodate that right now. His eyes demand absolute focus.

Bringing his hand down to his heart, he nods at Dobbs to do the same thing before gently swaying his hand whist gesturing breathing. He's telling Dobbs to breathe. He opens his mouth and slowly attempts to draw air into his lungs and feels his Earth bound body suddenly breathing that is now almost for gasping. Now he senses what's happening more. This is his human body, the biological living mechanism that is being allowed to see the other light body his soul uses beyond this world.

Doddi keeps his eyes on Dobbs who's now becoming acutely aware of his Earth body and nearly pulls out of the vision but Doddi keeps his hand upon his solar plexus holding Dobbs's attention with eyes fixed like stars in the night sky, holding his awe with pin point focus.

Every breath seems almost unbearably blissful now and as Doddi just nods at him, smiling, he can feel tears running down his cheeks, like they might be real tears running down his real cheeks. He keeps on breathing, even though his whole being is now shuddering with the intensity. Whatever is now happening, it connects directly into his physical state of being and can literally feel the sensation of his earthly body still lying on the bench.

Doddi just keeps on gently nodding with his hand on his heart, encouraging Dobbs to keep all his attention on the sensation of burning bliss building up within his heart. The more he homes in on it the more powerful and intense it becomes until it almost feels like he's going to explode with the ecstasy. Suddenly something with the intensity of the bliss now thundering through him and he is consumed with the most intense light and he feels himself rising out of his new *light* body and is now escalating rapidly upwards in what seems to be, effectively, a vertical corridor, barely visible in its burning brightness.

Set into the walls of this tower of light are terraces and balconies. They are too bright to get any real sense of form and only really the beings that line them stand out; the guardians of the door. Their faces look so beautiful and are blazing so brightly he can only weep at their unimaginable grace. Then he sees a lady that he recognises. She curtsies ever so slightly and in so doing drops her head, almost obscuring her face, but Dobbs knows immediately it is Gatita, and suddenly he feels the pang of the twisted emotional tale that he wouldn't ever want Doddi to know about and feels so bare and exposed in all the brightness.

It is as though these beings are ambassadors, greeting him as he moves through, but the intensity of the burning bliss is becoming so bright and intense it is as though he is being lifted by this thing blasting through his solar plexus, as though his core is the centre of a massive jet turbine or the central vortex of a white hole. Finally the feeling of electrifying elevation begins to subside and he finds himself in a bodiless state, just a point of bright light, as though he is now in the centre of a star. Now he doesn't know if he has truly passed over to the other side.

'Have I died?' he thinks.

And then he hears the oddest sound: mosquitoes, a whole swarm of them. He can feel them landing on him and somehow, suddenly, he's in three places. His physical body is down on Earth, lying on the bench, and yet his soul is sitting on a log in heaven with Doddi, Agent6 and The Brigadier, yet at the same time there is yet another completely higher realm of consciousness, just witnessing the whole thing.

He tries to raise a hand to scare off the mozzies but as he does so a clear, resonant voice bellows,

"Where would you rather be?"

Dobbs freezes, dropping his arms by his side and listens. He can hear the mosquitoes swarming and feels them biting his body from head to toe, and the soft wet tears running down his face but now he just lays there and lets the little critters take their fill of him. In truth they make him aware of his physical body, and he's quite relieved to find that he's still alive.

Wow! he says in his mind, this is something else! and he tries to relax into the sensation of being swarmed upon as though lying on a bed of nails, regulating and harmonizing his breathing again.

"Here," he finally says in his mind; "I want to be here, with You."

And as he feels the peace of that take him for a few moments. He allows his body to completely relax and feel the awe of bliss coursing through him. He is pure blissful feeling now and he exits at the complete disposal of the bliss that holds him, waiting.

"You're going to write a book."

Dobbs wants to say something half-cocky but the intensity of what is happening is just too big to question. Even to ask who it is who speaks would be a silly question, so he just waits, quietly, almost scared to ask about what he should say in this book.

"I want you to invite them in," says the voice, as if reading his thoughts, and then, after a short silence it speaks again.

"I want you to give them the rule. The one and only rule that grants entry. You *know* that rule."

"Yes," he answers, feeling the unbridled volume of the unobstructed commodity blasting through him in its most purest state in quantities so huge he could not *not* understand.

"Peace."

"Yes. Peace. Peace is the rule. Peace is the only rule. In thought, in word, in action, declare your peaceful intent when departing this world and it will be denoted as understanding the rule to enter this world and it will be our binding contract that those who wish to enter have understood. A contract to which all will be bound, to occupy the space provided. All understand that rule now. Is it not very simple? Is the rule not obvious?"

"Yes. But what will I say? Where will I start?"

As he speaks the words he feels a flood of what could be described as energy coursing through his Earth bound body, like information but too fast for him to comprehend. It tingles and jars as it rips through his physical system, though far away. At first it feels like his body is going into muscular spasms but it almost immediately becomes so much more as the energy torrents literally thunder through his liver and kidneys, juddering painfully like a heavy sub bass reverberating through him followed by a feeling akin to an electric shock or plugging in loud speakers whilst they're switched on and turned up high. A sensation like lightning shoots through his kidneys, seeming to circle almost as if scanning. The sensation is positively painful, especially on his right side. It is as if something is scanning his whole body, like a computer reading a hard drive being uploaded with information.

Finally it calms down and his body is able to breathe easily again. Now he's lying there, taking deep breaths and wondering what the hell just happened to him when he hears the voice again:

'It will come. It will all just come.'

385

Dobbs is listening to the words but what is more perplexing is the vision he's seeing. His writing bureau, rather than closed up with all the papers and other mess and odd things he's normally got crammed in there bursting out the side are all gone. Now it's immaculately clean and organised, with his desktop lamp, which never worked, illuminated.

As he observes the desk, he is lost in a flood of many things running through him but much more smoothly than before. The process is quite soothing in fact; like millions of tiny switches being clicked open, as though his whole body is somehow being calibrated. It feels so caressing and calming and he just lies there, simultaneously present in all these multiple places, feeling tears just flowing down his face. He'd never been aware of his body in this state. To experience this sense of open awareness grounded in the physical body is something totally new and indescribably powerful.

Finally the intense peace and overwhelming love begins to fade into the background as the feeling of his body, heavy on the hard surface comes to the fore until he feels located, once more, right behind his eyelids again and between his ears, listening to the sound of the jungle. At first all seems unnaturally quiet but then, as he listens, he begins to pick out a myriad of tiny twitches and hums, croaks and creaks, Earthly sounds, guiding him back into his body. Reaching down, he touches the bare earth with his finger tips, as if reading her frequency like a needle on a record. And then, at last, he does the thing he knows he must; the thing that one day everyone will have to do. He opens his eyes.

After a few seconds he checks to see how his little friend is coping, but the spider is gone. His whole body is itching all over from head to toe from where he's been bitten, but rather than scratch he just lets himself sink into the odd sensation. Agent6 is sitting up, but with his head resting to one side, asleep. Looking at him, Dobbs marvels at how lucky he is to have such a beautiful friend and his eyes fill with tears once more at the thought of at all the fantastic adventures they've had together over the past twelve years. He is a true brother.

Suddenly Dobbs has a thought that makes him shudder from head to toe.

But I never came to find out about that world really. What about this world? What about my world? What about my country? I can't write about this other Earth or whatever that place is if there's no resolution for my home. What of this beautiful Earth that is being plundered? It's this world I want to save. I know I must seem so stupidly naive but what about Earth?

No sooner has he uttered the question than his mind starts to grasp once again for that painful space that has ruled his being with torment: the whole cluster fuck of doom and gloom scenarios that he so desperately does not wish to carry anymore. Just as he's about to go down that old familiar route into that quagmire of guilt and pain, all his woes are suddenly vaporised like morning mist by a peace so serene that it just washes through him like an aftershock and nearly sweeps him, leaving only an unutterable sense of calm and the words, lingering in his heart like a fragrance hanging in the air: "Don't worry, I've already deployed my best. Unprecedented peace will now be waged upon your Earth." The words are drenched in such bliss that he feels like he could curl up inside them as tears flood from his eyes.

"Thank you, thank you."

A Heavy Load

Pulling himself up, Dobbs finds he's feeling quite battered. His whole body is itching from head to toe – so much so that the sensation is bordering on pain, and it's difficult for him to relax and let his mind float free. Instead he just sits and watches Agent6 for a few moments, appreciating his friend for all his positive efforts and intentions as he quietly drifts to and fro, slowly returning to the world.

The effects of the *Ayahuasca* are still very much active but the main ride is over for Dobbs and it seems strange to him now how sometimes so little seems to happen on a journey whereas at others something so massive comes through that it can take years to truly get your head round it. What's just occurred has completely blown his mind. In fact it's quite literally the most powerful experience he's ever had and right now he feels as if he's been blown clean out of the *thunderdome* of his own nagging doubts and fears. Breathing into his heart, he finds the pain has gone and in its place is something different, a calmness and a sense of conviction which dwarfs the sorrow he has carried for too long. At last he has found what he has been searching for all his life: his purpose for being on this Earth.

In his heart he now knows that the Divine Creator has a plan for the depleted gang and all who sail upon their ship of misery. If they love their thoughts so much then they can become them. Why not, if a human is willing to abandon themselves to a lower astral energy that is intent on killing, maiming, raping, polluting, and all the other abominable crimes being used to generate fear amongst the populace?

'Let's see the real wizard hiding behind the person who believe they are the racist bankers they think they are.'

Shit; that's what this is isn't it? It's the end of duality isn't it. A choice between head and heart.'

The hopers and wanters who back war with their silent cowardly consent on one side of the equation and those who are willing to stand up against fascism on the other: to stand in peace and to be of peace, not just another hypocrite who preaches one thing and then practices the opposite. Isn't that the *real* reason the cops 'kettle' the crowd? The clue is in the word; a term created by the Police themselves to describe how to turn a peaceful protest into a seething cauldron of discontent. Surround the people with terrifying looking black-clad ninja turtles, then squeeze them like a boa constrictor until they reach critical mass, unable to escape, denied even the dignity to take a piss or shit. So ordinary men, women and children protesting against war, corporate control and the grand theft of everything that goes to make up a wholesome community are effectively punished because they believe in *peace*.

'*Holy fuckerony!*' Dobbs thinks to himself. 'People are not just choosing a *side* in this war, they're choosing a *soul*!' At last, he's clear of the pain he's been carrying, but he knows the energy of it is not gone; instead it has been transformed into conviction. The emotional mass of sadness and joy are just two sides of the same coin that is the currency of the human condition - a condition which, properly understood, is a doorway into another world. He is now merely on the other side of his pain. He has hauled his state of consciousness through the centre of the world of suffering and found his purpose here on this Earth in the bliss beyond. He is cured.

When he first came to South America to cure his knee, ten years before, he had had such a seismic ceremony that his knee had indeed been *cured*. Not just improved but, unequivocally, cured. He'd literally climbed a mountain the following day with The Brigadier and then bounded down and the biggest struggle he'd had the whole way was no longer the previously perennial pain, or the massive swelling but merely to remember which knee it *was* that had been plaguing him with pain for the past two years.

In the same way, now, breathing into his heart, he can feel that the agony that drove him here this time round has been replaced by something different; a calmness and clarity created by the knowledge that something much bigger and more powerful than him is in charge, a grace so pure and sublime that he can only surrender himself to the new-found knowledge that, for better or worse, he is now an agent of Divine Providence. For all his rights and wrongs, the fine embroidery where he's made real effort and the shabby patches where he's fallen seriously short, here he is, renewed and charged with a sense of conviction capable of dwarfing the woes of the world.

He thinks of his parents and all those who have taken a stand for peace like Hicksy and lived from the conviction that peaceful conduct is a virtue to live for in itself, a purpose greater than any other - especially in these times of global conflict and scientifically generated terror. Not to just think of peace or want for peace, but to hold the spear of peace aloft and carry it like the Olympic Flame, inciting all who witness it to wage peace within every cell of their being and shine the light of awareness into all the dingy nooks and crannies of divisive bitterness that threaten to drive this beautiful planet to destruction.

Still there is so much of the message he doesn't really understand, but now it's like he's staring at the same window from the other side, through eyes wide with the bliss of the opportunity to shine like never before, even in the face of the global conspiracy of corporate control. It feels as though a new tune is being feathered into to the mundane marching music that for so long has ridden roughshod over his world. A new beat, the sweet rhythm of raging bliss, has now become a thunderous fanfare in his heart, the herald of a whole new Age.

Dobbs feels so charged he's almost jumping out of his skin and he's frustrated that Agent6 is still not back yet; he just wants to tell someone what has happened and try to make some sense of it. The sense of spaciousness inside of him now is vast, a boundlessness that can barely be contained by the paltry confines of his corporeality. He feels as if he wants to get up and stride through that invisible landscape, to hike forever across the rolling hills and majestic valleys of that other Earth where the open expanse of a never ending horizon spans a thousand new lives to the timeless oceans beyond. He craves open fields and floral paths and a healthy breeze to fill his lungs, and to just walk until there's not a step left in him and this cloying flesh that clings like mud to his body of light has been burned away and he can once more soar like an eagle, casting his vision ever outwards like the morning star shining down at the dawn of a brave new world.

Back here in his earthly body however it's still dark, and even if it was light he could not go far before the impenetrable jungle turned him back. Not that he'd leave the space until the ceremony is over anyway, so for now he must just sit tight and wait until Agent6 is safely back. 'Follow your heart, but never forget the power of a circle - even of just two people,' he thinks to himself. Agent6 has been such a pillar of support in his life that another tear runs down his cheek just to think of it. No, he would never leave the circle whilst his wingman was still out there so, visualizing a golden ring around him, he leaves him in peace and lies back down on the bench to wonder once more at the message he'd received and bask in the sheer bliss of it.

Suddenly though he feels a sharp pain in his right kidney that causes him to tense his lower back involuntarily. The same pain had come up a few times over the last few years, most commonly at festivals when he was dehydrated from wandering about under the hot sun, shouting his mouth off all day selling his wares. He's fully down from the brew now so he tries to position his back more comfortably and eventually the sharpness subsides to a dull ache before finally fading away to leave him once more in the comfort of his metaphorical bed of roses, complete with all its thorns of doubt spiking through the serenity. He tries to distribute his entire body weight upon the tingling pains as more tears run down his face with each shard of disbelief and stagnation he moves through. It seems strange to him, but the plank on which he's lying somehow feels so comfortable. The dull ache of his limbs pressed against the rough sawn timber coupled with the more visceral judders of pain darting through his body fuse with the hum of mosquitoes biting and the itch of irritation all across his body but he allows it all to become like the bed of nails technique his mum had taught him. To completely arrive in your state of being no matter how good or bad and track it back to the bliss of non-judgmental awareness is the doorway to dive into the majestic mystery where spirit and matter merge and all vectors equal out in the silent centre of the soul. She is such a beautiful mother and a wise old fish; he owes her so much. Upon the blank white canvas of his bliss even the imperfections of the world feel like the brushstrokes of a master. The sheer wonder of existence is thrilling through his entire body, right down to the tips of his fingers and toes and, as he floats back into the bliss, tears run from the corners of his eyes. He can hear a mosquito humming right next to his ear but he doesn't care anymore and the only word that comes into his mind is "Thank you." He can feel himself starting to move back into the interstellar transit lounge once more, but this time his human consciousness does not follow and his body, which has been properly pounded again, finally falls into sleep.

***

Several hours have passed by the time he wakes again and for a moment he completely forgets where he is before the realisation of all that has just happened comes crashing back like a fully loaded freight train smashing into the empty platform of his being: Boom! He remains motionless as it impacts his conscious mind but the experience is intense and, like a child waking on Christmas morning, he can't wait to unpack his thoughts and examine them through the looking glass of this new alignment that he has connected with - or that has connected with him. He feels both calmer and somehow more delicate, more serene. It's still completely dark in the *maloka*, but peering through the doorway again he can see the first, pale luminance of the dawn revealing the world outside. Though his mind is back on line, his body feels tired.

'Man, I'm going to need some serious powers of containment to deal with all this new stuff,' he thinks to himself. 'But is it really new? I *did* come to Peru in search of an adventure. In search of a book, in fact. So is this, like, the core of it now?'

"It will come,"' he hears the echo of that clarion call. But what does that mean?

Excitement starts to rise up in him again.

'But is this 'just' an *Ayahuasca* vision,' he ponders. 'Can I take it as real? Would anyone believe it? Is it even something to believe?'

One thing's for sure through all the questioning though; it's real to him - *absolutely* real – even if it is nothing short of heretical. The breakthrough - although it was never really about finding a way through - is about just one thing and one thing alone: INVITATION.

That, he now realises, is what brought him into this world so that he could incarnate in this body and is also what allows passage to see the realms beyond this world. He'd always thought he was lucky that he'd been able to see more than most but then he had been brought up by channellers so it was always easier for him to open himself to the Vision. His mum told him about the law of *Karma* when he was just four years of age and he understood it perfectly and even argued the case with the school vicar, who thoroughly disagreed with the whole concept and got quite angry with Dobbs, to his great amusement.

Suddenly though, it seems that his ability has become a double edged sword. There are very few, even amongst his own friends who he feels he could openly talk to about such an experience without being met by a look of glazed vagueness. In fact the only time any of his friends ever really wanted to discuss the other side was when they'd suffered bereavement and felt they couldn't cope. After a while, he'd started to understand that bereavement itself is simply an invitation to a higher state of consciousness as it imposes the illusion of the loss of love and drives us to dig deeper in search of the realisation that actually love can never be destroyed as it is the true unbridled power of the Universe that drives the cogs of perpetual change and discovery. Bereavement is often the only mechanism that life has to drive us to the threshold of our own limited sense of self. It is a hand that reaches out from the unknown to guide one through the gateway of sadness to the loving bliss beyond.

But, just like everyone else, he can't simply bust his way in: Spirit is smarter than that. This thing suddenly feels bigger than he ever imagined. The invisible landscape suddenly has dimensions, and what had once only existed in fairytales has now stepped clean out of the storybook and into his life - and it's not fiction. It would probably be a lot easier if it was fiction, he thinks, and suddenly he finds himself laughing uncontrollably at the notion.

Dobbs feels as though he's going to explode but he can't. It's as if now he is haemorrhaging bliss instead of sadness. He wants to just bask in the wonder of what has just happened but he's struggling to just sit with it. His most fervent prayer has been answered and he has experienced something he never imagined he would – or could - and yet, somehow, he knows that the space he now finds himself in is even more treacherous than the one he's finally escaped. The Vision of Sorrow that had been visited upon him after that blast of laughing gas that he still did not understand that perhaps showed him the dark forces that attempt to enter this world through psychic black holes that are opened because they can legally operate below common decency and thus allow the Hungry Ghosts of the lower astral to enter and sabotage any kind of sustainable, wholesome existence with their insatiable greed. 'These days it seems, with people's shields so *depleted*. I guess they've still got a choice like everyone else. But, whatever or whoever they are, if they want in, and that is the human's individual choice, Well I guess then they can come in. Then so be it.

"Let's have ya. Let's fuckin' have ya then!" he mutters under his breath. *"Better the Devil you know*, ah? One or the other."

And suddenly his mind is running with that old egotistic thought-surge as doubt springs in from nowhere;

'Shit! Out of the frying pan and into the fire. What the fuck am I going to do about it all? Write a book? I mean, you've got to be having a laugh haven't you? "Invite them in?" You cannot be serious! That's not where I thought this was going. I mean that's going to be met with a bit of a...well, a reaction. I thought I was

393

here to work out, I don't know, the origin of Shakespeare, the hidden cabals of the Secret Chiefs – and, most of all, who the hell is *doing* all this shit. I wanted to know who *they* actually are. What or who is the big *THEY*: The big *THEM*?'

Dobbs runs his fingers through his hair, staring up at the half-collapsed roof of the *maloka* and as he lies there in the pale, cool light of a new day tears flood once more from his eyes as he feels the intense bliss taking him again burnt, over loaded mind. He feels torn open with love and as he drifts again, his departing though:

'And I thought I was here to work out who the *real* Shakespeare was. So silly…' And he's gone.

Something to Soothe the Bliss

Waking suddenly from a deep sleep Dobbs opens his eyes, momentarily clueless to the world. One tiny word is still echoing in his mind like a trip wire upon which his slumber has been snared, causing an abrupt seizure the psychic equivalent of realizing you're going in completely the wrong direction and hitting the brakes while bombing along, pedal-to-the-metal on the motorway. He was going somewhere but now he can't quite remember where and as he lies there, too scared to look in the rear view mirror, the word slams into his back brain like a hammer hitting a bell:

"WHAT," he feigns bemused.

He's come all the way to the Amazon to work out *who* Shakespeare was, but now the more pertinent question seems to be *what* Shakespeare was. And then, like a pile-up in the fog of his hypnogogic mental highway the whole dialogue comes crashing back into his conscious mind, all mixed up with the memory of everything that happened in the ceremony. The bliss returns, burning through his body in a seemingly unstoppable torrent that feels like lying in the sun after some wild illegal party, unable even to conceive that it's possible to share that level of joy with so many other people. It's as if his soul has actually come down and is dancing inside of him and he can't stop bouncing until there's nothing left. He doesn't ever want to leave this state of bliss and the feeling of coming back to consensus reality is almost like a pestilence rattle but he knows he can't keep conscious to appreciate it for very long and already he can feel himself departing again.

"You back, Cowboy?"Agent6 says, observing him from his bench.

"Yeah, kind of. How was it for you?" Dobbs replies.

"Strange one. Don't know where I was for most of it; just gone, like I was asleep," Agent6 says, massaging his eyes and temples with the balls of his palms.

"You were there with me. You were my wingman again. I saw you. *Muchas gracias, amigo.*"

Agent6 just nods, half squinting and half smiling. Dobbs wants to say so much more, to share his euphoria, but Agent6 is not ready yet so, satisfied his friend is finally back he gets to his feet and walks out of the *maloka* into the dawning day. Climbing the stairway into the main lodge, he becomes aware that his kidney is strangely achy again - clearly a reminder to begin the process of rehydration - so he downs almost a litre of water in the hope that it will ease the pain.

Staring out the front of the *maloka* his mind feels completely blown open, but he knows the shockwaves of what just happened will continue to impact him as the full implications of his Vision seep into his conscious being.

'Fucking hell. It really is a big old thing. You've revealed so much and yet I feel more clueless than ever before. "Invite them in"? I just don't get it. *Them*? Is there another side of this message that I'm not seeing?' he says under his breath to the wind.

Swaying, still off-balance from the intensity of his experience, he tries to remain present by focusing on the minutiae of his physical state to calm him. He feels completely clueless as to how he will achieve whatever it is he has to do and as his waking mind kicks in doubt is starting to gnaw at him again, so he does the only thing he can do and surrenders to it, allowing it to just move through him like a juddering wave.

'I'm missing a part of the picture here, aren't I? Something else is supposed to happen here and I just can't quite see it.'

As he tries to contain this huge thing that somehow feels like it is swelling inside of him tears begin to run down his face.

'How will it come though?' he finds himself asking.

Immediately, he remembers his father giving him a piggy bank when he was a child and trying to encourage him to make the effort to save his money, saying: "For every pound you save, I'll give you another."

He was hooked, and on hearing the news all his relatives had given him fifty pence pieces too until, in just a few days, he'd saved a tidy sum. His father, who prided himself that he always did exactly what he said he'd do - which for the most part seemed to mean enforcing specific punishments for specific wrongdoings - had observed the money presented, nodded at the sum, and, to Dobbs's complete amazement, banged down his share on the table. As the memory comes rushing back he hears the words, crystal clear, in his heart;

"You write half and I'll write half." Each syllable is drenched in buckling bliss.

Wandering down the steps to the front of the *maloka* he sits on one of the logs embedded in the riverbank and just stares out at the jungle around him, soaking up the glorious cacophony of a million different birds and beasts all seemingly competing to greet the dawn with the most beautiful song, the shrillest shriek or the most awesome roar. Tears of bliss are still rolling down his cheeks and he can still feel the echo of the *Ayahuasca* in his system, a healing euphoria like he's just made love with a goddess. There are plenty of mozzies still buzzing about by the shady riverbank but whereas before they'd triggered panic now they seem merely amusing. It's way too late to start worrying about Malaria or Dengue Fever now and as he watches them touch down and take their fill the very thought of it sends more tears, this time of laughter, running in glistening rivulets down his cheeks.

His knuckles are swollen and aching from all the bites and now, in the daylight, he can see he's absolutely covered in bumps and blotches. Far from being in pain though, his overwhelming feeling is one of blasting, triumphant euphoria to be alive and on the other side, looking back, at the vastness of the vista that has been opened up to him. He'd always believed the other world existed, but now he knows beyond doubt. Now it is time to buckle up and remember why he came to planet Earth in the first place; through this existence his soul has gained access to that other world and now he knows that all this is nothing more than Mr Ben's fitting service. Earth, it seems, is merely the dressing room of the gods.

He feels battered, but beautiful. Nothing in the heavenly scene sparkling before him in the shimmering light of dawn seems isolated or stand-alone anymore. It is all one, gloriously intermeshing web of life, reaching up through the early morning mist floating above the glassy, almost motionless river. Above and below, mirrored in perfection.

'Maybe it's time to make some ripples,' he suddenly thinks to himself and is just about to head down to the landing and climb aboard the *Christina* when he remembers that The Brigadier has taken her back to Iquitos and, at least until his return, they are all truly marooned out here in the jungle. Instead, he switches on his voice recorder and tries to record as much of his experience as he can to ensure the memory of it is burnt into his very being but before long the kids come down to play by the river and the sight of their freshness reminds him just how exhausted he really is. It seems it is finally bedtime for Dobbs so, after gulping down some more water, he makes his way back to his hammock.

Lying down to sleep, he can feel the familiar chorus of doubt beginning to batter at the front door of his mind but, determined to stay in the peace, he focuses instead on the sense of awe still smouldering within. It's almost as though Gatita is there beside him, cocooning him in love, her unconditional affection wrapping him up safe and shielding him from the voices trying to say 'no way was any of that real: you must be mad to even let your mind go there.' Enfolded in the living memory of Billi's warm embrace, all those doubts seem far, far away.

'You can't touch me here,' he recklessly throws back at them, feeling like a little prince, flicking pebbles at the hungry crocodiles circling the moat of his father's castle.

Finally, slipping back into the bliss, he falls into a deep and peaceful sleep.

When he wakes, hours later, the first thing he notices is that dull ache in his right kidney again. It's not so much a pain as the feeling that somehow something is in there.

'I hope it's not a stone,' he thinks, and mentally reminds himself to drink more water - lots of water.

Swinging his legs out of his hammock, he makes his way into the main net. The workers have all long since eaten breakfast by the looks of things and the little temple is now a kitchen once more in which lunch is being prepared.

"How's you?" Dobbs addresses Swifty, who is sitting making notes in his notebook.

Swifty just nods and carries on but then, suddenly remembering the ceremony, he says

"Oh yeah! How was it?"

"It was *interesting*," replies Dobbs, starting to smile. Then, bursting into a chuckle, "Ve-r-r-y interesting."

"Didn't die or anything too gruesome this time then?"

Dobbs chuckles. "No, I survived. It *was* pretty full on though."

"Yeah?"

Staring at Swifty, Dobbs wants to say more, but he just can't seem to find words so in the end he just nods.

 It was full on Swifty, full on, he says."

"You OK?"

"Yeah. It was a good ceremony; beautiful, very beautiful, but I'm still kind of, you know, trying to digest it all at the moment," Dobbs replies.

The smell of fish-scented barbeque smoke emanating from the little maloka offers more than just olfactory stimulation and

398

Bolivar is sat in the haze, taking refuge from the mozzies. Observing him, Dobbs feels a tear well up in his eye. He has such a friendly face, even in the morning when he's a little grumpy and he's never unapproachable and difficult, even if he's really moody; he owns his own shit. Now, seeing Dobbs is finally awake, he gets up and enters the net before plonking himself down beside him.

"Bastard. I bet you had a great time," Bolivar says finally.

"I wish my kidneys shared the same optimism," Dobbs replies, doing his best to find the most comfortable position to take the pressure off his throbbing back.

Observing Dobbs massaging the offending area, he is about to add something but just then Agent6 wanders in, still looking a bit out of it. For a while they all just sit there in a mood of quiet contemplation but finally Swifty breaks the silence.

"Well come on then, spill the fucking beans," he says. "What happened? Fuck me, you lot are making me want to go back to bed."

Bolivar looks up for a moment before quickly drifting back into his sleepy state.

"Man, I really slept last night," he yawns.

Ignoring him, Swifty diverts his attention to Agent6.

"Good one?"

Agent6 shakes his head, as if unsure himself.

"Lost a lot of it," he sighs, resting his head in his hands and massaging his eyes again.

"You had a mad one again, didn't you?" Bolivar chuckles at Dobbs.

"Yeah," he peers at Bolivar and then back down, "I really did. The maddest so far." But as he thinks to enlarge on it a sharp, shooting shock of pain from his kidney stops him dead. The magnitude of the feeling inside of him is almost overwhelming and all he can do is take a breath, let out a deep sigh then sit in silence for a few moments until the pain has gone. Finally he adds,

"Actually, I was told I'm going to write a book."

Everyone is silent, obviously waiting for more, but Dobbs just shakes his head and raises his hands slightly as if he is none the wiser than anyone else.

"Well you kind of knew that anyway, didn't you. So maybe that's just you confirming to yourself what you already knew - a self-fulfilling prophecy?" Bolivar offers.

"Yeah, maybe."

But then Agent6 looks up.

"About what?" he asks.

Dobbs opens his mouth to speak but the vastness of what is inside of him feels like it is going to flatten him. The feeling is all encompassing but its main focus is in just one place: his right kidney. It's almost as if the whole meat of the matter just rests uncomfortably there, like a finger, gently but constantly prodding him so that he constantly has to adjust his position to alleviate the pain. Shaking his head, he looks at Agent6.

"About," he says, moving his body slightly so he can utter the word, "Peace."

Agent6 nods, then half chuckles before looking away down towards the water.

"Good," he says eventually, and then looks back at Dobbs as if considering something before nodding again. "Very good."

As Dobbs bursts out laughing he reflexively clutches his side but the more it hurts, the more he laughs.

"You alright?" Bolivar asks.

"Yeah, sure, just dehydrated I think, or maybe I pulled a muscle."

"This is what you came here for though isn't it?" Bolivar says.

"It's exactly what you wanted, isn't it Dobbs?" Swifty follows.

"Go on then, spill the fucking beans. What happened next?"

Dobbs pours water down his throat, praying it's not a stone he can feel in his kidney. He's right at the perfect age for them but in absolutely the wrong place to be trying to clear one.

'Shit,' he thinks to himself, panic rising up within him, 'there's not even a boat to get back.'

Instead he just downs more water and to his relief the pain subsides a little, allowing him to relax enough to start to recount how he'd seen Agent6 and The Brigadier. The further he gets into the story though, the more he finds himself struggling to believe it. It's almost as though his words are being governed by this pain in his kidney and eventually he just dries up after he reaches the part where the mosquitoes landed all over him.

"'Where would you rather be?' Bolivar muses, staring at him. "What was that then? Who was it?"

"I don't know," he lies, looking away and contorting his body uncomfortably.

"You sure you're alright, man?" Bolivar asks again, looking concerned.

"Shit. You gotta get this down Dobbsy," Swifty blasts as he gets up and goes to see how lunch is developing. He returns a few moments later with the news that it's all ready and they all go into the small *maloka* and huddle round the smoky fire for protection against the mosquitoes as they eat. Juan, the caretaker who looks after the place when Agent6 is not about has, as always, arisen before the sun and caught enough fish for the whole day and a huge pile of them, all absolutely crammed with tiny bones, circle the grate on the fire. Agent6 and the indigenous workers dig in, skillfully removing the bones, whilst Dobbs and Bolivar have to spend five minutes on each mouthful, plucking the tiny spines from their mouths one or two at a time. Nonetheless they're a crispy delight and, served with boiled eggs and rice followed by a fruit salad, it's simply heavenly.

Lunch over, Swifty disappears off to allocate tasks whilst Agent6 gets the backgammon board ready for the first game. Meanwhile Dobbs is so overflowing with energy that he has to go and sit on his own down by the water and start ranting into his voice recorder. Soon enough, the children come down again, drawn by the sight of the crazy gringo talking to himself. He tries to communicate with odd words but they're far more fascinated by the phone and listening to themselves on playback than trying to make sense of his crap Spanish and before long the mozzies are back and everything just begins to seem a bit too much for him. The pain in his kidney is starting to make him feel like he's close to a complete nervous breakdown, unable to contain the energy of this burning bliss which is now so intense it's driving him almost to the point of screaming rage. Those nasty crocodiles in his mind are back too, thoughts he so wishes he could push back down, but which keep surfacing and circling closer until he's in such an unstable space that his only hope is to simply stay with his breath, sometimes panting fast and shallow then taking slow, deep breaths immediately followed by long, laboured exhalations through pursed lips as if trying to blow a trumpet. In short, Dobbs is struggling. He'd love to just take off in the boat and find Gatita but that's all too much of a complicated story for his mind to engage with too. Strangely though, he can't help feeling she's somehow there with him already, just like that first time they'd met and he'd felt her presence before he'd seen her.

But alas, there's no boat and no Gatita, nor has anyone mentioned The Brigadier since the previous night. Whether he made it back or not, no one would cast aspersions on his character; they all know the weight he is carrying.

'But he'll make it back,' Dobbs thinks. 'One way or another, he'll come back with that chainsaw.'

Finally, he retreats back to the net with the others. Agent6 and Bolivar are in the last throes of a game of backgammon whilst Swifty, as always, is in the middle of a million tasks, like a kid in an adventure playground building a camp. Dobbs just sits and strums his ukulele.

Then, in the distance, a faint noise becomes audible, gradually getting louder until it is unmistakable. Agent6 glances across at Dobbs, holding his gaze for a moment. Sure enough the distant sound develops into a distinct frequency and suddenly everyone's ears prick up. Agent6 jumps up and immediately heads down to the water's edge with Bolivar slowly lagging behind, rolling a cigarette. As they stand there Swifty and some of the indigenous workers join them to see what boat the pecki-pecki's pushing.

Dobbs just watches from the net. He can hear the sound of the *pecki-pecki* getting closer and closer and just when it sounds crystal clear the revs drop down. All eyes are now focused on the river as the *Christina* suddenly slips into sight, The Brigadier standing at the bow like an Indian chieftain with the biggest smile across his face. The sight brings a tear to Dobbs's eye. He watches as The Brigadier jumps off the vessel, painter in hand, and ties her to her mooring. Dobbs can see him greeting everyone then casting about as if looking for something before narrowing his eyes and glancing up at the main *maloka* to where Dobbs is sitting and giving a nod of greeting. He suspects The Brigadier can't actually see him in the shaded recess of the net but he waves back anyway and after a moment Elder comes out from below the *techo* roofing of the boat laden with bags and followed by a girl who Dobbs doesn't recognize, shorter than The Brigadier and, by the looks of her, a bit of a character.

Then, finally, one last passenger emerges. Unmistakably female, she's taller than the first girl. A baseball cap conceals her face but something about her has Dobbs transfixed. Stepping ashore, she removes the cap to let her long, silky hair fall free, catching the golden rays of sun as it ruffles in the gentle breeze. Dobbs's mouth drops open in utter disbelief. It's his dream come true.

'Brigadier,' he thinks to himself, 'you little beauty! You really are an angel with a dirty face, aren't you? This must be my bloody birthday.'

God Spotting

"What's the word for the day then, Dobbs?" Bolivar shouts as he enters the net. All the others apart from Gatita, who is lagging back just checking out the space, follow close behind.

"*Loco. Muy loco,*" replies Dobbs, still sitting in front of his notepad in shock. Bolivar just beams the broadest grin, shaking his head at his expression.

Meanwhile Gatita's looking round at the *maloka*, checking out the space. She still hasn't actually made eye contact with Dobbs who's holding his space steady, wondering what she's doing here and hoping it's as obvious as the nose on his face. Finally she turns to face him though and there's a distinct moment as everyone seems to sense how much Dobbs is struggling with the intensity of the situation. Gatita can clearly tell it's difficult for him but at the same time absolutely everything he could ever ask for in the whole universe is here right now. To Dobbs it seems she's literally been sent by the gods to stop him from blowing his mind - express delivery, straight into jungle. "*Como estas?*" she says at last, pouting a smile that seems more curiosity than come-on.

Dobbs is so overwhelmed he doesn't quite know what to say so he says nothing, just bites his lip, nods and smiles without ever taking his eyes off her.

"*Bien,*" he finally whispers.

The Brigadier is looking unfeasibly cool and wearing a half-smarmy grin that somehow seems to span right across his face as he gestures at Dobbs, giving him the exact same wink as in the *Ayahuasca* vision the previous night.

"You drank again?" It's more of a statement than an answer.

"Yeah. I saw you, funnily enough - on the other side."

"I know," he responds immediately, a strange twinkle in his eye.

Dobbs chuckles at that but knowing The Brigadier he probably really does know, on some crazy level.

"Heavy night with the mosquitoes though. I woke with…"

"Yeah, we know what you woke with Dobbs: Morning Glory," The Brigadier shoots out across the space, sniggering away as he catches Bolivar's eye.

Gatita looks over at Agent6quizzically but in the end it's Bolivar who fills in the details.

"Morning Glory; when a man wakes up with a – you know," and places his left hand on the back of his right elbow whilst bringing his forearm up, fist clenched, grinning at Gatita.

Dobbs blushes butGatita laughs along with everyone else. He feels very out of his depth, especially with Agent6 and The Brigadier racing off in Spanish twenty to the dozen. The other girl, to whom Dobbs has not yet been introduced, has seated herself on one of the two chairs hand crafted by the indigenous work crew which, considering they were carved with a chainsaw, appear very elegant. Their chunky bases are set low to the ground like coffee tables and their reclined backrestsare built for just kicking back, feet up, and soaking up the utter fullness of the Amazon experience. Whoever she is, she looks a picture perched on that chair, giggling along to the tone of the whole conversation. Dobbs catches her eye;

"Hola."

As he does so both Agent6 and The Brigadier shout, in unison,

"Don't go changing lanes, Dobbs!"

Dobbs doesn't respond to the comment at all but keeps his eyes on the girl, smiling.She rattles something off to him in Spanish. He picks up odd bits but when he tries to respond he's so nervous everything comes out all wrong.

"Ah, perdon, me Espanol no esbueno. Como se llama?"

"Estella. Errr - no problema, ah. Me entiendo pocito English and you entiendo a little Spanish tambien."

He can immediately see how relaxed the girl is but also that she's a wild one at the same time. She's short and cute with revealing rips in her jeans and a t-shirt that, without any bra beneath, leaves very little to the imagination. She's very sexy in a scruffy kind of way but relaxed with it and she looks easily versatile enough to cope with The Brigadier's crazy energy. She's clearly taken by his wild blue eyes and his deep, croaky voice, along with his super cool, Iquitos slang and his wildly animated faces. When he's on form he's such a kid, a born performer. Agent6 can play that game with him as far as it goes and suddenly they're a double act again, just like old times.

"Pocito - si," Dobbs answers but he's a little overwhelmed to even try to compete with all the banter. Instead he just stares at Gatita, nodding. Her presence seems so surreal, almost merging with the jungle, unlike Estella who seems more of a late night city, down

and dirty street performer type. She's right up The Brigadier's street.

Agent6 turns to Dobbs. "So, what *is* the word for the day then, Dobbs?"

Dobbs doesn't look at Agent6. He's really struggling with the intensity and perhaps Agent6 is sensing he needs a bit of encouragement to break the ice of his own disbelief. He takes a deep breath, keeping his eyes on Gatita. He wants to say 'Peace', as that is the overriding emotion which is juddering through him in such massive bolts, or perhaps even 'Love, but it would all just sound too hippie and not really busting through to where he's at. Instead he stares into Gatita's eyes and says the first Spanish word that comes to mind:

"*Quiero.*"

Agent6 bursts out laughing. "Want? Yeah, we all know what you want!"

Gatita immediately looks away but at least she knows exactly where she stands with Dobbs right now. As for Dobbs it's a bit embarrassing to be put so much on the spot, especially in the state he is in, completely blown open and so obviously wanting Gatita so very badly – both for her beautiful soul and her sweet, gorgeous humanity. He wishes he could move through the fear of what he wants and overcome the torture of the doubt and disbelief of everything that's going down right now, the feeling the of absolute insanity inside. There's nothing else he can say right now, though; this world in which he has incarnated has finally and properly done him in.

Turning to Gatita, Agent6 smiles.

"Teach him some new words Gatita, for fuck's sake," he says.

Dobbs half chuckles at the comment. She's not really catching him at his best. He doesn't even know if he really *has* a best and just wants to weep, to cry his eyes out like a baby. He's just feels laid so bare. The intentions of his friends have been so utterly beautiful it almost burns him to feel all the support they have given him through his crazy process. They had all become true men through the endeavour of living their lives to the absolute fullest; always up for it. They've all come through for him in their own way and he feels he could ask for no more of the universe than to have friends of this calibre by his side. They are all more than merely Earth brothers now. They are Soul brothers.

Gatita peers up at Dobbs and smiles briefly at him before disappearing behind those shields of hers again, almost as if she's barely there. The boyish banter is intense and Dobbs knows it was probably a daft thing to say that he wants her so blatantly but it sometimes seems to him that only the blatant truth is destined to come out of his mouth, and he feels unable to play any games with Gatita at all. His only hope is the absolute truth. There's always more comfort in the truth, and besides he's got no fast quips in him whatsoever. She's a sophisticated lady and he's only met a handful of women that manage to exist in the space she occupies, beyond the realms of their governing doubt. Then again perhaps behind that cool façade she too is struggling with where she stands with him?

"Where is it then?" Demands Swifty, who's been calmly observing the whole goings on with a subtle grin across his face.

"What?" The Brigadier asks.

"*What*? The fucking chainsaw. They fix it?"

"Nah. Got another one off 'em. Made sure it was a good one though. Not like that piece of shit."

Swifty nods at him, half looking away in guilt at buying it in the first place. Then he chuckles.

"Nice one."

"He didn't want to, mind, and then he wanted more money."

"You give it him?" Agent6 immediately asks.

"Did I fuck!"

Dobbs is half listening to the conversation but more paying attention to Gatita, who has now retrieved something from her bag. It looks like a bonsai tree made of thick copper or bronze wire. She then pulls out a selection of tools and places them on the table before sitting down and just observing the tree.

"Wow, so this is one of your trees?"

Gatita looks up, smiling. "Si," she says simply.

"Can I see?"

She nods but doesn't pass it straight away so he reaches over to take the tree off her but as he does he slowly runs his fingertips up the back of her hands, wanting just to feel her skin and to know that all this is really happening and not just some extension of his dream. Finally he picks up the tree. Holding it high enough so he can cast his gaze upon her as well as the tree, he examines the exquisite beauty of her work.

"Beautiful. It's like the trees in the dream world Gatita. The copper somehow captures that effect you see where everything is illuminated by its own inner light," he says, turning the tree and observing the countless stretches of wires doubled up and coiled round at the core. The densest mass serves as the trunk and then it splits off into thinner sections acting as the branches. Finally they divide into countless double lengths which serve as the twigs with tiny leaves, carefully twisted and shaped, running along each length and intricately positioned beads serving as the fruits.

"It seems so oddly animated, so elegant, Gatita," he whispers, admiring the tree and then placing it back before her.

Gatita just smiles and disappears into back into her tree-craft, giggling a bit at the endless innuendo and banter as Dobbs sits, trying to be social but just feeling her presence and wanting her.

Finally everyone gets up to check out the new chainsaw and Dobbs seizes the opportunity to sit next to Gatita and puts his hand on her leg. She just calmly smiles and then he pulls her leg back over the bench so that she faces him. He pulls off her sun glasses and pushes her hair back behind her ears, examining her face.

"You are so beautiful, Gatita."

She really has absolutely blown his mind. She wears no makeup and seems totally unaffected by the temperature apart from her hair, which has a silky dampness. She's clearly aware that that he's transfixed by her presence and yet seems completely uncompromised by that or by the instability he could bring into her life with his impermanence.

That's mainly what's tearing him apart - the notion that he's deceiving her, as he's stuck in the middle of everything. He could hurt her - he could hurt himself - and yet she feels like an agent sent from that place he's just visited, sent here to hold his hand and help him deal with whatever is happening to him so he doesn't go 'ping'. He feels as if she's come to stop him falling into that terrible abyss of doubt that imprisons direct action in the impotent prism of hope and want and so, moving through his want, he finally leans forward and kisses her. He'd thought it might be awkward but it's so stupidly easy and just like that the noise of all the interference, of all the doubt and anxiety in his head just dissipates into thin air.

When he finally pulls away from their embrace her eyes are locked onto his, yet searching his whole face.

"What do you want to do?" she finally asks.

"There's a question!"

But she does not blush or shy from the comment. She is as cool as ice, waiting for his response.

"Well...I want to slope off with you."

Gatita looks around and then back at Dobbs.

"Where?"

Dobbs looks about and as he does he realizes how rude it would be to drag her off somewhere for the intimacy he has running through his head. Not that there is anywhere to drag her off *to*. And then he looks down at the river.

"Let's take the boat."

"OK," she says without delay.

"Great. You want the very fine and dandy *Christina* or you want a dugout?"

Gatita peers down at the water. The scene is so utterly beautiful, the river drenched in the golden rays raining down on the water and busting through the trees in beams and shards. The tiny dugout looks so romantic. She smiles as she takes in the scene.

"Dugout!"

"Good choice. We can do some *God-spotting*," Dobbs whispers, wondering how she'll respond to that idea and even if she knows what he's talking about. Of course she knows *God-spotting*. She's a jungle goddess, he suddenly thinks.

She just nods at the idea.

In less than half an hour they've paddled far enough up river to stop and let the boat drift back down slowly with the current. Only the ripples caused by its slow movement can be seen now in the still water, slowly moving out from the vessel. They're tiny. Dobbs lies back, gently pulling Gatita with him so they're both lying with their heads resting on the side of the hull, looking out at the jungle's reflection in the water.

The tiny dugout - effectively half a log carved into a canoe shape has apparently been hollowed out with a controlled fire. The hull, which has to be kept wet to stop it cracking, would be uncomfortable but for the pure bliss of holding Gatita. Just to be able to run his hands through her hair is heavenly.

"You know what we're doing, right?" he asks, chuckling.

"*Si. God spotting*," Gatita whispers with a dry chuckle loaded with a warm, calming depth and undertones of utter seduction which drive Dobbs crazy. He squeezes her even tighter.

"This must be regular practice for a shamanic jungle *chica* like you," he whispers.

Gatita doesn't respond to the comment. She seems only to respond to his touch.

He senses that her position must be a little difficult on her lower back although it feels as if she has a good proportion of her body weight supported on his.

"Your back is OK like that, Gatita?" he asks.

"It's OK."

They lie in the boat, loosely holding their gaze at the focal point where land meets water and watching the world pass by as the river takes them slowly back down towards the retreat. The water is like a mirror and the sun is still quite high above, saturating them with radiant rays of warmth balanced by a gentle breeze loaded with the rich, sweet aroma of vibrant green Amazonas. The airways are jam-packed with animal mating calls and it is pure heaven on a stick. They just lie very still, allowing the reflection in the water to merge with the jungle above and the faces of the gods to spring forth in completely three-dimensional flashes that disappear as fast as they appear. They seem so unbelievably similar to the *Ayahuasca* visions. Suddenly a dragon's face appears, but a Chinese dragon, or perhaps, Tibetan.

"Wow!" whispers Dobbs. And just as he takes sight of the god face it disorganises itself back into the chaos of the jungle again. Then a steady flow of faces appear one after the other, like angelic beings - or sometimes just eyes, peering at them.

"Isn't it amazing how nature creates half and light creates the other half," Dobbs says, observing how they exist only in the symmetry of reflection and are revealed only by looking sideways.

"It makes me think of the words spoken to me last night. I was told I'm going to write a book and when I asked, 'what will I say?' the Voice said, 'you write half and I'll write half.'"

Gatita tries to look round, as if expecting something more.

"It's all so stupidly incredible. It's beyond anything fictional I could ever think of writing."

He tries to breathe through the intensity of what that means. The emotional mass that the message carried. The apparent building material of this other world. The bricks humanity carries up the mountain to build its castle in the skies.

"I think this is what heaven is like Gatita," he says, tears running down his face. "Being here with you I can exist in that space I was in last night without any sense of disbelief in anything anymore."

The whole world seems restored into the great miracle it truly is again. He can see it and he can feel it as he runs his fingers through Gatita's hair.

"La selva?" Gatita whispers observing his fascination with the jungle.

"Yeah. I can feel it Gatita. I can feel the intensity of the beauty. This is what the ego opted out of, isn't it? This is why the ego only comes in thought. It cried out to God: 'Why do I have to feel sadness when I do wrong?' It wanted to break from the sadness but it cannot come with us in just thought anymore Gatita. It looks like we're all about to find out what the ego really is at last. It's about to enter."

"You were told this? You went to the same place?"

"Yeah, but I didn't have to die to go through this time. It's just equality, isn't it? What's right for one soul *must* be right for all souls. The universe is utterly equal and fair. If death grants access to the other side than that has to be the rule for all souls. I had to die to see the other side. To completely let go of this world is to completely take a grip on another world. It's a gamble. A leap of faith. Trust; the emotional mass that empowers all manifestation. I'm beginning to think it might manifest miracles. Something brought you to me and something brought me here. But it's here Gatita: Heaven. All this beauty with this feeling of being, well, with you right here. It seems impossible that this feeling can exist. It just makes me want to kiss you Gatita, but I'll probably sink the boat," he laughs, squeezing her tighter.

"It just seems impossible that you're here, with me, right now. Like right now. It's more than just good timing." Tears run down his face.

She can no more see his face then he can see hers but he can feel her energy.

"It's as impossible as seeing these gods I see right now in the reflections and is no more impossible than what happened last night."

"You all drank?"

"No, just me and Agent6. The others didn't want to. I think I'm scaring them off a bit Gatita."

"Was it good or bad?"

411

"It was…" And he's really not sure how to describe the events, "…very good. I saw you and you…you were an angel. You *are* an angel Gatita. You're incredibly beautiful on this side, but on the other side? You're a goddess. You are an ambassador of whoever or whatever that thing is on the other side that spoke to me. I think, somehow, we all are. You are pure, blinding radiance Gatita. I don't know what the bloody hell is going on, but all my friends seem to be turning into angels. It was all so amazing and all so very full on."

"It just said you'd write a book?"

Dobbs can't bring himself to utter the fundamental words he'd been given to pass on. They were simply too mad. The exact words could *only* ever exist in a book. He could never utter them. Though he could try to translate them as he understood them the message burns not just in his mind but in every cell of his body. He doesn't understand yet but somehow everything still seems to rest on just one point. To be specific, it seems to rest on his kidney.

"It was the single most intense thing that has ever happened to me, Gatita. It said I'd write about peace. And when I asked 'what will I say?' It said; 'you write half, and I'll write half'."

"It was strong?"

"I don't know. It was very intense. It just feels like a massive ball of emotion inside of me now but a ball of bliss instead of this pain I feel I've been carrying. It's done something to my side, too" he says, suddenly deciding not to get too visceral and to try to ignore the kidney ache, which is now adding to the discomfort of his position.

"When I touch it I think of…Hong Kong. How mad is that?"

"'You write half and I'll write half?'" Gatita repeats. "What does that mean?"

"I'm not sure. I think it's going to tell me the story of the ego, whatever it really is. I'm not sure how it will tell me."

"You never wonder why you chose parents that channel?"

"Yeah," and tears run down his cheeks at the thought. "Yeah, but it kind of freaked me out as well, you know. An endless flow of terminally ill people coming…and going."

"You think I'm becoming a channel?"

"I think you are a channel. All are channels…ah?"

"Yeah, it's true."

"I never wanted much to be a channel though. I found it all a bit too weird I suppose. I much prefer the…"

412

"The *Ayahuasca* adventure? Where you get to remember everything - rather than the channelling, when someone else gets a message but you remember nothing?"

"Yeah," he says over a half chuckle, "I suppose I kind of want to be in on the show as well. I used to find the whole thing a bit creepy when I was a kid. No one ever had an opinion on it. They didn't know what to say. It's strange, this place I'm in now. I'm in this blissful cocoon that seems to allow me to see everything so clearly. Of course God, or whatever that is, meets us at the doorway of ourselves, a door we can only knock upon with our peaceful intentions alone, wherever we choose to find it. It could be through making a tree Gatita. Gandhi found that door weaving cloth. I can see why the governments of the world so often want to keep us in war and chaos. It blinds us from the truth. They cause us to disconnect from our higher state of consciousness by simply pushing us below the karmic threshold where the door to ourselves opens by making us ashamed to look at ourselves."

And as he ponders on those words suddenly he exclaims, "I mean - fuck - what makes a person want to become a channel? Few would surely want to do it as, like, a career option. There has to be a driving force? It's such a weird thing to want to do. Well, in Britain at least, where the witch hunt will allow the nuclear obsession to continue until God is scientifically proven and labelled in a jar, ready to be sold to the highest bidder, and anyone who threatens a Godless realm and stands up in the name of true peace is frowned upon. It won't be too long before they're locking up the shamans again in my homeland. Already the ceremonies are all going underground and soon the only way to pass on the whereabouts of sacred ceremonies will be by not letting the information come close to anything electronic; like non-electronic transfer."

Suddenly he stops to think of the words he's spoken.

"Non-electronic transfer; NET. Shit! Soon only spoken word will be a clear channel to organise ceremonies and free parties in my country. Maybe now is a good time to learn how to connect - like my folks - without taking anything. Maybe I'm hiding behind the *Ayahuasca* because the truth scares me - or at least scares part of me."

"Why?"

"I think it takes a genuine desperation to be a channel. I don't think want or hope cuts it like something stuck on the wish list along with the standard threesome and world peace."

He squeezes her tighter and runs his fingers through her hair. Her whole posture seems to curl over his abdomen like a snake and she feels so fluid in his arms.

"There's something locked in my side Gatita. I feel that the *Ayahuasca* is asking me to let go of all my old pain: to make room for something new and exciting."

"Your lives are all so exciting."

"It seems that way Gatita but Britain is a battlefield of utter self doubt. Few see their own beauty. They are blinded by perpetual war and lost in the world of television that peddles a message offear, debt, and obsolescence."

Suddenly he curves away from her with the pain in his kidney.

"Pain?"

"Yeah. This fucker's going to take me on a bit of a journey, that's all. I think I'm going to release a stone Gatita. Seems like there's nothing like a bit of excruciating pain to wake you up sometimes and bring you back from your thoughts to the vibrancy of the absolute here-and-now, even if it has to nearly fucking kill you in the process."

"The pain takes me to a place I'd forgotten," he says, moving as if trying to stir it up and touch the emotional mass that has perhaps compressed itself into a stone.

"Ahh," he gently cries, tears running down his face. "I'm such a fool Gatita. I came here trying to work out who Shakespeare was, like I thought through tracking the emotional mass that it might lead to a secret wisdom that could stop the endless suffering and bring peace back to Earth. It's such a childlike view - silly and innocent really – to think there really is a mindset out there that could break through the pain, like some Secret Power. But of course Shakespeare wasn't a man or a woman: it was a *movement* concealed as a superhero."

Dobbs runs his hands up Gatita's arm, luxuriating in the feeling of her soft, silky skin and the sensation of just her presence with him.

"This must all seem so mad to you Gatita. The *Ayahuasca* has just unlocked so much for me. Everything seems so stupidly obvious from this place. I've been locked onto the idea of an individual who wrote the works of Shakespeare but it's nothing less than the crazy American superhero mentality that has infected my mind; the notion that it takes just one to break through and free the rest. So stupid, so...childish. It was a *movement*. That is what all this has been trying to show me. A political movement boiled down to a single individual. To capture its magic but hide it from those that feared free speech. I'd thought perhaps Francis Bacon had had some vision that enabled him to unify his country: that he'd had a bolt of genius. That it was *his* secret and anonymous name. But I've been so silly, Gatita. Shakespeare was never a man. This has been the whole blag, the big secret that has been carefully concealed that no one should ever know - that Shakespeare was neither man nor woman but a movement that rose up against the Catholic Church, a political peace movement. The thing our governments fear most is that we might know our own minds and, even more terrifying, that we might know our own hearts and unite against the common threat. That humanity can unite not only in war but also in peace. That we can wage peace against war."

"Imagine that; an anonymous peace movement that was up against radical Christians that had taken the word of Jesus to drive war and hate and violate Christ's true teachings of love, peace, compassion and, above all, forgiveness. To step out of oneself and see through another's eyes: true compassion. It was literally a political freedom of speech movement concealing the true teachings of what Christ and every other prophet coming from true peace and love had not merely preached but lived out by the example of their peaceful lives. It was many works from many educated scholars that would have been burnt at the stake for writing such tales of love and light without the full permission and subsequent edit by the Catholic Church, so they used the name Shakespeare - as in to shake a spear and demand the right to speak and to be heard. The Works of Shakespeare are merely the best selection of the whole movement, assembled by Sir Francis Bacon - who ran the literary think tank with the total support of Queen Elizabeth most probably, in an effort to unify the country through a single language: *The Queen's English*."

"Most likely he added *The Tempest* himself, or perhaps his specialty was being a grammarian..."

"Gramm...?"

"Someone who understood and actually invented grammar. They give language dimension. Past present and future. A Grammarian is a Time Lord. I'm nearly forty, Gatita, and I'm just learning Grammar now. Imagine writing always in the now and always

415

observing yourself from beyond yourself, abandoning the concept of 'I'. To witness yourself through new eyes, like seeing an alien. Not who you thought you were but what you are by the toils of what you actually fucking do.

"And the real Shakespeare? It was the Renaissance, Gatita, an awakening to the fact that these Catholic priests peddling death hadn't spoken to God to gain permission to kill in His or Her name. They simply disguised themselves as God and killed whoever questioned their word. They had their codes in dress and manner, which they no doubt actually believed dignified their killing ways and ordained executing our shamans or sending them to prisons to be raped by murderers.

"You see it in every Hollywood blockbuster; the individual super hero mentality. That you can do it on your own and bust through, when it's really a group effort of many. A brotherhood...a sisterhood: Shakespeare represented the peaceful rights of a unified community. A peaceful revolution that rocked the land but discreetly boiled down to a single superhero. It was equivalent of *Reclaim The Streets* in today's world.

"Humanity is finally going to find out who the big, horrible *They* really are, Gatita."

"The Ego?"

"Yeah, I think it's going to tell me the story of The Ego. I don't know how."

How did your parents learn to channel?

"You think I'm becoming a channel like my folks?"

"What do you think?" Gatita says with almost a chuckle.

"I think I just have to write and stay clear of wanting to write and hoping to find the time and just get on it."

"You are...on it."

"Yeah, but nothing's actually written yet. But I've got a funny feeling that if I write this story it will tell me the story of Ego. I think it's all been about the relationship. If The Ego's been pulling us down, we must have been pulling *It* up."

Gatita struggles to look back at Dobbs's face but more acknowledges his presence in the attempt to see him.

"So you found your story?"

"Yeah. It's just a long version of a children's rhyme I realise now:
Humpty Dumpty sat on a wall
Humpty Dumpty had a great fall.

All the King's horses and all the King's men
Couldn't put Humpty together again.
"Do you know it?"

"I've heard it."

"The message is so simple. We all need to step off the dividing wall between war and peace and be, speak...vote for one or the other: War or Peace."

"It's choice time. Judgment Day is finally here. The wall that will allow only one to enter. Shakespeare was just one of the bricks in the wall of awareness that was the Renaissance. The impenetrable wall that I'm sensing is a new level of that same awareness. War will not break through. People in my country and the whole wide world will no longer be able to live in a tyranny that imposes the order of war and the dumping of depleted uranium on those who will not live under the order of pain to fund the lifestyles of the elite. They will wake to realize that there is no wall other than themselves. They are the walls and they are the fence sitters in their silent consent. Only a Humpty sits on the dividing wall of *decisionlessness*. Many will doubt, because doubt is what the ego does.

"Doubt is the Ego's only tool. If one Englishman or Englishwoman comes forth and says 'I voted for depleted uranium to be dumped on innocent women and children,' I'll stand corrected. Ten million people died in the last war when Iraq invaded Iran. Ten million, Gatita. But this time Iraq will not be invading for us. It will be Britain that has to fight this fight and we'll be on our own. All other nations will stand aside and abandon us in our time of need."

"It's so clear to you?"

"Painfully clear Gatita. It's all just pure karma. You know, my stepfather who's the channel only ever told me one bedtime story: The Tale of, *The Little Boy Who Cried Wolf.* You know the tale?"

"Si."

"If we cry wolf again we won't have a chance. Something is driving us into this wall. It's as though the whole thing is being set to collide with the wall of a raised karmic vibration. It's like The Ego wants humanity to bust through its own feelings. But it won't work, whatever they're up to. No other country will be able to gain support from their people to join our crusade. We are simply being sacrificed to implement a New World Order; an order that simply cannot be. We need a New World Consensus. An economy built on peace and wellbeing, not war, pain, obsolescence and debt."

"Everyone knows how our governments ask us if we are willing to fight. They cut off our money and food and then they make the sacrifice, an offering to the gods of war. The big *They* - whoever they are – who seem terrified of this prophesised new level of awareness, judging by all the so called 'anti-terrorism' laws that have been implemented to restrict the people's freedom of expression at every juncture. I'm guessing that whoever *they* are, they've hit this same wall before, a long time ago. Either way, when humanity goes into the house of feeling, overriding thought, only a global consensus can operate. Because emotion is like water; you can only compress it so much before it explodes, whereby it immediately equalises the force acting upon it. Hydrogen and oxygen, together, are highly explosive. Trying to 'kettle' emotion is big bang material. The masses will not take orders any more. It's the order of the dollar, isn't it? The order to give nine-tenths of all that we are to war. The dollar is the pain that is killing us. Is it so hard to flick the switch from 'War' to 'Peace', rather than continue to accept this pernicious order of perpetuated war with only a *hope* for peace? Is that all humanity is worth: Just a little splash of hope? That's not enough anymore."

"I don't even know if I could find the words to capture just one of the tiny sun beams raining down on your face right now," he whispers, squeezing her tight and half laughing, half crying at the impossibility of the task.

"The wonder of what it is to breathe just one lungful of jungle air into my core. How do you touch any of that with words Gatita? Let alone even *begin* to touch that other world that we seem to have another foot in. It all feels a little impossible right now. I'm not sure how to lock my sights on to it at all. It's there though Gatita. And at the same time it's like the answers are also right there, just waiting, in the abundance of the Unified Field. the Field of Peace. I can literally feel the answers there. It's like Stephen Hawking's said: '*Knowledge is what you know. Wisdom is what you are.*' We can learn the words Christ spoke, like an actor learning a script, or we can embody the wisdom of Peace and then speak the wisdom of Christ. Fear is the only thing that stands between me and that wisdom now."

He sighs, feeling his throbbing kidney.

"An emotional wall?"

"Yeah. The Cleaners are coming. I don't know how it works. Maybe our solar system hits this place every twenty six thousand years as it cuts through the central plane of the Galaxy. It takes about a thousand years to move through and to get the same distance on the other side, some reckon. I don't know how it happens but I sense something big is happening inside of me that's brought me here."

"Humanity, whether it likes it or not, has a thousand years of quite intense feeling ahead of it. What feels wrong will feel really wrong. Racial cleansing is seriously going to increase the need for Prozac, but it just won't touch the sides of this sadness. But then genocide never bodes well. If we are coming into the cycle of our sun, when it docks into the pit stop for overhaul and repairs then we must become the technicians. We are becoming the cleaners to sort out the mess. It is the wall of our true nature. Feelings: coming back to the heart. It's encoded in our genes, what scientists call 'Junk DNA'. For the first time, the masses will be able to feel what is being done in their name and be forced to take emotional responsibility, an unnecessary burden for those who aren't directly perpetrating the crimes other than with their silent consent, just hoping as hard as they can and wondering why their hope isn't actually stopping anything. Even if it they stand on tiptoe, twist their right ear with their left hand, place the pinky of the right hand up their bloody nose and waggle two fingers at *Proslairo* whilst hoping so hard they could pinch off a loaf, he still won't stop the killing. That kind of hope is only sadness if it is not hooked up to direct action, and only serves to perpetuates war. It's a *prayerless*, Godless, gutless *want*."

"I tell you, Gatita, no amount of Prozac will be able to ease the pain of this coming war and the more debt they throw at it, the worse it will get. Only the recognition of *real value* can stop this. Debt is effectively being used to rob the people and make them pay interest on their own wealth, to fund war and pain. In its current state, it attempts to take that which is not being given. Thus it attracts a karmic debt by its very action and it's going to hit this karmic wall. It will be like a tsunami. An economic tsunami."

Dobbs peers out at the jungle around him. They've long since drifted past the lodge and the sun is falling behind the trees a little now. He feels like he's in a cocoon with Gatita. Perhaps when he finally emerges from the dugout he will be a butterfly.

"I think we've gone with the flow long enough, Gatita. Might be time to start paddling."

After some time, they've finally paddled all the way back up to the lodge. The light will soon be failing and, Dobbs knows, the mozzies are on their way. Now is the perfect time to create a secluded space where he and Gatita can spend the night. There's only one obvious place and no sooner has he cast his eyes on it than Agent6 notices. Wandering over, he brings his hand down on Dobbs's shoulder.

"Eyeing up the Don suite, I see."

"Well, funny you should say that. Is that cool?"

Agent6 nods.

"How come you never got it on with Gatita?" Dobbs asks. "How is that possible?"

"Had another story. She's just been a mate. And you know Iquitos; there's lots of stories going on here. It's a crazy city full of, well…

"Crazy fucking people!" Dobbs finishes the sentence, grinning. "I fit right in here."

After food, chat and laughter, Dobbs gently squeezes Gatita's hand and they slope off together toAgent6's *maloka* where he has already hung his new, completely sealed mosquito net and made up a little love nest of sleeping bags and blankets. The pain in his side is still persisting, seeming to almost earth his focus to the here-and-now.

Lying down on his belly, Gatita massages his back, applying light pressure between his ribs, and each time it just releases massive floods of emotion and endless streams of tears. It's like bolts of lightning are shooting from her fingers with every stroke, and yet her touch is so gentle. He can't understand where all this pain and sadness is coming from. It's as though a lifetime of sadness has been stored in his back. All he can do is weep, and try to release the intensity of all that surfaces. He doesn't know if she truly understands the burden she is helping him to bear but eventually the massage fuses into an embrace and they make love for what seems all night long.

When he wakes to the splendour of the jungle and the gorgeous woman lying next to him he can barely believe she is really there. It all just seems unbelievable. He wants to pull her close and make love to her again but she's somewhere far away. Suddenly the pain in his side flares again but this time far more intense. A part of him wants to run from what he knows he has to release. That his ego is apparently centred mostly there seems utterly bizarre and yet that is how it feels. Part of him wants to deny it. The ultimate fear is still locked inside of him - the fear of arriving at himself. He's travelled all over the world to realize that *he* is his final destination, that all he has been through was not so much a separation from ego as much as the knowledge of its true state of being. That it really was a *Being*.

Silent Consent

Gatita and Dobbs spend Friday enjoying the day with the whole crew. It's a fun day, with trips up the river, swimming, fetching *techo*, smoking reefers and playing music. Dobbs is endlessly stealing kisses from Gatita, who knows she's doing something massive for his process, providing psychic tuning variations to the vehicle of his intention.

Dobbs's entire life, wherever it had seemingly been heading, has completely altered its course. For two years he's been trapped in the eye of a terrible storm, totally snared in that tiny space that exists between past and future. He has been blown along by a blast of laughing gas that turned time into a tempest, and thus could only go where the moment blew him. Finally, though, he has found himself, in the centre of the Amazon, beached on the island of his own bliss with only forgiveness for all beings in his heart. The temple of Now has become the only sanctuary from all the insanity he has left behind.

All, however, is not as fine and dandy as it looks. Another storm is brewing up and a divide is rapidly developing between The Brigadier and Estella. Well, The Brigadier and everyone really. But Estella is definitely getting the brunt of it, as no one else is prepared to go under the wheels of that anymore. Not unless there's a concerted effort to firstly acknowledge the fundamental problem and at least a want or hope to remedy it, or even a genuine moment of awareness to assess the true prognosis of his present condition. Nothing the poor girl says or does can bring a smile to his face and she is only just starting to understand the severity of his problem. He's heading right back into rage, rattling. No one can do anything do for him when he's in that state.

Gatita sits, crafting her tree, and Dobbs is finally writing in the pad that he's carried around for the last two years. He knows in his heart that The Brigadier has always lived his life more than to the brim. He overflows with life, hungry for the maximum of adventure all of the time. His objective has always been to just bust through fear and make everyone feel special and worthy and even in this terrible dog fight with the devil he's the only victim really. He's always tried his absolute best and wanted the best for all he loves in Dobbs's eyes but it seems he feels he's failed in places and the guilt of that has driven him ever deeper into his dependence upon pestilence, especially in the last few years. To

Dobbs it seems that sometimes a tempest just comes and takes you away and all the love in the world is not enough to alter the course of the bigger, divine plan that has decided to temporarily make you the lead role in the greatest performance ever known. However mad it might sometimes have seemed though, and however relentlessly those winds of change bore down, The Brigadier, has never just let life happen to him. He's chosen wild adventure every time; he never left it down to merely hope and want but grabbed it with both hands. If all you ever take from this world is your character, then when The Brigadier does finally leaves this world it won't be empty handed. In Dobbs's eyes he's filled his boots.

It has been blissful to see him just like the old days for a while, coming through for his friends even when the odds were so stacked against him. Dobbs so doesn't want to lose him to this monster but it is painful to watch how he is being consumed by the wild withdrawal which comes in bouts, moment by moment, minute by minute, hour by hour. All Dobbs can do is put a golden ring of light around him and feel the pain in his kidney, which somehow helps him touch The Brigadier's pain a little.

But his kidney is starting to get considerably worse and it demands his moment-to-moment attention to bring his awareness to bear and gently breathe through the pain and fear he's carried, concealed in his denial and doubt and lodged in the viscera of his body, waiting for the day when he's man enough to confront his own karma. A karma he is now convinced will make clear his own sacred path on this Earth, and give him the courage to walk it. Only by moving through his fear can he unlock the disbelief that stands between him and his divine purpose.

Beyond the nagging pain and The Brigadier's struggles the days have been pure bliss though. All of them, together, happily building their dreams, loving their lives and walking their talk. Dobbs can see that no way is The Brigadier going to stay at the retreat and do what he so needs to do. He needs professional help but no one can afford it, he doesn't want it and there's no way he's going back to the UK anyway - well not yet at least. He's burnt all his bridges back there so it seems he's going to have to ride this crazy fish all the way and give himself to Ego, or whatever that thing is, wholly and completely. On his current bearing the odds are all stacked against him, and yet perhaps his mission has all but been accomplished, and who among us ever really gets out of here alive?

By Saturday the energy has changed even more, and The Brigadier is crumbling. At about the same time, still early in the day, Swifty treads on a nail - a big one - that goes straight through his boot and deep into his foot. He reckons it's not rusty and he doesn't need hospital treatment but he does a big clean up on it anyway, keeping it raised and dosing himself with painkillers and antibiotics - everything that they would probably do in hospital but without all the physical stress of actually getting there.

The Brigadier offers to take Swifty to the hospital but Swifty just wants to keep it up, keep it clean, drink lots of lemon juice and antibiotics and take a rest. Dobbs has to take his hat off to his preparedness - his extensive medical kit far outstrips the description 'first aid' and he could probably perform a full-scale amputation if he needed to - which is, thankfully, doubtful. He's properly cleaned the wound and done all that a hospital would have, plus he doesn't want to give The Brigadier any more of an excuse to bail out on the jungle plan. He's dealt with the problem, and now he just wants some peace and time to recuperate, to clean and dress the wound then sit back and watch the whole place come together from the sidelines like Agent6 - who needs no nails through his feet before he's ready to kick back and put them up. For him a fat spliff suffices just fine. It all seems a very sensible choice to Dobbs and once Swifty's lying in his hammock with Gatita pampering him he seems fine. It's all perfect, except that as soon as Swifty has said he's not going back The Brigadier just says,

"Well I'm going back anyway. Come or don't come."

Everyone tries to persuade him to stay and endure but he won't have it. Finally, just as he's about to leave, Agent6 and Bolivar, no doubt a little green from watching Dobbs get all the booty, decide to go too. After all, a wild city all primed and ready for a bunch of likely lads with the notion of a party on their mind is merely hours away.

"OK, you win. I'll come with ya," Agent6 finally concedes.

"Yeah, wicked," The Brigadier replies, unable to conceal a look of surprise and relief.

"Iquitos on a Saturday night gentleman? Without me? I don't think so!" Bolivar chips in.

It's perfect for Agent6. He's got a foreman left on site with all the workers - an injured foreman who can't speak Spanish, admittedly, but Gatita can happily translate - plus his wingman seems to have

424

disappeared off the radar again. Although at least this time Dobb is lost in bliss and acceptance instead of worry and fear. Besides, his work here is kind of done for the week. It's all just another day in the jungle for a shaman; a *curandero* which, for all intents and purposes, is what he's become. For Dobbs there's still hope for The Brigadier – hope that he might choose a different pathway - but without the *choice* to take on the challenge of withdrawal, hope is all that remains.

***

The others have gone, and Dobbs is lying face down on the floorboards with Gatita massaging him. The pain is now reaching excruciating new peaks, moving in cycles that cause his whole lower back to go into spasms.

"Wow. Shit, it's so painful Gatita. Maybe I should have gone back with the others; it's absolute agony. It's like the base of all my doubt is held in there."

"It's OK."

"It doesn't feel OK," Dobbs grimaces, holding his back as straight as he can and breathing through gritted teeth.

Swifty, wearing a similarly perplexed look, is flat out on the bench on the far side of the net, lost in his own pain and now fighting a fever too. Somehow Dobbs finds it all just so funny and every time the pain reaches its peak he can't help but laugh at the ridiculousness of the situation. Now it's just them in the net and the indigenous workers all in Swifty's *maloka* listening to a tiny radio and preparing for bed, if not already fast asleep. It's very warm and humid and despite his pain Swifty looks so happy it all seems a little surreal. He's lying on the narrow bench almost cocooning himself up in his fever, drifting in and out of consciousness but somehow looking uncharacteristically blissed out.

Suddenly the pain comes. It's the time Dobbs always knew was on its way; a whole new threshold. He groans but it is more of a scream, almost a roar from his very core, and as he does so the words 'olive oil' come into his head.

"Ah, fuck, have we got any olive oil here, Swifty?" he says, half chuckling with the intensity of the pain and half wanting to cry. "Ah, why didn't I get on the fucking boat? I fucking hate hospitals but no way have we got any fucking olive oil here, have we?"

"I can have a look in the kitchen?" Gatita says, trying to help, but Dobbs knows there's none.

"Olive oil?" Swifty suddenly says deliriously, pulling himself from his near slumber.

"Yeah!" Dobbs shrieks, chuckling and yet buckled over in pain, tears running down his face. "Ah, fuck! It's like agonizing bliss!"

"I got a little bit of olive oil in my bag, I think. Side pocket of me rucksack," Swifty says, raising his arm and pointing.

"You're fucking joking!"

Dobbs doesn't wait. He jumps up and runs to the rucksack, ignoring the agony. The tiny bottle is only half full, it's lid taped on with *Gaffer* tape. Dobbs can't help but piss himself laughing at the sight of it as he holds it up.

'What else?' he asks, and the answer that comes to mind is 'Salt, and lemon.' He grabs the salt and finds two huge lemons just sitting on the table in front of him which Swifty must have brought in earlier. Picking up a cup, he pours in the olive oil and half a teaspoon of salt before cutting the lemons in half and squeezing them into the cup. Then, placing his hand over the top of the metal beaker, he shakes it like a fine cocktail. He's of a mind that getting the mixture down might be like drinking *Ayahuasca* so he downs it in one motion, expecting to gag but in fact it's almost pleasant.

Almost immediately the pain morphs into an emotional judder that feels just like that old roller coaster ride at the end of Brighton Pier. He groans again.

"Ahhh! Sorry to sound so weird! I don't think you're quite seeing me at my best, Gatita."

At this Swifty starts laughing which makes Dobbs laugh even more, until tears are running down his face.

"I never thought agony could be so hysterical," he manages to say, and that sets Gatita off too.

"I feel like I'm being transported back to Hong Kong again," he says. It's so painful to touch that space. I'm climbing a mountain. I'm crying my eyes out. Fuck, for a man I seem to have cried so much."

"Only a real man can cry," Gatita whispers, massaging his back

"Ahhh, thank you Gatita," he whispers back, half shaking with the agony and the ecstasy.

"That stuff's like drinking *Ayahuasca*!" he screams out, louder this time. "Ah, just to see the mountain track I'm climbing hurts."

Dobbs knows the mountain well. It was what some called *Lion mountain* on Lantau Island, one of the many outlying islands off Hong Kong and is so called on account of its similarity to a lion, proudly lying recumbent. Dobbs used to love it up there and would be up there almost every day. From the top you can see all of Hong Kong, the New Territories and many other outlying islands.

"I'm at the top of the mountain Gatita, and I'm looking out. Hong Kong is so beautiful. It's not just a big city; it's a massive nature reserve."

"Keep breathing. Deep breaths," Gatita says softly, continuing to massage his back.

"OK," he screams out again, "I remember now. There's been a massive bust on our house and the police had smashed down the door."

"Where?"

"Same place, where I lived in Hong Kong." Tears run down his face. "Ahhh, so sad. Such a mad time. My mate was holding the door with all his might whilst I was throwing all the ganja out the window. But the cops were everywhere and there was, like, two hundred tabs of acid in the fridge. So they got the weed but they never looked in the fridge. It was the acid they were looking for. They kept demanding we tell them where it was, trying to scare us with beatings and long jail sentences. We were shitting bricks. It was the end of a long run of crazy shit and this girl who was hanging out with us all, she kind of lost it in the process. She was a delicate little thing and I had to take her to the loony bin after... I'll never forget her face when I left her there. Fuck me, the way I'm going I might have to pay a visit myself."

"You're not so mad."

"Thank you, Gatita. I guess it was just a long run of...well, life I suppose; of crazy choices. The same shit kept happening over and over. I was always just fucking up and moving on, running from the previous mess. So there I am, climbing Lion Mountain. Crying my eyes out that I'm such a lowly piece of shit. It was like the end of a long ride of total shit. I was a total shit," he sobs, as the tears course freely down his face.

"The only reason I was in Hong Kong was because I'd fucked everything up." He clutches his side, shaking with the memory.

"Ahh, it's so fucking painful. I'd forgotten about all that."

Suddenly he screams out again as a rush of images, snapshots from a forgotten story flood his mind's eye.

427

"I can see myself, Gatita! I'm kneeling at the temple at the top of the mountain and I'm crying my eyes out. I can feel my desperate sadness. Everything just perpetually fucking up. I'm praying. I'm more than praying; I'm shouting. I'm begging to be more than this thing that I am, screaming at…God." Tears run down his cheeks. "I'm begging to be given an opportunity to be better than what I am." And he chuckles suddenly. "And I'm shouting out, over and over again, 'I want to be a writer! I want to be a writer! Is that so much to ask? I just need a break.'"

The tears are streaming down his face in hot torrents now as he sees himself, on his knees, utterly lost in this moment of existential agony.

"This is so crazy! I can see myself, I'm right there. I'm literally right behind myself, watching my past self from behind."

He clutches his side in absolute agony.

"What the fuck is going on, Gatita?" he says as he just observes himself in that other time, more than fifteen years before, a young man crying like a child at the terrible state of his life but beyond the blame of anyone else but himself.

Gatita doesn't answer. She just runs her fingers through his hair, soothing his process.

And then suddenly the words come into his heart, as clear as a bell: 'You see now how you asked for this opportunity. You asked for this. You prayed for this opportunity.'

"Yes," he sobs. "Yes, it's true!" And suddenly he remembers it all. "Yes. I'll do it. I don't know how but I'll do it. I'll do whatever it takes to complete my mission here on Earth. I've come too far to turn back now. There's no way back anyway. Thank you. Thank you." And finally he surrenders and let's go.

Suddenly the pain spikes to an all time excruciating high.

"Ahhhh," he screams out as the feeling of euphoric bliss, near to an all body orgasm moves through him, as he finds himself moving forward, and fusing into the vision of himself on top of that mountain. As he does, he momentarily remembers the beauty that had entered his life right at that moment all those years back - almost looking round to see if he could notice the seamlessly seismic shift that had just occurred in his life without any knowledge whatsoever. The sadness and shame that had just vanished. As he feels the bliss coursing through him now butting hard up against this solid lump of emotional mass in his kidney; his nails, clawing into the floor boards, it finally shifts. And his whole body is consumed into euphoria.

"Ahhh," he screams out, now laughing through the tears. "Ahh, Gatita! I know I keep saying it but you do know that you're beautiful?" And as he pulls her close and kisses here. Thank you. I'm not always this mad, Gatita, I promise. Well, I mean I am. But I'm kind of a nice mad normally. You know what I mean?"

"Si."

The tears are still flooding down his face but they're tears of joy now as all the pain just dissipates into absolute bliss.

"You feel OK?"

"Yeah," and he chuckles, "it's gone. Wow. You know what Gatita; I'm not becoming a channel, I'm becoming a...well, a *psychic detective*. It seems what we're looking at here, Dr Watson, is actually a...a heist.

"A *heist*?" Gatita says with a curious smile.

"Yeah. A robbery. Holy shit, this is nothing short of the greatest gold robbery ever conceived.

"I thought it was showing me the gold because that proved the bankers were shitting bricks. That it was the single pin point evidence of what is driving the Federal Government into war, that this was all economic hegemony. I've been so silly. It's always been about gold from the very beginning. That's what they want; whoever *they* are. I mean, how is it possible to plan a robbery for thousands and thousands of years? Unless Earth is a...vaulted time lock." And he runs his hand up through his sweaty hair. "How do you blow the safe door off one of those? How do you smash a hole through the walls of a dimension?"

"Sounds dark."

"*Dark*," and he considers the word. "yeah, it does rather smell of a somewhat, *dark matter*. Shit! So that's why they need our silent consent; to generate the negative karma. That *is* the incendiary component. One is merely the karmic reflection of the other."

"What?"

"Oh Gatita, I've been so silly. A *black* hole. That's what I saw on a blast of laughing gas at *Reading Rock Festival*. Of course...I just had...I had...doubts. The question is how do you focus all that negativity into one tiny space to bust a hole open through the very fabric of, well, matter and tear open the walls of a world and... do it all with our consent? Holy shit...we've been hacked."

"I tell you one thing, it spells out that we have some Divine Birth Right that whoever they are, they're terrified of. A peaceful Birth Right. That's why we celebrate our Birthday parties. We have true sovereignty." And again he chuckles, "And all nullified if we choose to sit on the fence between war and peace. The true creator, whatever that truly is, needs to know which side of the fence we all stand. It really is Judgment Day. I mean, how bloody hard is it to stand in peace, in your brightest colours, so no one is in doubt, even God himself, to which side of the fence you truly stand and shout out for all to see, 'NO, NOT IN MY NAME?'"

…to be - or not to be - continued.

Don't just leave it on the shelf to gather dust. Pass it on to someone you love… And please leave a review on Amazon if you get a mo. Wishing you all the love and success in your endeavours, no matter how crazy they might seem. And don't forget to track your intentions. Get out there and make it happen!

Dave xxx